PRAISE FOR *IN SEARCH OF MARY SHELLEY*

'Even for those of us who thought we knew everything about the young author of *Frankenstein*, Fiona Sampson's brilliant new biography, *In Search of Mary Shelley*, has many surprises in store ... This is not so different a project from Mary Shelley's own: to breathe life into the dead, to bring new life to the archives of the past.' *Washington Post*

'Sampson wields her vivid imagination to effect, quickening a dead woman's being into reanimated life.' *Telegraph*

'It is a passionate demonstration of the elements that have kept her story vibrant for 200 years. It is moving, it is alive, it is a success.' *Spectator*

'A detailed and intimate portrait of the real person behind *Frankenstein*.' *Stylist*

'Fiona Sampson is a sleuth of a biographer ... rarely has my jaw dropped on so many occasions while reading a biography.' *Daily Mail*

'A daringly swift and enjoyably irreverent retelling of Shelley's life.' *Observer*

'Sampson, a poet, has a visual sense of biography.' *Times Literary Supplement*

'Mary Shelley emerges from Sampson's book as an intellectual interested in moral codes or laws: a daughter of whom Wollstonecraft would have been deeply proud.' *FT*

'Whatever her mood, speculative or assertive, Sampson's gift is for interpretation and analysis ... by the end of her book, you have the sense of having seen Mary Shelley through her own unique lens.' *Literary Review*

'If you are after bravura scene-setting ... and an ardent inhabiting of the book's subject, Ms Sampson car'‚ ' '
throws her
psychologi

LONDON BOROU(

D0262866

FIONA SAMPSON is a prize-winning poet and writer. She has been published in more than thirty languages and received an MBE for services to literature. A Fellow of the Royal Society for Literature and the recipient of a number of national and international honours for her poetry, she has worked in healthcare, as a violinist, and as an editor. *www.fionasampson.co.uk*

In Search of

MARY
SHELLEY

In Search of

MARY SHELLEY

The Girl Who Wrote Frankenstein

FIONA SAMPSON

P

PROFILE BOOKS

This paperback edition published in 2018

First published in Great Britain in 2018 by
PROFILE BOOKS LTD
3 Holford Yard
Bevin Way
London WC1X 9HD
www.profilebooks.com

1 3 5 7 9 10 8 6 4 2

Typeset in Caslon by MacGuru Ltd

Printed and bound in Great Britain by CPI Group (UK) Ltd, Croydon CR0 4YY

A CIP catalogue record for this book is available from the British Library.

ISBN 978 1 78125 529 2
eISBN 978 1 78283 195 2

Contents

For AAS, PMS & PWPS

Acknowledgements

A book like this is a sally into the unknown, for its writer at least, and I'm very grateful to a number of people.

My path has been lit by inspiring and distinguished biographers, and by the forensically gifted editors who have prepared the editions of letters and journals that allow the general reader to follow otherwise archival material. I have tried to repay a little of this debt by signposting the reader to their editions in the Notes, and the Bibliography gives a taste of the bibliographies, single and group, that I've been most attracted to.

My warmest thanks go to: Mike Jones, whose idea this book was and who commissioned it; everyone at Profile, including Penny Daniel, Cecily Gayford, Hannah Ross and Valentina Zanca, who have so calmly and generously seen a complicated 'creature' through publication; and Peter Salmon, first reader, indexer, and a man who has put up with more Mary talk than anyone should reasonably be expected to.

List of Illustrations

Introduction

Henry Frankenstein: Look! It's moving. It's alive. It's alive … It's alive,
it's moving. It's alive! It's alive, it's alive, it's alive!

    It's ALIVE!

Victor Moritz: In the name of God!

Henry: Now I know what it feels like to BE God!

Frankenstein, 1931 film

IT'S ONE OF THE MOST FAMOUS, and most parodied, moments
in cinema. The set piece twenty-five minutes into the first feature-length
Frankenstein film, in which Dr Frankenstein exults as his monster's fingers
begin to move, is genuinely uncanny. It is also very funny.

Generations have found this mixture of hilarity and horror irresist-
ible. I remember primary school playtimes when we ran screaming round
the yard while boys lurched after us with their arms held rigidly in front
of them. We didn't really know whether they were being Frankenstein's
Monster, the Curse of the Mummy's Tomb or one of the Living Dead,
and that was part of the point. The monster had stopped being a specific
character in some long-ago book or film. He had become part of our
shared imagination, and he could do whatever we thought he could. In

the rainy yard we used him in games about pirates, games of tag and especially, of course, in kiss chase. At any moment a boy could turn into the Monster, trumping the rules of whatever we were playing – and we'd scatter screaming. To be the one he singled out was a thrill and a terror, because there's something uncanny about the human who isn't quite a human. Masks serve purposes of enchantment, turning priests and actors alike into something more than their ordinary selves. And Frankenstein's Monster, as acted out in the schoolyard, was genuinely frightening and unpredictable in ways that the boys themselves were not.

'Frankenstein films' have had their own spawning, every bit as monstrous as the creature's own. They've become both a discrete horror movie sub-genre and one of the most fertile grounds of remakes ever. The classic 1931 film of *Frankenstein* alone remade the three silent movies that had preceded it, and launched a Universal Studios series of eight Frankenstein-themed movies in the 1930s and 1940s. Later the baton would pass across the Atlantic to Hammer Film Productions, who between 1957 and 1974 released a further seven movies, most starring Peter Cushing as Dr Frankenstein. These serial shlock horrors had brilliantly broad-brush titles: the American series included *Frankenstein Meets the Wolf Man* and *Abbott and Costello Meet Frankenstein,* the British *Frankenstein Created Woman* and *Frankenstein and the Monster from Hell.* At least a dozen further films that retell the original story – or at least *a* story – of the monster's creation have appeared since then. Which is to say nothing of the tremendous mushrooming, since the Sixties, of Frankenstein-themed TV programmes, comic books, graphic novels and manga, video games, jokes, music, stage shows, popular fiction, toys, and allusions from *Blade Runner* to *The Rocky Horror Picture Show.*

Much of the genre's appeal stems from its sheer unbelievability. Like pantomime Dames, who fail gleefully in their attempts to impersonate women, the Frankenstein genre revels in implausibility. It is so much camp nonsense and yet, as is the way of camp, it gives us a peek at one of our primitive anxieties – before we run off screaming. If the Dame lets us play with our anxieties about gender, Frankenstein's monster lets us play with the anxieties we have about human nature itself. James Whale's 1931 *Frankenstein,* badly acted by badly made-up actors in a magnificent set, is perfect camp. But even it manages to include genuine sentimentality: *the miracle of life!* It's this oscillation between the meaningful and the ridiculous that our culture has been playing with for decades.

Yet in Mary Shelley's original novel *Frankenstein* the weird nativity is completed in just one sentence:

> It was already one in the morning; the rain pattered dismally against the panes, and my candle was nearly burnt out, when, by the glimmer of the half-extinguished light, I saw the dull yellow eye of the creature open; it breathed hard, and a convulsive motion agitated its limbs.

And almost everything about this scene differs from the one popular culture has fixed in our minds. The moment in which Mary's creature comes to life is un-witnessed, except by a far from exultant Dr Frankenstein himself. The setting for the transformation isn't a laboratory, just a 'solitary chamber, or rather a cell, at the top of the house'. Man and monster aren't surrounded by gleaming equipment, occult with modernity, or even by nonsense machinery in the great British tradition that runs from William Heath Robinson to Nick Park's *Wallace and Gromit*. Above all, the novel gives us a scene not of success but of failure.

For Mary Shelley's imagination doesn't snag on the apparatus of physical transformation. Her novel is an exploration of the consequences of *being* a monster, and it is not a comedy but a tragedy, as her choice for the book's epigraph makes clear:

> Did I request thee, Maker, from my clay
> To mould me Man? Did I solicit thee
> From darkness to promote me?

It's the cry of protest that Adam makes to God in *Paradise Lost*, John Milton's tough, often bitter, retelling of the Biblical account of human creation. When I actually read *Frankenstein*, some time in my teens, I was astonished and relieved to discover that this was a story about selves and their feelings. I was moved by Frankenstein's creature, destined by an ugliness that's not of his choosing to a life of loneliness. He's an easy figure to identify with for any teenager coping with a newly grown body and not yet, perhaps, feeling secure about the world of sexual agency – or even dating. I had less sympathy for Frankenstein himself. His good looks seemed to me no excuse for a failure to live up to his moral obligations. All the same, I was caught by the book's shifting, ambivalent sympathies. Although its narrator insisted that Frankenstein was good, the narrative only seemed to show him being bad. It was the first time I had found myself being forced by a story to decide who was right – to choose between two truths – and I was shaken.

I had anticipated a sci-fi novel crammed with hardware, and instead, against all expectations, I was thoroughly engaged. But of course Mary Shelley would never have written science fiction. Modernity was not her chief concern, even if experiments in living were, and she could certainly have had no way to understand modernism – leave alone postmodernity. She lived in the Romantic era, when European culture was trying to build sense outwards from the individual self. The investigation of human experience by Idealist philosophers such as Immanuel Kant, Friedrich Schiller and Georg Wilhelm Friedrich Hegel had led to revolutionary questioning of that human's rights across Europe, and would also define some of the forms that human knowledge could take. 'Romanticism' was the term invented around the turn of the century for the effect of this new way of thinking on the arts, where it made emotion and experience primary.

Mary's version of this *zeitgeist* was both very new and rooted in a Classical education. *Frankenstein*'s subtitle is 'The Modern Prometheus', and the Greek myth of the Titan who creates humans in an almost mechanical way was being revisited by Romantic artists as an alternative to the story of divine creation. Goethe had published his poem 'Prometheus' in 1789; Beethoven composed his *The Creatures of Prometheus* in 1801 (the ballet has disappeared, but the overture entered the repertoire). In the year of *Frankenstein*'s publication, Mary's husband, Percy Bysshe Shelley, started work on his own verse drama on the theme, *Prometheus Unbound*.

I don't think I was alone in my ignorance about Mary Shelley and her novel. When I was a teenager, its author was chiefly remembered as the poet's wife. Sometimes she also had an honourable mention as a one-hit wonder who had somehow – perhaps inadvertently? – come up with 'the Frankenstein idea': the notion that if humans play God with the 'instruments of life' they will produce something monstrous. The date stamps showed that my battered library copy of *Frankenstein* had not been borrowed recently. Though in the late twentieth century the novel form was seen, at least in the West, as *the* 'great' literary form, and that greatness often seemed to be as much a question of scale as of depth. The model, at least for a non-academic, general reader like me, was still late nineteenth-century fiction – that almost symphonic creation – and its reception not dissimilar to that for the bloated symphonic orchestral pieces of that same period. Eighteenth- and early nineteenth-century work like *Frankenstein* was seen as transitional, primitive: the first steps towards inventing a form that would become fully fledged only once it had sized up.

None of this is how we think about Mary Shelley now. She has been claimed by scholars and literary biographers, contradictorily both as the author of a canonical novel and as part of a tradition of serious women writers largely excluded from that very canon. The facts of her life have been excavated by her biographers. They've also been revisited by those more interested in her husband. Some have believed the poet's grumbles about her, not remembering that he was at the very least a subjective, embroiled witness to his own marriage: hardly a reliable narrator. One cohort, who accuse Mary of unfaithful editing of her husband's poems, even seem to assume that the grieving widow had access to twenty-first-century research facilities and training in today's archival best practice: a curious precursor of how the survivor of another great British literary couple, Ted Hughes, would face similar accusations when he produced the posthumous editions that ensured Sylvia Plath's reputation.

Reading these multiplying accounts can feel like squinting at a radar screen. Mary Shelley was a literary star. But too often she appears as little more than a bright spot being tracked as she moves from one location to another. This is no replacement for encountering the person herself. We know *where* Mary Shelley was, yet I still find myself looking for her. Like the monster she created in *Frankenstein*, she seems to race ahead of us 'with more than mortal speed':

> Amidst the wilds of Tartary and Russia, although he still evaded me,
> I have ever followed in his track. Sometimes the peasants, scared
> by this horrid apparition, informed me of his path; sometimes he
> himself, who feared that if I lost all traces of him, I should despair

and die, left some mark to guide me. The snows descended on my head, and I saw the print of his huge step on the white plain.

But, unlike her monster, Mary Shelley does not need fictionalising. She deserves better than imaginative reconstruction: she deserves to be listened to. Her letters, journals and publications, and those of her friends and colleagues, tell us a great deal about what she actually felt and thought. Mary Shelley is not a fictional character. She was a real person, sometimes paradoxical and at other times predictable, and as complicated to get to know as anyone else. It's this real person, full of living contradictions, who often seems to be hollowed out from accounts of her life and of her circle. This all the more surprising because the Romantic movement in general, and Mary's writing in particular, is so much concerned with the psychological. After all, the great plea of her most famous novel is that we should understand who Frankenstein's creature is *to himself* – his own feelings and motives – rather than judging on appearances.

Mary wrote that plea astonishingly early in what was already becoming a sometimes heartbreakingly difficult life. She started work on her most famous novel when she was only eighteen, and when it was published she was still no more than twenty. Each time, over the years, that I reread her *Frankenstein*, its plea for understanding seemed more audible. I wondered who she could possibly be, this teenage author of not one but two of our culture's most enduring archetypes: the inventor not just of the scientist with no thought for consequences but also of the near-human that he creates. Who *was* the unmarried teenage mother who attended Lord Byron's house party on Lake Geneva and responded to his playful challenge to write a ghost story, one of the first and surely among the most influential 'creative writing' exercises in literary history? What extraordinary resources did she draw on to become a major writer, in an era when women mostly 'knew their place' as literary muses rather than protagonists? And what was it about her – as well as her pure exceptionalism – that so often seemed to bring out the worst in those around her?

The most enduring image of Mary's *Frankenstein* is, for me, her story's ending, in which the creature goes out, alone again, onto the Arctic ice to die. It is the original 'fade to white'. If we're not careful, the same thing happens – again and again – to the woman who created that image. I want to rewind the film: to bring Mary closer to us, and closer again, until she's hugely enlarged in close-up. I want to see the actual texture of her existence, caught in freeze-frame. I want to ask what we do in fact know about who and how and why she is – who she is – and about *how it is for her*.

Of course, there are disadvantages to this approach. One is that a freeze-frame is a form of tableau, which asks a single moment to represent a wealth of incident and information that doesn't make it into the chosen image. Another is that viewing Mary like this produces a kind of foreshortening. To put it another way: we see everything that's 'in front of', or leads up to, the given moment; we don't necessarily see what happens when our characters are released into movement after that moment has passed. But this, of course, is how we picture human events. We see the motivation prior to the action, and think in terms of decisions that get us to certain points at certain junctures. Indeed we visualise entire life stories this way: it isn't only psychoanalysts, or Jesuits, who believe that the child is father to the man.

And so it is that the rules of perspective apply even to a freeze-frame biography. Mary's youth, and her life with Percy Bysshe Shelley, take up more space in this kind of storytelling than the equal number of years of her widowhood, in which she was able to settle into a literary life of her own. This isn't because she was a one-hit wonder; she was not. It is because the later years of a life – of anyone's life – do not build a personality, and they don't go on to affect a future. They *are* that future. *Frankenstein* is not unconnected to what comes after it in Mary's life. On the contrary, it changed her life just as it has changed our cultural imagination. But that's the thing: Mary's first novel informs her future; her last does not inform her past.

When Mary's silver ghost steps away from her and comes towards us it's the future, not the past, that it is on its way to haunt. We are all haunted by our own childhoods, with their particular dreams and nightmares. The Frankensteins of the schoolyard that haunt my dreams – or yours – aren't quite the monsters that haunted Mary's. But they are kissing kin.

Part One

THE
INSTRUMENTS
OF LIFE

Chapter 1

The Instruments of Life

To examine the causes of life, we must first have recourse to death.

WE KNOW A GOOD DEAL about the circumstances of Mary's birth in 1797, in an August bedroom in Middlesex, on the outskirts of London. We know, for example, that it is nearly midnight on 30 August, and that there's a smell of damp countryside coming in at the window on the night air. Attracted by the light, crane flies and moths skitter on the windowsill. The waxing moon is only just half full.

A new family – the Godwins – are grouped together at the bed. The healthy baby who's just been born is being introduced by her mother, the famous radical writer Mary Wollstonecraft, to the delighted father, fellow radical and philosopher William Godwin. Light from the household's oil lamps – brought upstairs for the tremendous occasion of this birth – concentrates in all three faces, finding them the way it does in one of those studies of the Holy Family by Rembrandt, where lantern light falls out of a tender chiaroscuro darkness on to the family group. Rembrandt's paintings tell us to trust the light because it finds where the action is, and is always on the side of the protagonists. And tonight's lamplight gives everyone a healthy glow even as it covers up less attractive details, such as blood-stained sheets and towels, with tactful shadow.

The bedroom is at the top of a smart four-storey town house: actually there are five storeys if you count the garrets overhead. The house has only recently been built in low-lying, clay fields just north of London. On farmland to the east and south, ghostly roads have been marked up. A small grid of streets peters out between half-built shells, the bumpy outline of foundations, surveyor's tape straggling between clumps of dock and nettle. In the dark it would be hard to tell whether these are ruins disappearing into the soil or new structures rising out of it. In fact, they are what's left of Brill Farm. Its upwardly mobile owner, Charles Cocks, recently elevated to become First Baron Somers of Evesham, has leased them to a local architect, Jacob Leroux, who has great plans as well as a fine track record. He's already made a career on the south coast. But he also has a decidedly un-English name. Perhaps it's for this reason – or perhaps just to clinch the deal – that he has flatteringly called the development that will surely make his *own* name after its landlord.

In the summer of 1797 Somers Town is not yet in the shadow of the still un-envisaged railways that will slice up this northern entrance to the metropolis. Tonight it remains an aspirational address, the sort of place where respectability can be invented and rehearsed until, with a bit of luck, it turns into security. This is an immigrant area, where many inhabitants are learning how to be bourgeois in the English way. Life here must sometimes feel like playing at house, and not only for newly-weds like the parents in our nativity tableau. There are strange clothes to try on. Contemporary Englishwomen's fashion nods towards the neo-Classical in a way that echoes French Directoire style, with its high-pitched, largely exposed breasts; and Beau Brummell is cutting a high-society dash that puts pressure on men to keep up with their women. Then there's the odd diet. The British are obsessed with meat. Currently fashionable is the Revd Dr John Trusler's 1788 tome *The Honours of the Table* (which includes a guide to the arts of carving so thorough that it will still be a key text in the 1930s). More coffee is being drunk in England than anywhere else in the world, but the ruinously expensive national drink is tea. In fact, so expensive has it become that a special offence of reusing tea-leaves has been created.

All this may seem like costume drama to us, but it is being played for real. The high stakes for these tenants include staying out of debtor's prison, particularly in the current economic downturn. The Panic of 1796–7, though largely North American, has added to the strains already placed on the British economy by war with France, which has been dragging on since 1793. Indeed, when the architect of this whole ambitious development dies, less than two years from now, his executors will auction off the entire half-built estate. The sale that takes place at the Somers Town Coffee House on 30 June 1799 exposes shaky foundations to Jacob Leroux's prosperity – and to the district he has created: 'the whole held for long terms at very low ground-rents, part let on lease and part to tenants at will; the annual rental £62 8s. per annum.' Even the sale announcement in *The Times* acknowledges that this does not amount to a profitable investment. Forty lots 'will be sold without the least reserve' – with no reserve price – as will Leroux's own 'capital spacious family home' near by, with its 'coach-house, stable, and garden about three quarters of an acre'. The chaotic, inconsistent system of tenancies he leaves behind reveals that Somers Town has Leroux in over his head: a gifted architect isn't necessarily a gifted speculator.

It's Leroux himself, for example, who tipped off baby Mary's father about a cheap let going at 29 the Polygon. The tip-off seems characteristically generous on Leroux's part, but it may also be politically motivated. Although he's Covent Garden born and bred, Leroux's surname is undeniably French in origin. His mother's maiden name, Bonet, is French too. This may be coincidence, but it's the kind that goes along with membership of a community. A century earlier, after the 1685 Edict of Fontainebleau made Protestantism in France illegal, up to fifty thousand Huguenots arrived in England. These were skilled migrants, glass and textile workers with the latest techniques up their sleeves, and they were welcomed with governmental and charitable subsidies, and by the naturalisation offered under the 1708 Foreign Protestants Naturalisation Act. In contrast, just the year before this story opens, the 1796 renewal of the Aliens Act has forced all *émigrés* away from coastal areas, causing the thousands of more recent – and Catholic – refugees from the French Revolution of 1789 to settle in the English capital. Despite their religious differences, the Huguenot community is helping these newcomers.

Somers Town is particularly welcoming: it has the closest housing to St Pancras Church, which is one of the few sites in London where Catholics can be buried. The Abbé Carron, practical and spiritual leader of the local refugee community, lives at 1 the Polygon itself.

Tonight's new mother is in a sense also a refugee from the Revolution. Mary Wollstonecraft Godwin, who on the August night when she gives birth to her second daughter, Mary, is well known for the revolutionary *A Vindication of the Rights of Men* (1790) and *A Vindication of the Rights of Woman* (1792), has recently escaped France with her first child, Fanny, who was born there. Her husband, William Godwin, anarchist and utilitarian, published the equally influential and similarly radical *An Enquiry Concerning Political Justice* just four years ago.

The couple's new baby daughter will remain at 29 the Polygon for the first ten years of her life. During that decade Bloomsbury will fill the fields that at present lie beyond the new road to Paddington, and settlement will straggle up Pancras Place. Soon cheap rents and multiple occupancies will come to characterise a neighbourhood that symbolises the very opposite of respectability. Within thirty years of their construction its new houses will be a slum whose notoriety persists for a century and a half, into the eras of public housing, gang culture and the anxious socio-political footage of Shane Meadows's 2008 film *Somers Town*.

Children like Mary Godwin, who grow up on estates that are still being built out of the surrounding countryside, have a special sense of how precarious that habitation is. They see how society is a matter of invention. Often it's only one house deep, sometimes a matter of weeks old. The finished streets on which they and their friends live resemble suburbs yet seem little more than stage sets when they give way abruptly to farms and fields. But at the pre-dawn of the nineteenth century – as in the twenty-first – children of respectable but not wealthy middle-class families cannot play outside, however seductive the environment. Crime rates are high, and the sixty-eight men who make up the Bow Street Runners are the only professional policing force anywhere in London. Beyond the little glow cast by house lights, the roads are unlit; even darker is the dangerous, unvisited land beyond 'each charter'd street'. William Blake's dystopian vision, in his poem 'London', of a city full of 'hapless

Soldiers' and 'youthful Harlots' dates from just three years before the night of Mary's birth.

The problem of playing outside has not yet arisen in the Godwin house. Until today there has been only one child, three-year-old Fanny, living at 29 the Polygon. It is a grand house, with 'iron balconies [...] two marble mantelpieces at least [...] and the remainder of Portland Stone [...] wood dados and mouldings and double deal six-panelled doors to the two principal storeys', according to the architect's contract. Fanny's small person makes little impression on it. It seems she's already becoming that well-behaved elder child whose stepfather will later describe her as being 'of a quiet, modest, unshowy disposition'. Besides, outdoor activity of any kind is difficult in the rain, and it's been a wet summer. We can imagine what a combination of rain, clay soil and the perpetual building site of the surrounding developments have done to domestic order. To make matters worse, there are as yet no default routines in what is a house of newly-weds. The couple who live here have only been married since March, and the husband arranged the bargain lease only on the eve of their wedding.

Still, they must have known about the mud in advance, since both were already living in the area. William's kept lodgings round the corner in Chalton Street since 1793. This relationship developed after Mary moved down from Pentonville in July 1796 to live nearby. Like other people's money, other people's partnerships work in ways that only their protagonists understand. But these protagonists are both writers, and their compulsion to record means that we know a great deal more than we might expect or want about their private lives. We know, for example, that the affair between Mary Wollstonecraft and William Godwin was first consummated on a Sunday evening, 21 August 1796, almost exactly a year before Mary's birth, when Godwin wrote in his diary 'chez moi, toute'.

So Mary Godwin's story starts in what a century later the actor Mrs Patrick Campbell will call the 'hurly-burly of the chaise longue'. Although her parents will marry by the time she's born, the scene on 30 August 1797 is in no sense a Christian nativity.

The baby's father, one of the leading atheists of the day, will have a free hand in her upbringing. Besides, this is an era before Queen Victoria, her German prince and the domestic pieties they will import. In the world this baby is born into, even carols that are today's Christmas clichés – 'Away in a Manger', 'Once in Royal David's City', 'It Came Upon a Midnight Clear' – have yet to be written. It's a time before nostalgia, before *The Old Curiosity Shop* and teddy bears. An era of progress, of science and of reason – even of revolution. It is the moment before kitsch revives the fortunes of the British monarchy; the instant when Britain comes nearest to creating its own Second Republic.

Baby Mary's parents are part of this radical moment. In Revolutionary France Mary Wollstonecraft had the affair, with an American adventurer called Gilbert Imlay, that resulted in her first child, Fanny. Abandoned by Imlay, Wollstonecraft has returned to Britain and, to support herself and Fanny, resumed her writing career. After starting the affair with Godwin she has quickly fallen pregnant. Despite her earlier statement, in *A Vindication of the Rights of Woman*, that 'the divine right of husbands, like the divine right of kings may […] be contested', the couple marry when she is four months gone. After all, this is an era when illegitimate children, if abandoned, face a lifetime of social exclusion – should they even reach adulthood. (The life expectancy of foundlings in institutions is very low.)

It seems astonishing that Mary Wollstonecraft is able to trust another lover at all, especially so soon after Imlay. Does she know in her bones that this time Godwin is what W. H. Auden calls 'the more loving one'? Or does she simply feel that he's a very different bet from the American: a bookish, indoor man, not rogue material? Finally – a question that will arise again and again in the course of this story – don't any of these protagonists at least *try* for some form of birth control? William Godwin and Mary Wollstonecraft are two of the most politically, socially and intellectually sophisticated people in London, and, by extension, among the most sophisticated in the Europe of their day. They are politically radical, socially nonconformist, not 'family values' conservatives. Sex matters to them: certainly to Godwin, who keeps a slightly creepy diary record involving em dashes. Sponges and condoms, which are called 'gloves', have long been available to people in the know and with a little disposable income: just such people as Godwin and Wollstonecraft. Both are discussed, for example, in Thomas Stretzer's *A New Description of Merryland Containing a Topographical, Geographical and Natural History of That Country*, the Dr Alex Comfort of its day, which had entered a fourth edition back in 1741. Of course, contraception is always inexact. But Godwin is forty, and Mary by now not a super-fertile teenager but a thirty-eight-year-old mother, and they surely have to try a *little* to have an 'accident'.

Or do they *want* a child: quickly, before it's too late? After all they are a progressive household, now occupying a home built with an eye to the future. Out beyond the smallpox hospital on Bachelors Row and the Pancras Place turnpike, the Polygon must be a striking development among the district's brickfields and market gardens. It's a bumpy ring, built high and sixteen-sided: 'The Hexadecagon' presumably considered too much of a mouthful for commercial reality even by the impractical Jacob Leroux. There are to be thirty-two houses, arranged in pairs joined by stepped porches that builders would probably now call link-attached. Within the ring thirty-two cake slices of garden are proposed.

The great residential doughnut is still incomplete on this night in 1797, and it will remain that way. Still, feeling nature break in around them, the householders of this utopian development play at country living, taking walks in the fields and maintaining gardens, as a hundred and fifty years later their successors will play at cottages in the hygienic half-timbering of Metroland a few miles further north again, on the ever-encroaching outer rim of London. And it *is* play. The Polygon is an urban, not a rural, phenomenon, tuned to the busy city of coffee shops, publishers and booksellers that is visible – and must be audible – just across the fields. Society is being urgently questioned there right now: this is the era of thinkers as energetic and disparate as Jeremy Bentham and, dead less than two months, Edmund Burke. Number 29 has its own library of serious, radical books, while for further intellectual stimulation the British Museum, open to the public since 1759, is just a country stroll away by footpath or down Duke of Bedford Road.

On the whole, social revolutionaries like William Godwin and Mary Wollstonecraft believe more, not less, than other people that where and when a child is born affects his or her life chances so materially as almost to define it. This logic extends to maternal health. There have always been large numbers of maternal orphans, whose mothers die during or because of their birth. In England between 1750 and 1800 an average of 7.5 live births per thousand result in maternal mortality; in London, with its overcrowding and poverty, the figures are worse. Although by the 1790s London has managed to get its death rate down closer to the national average, the reduction can hardly be much consolation for women facing childbirth. Even at the new rates, your risk of death from pregnancy may be less than one in a thousand on each occasion, but for two pregnancies it still becomes greater than 1 per cent and so on. These are scary odds. Among other things, they transform marriage and sex from romantic entertainment into the most dangerous undertakings of a woman's life.

Is this why Mary Wollstonecraft refuses to have a doctor in attendance for her second delivery, relying instead on a midwife? Faced with such odds, do you find ways to diminish the risk in your own mind, to believe that 'it won't happen to me'? Her first labour, with Fanny, was relatively easy: certainly it lasted fewer than the sixteen hours it will take to deliver her second child. Perhaps she uses this experience as a touchstone to help her through anticipation of the delivery. 'She was so far from being under any apprehension as to the difficulties of child-birth, as frequently to ridicule the fashion of ladies in England, who keep their chamber for one full month after delivery', Godwin reports. She has had a healthy pregnancy, after all, with plenty of walks (when it isn't raining) through the surrounding fields, to Sadler's Wells, to the bookshops on Ludgate Hill or on to Lamb's Conduit Fields. She is at the height of her personal and intellectual powers and – a near-inconceivable feat for a woman – a well-known writer. She has found love when she might never have expected to again, and at what may seem to her a great age for doing so. She has managed to secure the future of both her first daughter and this new baby through marriage. Above all, she has seen and survived the Reign of Terror that grew out of the French Revolution in 1793–4. Indeed, she gave birth the first time, in Le Havre on 14 May 1794, during the Terror and while her own country was at war with France. She must be feeling pretty invincible.

What *is* Mary Wollstonecraft's relationship with danger? Does it simply not enter her calculations? Does she think, as so many women must even today, in the developing world, that some things – to do with love, or social conformity – are worth taking a risk for? Or does she court danger? Does she so want to live 'manfully' that she will risk her own life? In 1795, after all, she undertook a three-month-long business trip to Scandinavia on behalf of Fanny's unreliable father, who was also a blockade runner: from 1793 he organised the British blockade of France's Channel ports even while serving as an American diplomatic representative to that country. Imlay abandoned her and their child twice – in France and then again in Britain – yet Wollstonecraft undertook this wartime trip, alone apart from a lady's maid and an infant Fanny. Her letters show that she thought this would secure both Imlay's financial future and his love. Possibly that wasn't pure romantic hot-headedness; it may also have had to do with Fanny's future, both financial and legal. Or perhaps she's good at compartmentalising. After all, she turned the trip into the book that becomes her best-seller *Letters Written during a Short Residence in Sweden, Norway, and Denmark*.

Or is Mary Wollstonecraft, as she embarks on this second labour, simply showing grace under pressure? Is she protecting William the first-time father, who is besotted by her, from his own anxiety? Later William will present himself as overruled: 'She had already had some experience on the subject in the case of Fanny; and I cheerfully submitted in every point to her judgment and her wisdom.' Not so 'cheerfully', in fact. Godwin has his resistances: 'Influenced by ideas of decorum, which certainly ought to have no place, at least in cases of danger, she determined to have a woman to attend her in the capacity of midwife.' Does Mary care about 'decorum', or is it just that she trusts women more than men, when it comes to childbirth? Godwin is right that many things no longer matter 'in cases of danger', and hers is unlikely to be a political choice. It's no more likely that choosing the Matron of Westminster Lying-In Hospital as her midwife is a gesture of political solidarity with its largely impoverished clientele. Instead it looks like a loving domestic compromise between Mary's desire to use a midwife and her anxious husband's friendship with Anthony Carlisle, the principal surgeon at the Westminster hospital.

If it's meant as reassurance, it works. When the first contractions wake

Mary at five in the morning on 30 August, the father-to-be feels able to go off as usual to rooms he has kept on to work in, round the corner in Evesham Buildings. Mary has told him she plans on 'coming down to dinner on the day immediately following'. In any case, her instincts are correct. There seems to be no problem with the midwife's care. The labour may be slower than her first time around, but Mrs Blenkinsop is experienced, and all goes well. The baby arrives safely, at twenty to midnight. And this, surely, is the moment for our lamp-lit nativity scene. The baby has been born healthy, and so, it seems, is the mother. Although the parents' love talk has circled for weeks around an infant William, the fact that they have a daughter instead no longer matters a jot.

This must be the scene Mary imagines as she sends a message for William to come and meet his baby. Once 'all was over', she has always planned to perform 'the interesting office of presenting the new-born child to its father'. It must also be the scene William imagines as he waits downstairs for the call to come. But it is not what happens. William waits and waits. It is not 'all … over'. Time stretches out. One imagines a clock ticking. It is the wolf hour. Does he feel tired? Or is he wired by adrenalin? Does he long for a coffee? Can he make one unaided? If not, impotent in the kitchen as he is to help the difficult and mysterious business going on in the bedroom upstairs, does he resort to water – or wine?

Shortly before 2 a.m. Mrs Blenkinsop asks him to fetch help. Things are going wrong. The afterbirth hasn't come away. In the orthodoxy of the time, this should have happened almost immediately. The glowing tableau, which has been fading for hours, vanishes abruptly. Godwin takes a carriage to the Westminster Hospital. But the Lying-In Hospital, where Mrs Blenkinsop works, is separate from the main hospital. He returns in about an hour, bringing with him not Anthony Carlisle but a Frenchman, Louis Poignand. Poignand is no surgeon, though he is a Licentiate in Midwifery of the Royal College of Surgeons.

What does William feel at this point? Does he think he has retrieved the situation, placing it in the hands of a man of science? Is he in any case too buoyed up by the safe arrival of his child to believe that things will go badly wrong – now, at this late stage? No: I think he is hovering. He knows things are bad. The house must be full of hurried activity, anxious expressions; perhaps there are screams. A few months later, in his *Memoirs of the Author of A Vindication of the Rights of Woman,* he will write, 'The period [...] till about eight o'clock the next morning was a period full of peril and alarm. The loss of blood was considerable, and produced an almost uninterrupted series of fainting fits.'

Dr Poignand pulls away the afterbirth in pieces, by hand. There is, of course, no anaesthetic. Mary Wollstonecraft tells her husband afterwards that it was the most severe pain she has ever known. Still, it seems the worst is over, and by Friday Godwin is recording 'favourable appearances' in his diary. Some time on Thursday or Friday the long-imagined tableau, in which the parents dote together on their newborn, must take place. But the worst is not over. It turns out that in saving Mary Wollstonecraft Dr Poignand has in fact condemned her. On Saturday she suffers a series of shivering fits so violent that the whole bed shakes. The guests invited to supper are put off. It is the start of her fatal illness.

When Mary dies on 10 September of puerperal fever – that's to say, of infection introduced by Dr Poignand's unsterile hands – it is an agonising, unnecessary death. The cause of puerperal fever has already been identified by Alexander Gordon, an Aberdeen obstetrician who two years earlier published his *Treatise on the Epidemic of Puerperal Fever*: 'It is a disagreeable declaration for me to mention, that I myself was the means of carrying the infection to a great number of women.' So 'disagreeable' *is* this declaration to the rest of the medical profession that, far from trying out his ideas in case they save lives, they have attacked Gordon. In fact, clinicians' continuing resistance to the idea that they fatally infect women during childbirth will remain so violently entrenched for nearly another century and a half that it gives its name to the more general phenomenon of knee-jerk resistance to new knowledge. The Semmelweis Effect is named after Ignaz Semmelweis, who over half a century after Mary Wollstonecraft's death will be confined to an asylum for pointing out the fatal connection between poor hygiene and maternal mortality.

William Godwin doesn't care about the thousands of other women who will continue to die because of clinical arrogance. He cares about Mary. During the ten days that she lies dying he sends for four different doctors and consults several more. But in the era before antibiotics there's nothing with which to fight the septicaemia as it takes hold. And this is no gentle fading away. It is a bad death. Alexander Gordon reports:

> The situation of the patient, at this period of the disease, was truly deplorable; for the pain of the abdomen, already excruciating, was aggravated by the act of respiration, and by the smallest motion of the trunk. The miserable patient, therefore, lay on her back incapable of turning on either side, and unable to breathe. Death, in such circumstances, was an event to be much wished for.

Before this there has been vomiting and, usually, diarrhoea, eventually containing the black 'coffee grounds' of blood. Mary, who must be unusually strong, takes longer to die than most women. By the end she cannot 'follow any train of ideas with force or any accuracy of connection'. For the last five days of her life she has been fed a 'wine diet', as recommended by both Carlisle and another of the physicians in attendance, John Clarke.

It's not clear whether this is palliative or designed to help the body's 'constitution' cope with the effects of retained placenta, which Clarke seems to believe is what is making Mary ill. William is initially reluctant to, in effect, keep his wife permanently drunk: 'thus to play with a life that seemed all that was dear to me in the universe.' The moment at which he agrees to it, on the afternoon of 6 September, looks like the moment at which he realises he's going to lose her. The brevity of the day's entry in his journal is not unusual for Godwin, but its content, little more than a list of helpless attendants, is cheerless: 'Carlisle calls: wine diet: Carlisle from Brixton: Miss Jones sleeps.' Worse is the next day: 'Barry, Reveley and Lowry call: dying in the evening.' On the next, 'Opie & Tuthil call. Idea of Death: solemn communication. Barry: Miss J sleeps.'

Where is the baby in all of this? Mary Wollstonecraft has nursed her second daughter for the first three days of life. Then she stops, because her septicaemia becomes apparent and could infect the child. A wet-nurse is found, and the infant Mary is sent away to join Fanny in the care of a family friend, Maria Reveley. Meanwhile, puppies are brought in to drain off the new mother's milk. How could this reduction to the purely animal not be humiliating, as well as a terrifying sign that she is really ill? There's no privacy at the sick bed. The puppies 'occasioned some pleasantry of Mary with me and the other attendants', says Godwin, with

surprising lack of insight; for what could this possibly mean to a revolutionary writer who has struggled against the reduction of women to
the purely creaturely? Just five years earlier, in *A Vindication of the Rights
of Woman*, she has written about 'those talents and virtues, the exercise
of which ennobles the human character, and which raise females in the
scale of animal being, when they are comprehensively termed mankind'.
In her last days little of that 'grand light' of humanity remains for Mary
Wollstonecraft to hold on to – apart from courage. And she is a coura-
geous patient. Even fatally ill, she is 'affectionate and compliant to the
last'. Godwin will describe her as 'perfectly cheerful' 'the whole day' of
her labour. Indeed, the most touching of the notes she sent him that day
is consummate in its understatement:

> I have no doubt of seeing the animal to day; but must wait for Mrs
> Blenkinsop to guess at the hour—I have sent for her—Pray send me
> the newspaper—I wish I had a novel, or some book of sheer amuse-
> ment, to excite curiosity, and while away the time—Have you any
> thing of the kind?

Godwin publishes his *Memoirs of the Author of A Vindication of the
Rights of Woman*, from which his account of her last days comes, within
four months of Mary Wollstonecraft's death. Perhaps rushed unwisely
into print by grief, its unapologetic discussion of her personal life exposes
its subject to a public opprobrium that results in her work being almost
completely dismissed for decades. This reception isn't simple moral
hypocrisy, however. Her unconventional private and professional life, as a
woman writer and intellectual whose first child is illegitimate and whose
second is conceived out of wedlock, reveals to contemporaries that Wollstonecraft really did live in pioneering ways. She was truly as radical as
her books suggest; and radicalism, in this era, isn't simply a live-and-let-
live lifestyle choice. It poses a threat to the very fabric of civil society.
After all, it was armed revolution that attracted Wollstonecraft to France.

Civil society fights back with all the resources, from ridicule to moral
disapprobation, at its disposal. But Godwin's book is a work of personal mourning: 'This light was lent to me for a very short period, and
is now extinguished for ever!' It evokes a marriage that, though short,
has found out how to work: 'My oscillation and scepticism were fixed by

her boldness.' It ends with a curious summary of the character of Mary Wollstonecraft's intelligence:

> The strength of her mind lay in intuition. [...] She adopted one opinion, and rejected another, spontaneously, by a sort of tact, and the force of a cultivated imagination; [...] though perhaps, in the strict sense of the term, she reasoned little [...]. In a robust and unwavering judgment of this sort, there is a kind of witchcraft; when it decides justly, it produces a responsive vibration in every ingenuous mind.

This is a portrait of a Romantic ideal: the kind of thinking most valued by the writers and artists of the new school. A leaping intuition, taking its own intelligence as touchstone, is led by process and feeling, rather than by structures of logic or citation. Godwin's portrait of his wife's mind bears a startling resemblance to the way their little daughter, when she comes to write her first novel nineteen years from now, will portray the thought processes of her Romantic protagonist. It is Dr Frankenstein's 'intuitive discernment; a quick but never-failing power of judgment; a penetration into the causes of things' that is the very proof of his worth.

Mary Wollstonecraft dies at 7.40 on the morning of Sunday, 10 September: '20 minutes before 8', Godwin writes in his diary, starting – as is his custom on Sundays, the entries printed at the top of each leaf – in the middle of the allocated space. He completes the line by drawing a rule, as if he were signing off a cheque. Surely he must feel, as he does so, a grotesque echo of all those sexy em-dashes of his courtship? He rules through the rest of the space his diary gives for the day as if to cross them out:

20 minutes before 8. _____

_____

_____

_____

_____

It's a wordless acknowledgment of everything he is feeling. He cannot bear to write the words that would record *what* has happened. Later something – a desire for order in emotional chaos? The habit of a lifetime?

– forces him to reconsider. A line of writing is added. When I enlarge the facsimile, I believe I can see the difference in colour of ink where he squeezes in the rest of his day below the crossing-through: 'Montagu, M, Miss G & Fanny dine.'

Yet, once the worst has happened, William Godwin seems to pull himself together. He throws himself – particularly by the standards of his time – into life with the two small children Mary Wollstonecraft has left him, bringing his three-year-old stepdaughter Fanny home less than a week after her mother has died: on 16 September his journal records, 'Fanny home'. The next day we read, 'Mary home'.

He also throws himself into memorialising his late wife. The portrait John Opie has painted of her during her second pregnancy is hung above the fireplace in his study. In the picture, which now hangs in the National Portrait Gallery, Mary's ever so slightly equine long upper lip makes a forceful horizontal of her mouth, whose corners are just lifted. It looks as though she's repressing a thought: something wry, or funny. It also looks as though she would be – charmingly, lightly – stubborn. Although she's posed looking thoughtfully off to one side, Mary's face is lively and inhabited, more enquiring than authoritative. She looks like someone you'd want as a friend; I wonder whether her daughters, growing up with this image of her, feel the same. Despite the relaxed way she holds her body, she does not particularly resemble a mother.

It's a sympathetic image, far removed from John Chapman's engraving of a clownish figure in a top hat, produced the following year when derision is already *de rigueur*. No surprise that, a century from now, her grandson's widow, Lady Jane Shelley, will choose this painting of Wollstonecraft to give to the nation. The artist John Opie, just a couple of years younger than Mary, has been rescued from a provincial, working-class background by precocious artistic talent: he's known as 'the Cornish wonder'. The picture is a commission, but it reveals genuine understanding of this remarkable woman and her ideas about equality and freedom. Opie even paints her wearing the Phrygian cap of liberty, though hers isn't red like those favoured by French Revolutionaries. Indeed, she looks a little like a Marianne, that personification of the French Republic, albeit a thoughtful one whom we might expect to ignore the shield and fasces we can imagine propped beside her just out of frame. This mixture of public pose and private expression is strange yet attractive; in a younger man's admiring gaze we catch a glimpse of the Wollstonecraft that Godwin himself found so compelling.

As well as publishing the *Memoirs*, the widower commissions a substantial monument at the grave in St Pancras Old Churchyard. It's a square stele, a kind of *faux* sarcophagus, with a neo-Classical architrave and squared-off Doric base. The name MARY WOLLSTONECRAFT just fits across the width; his wife's married name, GODWIN, standing shyly alone on the next line. 'Author of A Vindication of the Rights of Woman' is followed simply by birth and death dates. Unsoftened by pious expression, this is a bald declaration that 'by their works shall you know them'.

Mary Wollstonecraft's epitaph will find an uncanny echo in 'Ozymandias', the sonnet Percy Bysshe Shelley publishes in 1818, four years after courting her daughter at this very grave. 'Look on my works, ye Mighty, and despair!' his imagined statue commands. The poem adds, 'Nothing beside remains'. In the twenty-first century little remains beside the monument in St Pancras Old Churchyard. Wollstonecraft's is one among a handful of memorials for the famous that dot a muddy, rather bare patch of grass below tall trees. Dog-walkers track up and down the paths. A couple of homeless guys drink on the vestry steps. The traffic on the Pancras Road is ceaseless. The whole churchyard, wedged between road and railway in the shadow not only of the new St Pancras development but also of the even newer Francis Crick Institute, feels bleakly transitional. Even the church that Godwin would have recognised has been vandalised by the Victorian 'restorers' R. L. Roumieu and A. D. Gough, who in 1847–8 pulled down the distinctive west tower and clad the rest of the mainly Tudor structure in hefty *faux* Norman stonework. In the mid-1860s the building of the Midland Railway's line into St Pancras Station led to land requisition. Graves had to be moved. It was the young Thomas Hardy, still a student architect, who was in charge of reinterring remains that had been disturbed – in St Pancras Cemetery, Finchley – and of re-erecting substantial monuments, Mary Wollstonecraft's among them, further west across the Old Churchyard. Simple headstones he set in radial lines around the bole of an ash tree, back to back as if *do–si–do* in some old Wessex round dance. A hundred and fifty years later they're still there, the elderly dead – some thrown a little off-kilter by tree-roots – moved aside in the name of progress. But Wollstonecraft is long gone, moved the decade before Hardy arrived to be reburied with her Somers Town baby, in, of all places, Bournemouth.

Still, when Wollstonecraft was first interred this was a country churchyard, and the original site of her grave is a grassy slope down to the River Fleet. In the years after her death it's somewhere her two young daughters are often brought. The younger girl, a precocious child, even learns to read by tracing the letters on her mother's grave. For Mary Godwin and her older sister, Fanny, it must be as if their mother is in two places at once. She is the life-size figure in the chiaroscuro Opie portrait in their father's study: a pretty lady in a ghostly white dress. Afloat in the painterly murk, she looks as though she could really be in the shadowy room with them. But this masculine sanctum from which the household is run is hedged about with *Don't touch!* Luckily, their mother's also to be found outdoors, in the sunny churchyard at St Pancras. Here they both can and cannot touch her. Little Mary's fingers fit inside the grooved letters carved on the memorial. Learning to read involves repetition; it's easy to imagine her tracing them over and over.

The abandonment fury of the bereaved is a truism of twenty-first-century grief management. But the eighteenth century has no Elisabeth Kübler-Ross, and fury with no channel for expression can quickly turn to melancholia. Both Mary Wollstonecraft's daughters will struggle with circular, claustrophobic feelings of depression in their adult lives. What must it be like for a child to grow up in the house where her mother has died, to pass the door of the death chamber on the landing every day? Perhaps Wollstonecraft's daughters open it sometimes and step inside, looking around at the smallish, ordinary bedroom. Do they expect its banal bed and dressing table to communicate something? How can such big meaning be crammed into such a domestic space? And does this upper-floor room become the 'solitary chamber, or rather cell, at the top of the house, and separated from all the other apartments by a gallery and staircase' that the younger girl will grow up to imagine as a 'workshop of filthy creation'?

Mary will be just a teenager when she produces this claustrophobic description of the scientist's workshop in *Frankenstein*. A couple of pages later on in the novel she uses a similarly claustrophobic chiaroscuro in that famous focus on a catastrophic fictional nativity:

> With an anxiety that amounted almost to agony, I collected the instruments of life around me, that I might infuse a spark of being into the lifeless thing that lay at my feet. It was already one in the morning; the rain pattered dismally against the panes, and my candle was nearly burnt out, when, by the glimmer of the half-extinguished light, I saw the dull yellow eye of the creature open; it breathed hard, and a convulsive motion agitated its limbs.

This is the very same technique as Rembrandt's. But here the details that guttering candlelight catches on – the window panes, the 'dull yellow eye' – seem better suited to a deathbed than to a birth. Rembrandt's paintings use the portrayal of light to affirm their protagonists, create a sense of something shared, and invite us in. Mary's chiaroscuro works the opposite way. It seems to ask us to look, yet also to look away.

For now, though, Mary Godwin is just a little girl who lives at 29 the Polygon, in the house where she was born. Her famous father and her sister Fanny are her world; her famous mother hangs above the fireplace. It is a tenuous security, and it will be shaken when she turns four.

Chapter 2

Learning to Look

While I watched the tempest, so beautiful yet terrific, I wandered on with hasty step.

NUMBER 29 THE POLYGON has tall, modern windows. Sunlight reaches right into the rooms. As yet there are no buildings close by to interrupt its progress across their polished floors, and the people who live here can always tell roughly what time of day it is. At the turn of the new century, letting light in has become more important than keeping out the cold: at least, for fashionable architects and their patrons. Households like this one can afford coal – the hot-burning new fuel of choice – and the labour of domestic servants required to keep the grates clean and many fires set.

But smaller, old-fashioned windows shut out more than the cold. They also exclude the outside world. There's an aspect of display to the big windows of houses built, like this, in the Palladian style. Through their multiplying panes passers-by can see every detail of the rooms and the people who live in them. At times it's almost as if the households of the Polygon are performing for the street.

Of course they have curtains, though not the heavy draperies that will become the fashion in later decades, when Victorian culture takes hold of domestic style. As the nineteenth century dawns, excessive anxiety about concealment and modesty is still in the future. Curtains carry other connotations. Theatres expanded hugely in popularity during the eighteenth century, and their new audiences are discovering that stage curtains serve to frame rather than hide what happens on-stage. Indeed, it transpires that they perform a similar function for the newly developed theatre boxes. Curtains reveal how individuals, and the spaces they occupy, can be both private and public at the same time.

This fusing of public and private was formerly the preserve of royalty, or at least of political leaders. In 1801 it's part of the *zeitgeist*. Traditionally how palaces work, it remains a sign of authority. But authority itself is shifting. The two volumes of his *An Enquiry Concerning Political Justice*, published in 1793, have confirmed William Godwin as a leading social philosopher, and his lifestyle is designed as a model. A literally revolutionary era gives real urgency to questions about how to live; actual lives are the experiments through which these can be researched. As Jean-Jacques Rousseau, who has greatly influenced Godwin, puts it at the outset of his *Confessions*, of 1782, 'My purpose is to display to my kind a portrait in every way true to nature, and the man I shall portray will be myself.' Godwin's domestic display springs from the same source as the new interest in biography, to which he has also contributed with his controversial *Memoirs of the Author of A Vindication of the Rights of Woman*.

Questions about how to live are being repositioned somewhere between what we would nowadays call a political and a social science. This is an era of public knowledge, in which the idea of the professional researcher 'scientist' is about to be invented, and the experimental discipline of Natural Philosophy is publicly disseminated by lectures and publications. The possibilities of model communities are also being explored – a project that, as we'll see, the next generation of Romantics will make its own. (Already in 1800 Samuel Taylor Coleridge has joined the Wordsworths in the Lake District.) Contemporary Palladian architecture helps spread these and related ideas. Despite widespread use in the newly fashionable spa towns, it's not primarily a recreational toy. Instead, districts like Edinburgh's New Town, Bristol's Clifton and London's Bloomsbury both demonstrate and drive the mercantile and professional energy of their cities. Domestic monuments to the contemporary ascendancy of science and reason, the proportions of their façades repeat – and repeat – the Golden Section, while their outsize windows display the new possibilities of industrial rolled plate glass.

Growing up in this model home, Godwin's little daughter Mary takes glass for granted. But at four she still inhabits the underworld of infancy. Beyond the bright focus of her immediate attention, lots of things are unclear. Sometimes, like every child her age, she must be afraid of things she doesn't understand. For all that the daytime house is full of light, every evening it fills with shadow. On winter nights, even in the nursery, the leaping shadows cast by the fire seem more substantial than the candlelight. Things get lost in their obscurity. Every night her papa disappears in the darkness of downstairs. Even her sister, whose breathing she can hear in the other cot, seems vast distances away.

Sometimes Mary and her sister Fanny get taken out to play in the fields near by; sometimes they are taken to the churchyard where their mother is buried. One or two of these interludes may remain with her; most must disappear. Meanwhile, she's struggling with hooks and eyes, learning to dress herself and to do up her boots. At four she probably understands that sisters can be mean, and that sometimes people cheat at games, but she will still find it hard to keep up with the now seven-year-old Fanny.

Both sisters know the songs and games adults teach them but have almost no chance to pick up childhood lore, its codes and jokes. On the street and in schoolyards everything is fair game for games. Rules change. Songs mutate, misheard or deliberately borrowing from the here and now. Even names turn into nicknames: a child gains an extra moniker, like a new identity, in a moment. Language is pliable because it's made in the mouth, at the instant, on the fly. Sing-song skipping and clapping games generate rhyming variants that last an afternoon, or are repeated for years. Playing like this, children learn that language doesn't have to be a serious affair of literal meanings. It's just something you *do*. But, like many girls of their class and generation, Mary and Fanny are, and will largely remain, home-schooled. Even playing with each other is supervised and slightly claustrophobic.

It's hard to play when a writer is working in the house, especially when you're only four and that writer is your father. It's important not to make too much noise. Samuel Taylor Coleridge, a regular visitor to the household at the Polygon from 1799, finds the two Godwin girls delightful, but his initial reaction is that they are far too well behaved: 'the cadaverous Silence of Godwin's children is to me quite catacomb-ish: & thinking of Mary Wolstencroft [*sic*] I was oppressed by it', he tells Robert Southey.

Still, play they will. In 1801 the repertory of the middle-class nursery already includes such enduring staples as 'Hushaby baby on the tree-top', 'How many miles to Babylon?', 'Ride a cock horse to Banbury Cross', 'Who shot Cock Robin?', 'Oranges and lemons', 'Little Bo-Peep' and 'See-saw, Margery Daw'. We know this because the late eighteenth and early nineteenth centuries see a sudden flourishing in the publication of books for children: not least, collections of nursery rhymes. It's likely that a bookish household such as the Godwins' owns at least one of these, perhaps a newly republished *Mother Goose's Melody,* or *Gammer Gurton's Garland.* London's publishing and bookselling community encompasses both the bookshops on Ludgate Hill and the printers congregated around St Paul's Churchyard, where both Mary's parents have publishers. It would be nice to think that perhaps as she visited, in the spring of 1797, on business or just to browse, Mary Wollstonecraft picked up one of these collections for the baby she was expecting.

For she and Godwin can only approve of such modern, child-centred books: nursery rhymes work through delight, after all. Their lightly scrambled logic, their language blurred by repetition, are typical of oral transmission. Appealing to the imagination and the ear, they teach the child stories she at once believes in and knows are untrue, creating a jumbled imaginary, a half-human world of talking animals and people who are in some way not-quite-right. In her nursery Mary hears the bells of the City of London clearly, on still days and when the wind is from the east. She knows they're church bells, but thanks to nursery rhymes she also knows that they're saying, 'Here comes a chopper to chop off your head!' She knows that if, in a topsy-turvy world, a baby's cradle is stowed high up in the trees she sees from the nursery window, across the fields towards Camden Town, the wind will blow the 'baby, cradle and all' out, like a candle. She knows that just out of sight is a countryside populated with pigs who go marketing and Simple Simons who try to shop without money, where lambs have their tails sewn on instead of lopped off and sparrows turn into hunters with bows and arrows.

Short of playmates, Mary can enter an imaginary world that's not a million miles from the half-human creation of her most famous novel. The primal scene in the formation of the future writer, when her father teaches her to read by tracing the letters of her own name on her mother's tombstone, has probably taken place already, while he's still a widower without a new spouse – and a houseful of stepchildren – to distract him from his late wife's memory.

But when we ask what books Mary is reading when she's four, we come up against the frustrating near-silence that surrounds her growing up. Few records remain, not because no writing goes on either to or about her but because all her correspondence will subsequently be destroyed. The silence is deeper still because all that she herself chooses to save of her juvenilia will be lost in a trunk in Paris during her 1814 elopement. It's an astonishing deletion at the heart of a literary household with the habit of recording itself punctiliously for posterity. As a result, picturing Mary's childhood and adolescence means piecing together often circumstantial evidence. What we can guess is back-projected from what we know: enlarged and unclear, like nothing so much as those creatures generations of grown-ups have made out of the shadows of their hands against candle- and lamplight. Half-scared and half-delighted, the small child crows when wolves with sawing mouths chase rabbits across walls and ceiling: now stretching, now shrinking.

But these losses are yet to come. In August 1801, when she turns four, Mary is the apple of her father's eye. Godwin was himself a precociously brilliant child. At the age of five he was reading such age-inappropriate material as John Bunyan's *The Pilgrim's Progress*, James Janeway's grimly florid *A Token for Children, Being an Exact Account of the Conversion, Holy and Exemplary Lives and Joyful Deaths of Several Young Children* and religious verse by Dr Isaac Watts. He will expect no less precocity from a daughter he already sees as an infant Wollstonecraft. We also know that he is a man who bitterly resents his own upbringing and seeks to distance his parenting from the kind he received. So it's likely that Mary is encouraged to read, and to range relatively widely in her imagination even at four. She may need little encouragement. The era's children's books are frequently tiny, their pages less than half the size of a twenty-first-century paperback. Any little girl would treasure these volumes, which fit her hands the way an adult book does a grown-up grip.

We do know, though, that her first storybooks include her mother's own *Original Stories from Real Life*, in the 1791 edition. Its illustrations, etchings of unusual sophistication and delicacy, are by her mother's friend William Blake. In *Original Stories* a Mrs Mason, who rather resembles Mrs Doasyouwouldbedoneby in Charles Kingsley's *The Water Babies* almost a century later, teaches ethics to the two orphans she's raising by letting them experience moral choice in action. The child reader in turn observes and learns. It's just the strategy Mary will use to implicate her readers in *Frankenstein*, where our loyalties change as we learn more of the story, but not because the narrator tells us they should. A more widely read contemporary children's book using this method of moral instruction that she may also know is *The Looking-Glass for the Mind* – an abridged translation from the French of Arnaud Berquin – which is designed to make its child readers see their own behaviour 'reflected' in its pages. Hugely successful, it will be pseudonymously plagiarised by Mary's own father in a few years' time, when in 1805 'M. J. Godwin & Co.' publishes *The Looking Glass*, by 'Theophilus Marcliffe'.

Perhaps images from these books flicker at the extremities of Mary's imagination. But the whole house is her four-year-old's world. Surrounded by love, she can't remember a time without her foster mother: Louisa Jones arrived just days after she herself was brought home after her mother's funeral, at three weeks old. Louisa is no servant but a friend of Mary's aunt Hannah, who comes to dinner every fortnight. Somehow, even in the early days of his grief, Godwin has managed to find among his sister's friends a volunteer to run his household and act as foster mother for Mary Wollstonecraft's little girls. This kind of home is an article of belief with him. He resents having been sent away to a wet-nurse for the first two years of his own life. It seems to him further evidence of the parental neglect that saw him raised, at least until he went to boarding-school at the age of eleven, chiefly by one of his father's cousins. Now, the man who was 'sent from home to be nourished by a hireling' wants his own daughter raised within the family.

Such class distinctions might seem out of place in a social revolutionary. But Godwin's is neither the first nor the last social conscience to recognise precisely the difference that circumstances make to a child. Louisa Jones can create a nurturing, familial atmosphere for three-year-old Fanny and baby Mary, who is not at first expected to survive. Indeed, the infant's very frailty is possibly what has persuaded Louisa to try domestic life in the Godwin household. After all, 1797 is not a good year for a young woman who has to look to her marriage prospects to be living in a revolutionary household. But she may feel this is a temporary arrangement. Perhaps Godwin does too: it's ironic, after all, that he is a feminist philosopher, yet views a woman as necessary for the creation of domesticity. But then – as he admits to one of Wollstonecraft's close friends, Mrs Cotton – by the time Mary is two months old he already understands that, when it comes to child-rearing, 'I am the most unfit person for this office'.

Luckily, there's a cohort of women friends and family members to help raise the girls, or keep an eye on those who are doing so. Louisa moves out of number 29 after fifteen months, when she starts a relationship with one of her employer's protégés, but for more than two years she continues to come in daily. The girls are also visited frequently by one of their mother's closest friends, Eliza Fenwick, whose own children are already Fanny's playmates, and by Harriet Godwin, another aunt. Harriet is a slightly less genteel influence than some since Joseph, the Godwin brother she has married, works as a servant. Nevertheless, she is family. Isolated in the rural north of Norfolk, widowed Grandmother Godwin doesn't visit, but she does send numerous letters of advice, and gifts ranging from knitted socks to family heirlooms. Finally, too, there are the servants themselves: the nursemaid Cooper, and Marguerite Fournée, who was Wollstonecraft's maid and has cared for Fanny since her birth.

Baby Mary is helpless to do anything but love her caregiver. The same isn't true for Fanny, who is three when her mother disappears, to be replaced by a stranger. She forms no attachment with Louisa. Indeed, it's not clear to what extent she forms attachments to any of the women who humanise her childhood for the first four years of her orphanhood. After all, although she doesn't yet know it, Fanny isn't related to any member of her family. At least, she doesn't know this consciously: even the best-intentioned adult will sometimes make, perhaps unconsciously, a distinction between one of their 'own' and someone else's child. Is Fanny always the less fussed-over little girl? Is it taken relatively for granted that, having weathered the vulnerabilities of babyhood, she is the more likely to survive – and is this how taking her for granted could start? Two years after her mother's death, Fanny experiences another loss at the age of five, when Marguerite Fournée, the woman who has been her nursemaid since she was an infant, moves out of the Polygon to get married. Like Louisa, Marguerite returns daily to the house. But day labour isn't the same as living in: above all, not when it comes to a child's need to be cuddled, played with and listened to.

William Godwin's involvement in fathering the girls is up to date as well as a repudiation of his own parents' hands-off methods. He seems to have absorbed wholesale his late wife's belief that 'It is possible, I am convinced, to acquire the affection of a parent for an adopted child', and doesn't hesitate to raise Fanny as his own, encouraging her to call herself Fanny Godwin. During her childhood, at least until adolescence, she believes he is her father. Something much warmer than charity is clearly at work in this decision of Godwin's, which has the rapidity of instinct. Fanny and her baby sister are all he has left of his wife; and since the baby's life appears to be in danger, Fanny may be Wollstonecraft's sole posterity. Besides, the unexpected pleasure Fanny's presence seems to have brought him during their courtship is an inexpungible part of that history.

On the day after the infant Mary comes home from her wet-nurse, Godwin asks the famous physicist William Nicholson to conduct a phrenological examination in order to establish her personal qualities. Her father is the first, but not the last, of Mary's great loves to see her both as herself and as a kind of Russian Matryoshka doll: a toy 'darling Mary' whose parentage is packed inside her. Later in life Godwin will dismiss phrenology as superstitious essentialism. But grief is often the parent of superstition. And Mary's birth, like his grief for her mother, has rearranged his certainties. Having his own daughter shakes up his view on equality of talent, so key to the philosophy on which he has built his intellectual and political life. Before she is a year old, he has already decided that 'there exist differences of the highest importance between human beings from the period of their birth'.

For four years, until 1801, Godwin manages to sustain his model parenting despite everything going on in his own life. Even on a summer trip to Dublin that is otherwise professionally and personally highly satisfying, he can't resist writing home anxiously with questions about and kisses for the girls – in a letter that is equally revealing about Mary's insecurity and dependency:

> Tell Mary, I will not give her away, & she shall be nobody's little girl, but Papa's: papa is gone away, but papa will soon come back again, & look out at the coach-window, & see the Polygon across two fields, from the trunks of the trees at Camden Town. Will Mary and Fanny come and meet me?

Outside the home, however, these are years of disappointment. The rushed publication of *Memoirs of the Author* in January 1798 has made both his beloved late wife and himself into scapegoats, to be traduced and set slightly beyond the social and intellectual pale. His four-volume novel *St Leon*, published the following year, has not done what he hoped. He intended it as a novel of ideas, but it's widely read and reviewed as a straightforward historical novel, while his friends view it as schematic and disappointing. His 1800 verse-drama *Antonio* is a failure despite being produced at Drury Lane with the famous Mrs Sarah Siddons, who was a friend of his late wife, as the female lead. Positioned by the anti-Jacobin press as a crank at best, and dangerously immoral at worst, Godwin lacks the social graces that might, in compensation, turn him into a glamorous rebel.

Despite this, in these years of widowerhood Godwin's intellectual and artistic friendships remain numerous and strong, and colour the environment in which his children grow up. One fixture in his social diary for over ten years is his fortnightly Sunday evening dinner with fellow radical and writer Thomas Holcroft and other friends from early days. He goes to St Paul's Churchyard almost every week, to dine with Joseph Johnson above the publisher's offices. Johnson is not only his own publisher; he was also Wollstonecraft's mentor, who commissioned her first books, and her employer on the *Analytical Review*. Indeed, it was at one of Johnson's Monday dinners that Godwin and Wollstonecraft first met, although on that occasion they didn't 'take'. Many of the authors on Johnson's list join these famous evenings. A roster as distinguished as it is radical, it includes Thomas Paine, William Blake, William Cowper, William Wordsworth and Thomas Malthus. John Bonnycastle the mathematician and the artist Henry Fuseli – who was once Godwin's rival for Mary Wollstonecraft and is still disliked by him – are also regulars.

When these figures visit Godwin at home, their talk fills the rooms. Mary, who is allowed from early childhood to listen in and soon, while still a child, to join them for dinner, is surfacing into a world where talk is debate, and thinking the paramount human activity. Even in 1801 the words she's hearing, perhaps without understanding them, far outreach the language of children's stories. The political and philosophical terms her father and his friends repeat must sound charming in her babyish voice. But they are also becoming familiar, so that, as she continues to grow and meets them again and again, she will find she already understands them. She's a child raised by the intellectual *zeitgeist*.

If, despite these connections, Godwin's continued political reputation and a certain lack of charm make him a failure with the ladies, it's not for want of trying. Three months after Wollstonecraft's death he approaches his old flame Maria Reveley about some form of living-in, and perhaps proto-wifely, arrangement. After she is unexpectedly widowed in 1799, he returns to the theme and proposes to her: not surprisingly, she takes this as more the renewal of a domestic job offer than a romantic declaration. (When she refuses, arguing for the importance of love, he rather gracelessly writes back, pointing out the practical and worldly advantages she's turning down.) In 1798 Godwin proposes unsuccessfully to the Bath author Harriet Lee. When she too turns him down, he continues to pursue her for another half-year, advancing such attractive arguments as: 'Celibacy contracts and palsies the mind, and shuts us out from the most valuable topics of experience.' Godwin's belief in salutary honesty may derive from his background as a Dissenting minister: his education and first training in an era when to choose this alternative to the established church implied a literal belief in 'fire and brimstone', and entailed various forms of social exclusion. His plain speaking also faces forward into the Romantic preoccupation with the truth of what the individual actually experiences and feels. But there's no context in which it's seductive to tell a woman that she will be an old maid without you.

This graceless batting about appears like nothing so much as panic. There's an awkward disproportion between the feelings being expressed and their occasion. Embarrassing surviving letters include one in which Godwin comes on heavily to a woman he has just met in the street. Individual human lives are rarely ideal, their truths rarely tidy – something that Godwin's daughter will learn repeatedly in years to come. Indeed, resolving the awkwardnesses of the individual life story is destined to become one of her personal and professional preoccupations. But at four years old, of course, she's unaware of her father's undignified attempts at courtship – although they matter to her profoundly, because they are leading him into the arms of Mary Jane Clairmont, the woman who becomes her stepmother on 21 December 1801.

It's to be an expulsion from paradise. Yet things begin well enough, from Mary's point of view. Over the summer when she turns four, her father and Mrs Clairmont, who lives next door at number 27, spend increasing amounts of time together. For Mary and her sister this means play-dates with the young Clairmonts: Jane, who is eight months younger than Mary, and five-year-old Charles.

Mary Godwin is a child of startling precocity. Her close friendship with a child who is the best part of a year younger than herself must be one of her earliest lessons in compromise. Nevertheless, Jane *is* Mary's first best friend: as lively as herself, and a welcome change from the demure Fanny, she's also more amenable to fun, not least because she can be bossed about. The two girls are mirror images of each other: Jane dark and Mary fair. They're of an age to be fascinated by this, and to delight in recognising themselves as a pair. In the daily adventure of being three, then four, it's likely that they sometimes play at 'being' each other in games of let's pretend, swapping names or possessions: clothes, say, or a toy. Absorbed in the novelty of such a friendship, Mary's possessive instincts are unlikely to be aroused when the two families spend time together, even going to the pantomime as a party in July. For both Mary and her father this is a glorious season of affection of an unfamiliar kind. Each has the delightful experience of having a new, positive version of themselves mirrored back by someone they're just getting to know.

Is Godwin as naïve as his daughter? According to later accounts of this courtship, Mary Jane Clairmont makes the running, using the kind of shameless manipulation that shouts *man's woman*. We're told that, once they have been introduced or otherwise met in May 1801 – 'Do I have the honour of beholding the immortal author of *Political Justice*?', she's alleged to have cried – on subsequent occasions when her next-door neighbour is in his garden, she slips into her own, and then exclaims audibly, 'You great Being, how I adore you!' Whether this is the exact case or not, reports of her character once she becomes Mrs Godwin are certainly of a piece with such a stratagem. Godwin's soon displaced personal secretary James Marshall, admittedly a witness with no incentive to be generous, describes her as a 'clever, bustling, second-rate woman, glib of tongue and pen, with a temper undisciplined and uncontrolled; not bad-hearted, but with a complete absence of all the finer sensibilities'. Yet, to the mystification of his friends, Godwin is clearly delighted and enamoured. Charles Lamb describes how he

> bows when he is spoke to, and smiles without occasion, and wriggles as fantastically as Malvolio, and has more affectation than a canary bird pluming its feathers when he thinks somebody looks at him. He lays down his spectacles, as if in scorn, and takes 'em up again from necessity, and winks that she mayn't see he gets sleepy about eleven o'clock. You never saw such a philosophic coxcomb, nor any one play the Romeo so unnaturally.

Mary Jane is the canny survivor, a type instantly recognisable across the centuries. She is also a practical woman who, despite contemporary handicaps of gender, makes things happen. In the years to come she will even make an entrepreneur out of the unlikely Godwin. And she is at least thirty-five when she meets him. Time is running out for her to achieve the social and financial safety of marriage. She already has two illegitimate children, the offspring of different fathers. Of 'Mr Clairmont', that flag of social convenience, needless to say no trace has ever been found: Charles's father, Charles Gaulis, a Swiss merchant living in Bristol, died before Jane was conceived. What could be more natural, when she finds herself next door to an eligible – at any rate, eligible *enough* – widower, than that she should try her luck with him? What has she to lose? Her probable lack of subtlety might be apparent, even laughable, to the intelligentsia who make up Godwin's set; but it works. Her tactical assessment of the massageability of the male ego – call it the Clairmont Manoeuvre – still resonates today.

Besides, she has much to offer Godwin. She represents the domesticity he longs for. Indeed, she can supply it better than Mary Wollstonecraft, who explicitly rejected domestic responsibility for the joint household. Man's woman *contra* feminist, Mary Jane will exercise her very traditional source of power by seizing the domestic reins, not loosening her grip on them. Also, unlike the other women he has been courting recently, by July 1801 she is giving Godwin sex. Not surprisingly, given both protagonists' poor track records on contraception, she soon becomes pregnant. Perhaps she even does so deliberately, or at least half-consciously, knowing he will 'do the decent thing', whatever his intellectual reputation. After all, she knows the dates both of his marriage to Mary Wollstonecraft and of their daughter's birth: so she's fully aware that pregnancy precipitated his first wedding – and that he has no regrets about the marriage.

As for the happy chance of being William Godwin's neighbour: can we be absolutely sure that this is an accident either? Mary Jane Clairmont is intelligent enough: it is her own earnings as a translator and author of children's books that support her family in the stylish comfort of the Polygon. There is no reason she might not have heard through mutual publishing contacts about Godwin's increasingly desperate search for a wife. Eligible men prepared to marry are everywhere at a premium; a woman with a search of her own knows better than to pass up such a lead. Might 'Mrs Clairmont' have rented 27 the Polygon at around the time, in May 1801, that Godwin's diary first mentions her, *because* it's next door to his house?

Certainly her spectacularly rackety background reveals someone determined to take risks in search of a better life. Born in Exeter, she apparently ran away from home when still a child, after the death of her mother, to live – evidently in some style – with her father's relatives in France. Godwin rightly admires this precocious bravery. Of course, he has only his new wife's word for it that she *was* a child when she made this journey: in other words, that she is the age she says she is now. What he possibly doesn't know is that she and her sister Sophia were heirs to a pub, the Fleur de Lys, in the backstreets of Exeter; he may also not be aware that little Jane's actual father is a member of the Somerset gentry, Sir John Lethbridge of Sandhill Park, Taunton, who later becomes 'bored' of the pregnant Mary Jane and tries hard to avoid supporting her and his child. Lethbridge's reactions to Mary Jane as the mother of his child fascinatingly and uncannily prefigure Lord Byron's reactions to impregnating the adult Jane: 'this artful Harpey', Lethbridge tells his solicitor, 'is an extraordinary production in nature; & I had no business to have anything to do with her'. Godwin may be even less well aware that as a result the woman he is about to marry has been destitute, was examined by the Poor Board and spent about four months from 21 April 1799 imprisoned for debt in Ilchester Prison.

Nevertheless, by the time they wed Godwin does know something of Mary Jane's self-invention. On 21 December the couple have not one but two secret weddings. Presumably this is so that, if the untruth of their public narrative is discovered and the marriage made on its terms is annulled, the couple will remain legally married. So, at St Leonard's, Shoreditch, he marries 'Mary Clairmont, widow of this parish', with James Marshall as witness. Later the same day, at St Mary's, Whitechapel, he marries – using Mary Jane's correct maiden name – 'Mary Vial of Mary le Bone, spinster', with no friends present.

Whatever other compromises are going on, the pregnancy on which this marriage is based is not a fiction. Some time in the spring of 1802 a son, William, is born, stillborn or miscarried. Although the child does not survive, a second William, born just under a year later, in March 1803, does complete the family. Now with five children under ten, all of whom will make it to adulthood, Mary Jane's role as mother and stepmother is an important one, and she fills it energetically.

No sooner has she married Godwin than the informal arrangement with the coterie of petticoats in the nursery is swept away. So are the staff Godwin has employed. Gone, with Mary's foster mother Louisa, are Marguerite Fournée and Cooper, to be replaced by a Miss Hooley, along with a maid, a live-in governess and a male tutor. James Marshall is moved out of the house. And the precocious Mary is sent briefly and unsuccessfully to a local day school. At a stroke, in December 1801 the house becomes female-led, and Mary's infancy is over. Ceding her place as petted baby of the family first to Jane and then to William, she becomes merely a middle child. She also finds herself suddenly the middle of three daughters. It must be a fairly rude awakening, one that makes her, albeit in half-formed, childish ways, change her ideas about her place in the world.

In this newly feminised environment, for example, the importance of appearance, and so of mirrors, cannot be lost on her. At the start of the nineteenth century glass is still blown, then tooled in various ways, by hand. The results are uneven. Panes of hand-blown window glass make the view ripple and bulge. In domestic mirrors, glass distorts the person looking at herself. Sometimes this is funny, and must make the three little girls living at number 29 laugh at themselves and each other. At other times it's not fun at all. Mary looks at Jane, her sister–companion, and sees a stable, undistorted prettiness. But as she moves about in a mirror, her own image distends or atrophies. She knows this is an effect of the glass, but it shows her the possibility of being ugly, a 'mummy again endued with animation […] a thing such as even Dante could not have conceived': trapped, like Frankenstein's creature, by the reactions such ugliness elicits.

Looking is knowing, and what Mary can't see – her own face – she can't know. This is the lesson contemporary experimental research and philosophy have taught each other, and taught the world in which she lives. 'Natural philosophy is the genius that has regulated my fate', Mary's *Frankenstein* will one day declare. Empiricism – 'natural philosophy' – is seen as the way to understand the world. As its name suggests, the discipline assumes that existential questions have practical answers, that what we observe is the measure of what we know. Chairs, including one at Oxford University, have been established in the field, which becomes an explicit part of Mary's own understanding as she begins to grow up. Among her father's frequent visitors, for example, is Sir Humphry Davy, famous for his public scientific experiments, including demonstrations of the electrical 'galvanism' on which he's appointed to the Royal Institution in 1801 to work.

This, which seems to throw up questions about the nature of life itself, is among the most eagerly debated specialism of the day. Probably its most notorious public demonstration – passing an electrical current through various nerves in the body of a convicted murderer – is conducted by the Italian discoverer Luigi Galvani's own nephew Giovanni Aldini in January 1803:

> On the first application of the process to the face, the jaws of the deceased criminal began to quiver, and the adjoining muscles were horribly contorted, and one eye was actually opened. In the subsequent part of the process the right hand was raised and clenched, and the legs and thighs were set in motion.

Another of William Godwin's guests, Dr Henry Cline, eventually Master of the College of Surgeons, will become well known in 1814 for the clinical use of galvanism, successfully rousing a patient from a month's long coma.

Godwin's intellectual reputation may be undergoing vicissitudes at the time of his marriage to Mary Jane, but he remains at the leading edge of contemporary thought. And that thought is changing. In 1805 he publishes *Fleetwood,* a novel set in early eighteenth-century north Wales that portrays Rousseau-ian education as a dangerous naïvety. Appearing four years after the arrival of her stepmother, and in the year Godwin becomes a small businessman, *Fleetwood* is of particular significance for Mary because it rejects the educational theories on which her parents had agreed, and which he promised her dying mother to follow.

Yet these ideas are still the best clue we have to what and how Mary Godwin is taught in childhood, and they fit with the little we do know about her during these years. In 1783, when he left the Dissenting ministry, Godwin had briefly – and unsuccessfully – tried to start a school. Its prospectus, a fifty-four-page essay entitled *An Account of the Seminary,* was short on practical details but instead laid out educational beliefs informed by, in particular, Jean-Jacques Rousseau's *Emile, or On Education* (1762), John Locke's *An Essay Concerning Human Understanding* (1690) and *Some Thoughts Concerning Education* (1693), which argue respectively that the mind is a *tabula rasa*, filled by education, and that learning is done best when the body is healthy, and Claude Adrien Helvétius's *De l'esprit* (1758), which also held with the *tabula rasa*, arguing for the natural equality of intelligences and the consequently determining role of education. Godwin's own *An Account* takes up the *tabula rasa* principle, arguing that the child is born not in a state of original sin but, on the contrary, spotless. Teaching shouldn't mean, as it did in Godwin's own Calvinist childhood, driving out the child's 'fallen' nature; on the contrary, his (or her) intrinsic goodness must be preserved and encouraged. This is accomplished by teaching children about their own, human nature: something best done through history and, next to history, literature, the Classics and modern languages. Human stories – what we nowadays call the humanities – allow children to discriminate and to emulate: just like the moral primers of Mary's early childhood, in fact.

Mary Wollstonecraft's own ideas on child-rearing and education are based not only on personal experience with her first daughter, Fanny, but on the time she spent as a teacher and governess. Her first book, *Thoughts on the Education of Daughters* (1786), was written after the failure of a school she had set up with her sisters. Its ideas are rooted in the feminist philosophy – in other words, in ideas about how personhood is created and what it comprises – that she would explore more fully six years later in her *A Vindication of the Rights of Woman*. In that famous later work, Chapter 12 is titled 'On National Education', and Chapter 13 contains a section on the importance of educating women so that they develop good parenting skills, for 'so early do [children] catch a character, that the basis of the moral character, experience leads me to infer, is fixed before their seventh year'.

Today, Wollstonecraft's argument for girls' education seems unnecessarily conservative, both self-evident and open to question: women's education matters because it is they who raise children. She doesn't quite go so far as to say *which matters because half of these will be boys*, but she certainly focuses on boys' education. Her language here is gloriously rhetorical:

> And what nasty indecent tricks do they not also learn from each other, when a number of them pig together in the same bedchamber, not to speak of the vices, which render the body weak, whilst they effectually prevent the acquisition of any delicacy of mind.

The concise contempt of that verb 'to pig' is Wollstonecraft at her passionate and idiosyncratic best. Its force reminds us that she is truly no conservative but simply practising the philosophical method, which is never to speculate but to proceed only from what is known – and, in 1792, universal education for women has never been tried.

We should remember too that, though it may be the work for which we now value her most, this was Wollstonecraft's second *Vindication*. It was her *A Vindication of the Rights of Men*, appearing (initially anonymously) two years earlier, that had made her famous. In this first published response to Edmund Burke's anti-revolutionary *Reflections on the French Revolution* of 1790, she argued that the true 'Rights of Men' are intrinsic to everyone and arise from our human nature, rather than being the property rights of the wealthy few. It's a critique of a top-down political system, while *Rights of Woman* challenges the more intractable, bottom-up systems of actual social practice, but Wollstonecraft's argument in both proceeds from the same premise. To be human is to be born rational. The human who isn't allowed to exercise that rationality becomes damaged.

This was Wollstonecraft's common ground with Godwin, whose *Political Justice* makes similar arguments for and from reason on the larger canvas of whole societies, which, he argues, need no government – something that simply produces dependency and so prevents the individual from rational self-determination. This whole argument hangs, of course, on its own assumptions about humans' inherent and equal rationality. But as a basis for thinking about education, it becomes an argument for developing a child's reasoning rather than, for example, their obedience or memory. Godwin and Wollstonecraft were united in their opposition to rote learning, and their interest in developing enquiring minds. It's an intellectual version of learning by doing: languages ancient and modern, or the understanding of texts and facts, are skills to be mastered, not knowledge to be crammed.

From a twenty-first-century perspective, knowledge at the turn of the nineteenth century appears strikingly participative. Philosophers expect responses to their books: the five-year delay before the first published 'replies' to William Godwin's *Political Justice* is unusual. There will be no notion of the *professional* scientist until 1834. Contemporary popularisation of science has taught the lecture-going urban upper classes that observation *is* the scientific method, and that they themselves can make those same observations. *Nullius in verba*, 'take no one's word for it', is the motto of the Royal Society itself: 'received wisdom' is a contradiction in terms. The growing European publishing industry has led to a large number of books, periodicals – such as the Royal Society's *Philosophical Transactions* – and encyclopaedias, including several devoted to science, which can be purchased or read in coffee houses and reading rooms. Demonstrations are hugely popular, both in public and in the affluent home. Observatories and cabinets of scientific instruments are being developed both in Britain and overseas. These cabinets include telescopes, microscopes, lodestones, compasses and globes, barometers, thermometers, air and suction pumps, models of larger-scale machines such as mills, and numerous devices designed purely to demonstrate mechanical and physical properties, such as gravity or the workings of steam: a cornucopia of brass and glass.

To see is to know, and London is the world centre of scientific instrument-making. Rather like publishers, instrument-makers are at the same time shopkeepers and socially and intellectually distinguished specialists, the best of whom are elected Fellows of the Royal Society. The gifted craftsmen of families such as the Troughtons and the Adamses produce optical instruments that drive whole new areas of study, even though their glass itself is flawed: Michael Faraday's discovery of how to make accurate optical glass for lenses is still two decades away.

Examination is minute but also public. In a world where the corpses of criminals are 'experimented' on in public in the name of knowledge, moral inhibition is trumped by progress. Private, unannounced research seems a contradiction in terms: what would it be for? Some hangover from what Mary's Frankenstein calls 'the dreams of forgotten alchymists', perhaps, with their occult researches into 'the philosopher's stone and the elixir of life'. When Mary comes to write her first novel, one of the ways in which she flags such science as sinister is by having her researcher undertake it in isolation.

What can be seen defines what is the case. In the month that Mary turns ten, Mary Jane and the five children of the Godwin household move from the generous modernity of the Polygon to darker, more overlooked quarters in a house above a shop on a Holborn street corner. Her father doesn't follow till November: it's not altogether clear that he's wholly straightforward in his dealings with their Polygon landlady as he leaves. Intellectually, the philosopher may value truth, clarity and the 'light' of reason. But as the entrepreneur husband of Mary Jane he seems to have taken lessons in the usefulness of a little chiaroscuro.

Number 41 Skinner Street is a five-storey corner building facing two ways, on to Skinner Street and Fleet Market. It has no basement area: the street abuts the ground-floor windows. Like the Polygon, it's part of a half-failed and incomplete speculative build; the house has stood empty for the five or six years since its construction. The surrounding neighbour-hood is built up without necessarily being very lively. And with good reason. There are three prisons close by, and the house is within earshot of both Smithfield Market, where cattle are slaughtered nightly, and the New Drop at Old Bailey, where public executions take place every few weeks. The abattoir stink of the meat market and the threatening, noisy crowds who surge in to see the hangings seem to press up against the very walls of this new home. Unlike the Polygon, with its smells of fresh air and fields, this is a house in which to keep the windows shut. Gone is the garden of Mary's childhood, where she and Fanny helped Cooper pick the peas. Gone are the views of hills and trees. The windows at Skinner Street are large enough, but they look out on other shops and houses.

Because it occupies a corner site, the house buries the two sides that don't make up frontage in the terraces it joins on either side. Literally blind-sided, it faces only front – a house that is all show. It's also a home in which roles have been reversed. The powerhouse is no longer Mary's father's first-floor study but the unavoidable ground-floor shop, presided over by her stepmother. The house has no other entrance.

Writing, formerly sublimated as intellectual adventure, turns out to be something to sell. For number 41 is – at least – on a street of book-sellers. By now Godwin has been a publisher for around two years, and he has been writing pseudonymous books for children for three more. The names under which he writes seem almost to develop into hetero-nyms, each with its own specialism. Edward Baldwin, author of *Fables, Ancient and Modern* (1805) and *The History of England for the Use of Schools and Young Persons* (1806), is the historian. His *History of England* (1806), *History of Rome* (1809) and *History of Greece* (1821) will continue to be reprinted into the 1860s. William Scolfield retells *Bible Stories* for chil-dren. And Theophilus Marcliffe writes books with improving morals for the young, including his copycat *The Looking Glass*.

Godwin produces relatively little serious work during these years. No surprise: since 1805 he's been maintaining, as well as 29 the Polygon, a house off Oxford Street for use as a bookseller–publisher, and making the building pay by taking in lodgers. His notoriety means that these projects have had to be kept at arm's length. But secrets have a habit of running away with themselves. The bookshop, in Hanway Street, is set up in the name of Thomas Hodgkins, the man Godwin employs to run it. He's thus able to embezzle the money it makes – and he does.

At Skinner Street, where the new bookshop is set up in his wife's name as M. J. Godwin & Co., family life combines with business prem-ises. Soon these in turn combine with the Juvenile Library, which marries commerce with a discreet dissemination of liberal social and educational ideas. Publishing writing by fine radical contemporary minds, Charles and Mary Lamb's among them, is commercially attractive and keeps stan-dards high; it also keeps Godwin connected to his intellectual peers. His crack at integration, the move is presumably also an attempt to econo-mise after the financial disaster of Hanway Street, though Godwin has to borrow heavily to set up each successive business.

So far his signature single-mindedness has allowed Godwin to follow a line of intellectual enquiry with depth and determination, and propelled him from provincial Dissenting ministry into intellectual life at the heart of the metropolis. But it's a mixed blessing. He seems able to see only one possible course of action at any time. Merely a social embarrassment half a dozen years ago when he was chasing a wife, this character trait now mixes with financial investment and the volatile world of business to become a liability. It's as if the man himself, and not just his new home, is blind-sided. As a result of his new obsession with publishing, Godwin will continue to have financial problems for most of his life.

Of course, there are virtues to such monomania. It's the blind side of the glass that makes mirrors work. This paradox isn't lost on wider contemporary society. In nineteenth-century Europe, *Spiegelkabinette* (Mirror Cabinets) or *Lachkabinette* (Laughing Cabins) have quickly become popular. They're the poor man's version of the Halls of Mirrors and Mirror Labyrinths that eighteenth-century technology, and indulgent Romanticism, have already made possible in palaces and castles from Finland and Russia to Austria and France.

Like a giant version of the domestic mirrors of Mary's nursery, the *Spiegelkabinett* dares punters to step inside and discover a hitherto unsuspected ugliness in themselves. But ugliness and beauty are neither incidental nor superficial in Mary Godwin's world. As they grow up, she and her young peers are being shaped by the mood of their parents' times, and it's not only science that judges by appearances. This initial decade of the nineteenth century still belongs to the first generation of Romantics, for whom apprehension is everything. The first edition of *Lyrical Ballads* was published anonymously by Wordsworth and Coleridge in October 1798, just a year after Mary's birth. Wordsworth's *Poems in Two Volumes* appears in the year when she turns ten; she becomes eleven in the year in which Goethe publishes the first part of *Faust*; finally, the precocious first two cantos of Lord Byron's *Childe Harold's Pilgrimage* appear in the summer she turns fifteen.

It's unlikely that the young Mary reads these books as they're published. But they are in the cultural air, both inside and beyond her home. They share a moment, and a movement, with painters such as Godwin's old acquaintance Henry Fuseli or the giganticist painter and part-time sewage pioneer David Martin. Awe-inspiring, 'picturesque' or grotesque: in Romantic art and literature appearances are the measure of meaning.

The malleable emerging minds of Mary's generation absorb these measures wholesale.

Even before the Godwins move to Skinner Street, Coleridge reads *The Rime of the Ancient Mariner* to an audience that includes the eight-year-old Mary and Jane – until they're discovered, hiding behind the sofa. Only at Coleridge's pleading does Mary Jane allow the girls to stay for the remainder of the recitation, which makes a huge impression on Mary. An ice storm is added to her imaginative stock:

> And ice, mast-high, came floating by,
> As green as emerald.
>
> And through the drifts the snowy cliffs
> Did send a dismal sheen:
> Nor shapes of men nor beasts we ken –
> The ice was all between.
>
> The ice was here, the ice was there,
> The ice was all around:
> It cracked and growled, and roared and howled,
> Like noises in a swound!

This 'production of the most imaginative of modern poets' will make an explicit appearance in Mary's first novel when Walton, the narrator who frames her story, promises his sister that:

> I am going to unexplored regions, to 'the land of mist and snow'; but
> I shall kill no albatross, therefore do not be alarmed for my safety,
> or if I should come back to you as worn and woeful as the 'Ancient
> Mariner'.

Imagination is well and good, but by the time she arrives in Skinner Street, Mary has private anxieties to bring to the mirror. Even the liberal world she inhabits idealises the role of the mother and, as a maternal orphan who effectively killed her mother by being born, she is this ideal's opposite. Moreover, she has in the emotional and strong-willed Mary Jane a stepmother who seems to compete on her own daughter's behalf. As if to level some imagined privilege, the second Mrs Godwin provides Jane with advantages, such as music lessons, that are denied Mary. We know already that Mary Jane is a fabulist, and that she's good at managing – we might even say manipulating – Godwin. We also know that she has been unafraid to act to defend her interests. All these qualities, better in an ally than in an enemy, make her a formidable adult for a child to cross.

Even beyond the tensions of the actual relationship, Mary Jane's arrival must trigger, for Mary, a whole new understanding of what her mother's death means. It's the first time she's seen mothering up close and for any length of time. When she compares herself to her 'mirror', Jane, she can't miss the fact that chief among their opposites is the presence in the house of Jane's mother, and the absence of her own. This developing consciousness of her own lack coincides with the normal childish development of self-awareness. A ten-year-old notices things beyond and alongside the single object of her attention in a way no four-year-old, however precocious, does. At what point, for example, does Mary realise she is has something in common with the changelings of fairy tales, the stories she hears at bedtime and round the nursery fire? Fanny is also now motherless: but orphans are portrayed sympathetically, and often, in stories. It is her matricidal birth that sets Mary apart.

Nor are folk tales the only stories she must be absorbing about exceptions who – like Frankenstein's creature – were not born in the 'natural' way. It's reasonable to assume that Mary's schooling exposes her to the canonical myths, since the nineteenth century gives those children it does educate an early Classical grounding. It's likely she learns about the goddess Athena, born from Zeus's forehead, when she's still a child. Her father publishes the Lambs' famous *Tales from Shakespeare* in his Children's Library in 1807, when Mary turns ten; so she may also know at a young age about Macbeth's nemesis Macduff, 'none of woman born' because he was a Caesarean birth, 'from his mother's womb / Untimely ripped'.

Having no mother seems to confer some kind of uncanny, not quite human, status on a child. With their dark curls, Jane, her brother Charles and their mother, Mary Jane, resemble each other. Even Fanny is a brunette. But Mary is strawberry blonde. When she looks in the mirror, whom does she resemble? It's hard to detect her father, with his male pattern baldness and thin intellectual's nose, in her own image. Her mother, in the beautiful portrait from her father's study, is surely remoter still, veiled as she is in the unreality of paint. Most children pass through phases of self-consciousness and outgrow them. But there's something ineradicable about the experience of resembling no one as you grow up.

Since the years in which her stepmother takes over running the family are also the years in which Mary's education develops, is it any wonder she resorts to being a Clever Child? Intellectual knowledge probably appears more straightforward than the slippery human relationships around her. As this is her father's realm, intellectual work also allows her to get closer to him.

We know now that precocity is among the coping mechanisms of children without mothers, who can be over-invested in adult approval, or at least attention. It's as if, lacking a mother, they need some other mirror in which to see themselves affirmed. Mary may not become the child her father boasts of – 'singularly bold, somewhat imperious and active of mind, her desire of knowledge is great, and her perseverance in every thing she undertakes, almost invincible' – *because* she's in revolt against her stepmother or in mourning for her mother. But her troubled childhood relationship with mother figures is certainly likely to encourage an escape into the worlds of imagination and of books.

Chapter 3

Through a Door
Partly Opened

I ardently desired the acquisition of knowledge. I had often, when at home, thought it hard to remain during my youth cooped up in one place, and had longed to enter the world, and take my station among other human beings.

IT IS 8 JUNE 1814, in the rickety first-floor front room of 41 Skinner Street. Two young men about literary London, Percy Bysshe Shelley and Thomas Jefferson Hogg, have called to see Percy's intellectual mentor, William Godwin. But the philosopher is out, and the young men hang around awkwardly, pacing and browsing the bookshelves. All of a sudden:

the door was partially and softly opened. A thrilling voice called 'Shelley!' A thrilling voice answered, 'Mary!' And [Shelley] darted out of the room, like an arrow from the bow of the far-shooting king. A very young female, fair and fair-haired, pale indeed, and with a piercing look, wearing a frock of tartan, an unusual dress in London at that time, had called him out of the room. [...] It was but the glance of a moment, through a door partly opened. Her quietness certainly struck me, and possibly also, for I am not quite sure on this point, her paleness and piercing look.

Mary at sixteen: a murmur, and a glance caught through a partly opened door. This fleeting impression is more than forty years old by the time Hogg records it. No wonder he's 'not quite sure' what struck him at the time.

He will publish it after her death in the first instalment (published 1858) of a projected four-volume *The Life of Percy Bysshe Shelley*, commissioned and supported by the Shelley family. A quarter of a century earlier Mary herself will have been the first to suggest the project, prompted by Hogg's short 1833 memoir 'Shelley at Oxford'; it will prove a misjudgement. *The Life* makes for entertaining reading. Hogg is garrulous, easily distracted, self-indulgent to the point of self-absorption. Percy's old friend the autodidact and satirical writer Thomas Love Peacock even suggests its author should have called the work his autobiography. 'Shelley at Oxford' had appeared in the heavily edited context of a periodical, *The New Monthly Magazine*. But despite his youthful interest in writing, Hogg, who becomes a barrister and hobby classicist, seems simply unequal to the task of full-length biography: his casually uncomplimentary *Life* will receive almost uniformly hostile reviews and enrage the Shelleys.

In this context it might seem as though his decades-old 'memory' of Mary at sixteen is simply cobbled together, like the 'crazy […] ill-built, un-owned dwelling house' of Skinner Street itself. But it's not, after all, so very *en passant*. Hogg and Percy became close friends and even creative collaborators at Oxford, where they co-authored *The Necessity of Atheism*, and were sent down together as a result. Their friendship will remain close throughout the poet's short life, although Hogg's legal career will prevent his joining in Percy's European escapades.

At its heart is a boy-meets-boy rivalry that finds its outlet in sexual competition. There's nothing unusual about this: young men have presumably compared sexual conquests since the dawn of time. But what might normally have remained as drunken banter or solitary fantasy goes further with Hogg and Percy, not least because the doctrine of free love almost impels it. By the time they bump into each other on Cheapside this early June afternoon, their friendship has had to accommodate several years of advances made by Hogg to Shelley's young wife, Harriet, by now the mother of Percy's first child, Ianthe, and pregnant with his second, Charles. In the early stages of their relationship Harriet complained about this to her husband. But by 1814, Hogg recalls that:

> When I called on Bysshe, Harriet was often absent; she had gone out with Eliza, gone to her father's. Bysshe himself was sometimes in London, and sometimes at Bracknell, where he spent a good deal of his time in visiting certain friends, with whom, at that period, he was in very close alliance, and upon terms of the greatest intimacy, and by which connection his subsequent conduct, I think, was much influenced.

This is lightly done, but it sketches a sad, familiar picture of a couple gone adrift from each other. Percy's 'very close alliance' is with a married eighteen-year-old, Cornelia Turner, with whom he is 'reading the Italian poets', and whom he met at her mother's salon in 1813, when the widowed Mrs Boinville rented Percy and his young family a house there, called High Elms. Whether or not the Bracknell adventure is sexual – as it certainly appears to be from this distance – it is by now far advanced: far enough, a cynic might argue, for the poet to feel ready for something new.

Meanwhile, by 1814 Harriet has softened enough to enjoy Hogg's company:

> The good Harriet had fully recovered from the fatigues of her first effort of maternity, and, in fact, she had taken it easily. She was now in full force, vigour, and effect; roseate as ever, at times, perhaps, rather too rosy. She had entirely relinquished her favourite practice of reading aloud, which had been formerly a passion. I do not remember hearing her read even once after the birth of her child [...] Neither did she read much to herself; her studies, which had been so constant and exemplary, had dwindled away to nothing, and Bysshe had ceased to express any interest in them.

Instead, she asks her husband's friend to accompany her when she goes shopping for hats. It's a poor substitute for the excitements Hogg suspects Percy of, and it would be hard to avoid the conclusion that in fact both men are in fact 'much influenced' and ready to fall for the sixteen-year-old Mary Godwin, that 'very distinguished lady, of whom I have much to say hereafter'.

What do we know about Mary at this moment? Standing in the gloom of the landing, she must be barely visible from the comparatively well-lit library, with its bay front window. Still, we know from other sources that Hogg is right about her pallor and her pale strawberry-blonde hair. We know he's right to say that she is 'very young'. We also know that she must indeed push the library door ajar cautiously and do no more than whisper to Shelley. She's trying to escape detection in a house which, even when her father is out, is busy with siblings, servants and her hated stepmother. Her 'quietness' as she manoeuvres a situation where she can have a quick word alone with Shelley reveals not mousiness but a strong will. It's quite a contrast with Shelley's own 'uneasy promenade' around the room as he waits for her, and the general jumpiness Hogg records: '"Where is Godwin?" he asked me several times, as if I knew.' (And after all, is it just a word she manoeuvres? Or is it by now, a month after their first known meeting, a kiss?)

But the most telling detail of Hogg's picture is the one he would surely be least able to invent: her 'frock of tartan, an unusual dress in London at that time'. *This* is where we can recognise Mary, not just as the attractive blonde Hogg remarks but as herself. She is indeed a 'very young' sixteen, still too inexperienced or too bookish or both to get her dress quite right. In the nineteenth century, as in the twenty-first, London cares about fashion: Londoners have a quick and sophisticated eye for nuances of dress. And tartan is no nuance; in 1814 it's not even a cliché. The tartan industry will not take off for another eight years, until the state visit of George IV to Scotland.

Instead, the fabric is still rawly picturesque, and carries with it a faint association of rebellion. It's less than thirty years since the law forbidding the conquered Scots from wearing it was repealed. The daughter of Mary Wollstonecraft, and as someone whose own sister was born in the middle of the French Revolution, Mary is unlikely to have much hesitation in choosing which side in recent Scottish history to romanticise. She has just returned from nearly two years at Dundee, and this must be one of the first dresses she has chosen for herself; it's easy to imagine her in some provincial dressmaker's discovering how the tartan highlights her own classically Scots colouring.

Mary was very happy in Dundee. Perhaps she even wears the tartan dress as a reproach, a wordless symbol of how much she would have preferred to remain in Scotland than to be back here in Skinner Street under the sway of her stepmother – and, worse still, serving in the shop. Mary's sense of herself as the daughter, and so the heir, of the two leading political philosophers of her age was cultivated in early childhood. At sixteen she certainly sees herself as an intellectual; perhaps even as exceptionally gifted. Her intellect even forms part of her sexual allure. Four months from today Shelley will write to Hogg of his awe at her intelligence, which leaves him 'far surpassed in originality, in genuine elevation and magnificence'.

Nor is her sexual allure all that obscure, something to the taste of only a few like minds. Mary is no *jolie laide*. At fourteen and fifteen she is being complimented on her beauty by family friends who are sophisticated men of the world, among them the former US vice-president Aaron Burr. The result is a kind of self-belief that won't quite leave her even in widowhood. In 1830 the society portraitist James Northcote (who had painted her father in 1802) delivers a telling verdict in conversation with William Hazlitt:

> 'What!' he said, 'the beauty-daughter?' I said, 'Do you think her a beauty, then?'—'Why no, she rather thinks herself one, and yet there is something about her that would pass for such. Girls generally find out where to place themselves. She's clever, too; isn't she?'—'Oh! Yes.'

'She rather thinks herself one': this is not a humble young woman who accepts her natural destiny is to be a shop assistant. This despite the fact that she does it well: better in fact than her stepmother, as Mary Jane will herself later tell Lady Mountcashell. Although perhaps this is self-exoneration, since in her girlhood Lady Mountcashell, as Margaret King, was Mary Wollstonecraft's protégée; she can consequently be expected to have a potentially threatening loyalty to her old mentor's daughters.

Real tartan is certainly a remarkably heavy wool weave to be wearing in London in June, though in east-coast Dundee its warmth was probably necessary. Wearing it now might be an explicit choice, even a mark of stubbornness. Perhaps Mary *is* aware, after all, of how unusual her outfit is, and is determined to be special. Or else, quite the opposite: in this cash-strapped household the middle daughter is having to wear her badly chosen new dress, suitable or not, until it is worn out.

Either way, here she is: naïve, idealistic, intelligent, perhaps just a little vain, as every sixteen-year-old girl should be. In the half a dozen years since leaving the Polygon, Mary Godwin has spent almost as much time away from London as she has in Skinner Street. The library where Shelley and Hogg glimpse her on this afternoon in June 1814 is not somewhere she can truly call home, although it is at the heart of her sophistication. Her father's substantial collection of books is open to her, and she's not only unusually well read but reads with acuity. Yet, as we'll see, she has spent the majority of her adolescence away from her family, in provincial seaside towns in Kent and Scotland that, though far apart from each other, are equally likely to introduce even a metropolitan teenager to small-town mores, to encourage a gradually developing naïveté. A suggestible teenager can quickly lose touch with metropolitan convention.

And like every adolescent before or since, Mary has been shaped more than she realises by external influences. She has learned how to think not just through reading but directly from the important thinkers of the day who visit her father's home. Frequent visitors, such as the research chemist Sir Humphry Davy, the Quaker social reformer Robert Owen or the poet Samuel Taylor Coleridge, don't simply lock themselves away in Godwin's study. They take tea or dinner with the whole family, spending evenings in political, scientific and literary debate with Godwin and his, after all, somewhat educated second wife. The discussions continue even when there are no visitors present: Godwin invites his entire family to concern themselves with his publishing house, and the children even test out new material for his Juvenile Library.

Yet he has decided to send Mary away not once but twice. In 1811 she is sent to Ramsgate from 17 May to 19 December; and in 1812 she goes to Dundee in Scotland from 7 June to 10 November, returning there again from 3 June 1813 to 30 March 1814. All the household's children seem to have spent the summer of 1809 in the fresh air and familiar surroundings of Somers Town, where they stay with family friends the Hopwoods. But something – or some set of things – has made the choice to send Mary away desirable enough to trump the kind of homesickness Godwin felt for her and Fanny when they were infants. Perhaps it's simply that now, happily remarried, he's less needy. But if so this is a curious interlude, since it's not to be the pattern of a sometimes demandingly close relationship with his first-born in years to come. The truth seems more to be that as Mary develops into a young woman her father, like many men before and since, cannot understand that she is still his child and still needs his love and support. In the early nineteenth century, long before the social invention of the category of the teenager, this is particularly hard to understand. Until 1885 the British age of consent will remain, as it has since 1576, set at twelve. As a very young teenager, Mary can conveniently be regarded as an adult, even while she must obey her father and indeed continues her education.

It's hard not to suspect there's more to this new distance between father and daughter than strengthened parental boundaries. For between 1814 and today – or at least the mid-twentieth century, when Mary's life began to be seriously researched – some hidden hand destroys all Mary's childhood letters home to her father. Her father's correspondence with his young daughter also disappears. True, when Mary runs away from home later in the heady summer of 1814 she will take with her a box containing the papers she values most highly – among them, letters from her father – and promptly forget it in a Paris hotel. But it's hard to imagine that she has with her every single letter that indefatigable correspondent could have been expected to send during her three years of living away from home. Yet nothing that might have been left behind at Skinner Street survives: not a single letter to or from the teenaged Mary, or any of her juvenilia.

The Godwins' household is built on paper. Writing and reading are its *raison d'être* and, literally, its business. Godwin's notoriety means the family is always acutely aware of its posterity: 'my father, whose passion was posthumous fame', as Mary Shelley will describe him in a letter to Edward Trelawny in 1837. Any accident – a flying spark or a spilled water jug – that damaged or destroyed such a significant tranche of correspondence would surely have warranted a mention in journals or letters.

So what has happened, first to Mary and then to her correspondence?

Why would someone want to obliterate every trace of a high-spirited, intelligent child of thirteen, fourteen, fifteen? The obvious answer that presents itself is: someone who doesn't like her. One candidate is Mary herself. Perhaps she feels that as a teenager she let herself down in some way, and wants to clean up the record of her life. A later, wiser Mary – or someone protecting her reputation – might be mortified by the psychic growing pains of her adolescence and feel her enemies and naysayers have plenty of ammunition without any help from her own younger self. Or else, presumably, the hidden hand belongs to someone who destroyed the correspondence in a fit of exasperation, either with Mary or with Godwin, or because they're aware of having behaved badly themselves.

At the time of her absences Mary's own 'hand' – in fact, one entire arm – is often hidden in dressings. It has become mysteriously handicapped. She may have eczema: her father suffers from an undiagnosed recurring disease that resembles migraine, and we know now that eczema is partly genetic and connected with migraine, although triggers include stress and a woman's hormonal cycle. Mary does indeed develop her illness at puberty. Since migraine's hormonal links and 'additional' neurological symptoms have been known since at least the second century and are listed in the *Bibliotheca Anatomica, Medica, Chirurgica* of 1712, it's surprising that this is never postulated as a diagnosis for Godwin's condition or indeed for the agonising headaches and dizzy spells the adult Mary will suffer in the last years of her life.

The arm itself is treated with 'poultices', but Mary is unable to move it at times and uses a sling. Rigid, and huge with bandages, her limb must feel like a monstrous appendage stitched from some other body on to her own, as the creature she invents in her first novel will be stitched together by Frankenstein. Among the most common sites for atopic eczema are hands and elbows; a severe case might therefore easily seem to consume a whole arm, and though eczema is a disease of the skin only, it can be so severe that any movement of the affected area is extraordinarily painful. The skin can be as raw as a burn. Dr Cline, whom her father consults on Mary's behalf, can offer no twenty-first-century steroid creams to speed up healing. Nor is it easy to prevent infection of affected areas before the discovery of effective antiseptics and antibiotics.

Another candidate diagnosis is psoriasis, with its panoply of cruel and unsightly skin symptoms, including scaly plaques and pustules. In the roughly 30 per cent of cases that develop into psoriatic arthritis, these characteristic lesions are accompanied by localised symptoms of arthritis itself. These are asymmetric in 70 per cent of cases – meaning that with this disease it's more likely that Mary would have symptoms in just one arm, as indeed she does. They can also include an increased susceptibility to inflammatory bowel disease. Perhaps it's a good thing that we don't know how Mary's bowels are, but in the coming years she will certainly turn out to be a poor traveller, who suffers badly from seasickness and possibly even from motion sickness on land – illnesses that are nowadays associated in part with poor digestive health.

Like eczema, psoriasis can be stress-related, and heredity pays a significant role in its occurrence too. Both illnesses also have a relationship to environmental allergens: that's to say, things like house dust, woollen clothes and dairy foods, all of which form part of Mary's daily life. For all the violence of its symptoms, psoriasis can go into remission between flare-ups; it can also disappear completely. This is certainly the case with Mary's condition, which is not heard of again after her return from Scotland in 1814.

As far as we know, Mary first presents with her illness – or it becomes grave enough to warrant the family's attention – in 1811. At this time psoriasis has only recently been separated from a generalised diagnosis of 'leprosy', primarily through the work of Robert Willan, the London-based founder of the clinical discipline of dermatology. 'Leprosy' itself – what we now call Hansen's Disease – is, though unusual, not unknown in the London of the time. The city is tied to parts of the world where infection is endemic by a huge amount of trading and general colonising activity. Psoriasis is still frequently being treated with Fowler's solution, which contains arsenic, as well as with mercury. Sulphur or iodine is applied to prevent transmission, in the mistaken belief that this is an infectious disease: if Mary's 'poultices' are simply creams to reduce itching or dry chafing, she's luckier than many of her contemporaries.

But she may not be luckier in terms of family anxieties about the nature of her illness. Her stepmother – or stepsister – mentions tuberculosis in a much later letter, written by Mary Jane to Lady Mountcashell and redacted by Jane, who by the time she does so has a tubercular diagnosis herself. That Mary might have either TB – which has its own panoply of lesions – or leprosy, both infectious and potentially fatal conditions that could endanger other members of her family, would certainly account for her stepmother's anxiety about what she calls in a letter to Godwin 'the dreadful evil we apprehended'.

It would also be a compelling reason to send Mary away from the intimate conditions of the family home. Dr Cline's other recommendation, that Mary needs sea air, seems to fall in conveniently with such prophylaxis. It's also not far removed from today's clinical wisdom. In the hurly-burly of family life it's hard to isolate triggers for allergies and skin diseases. Such diseases are also triggered by poor general health, and Mary's symptoms have come on since the Godwins' move from the countryside of Somers Town to the inner-city streets of Holborn. Family friends comment that Mary at fourteen is beautiful but 'has not the air of strong health'.

So moving the girl to another, controlled environment – and one that is generally healthier than the stinking streets around Smithfield Market and the prisons – makes good clinical sense. Moreover, trigger stresses can be hidden. If any adult is putting pressure on Mary's still developing thirteen-year-old self, for example, it may not be that obvious suspect the 'wicked stepmother'. When it comes to it Mary Jane, not Godwin, accompanies her stepdaughter to Ramsgate on 17 May, just four days after receiving Cline's advice. It's also she who hesitates over leaving Mary there at Miss Pettman's Ladies' School for six months.

The letter Mary's father writes his wife as she hesitates, on 4 June, is as shocking in its coldness towards his daughter as it is revealing in the neediness it directs towards his wife. Mary's future merits a mere seven lines out of a three-page letter, which devotes more space to the theme of Godwin's own writing 'ease':

> When I do not answer any of the lesser points of your letters, it is because I agree with you, & therefore do not think it necessary to draw out an answer point by point, but am content to assent by silence. […] And this was the case as to Mary's being left in the care

of Miss Pettman. It was recommended by Mr Cline from the first, that she should stay six months; to this recommendation we both assented. It shall be so, if it can; [...] only I conceived you on the spot most competent to select the [best way to do so].

Tell Mary I do not write to her now, because it will be most natural, & will come most easily, for me to write to her, when I shall no longer have occasion to write to you every day at the same place. [Godwin's underlining]

By the time Godwin sends this letter, his wife, daughter and son have been taking the sea air of Ramsgate for nearly three weeks. He is becoming fractious at the delay in Mary Jane's return. She has told him she is no longer worried for William's health, so why is she delaying?

Have you altered your mind as to the confidence you had thus received? Or is it the altered face of our affairs that minds you to alter your plans? Do not imagine that I am not capable of sustaining my spirits, & doing everything that is right, without its being necessary to abridge on that account one hour that you had devoted to the care of your health. I am truly solicitous to understand what your plans are as to staying or returning, & the grounds of these now, as fully as it shall be possible to understand them when the whole has been determined and executed. Do not come away early from the place you are, at the expense of our both afterwards regretting that the resolution to return had been formed too hastily.

Mary's life has been turned upside down since those four days following her diagnosis in May. The speed with which her parents act to send her away suggests urgent concern. Yet Godwin's failure to write to his daughter during the weeks that follow because it isn't 'easy' enough hardly suggests he fears for her health. There's no tenderness either in his famous message, delivered not face to face or even in a letter to his daughter but via her stepmother, and written the day after he has sent her away: 'Tell Mary that, in spite of unfavourable appearances, I have still faith that she will become a wise and, what is more, a good and a happy woman.'

It's clearly a condemnation rather than the message of an anxious father. Mary is not yet fourteen. And this message to her is so sanctimonious in its phrasing, and so impossible to relay both accurately and kindly, that it's hard not to hear it as emotional cowardice. Is Godwin the kind of man whom it suits to let his adolescent daughter blame her stepmother for whatever he decides? His first letter written on this date is a four-page obsession about money, in which the news from Ramsgate gets no mention at all. Another puzzle: on 10 June Mary Jane reports that Mary is 'decisively better'. If this is the case, why must her stepdaughter remain in Kent for a further six months? Mary Jane seems more concerned with whether Mary is well enough to cope with Ramsgate than with whether Ramsgate is good for her health. But if the decision to leave the girl there isn't being made on the grounds of her physical health, what is going on?

Might Godwin, for example, be able to act so quickly because Cline's verdict is a foregone conclusion, delivered to an old friend and fellow radical who is also a customer? And does Mary Jane hesitate to leave her stepdaughter because she's faced with the reality of 92 High Street, where the school is housed? The street is narrow, and the houses terraced unevenly along its unfashionable top end are not as large as the Skinner Street home, leave alone the Polygon. The street leads down not to the town's fashionable esplanades but to Harbour Street and the working port itself: not the kind of area for a young lady to wander about. The establishment itself may at a stretch be described as cosy; it is clearly not elite. It would be hard to pretend that Mary, a highly intelligent, exceptionally widely read girl who lives at the sophisticated centre of London's radical establishment, is attending it for the sake of either her education or her social formation. The best we can say is that Mary Jane's own daughter Jane has already spent some time at Miss Pettman's in the summer of 1808, and so, clearly, the establishment is not actually exploitative or abusive.

Whether Jane comes home from that summer appreciably more grown up and poised, or whether she simply returns to London with healthy summer colouring, what has she told Mary about those weeks? Has she painted them as a privilege, an exciting time of new friendships and experiences? Does Mary go to Ramsgate willingly, thinking that the balance of favouritism is being redressed?

Whatever the feelings with which she arrives at 92 High Street, she remains there for not six but a full seven months. Her fourteenth birthday passes unremarked in Godwin's diary, and not because he is busy at work. The day before, he has left on a trip to the south coast: without his wife, who only moved back into Skinner Street four days earlier after a summer-long domestic – though not a professional – separation. If it were not clear enough already from his parting message to Mary, it becomes clear that she's no longer his favourite now when he chooses not to go to Kent, where he might see the birthday girl. Instead he is in Sussex, where he spends two nights at the Dolphin Hotel, Chichester at the start of a nine-day sightseeing excursion to the Isle of Wight and back through Hampshire and Surrey.

Mary is finally allowed home on 19 December. The next year, when her arm flares up again, she somehow manages to parley the terms of her exile into a stay with a family friend in Scotland. Or perhaps her wishes make no difference at all. Perhaps it's just that the school was fee-paying, and this will be free – apart from the obligation similarly to entertain one of her host's daughters in return?

Mary is to stay near Dundee with the family of William Baxter, who is father-in-law to one of her father's friends, David Booth. Baxter's household is Glasite, a breakaway strand of Christianity founded by the eponymous John Glas within the Dissenting tradition, which remains strong in Scotland, and to which Godwin's own childhood home belonged. Although life with Baxter's family turns out to be far removed from the extreme joylessness and rigour that have scarred Godwin, it is not clear how certain he can be about this when he commits his daughter to their care – or, indeed, whether he would mind if it turned out to be the case. The Baxters' invitation is extracted on 25 May; less than a fortnight later, Mary is already on her way to live with strangers. (She has met 'Baxter of Dundee' and one '*fille*' already, their visit to Skinner Street recorded in Godwin's diary, but that was when she had not yet turned twelve, an aeon ago in adolescent time.)

The letter Godwin sends Baxter the day after he has deposited Mary aboard the *Osnaburgh* – 'shipped off to you by yesterday's packet' is his opening joke – reveals just how tenuous are the terms on which her father is sending her away again: 'I am quite confounded to think […] to what a degree I may be said to have taken you in, when I took you at your word in your invitation upon so slight an acquaintance.' Once again, the famous philosopher delivers himself of some well-turned phrases on the need to develop the 'worth' of his daughter's 'character'; once again, he relies on someone else to deliver the tough love he believes Mary needs:

> I tremble for the trouble I may be bringing on you with this visit. In my last I desired that you would consider the first two or three weeks as a trial, how far you can ensure her, or, more fairly and impartially speaking, how far her habits and conceptions may be such as to put your family unreasonably out of their way [...]
>
> I do not desire that she should be treated with extraordinary attention, or that any one of your family should put themselves in the smallest degree out of their way on her account. I am anxious that she should be brought up (in this respect) like a philosopher, even a cynic. It will add greatly to the strength and worth of her character. [...] I wish too that she should be *excited* to industry. She has occasionally great perseverance; but occasionally too she stands in great need to be roused.

At fourteen, Mary may well have heard some of her father's stories about the upbringing his personal intellectual revolution protests. She has been brought up in a secular household that has at times paid a high price for its unorthodox belief that religion is unreasonable. It's hard to imagine she's ecstatic about being sent to a home about which she knows nothing except that it is Dissenting Christian, and that it is far away. Besides, one thing she does know with clarity is that she suffers badly from seasickness. She was even ill on the trip to Ramsgate, much of which is along the (admittedly tidal) River Thames and its estuary. The journey to Scotland, turning left out of that estuary and on up through the bumpy North Sea, takes about a week, and – even though she's sailing in June – she knows she can't expect a smooth ride. The *Osnaburgh* is a single-deck wooden sloop built in 1803, but fitted with new topsides since she is no longer young. She may well have only a single mast. In other words, she is quite small as well as reasonably fast: just the shape to bucket about as she speeds across the waves. And speed, rather than comfort, is of her essence. As a 'packet', she carries the mail between London and Dundee, part of the official network carrying national and international mail from ports all round the country.

Sure enough, Mary arrives in Scotland even more unwell than when she left London. Once again it's hard to believe that this is a trip made with her physical health foremost in mind. She has also been robbed. She tucked her travelling money in her stays for safekeeping; during the voyage it is stolen, something which is both difficult and easy to understand. Difficult, because who could get their hands in her underclothes without her noticing? Easy, because nausea is not only violently distracting: it undermines the will to resist even something so blatant. Mary's whole self is concentrated on trying to resist vomiting, to correct the motion of the boat. In that contraction of the self to a kernel of resistance – and a nausea that continues for around seven days – almost everything else becomes unimportant. It's likely, too, that Mary undresses and takes to her bunk. In the difficulty of doing so in a confined, vigorously rocking and dimly lit space while trying not to be sick, money can easily be dropped or forgotten. And it's just as easy for someone finding such money to tell themselves that they can't be sure whose it is; easy too for someone with a stronger stomach to move around the darkened space in ways that aren't quite clear to the sufferer on the bunk, to find the things they know to have been stowed carefully in a now discarded costume – perhaps even on their own advice. It seems likely that Mary's pickpocket is a woman, with free access to the cabin in which she has her bunk.

The Baxter family live in Broughty Ferry, in a house deprecatingly called The Cottage: probably in part because William is one of the less wealthy of the extended Baxter family, who have made fortunes in jute and linen. Partly too, perhaps, because the fiercely egalitarian congregational church to which he belongs believes that to 'lay up treasure on earth' its unlawful. Apart from some historic fishermen's cottages grouped along the waterfront and around the harbour, Broughty Ferry becomes known during the nineteenth century as 'the richest square mile in Europe'. It's where many of Dundee's commercial textile giants live, just upwind and east of the city whose prosperity they've helped build. The Baxters' substantial family house and grounds, with its large old trees on the front lawn facing the water, and thick stands of trees to the south and east to protect it from the sea winds, can be seen clearly on maps of the time.

Set just a little back from the main thoroughfare of Broughty Ferry Road, on what is now South Baffin Street, The Cottage is nevertheless firmly within sight, sound and above all within awareness of the shipping on which Dundee depends. No one can live here and be unaware of the brilliant east-coast marine light, the continual cry of gulls, the smell of the fishing fleet. The tall ships of the Dundee whaling fleet, active since the mid-eighteenth century, sail past on their way upstream to Dundee harbour. The ships' masts are higher even than the new harbour buildings; the sound of their ropes slapping against the mast-wood is a characteristic backdrop to any trip to town. As the whalers head out for their trips to Arctic waters, the family may be able to glimpse, fluttering from top masts, a coloured mass of ribbons. Sailors and their wives and sweethearts cut a ribbon in half; the men tie their halves to the mast, where they crowd, impossible to tell apart. Each departure is an occasion the community of Broughty Ferry turns out to witness, but the fleet usually leaves in March or April, so Mary will only witness this departure, if at all, at the very end of her second stay in Scotland.

These expensive, top-of-the-range vessels set out with large crews. Many of the up to fifty men on board are required not to sail the boats but to man the small open vessels that go harpooning once they make it through the Hudson Strait or arrive in Baffin Bay. If the battered boats do return, they are laden with cargoes from what Mary's Frankenstein will call 'the mountainous ices of the ocean', the mysterious north. Seal tusks and whale oil (for lighting and for the local cloth industry) are sometimes joined by the body of a polar bear. Whole whale carcasses may be brought in, tied alongside. Seen from the Broughty Ferry strand, these creatures appear monstrous, unsteady, ill adapted to motion even in the water. The first 'form which I cannot find words to describe, gigantic in stature, yet uncouth and distorted in its proportions' that Mary encounters is a marine, not a land-dwelling, creature. Frankenstein's fatal ice fields, and the explorer Walton, who braves them, come straight from these astonishing Tayside sightings.

Ships taking educated middle-class Scottish emigrants, and early victims of Highland clearances, across the Atlantic to new lives in Canada and North America also sail, oddly, from Dundee (and indeed Aberdeen) as well as from west-coast ports. There is much international trade. The adventurers of seafarers – however dimly imagined by a young girl who will never sit listening to their tall tales in some smoky pub – are part of the town's lifeblood, and make the windy foreshore as glamorous as the inland mountains that she will evoke in her Introduction to the 1831 edition of *Frankenstein* as 'the bleak sides of the woodless mountains [where] my true compositions, the airy flights of my imagination, were born and fostered'.

On the south side of the Tay, and a little further inland, is New-burgh, where Godwin's friend David Booth lives with his wife, the oldest of Baxter's four daughters. The Booths' home, Barns of Woodside, is an old house thought to be of seventeenth-century origin, lying just beyond the orchards for which the settlement is famous. The monks' well for the nearby Abbey of Lindores is in its grounds, and the Abbey stream runs though the garden; twelfth-century monastic masonry decorates the house, which sprouts ornamental turrets. It is a slightly fantastical, almost Gothic building, whose straggling floor-plan, offering plenty of private corners, couldn't be further removed from the well-lit, well-regulated spaces of the modern houses in which Mary has been brought up. These are all details to delight a bookish teenager, and Mary isn't alone in her enthusiasms but shares them with her new friend Isabella Baxter, the younger sister of Booth's wife.

Although she is the youngest of the Baxter sisters, Isabella is two years older than Mary. Unlike Jane – hitherto Mary's best friend – she is highly intelligent and passionately interested in history and French Revolution-ary politics. Isabella's mother, after whom she is named, has died only the year before. Like Mary, she is slightly adrift, as well as afloat, on the waters of an un-mothered adolescence; Isabella's eldest sister, Margaret, though married to Booth, is no substitute mother figure. Besides being just six years older, she is an invalid. With the ruthlessness of youth, the friends visit Barns of Woodside often, and even carve their names into the glass of a landing window. It is their home away from home: offering them a sense of escape that must feel doubled for Mary.

It's easy to imagine that the girls' appearance in their labyrinthine old house seems to the childless Booths like a compound, inseparable helping of delicious young femininity. But, as the elder unmarried sister, it's Christina Baxter – known as Christy – not Isabella who in November 1812 accompanies Mary back to Skinner Street for a promised stay in London. It is Christy, not Isabella, who meets Percy Bysshe Shelley and his beautifully dressed young wife, Harriet, there at supper on the 11th of that month.

Christy and Mary return to The Cottage in June 1813. And now the end of childhood begins to accelerate. Many things remain unchanged. There are still fascinating trips to the scenic and historic sights of east-coast Scotland, including St Andrews. The Booths still join the Baxter family in worshipping at the oddly domestic-looking eighteenth-century Glasite church on King Street, Dundee, where the soup served during the long Sunday services is a practical demonstration of the Glasite belief in equality and community. But other things are changing. Isabella and Christy's sister Margaret dies. The widower David Booth is on the look-out for a new wife. Glasites believe in marrying young, and fifteen-year-old Mary and seventeen-year-old Isabella are certainly not too young to escape his notice. In January 1813 Booth travels down to London to see William Godwin. Although Godwin's diary doesn't record what was said in their numerous meetings, on his return the Scot proposes to Isabella and is accepted.

Two explanations for Booth's trip to see Godwin seem possible. One is that his first choice is Mary; and that Godwin turns him down. The other possible explanation is that he asks the advice of his old friend, who has the reputation of being a philosopher of radical relationships, about his impending proposal to Isabella. Booth probably feels in need of advice about marrying his wife's sister, because this is regarded as illegal by both the Anglican and Glasite churches, after Leviticus 20:16: 'And if a man shall take his brother's wife, it is an unclean thing: he hath uncovered his brother's nakedness; they shall be childless.' Indeed David Booth, his new wife Isabella, and his father-in-law William Baxter, will all be excommunicated by the Glasites as a result of the match.

But making the arduous journey to London just to ask some advice seems both unnecessary and unlikely: surely Booth would simply have written to Godwin? Booth dines – each time alone – with Godwin on 8, 9, 11, 13, 16, 19, 23 and 26 January. He calls on Godwin on 10, 12, 15 and 21 January, and has tea with him on 14 and 17 January. On no occasion does Godwin call on Booth; instead, on 22 January, he 'adv', or advises, Booth. This pattern of visits suggests not so much a man who loves to eat as a siege laid and then gradually falling off. It also suggests obsessionality; and Booth will turn out to be unstable and abusive, as saturnine and romantic heroes can be. Isabella disappears into the marriage: soon Booth even forbids her to contact Mary. Indeed the controlling intensity he now reveals makes one wonder what exactly *was* wrong with his first wife. Could she possibly have been subjected to domestic violence?

Whether or not Mary is the first object of David Booth's affection, the fact that her best friend marries him while she's still in Dundee precipitates her out of a world of teenage crush and daydream into the midst of the real processes of marriage. In March, Isabella's brother Robert pays a visit home from Edinburgh, where he works as a merchant, and falls for Mary. It seems Godwin is somehow alerted to this fact. He writes to William Baxter on 15 March and to his own daughter on the 16th; just four days later, she is being rowed out to the *Osnaburgh* for the last time. Christy Baxter's journal records that the London-bound boat, captained by Captain Wishart, was late setting out from Dundee. The girls waiting at Broughty Ferry 'wandered about all the adjoining grounds till at length the vessel came out, and about three o'clock the boat came ashore and took her on Board from the Bottle-Work Rock'.

Robert Baxter will go on to marry a fellow Scot and settle in Lille. No record remains of whether Mary's heart is broken, though it seems likely, given the alacrity with which she's about to fall for Percy Bysshe Shelley, that the romantic injury itself is not grave. If anything, this brief romance – possibly itself a rebound from losing her closest friend to marriage – has been a useful rehearsal for the life-changing affair that is to follow. But she must be sorry to return to London, not only because it means saying goodbye to Dundee and the Baxters but also because of what she knows awaits her there. We can glimpse something of these feelings from the letter she will write from her widowhood nine years almost to the day, on

7 March 1823, to Jane Williams, the friend who will be widowed with her, as she contemplates having to return to her father's house:

> And I am threatened with a renewal of my girlish troubles. If I go back to my father's house—I know the person I have to deal with; all at first will be velvet—then thorns will come up—in fact it could not last long.

The adult Mary knows her father cannot, or will not, protect her. Does she already know this in her teens? The sententiousness on display in Godwin's letters to his wife suggests he is less likely to have destroyed the correspondence from Mary's youth than to have indulged in wordy self-exoneration. When he dies in 1836, he will be survived by Mary Jane. Emotional and well able to act out, she might in the last five years of her life want to 'set the record straight', perhaps to protect Godwin rather than herself. But she is relatively unlikely to possess the letters Mary received as a girl from Godwin. Not until Mary herself inherits some of her father's papers and begins, in late 1836 and early 1837, to think about writing his life, will anyone hold both sides of this correspondence and so be able comprehensively to delete it. Then, too, Mary will be able to see the whole pattern for the first time: both the daughter's bids for the attention of her adored father and his withholding of it.

Moreover, by this time she herself will be the fond mother of a teenager for whom she will have made many sacrifices. This happy parental relationship can't help but illuminate her own father's comparative coldness. In early 1837 she will struggle with a dichotomy between duty and love, between her 'duty' to write a biography of her father and the harm renewed family notoriety would do her seventeen-year-old son, and choose to protect the latter. In the same letter to Trelawny in which she identifies her father's obsession with posterity, she continues to meditate on reputation and family values:

> With regard to my Father's life—I certainly could not answer it to my conscience to give it up—I shall therefore do it—but I must wait. This year I have to fight my poor Percy's battle—to try to get him sent to College without further dilapidations on his ruined prospects—& he has to enter life at College—that this should be undertaken at a

moment when a cry was raised against his Mother—& that not on the question of <u>politics</u> but <u>religion,</u> would mar all—I must see him fairly launched, before I commit myself to the fury of the waves.

It's hard to imagine William Godwin making the same decision.

Still, the revenge of the writer is in writing. When Mary says, in her Introduction to the 1831 edition of *Frankenstein*, that 'I lived principally in the country as a girl, and passed a considerable time in Scotland', she is spinning 'airy flights of […] imagination'. Reimagining her youth without the years when she lived above the shop, she is still in many ways the same person as the teenager who – refusing to accept that Skinner Street is her real life – puts on a tartan dress, as a sign that she belongs elsewhere, to meet her lover.

Chapter 4

Elopement

My heart, which was before sorrowful, now swelled with something like joy.

IT'S EASY TO IMAGINE a Romantic portrait making the most of young Mary Godwin's ethereal pallor: unfortunate that we often catch her in the decidedly un-ethereal process of throwing up. In the next scene she lies exhausted by seasickness and fear on board a small wooden sailing vessel. The boat is being dwarfed by storm waves that swell under and around it in the moonlight. The time is just before midnight, and a crossing that the sailors promised would be 'only two hours' sail from the shore' has already been going on for more than six. The horizon is 'red and stormy'; there are vivid flashes of lightning.

Mary is only sixteen, and she is running away with Percy Bysshe Shelley, a man five years her senior who is not merely already married but the father of a young child. It's 28 July 1814, and they're in the middle of the English Channel, and of a summer storm that has come on with the night:

> Suddenly a thunder squall struck the sail and the waves rushed into
> the boat; even the sailors believed that our situation was perilous;
> the wind had now changed, and we drove before a wind, that came
> in violent gusts.

The crossing the lovers are attempting, between Dover and Calais, is a mere twenty-three nautical miles. When they left Dover at six in the evening on what was not only the hottest day of the year but 'a hotter day than has been known in this climate for many years', 'the evening was most beautiful; the sands slowly receded; we felt safe; there was little wind, the sails flapped in the flagging breeze'. But, like many straits, the Channel is concentrated into ferocious currents and susceptible to sudden storms. It's also markedly tidal, and the twelve or more hours this crossing takes pass through a complete cycle from one low tide to the next.

Eventually, at around 4.20 a.m., amid heavy wind and continuing lightning, a stormy dawn breaks over the labouring boat. Luckily, because the sailors 'succeeded in reefing the sail', the wind finally drives them 'upon the sands' of Calais, where 'suddenly the broad sun rose over France'. This is a striking image of rebirth: of near-death and the transfiguring experience of survival. But though taken from Mary's *Journal*, it's actually written by Percy. Mary herself won't write in what is the earliest surviving volume of her *Journal* until over a week later.

She will, though, rewrite this account within the next three years, when she publishes an account of the journey on which she and Percy have embarked, her *History of a Six Weeks' Tour*, of 1817. At this point – when she ghosts him as he has already ghosted her – the young lovers' voices overlap each other, like their limbs piled on each other's in exhaustion or sleep. Which is just how Percy portrays the crossing. In his account Mary lies all night between his knees, as he holds her head on his chest. 'She did not speak or look', and he believes she 'did not know our danger'.

But Mary knows the reality of shipwrecks from her time in Scotland. Who can say whether the too plausible estimate of a two-hour crossing the youngsters are given as they charter the boat is triggered by unusually anxious questioning on her part? Or is her famous pallor so deepened by the motion sickness she's already suffered earlier in the day, on the way to Dover, that even the boat's captain notices it? As Percy records:

> Mary was ill as we travelled, yet in that illness what pleasure and security did we not share! The heat made her faint; it was necessary at every stage that she should repose.

I've always wondered whether this passage is in code. What exactly does 'what pleasure and security did we not share' mean? Mary has always been a poor traveller, and her vulnerability may make her new lover feel protective and tender: able to be of intimate use. But she is also possibly in the earliest stages of pregnancy – just around the time, in other words, that she may be realising she could *be* pregnant. For in a famous entry in the *Journal* made just a few days later, on 4 August, Percy will record that he thinks of 27 June as his 'birthday': the date, just over a month earlier, on which Mary first either told him she loved him or made love with him, or both.

It's even possible that he realises, or at least suspects, that she's pregnant before she does. He has prior experience, after all – he's a married man with a small daughter and a pregnant wife – while Mary does not even have a mother to tell her about sex and pregnancy. (She was only a child of five when her stepbrother William was born: hardly of an age to witness and understand human reproduction.) Does Percy feel 'pleasure and security' in the signs of a pregnancy which he recognises, and which he knows binds Mary to him more surely than any choice she could now make? This is, after all, an elopement without the 'security' of a marriage at the end of it. Indeed, technically it's not elopement at all. Yet, because the couple believe in the 'common law' commitment of consummated romantic love rather than a legal contract, it *is* elopement in their terms. A 'common law elopement', as it were.

Next February, when Mary's baby is born on the 22nd, Percy will record, again in Mary's *Journal*, that the baby is premature, 'not quite seven months' and so not expected to live. In fact, she does survive – for just under a fortnight – something fairly exceptional before the days of intensive-care incubators. Percy's calculation assumes the baby was conceived around the date of this stormy night at sea. But if she was conceived not in France but a month earlier, in London, she would have been only one month premature.

This is something for which we can have no definite proof and only the circumstantial evidence of Mary's motion sickness and the baby's (brief) survival. But there's something else to bear in mind. Percy, as we're increasingly going to discover, has two equally powerful needs: to believe himself to be good, and to get what he wants. It would be entirely in character for him to feel guilt about seducing Mary while she's living under her father's roof, but to argue that once she runs away with him they are *de facto* – 'in the eyes of God' – married, and to adjust the date of the baby's conception accordingly.

Mary and Percy have risked the night crossing because they're too anxious or impatient to wait for the packet ship sailing the next day. They have already hired four horses instead of the more usual two at Dartford, 'that we might outstrip pursuit' on their race down to Dover. They aren't thinking clearly; they're in love. But it is, one can't help feeling, a typical piece of Romantic overreaching since their pursuer, Mary's stepmother, manages to arrive at their hotel at Calais on the very same day they do: presumably by the packet, presumably after a shorter, safer and altogether cheaper crossing. Or else you could view these big gestures as calculating rather than spontaneous. The advantage gained *is* just enough. Mary's stepmother does indeed catch up with the runaways in Calais. But by then it's too late: Mary has been publicly 'ruined', because she has passed that all-important (though as it happens entirely un-sexual, storm-tossed) night with Percy and because, arriving in another country and registering with him at a hotel there, she has definitively eloped. Percy, who has form in eloping with sixteen-year-olds – his wife, Harriet, was the same age when he ran off with her – must understand this, at least, perfectly well. Whatever happens next between him and Mary, he has ensured that there's no way back for her into ordinary society. He truly has snared her.

What *does* Mary think or know, as she lies in the paralysing grip of seasickness? Is she astonished by the speed of events that have got her on board this small craft, lurching so horribly in the grip of a Channel storm? Nausea turns the body into a liquefying burden. Does Mary really have no second thoughts, no longing to be safely back on dry land? Illness seems mercifully to embroil her, and 'as is my custom when thus affected, I slept during the greater part of the night, awaking only from time to time to ask where we were, and to receive the dismal answer each time – "Not quite half way".' Even a quarter of a century from now, looking back over her life from her forties, she will remember not this flight but her miscarriage in 1822 as her first near-death experience.

And after all, on 29 July 1814 the sun rises 'broad, red and cloud-less over the pier', and Mary, walking across the Calais sands, hears 'for the first time the confused buzz of voices speaking a different language from that to which I had been accustomed'. She observes the typical Normandy costumes: 'the women with high caps and short jackets; the men with earrings; ladies walking about with high bonnets or *coiffures* lodged on the top of the head […] without any stray curls to decorate the temples or cheeks.' She will never forget these initial impressions. She's a teenager, abroad for the first time in her life. Although Percy's *Journal* entries record the runaways' movements, Mary's recollections three years later are alive with observational detail. Like many a subsequent English traveller in France, she remarks that, 'The roads are excellent'; even so, she finds the cabriolet in which they embark for Paris 'irresistibly ludi-crous'. She remembers walking the outer earthworks fortifying Calais – 'they consisted of fields where the hay was making' – and notes, 'The first appearance that struck our English eyes was the want of enclosures; but the fields were flourishing with a plentiful harvest.'

Meanwhile Mary's stepmother has arrived, presumably on the same sailing as the runaways' boxes, something that we can guess helps her locate them at their hotel. The packet, too, has been 'detained by con-trary wind', and Mary Jane Godwin, who travelled through the night from London, must be exhausted. As usual, it's she who has the dirty work of trying to resolve the family's newest drama; as usual, William Godwin remains ensconced in London. And so she must face down the casual mockery a middle-aged woman travelling alone can expect. 'In the evening', Percy nastily comments in Mary's *Journal*, 'Captain Davison came and told us that a fat lady had arrived, who had said that I had run away with her daughter.'

The entry implies that this is hysterical exaggeration. But of course, it isn't. Besides, Mrs Godwin is not concerned with her stepdaughter Mary. She has come to rescue Jane. For here we need to pan out a little, and observe that Mary and Percy are not unaccompanied. Astonishingly, they've brought with them Mary's stepsister Jane. I want to write *for reasons best known to themselves*. But that would be a derogation of the biographer's duty, which is to try and understand the muddle these three young people – even Percy is at this date still only twenty-one, and both girls are sixteen – have got themselves into.

It's a muddle that will only get worse. Two's company, three's none, and Jane's triangulating presence will shape the young couple's entire relationship. For Mary's sake, one wishes Mrs Godwin could succeed in 'rescuing' Jane from this adventure and persuade her to return to England the next day. The worst of it is that she so nearly does. Mary Jane talks her daughter into spending the night with her in her own room, so she hasn't had an unchaperoned stay at a hotel but merely overnighted with her mother in another country. In the morning, Percy notes, 'Jane informs us that she is unable to resist the pathos of Mrs Godwin's appeal.'

'Pathos' is a privileged young man's shorthand for the whole complex of consequences that Mrs Godwin will try to unfold for her teenaged daughter – who can hardly be the most receptive of audiences. We know, as Jane probably does not, that Mary Jane has experienced at first hand the cost of toppling from respectability. She has since laboriously reconstructed herself, putting over a dozen years of hard work and sheer willpower into keeping the Godwin household financially and, despite the reputation of the first Mrs Godwin, socially respectable. That both these enterprises may actually have been complicated by her own and her husband's incompetence – the bookshop is in fact ruinously costly; it's Godwin himself who through that poorly judged biography made his first wife into a figure of ill-fame – is beside the point.

Mary Godwin will always be the controversial Mary Wollstonecraft's child but, in marrying Godwin, Mary Jane has gambled with the future of her own daughter. So she has been particularly keen to see the girls working with a private tutor, like young ladies rather than a shopkeeper's daughters, and assiduous in making sure that sulky, teenaged Mary and her unsightly skin disease are not on display at Skinner Street. If Jane returns home, both she and Fanny, who as Wollstonecraft's daughter is always going to be the harder sell – and whose prospects are in any case limited by her looks and lack of general sparkle, according to family lore – have at least the chance of marriage and a home of their own. If she does not, everything is changed not only for the two young women themselves but also for the rest of the family; and William and Mary Jane herself will for ever be figures of scandal.

In 1814 reputations have material consequences: unless, like Percy Bysshe Shelley, you are heir to a baronetcy and can buy the freedom to do as you want. With a hypocrisy that would be funny if it weren't so sorry, Percy, soaring above Mary Jane's 'pathos' on wings of aristocratic privilege, counters her arguments by encouraging Jane to think of own her situation in terms of the French Revolution, which has done away with the very privileges he himself enjoys; of France's 'past slavery and [...] future freedom'. Sure enough, Mary's stepsister changes her mind, telling her mother she won't return to England; whereupon, 'Mrs Godwin departed without answering a word'.

But it's Mrs Godwin who is right – about all of it. Jane will never marry; within twenty-six months Fanny, understanding her life to have been made supernumerary by her sisters' adventures, will kill herself. The rumour will go round London that Godwin has sold two daughters to Percy for £1,500; and this formerly distinguished philosopher will struggle for money and recognition for the rest of his life. Percy's fantasy of freedom will even infect the girls' little brother William junior, now just ten years old, who in a week's time, on 8 August, will run away from home. Luckily he is found safe and well: but not for two whole days.

Damage runs through the Godwin household like a rapid crack through the jerry-built Skinner Street property, as even Godwin himself has realised it will. Just three days before the elopement he had written to Percy, urging him to stay with his 'innocent and meritorious wife' Harriet, and to leave untouched 'the fair and spotless fame of my young child', adding that 'I could not believe that you would enter my house under the name of benefactor, to leave behind an endless poison to corrode my soul.' The letter is the near-culmination of nearly four weeks of push-me-pull-you during which Godwin grounds Mary in the upstairs schoolroom, admonishes both his daughter (on 8 July) and her accomplice his stepdaughter (on 22 July), and works hard and successfully on Harriet Shelley's behalf to separate her husband, Percy, from his other current amour, Cornelia Turner (after a visit from the girl's mother on 18 July, and one he pays to Harriet Shelley herself on 15 July).

He also stoutly refuses Percy a list of continental contacts to expedite the proposed elopement.

For Percy has announced his plan directly to Godwin on 6 July. This approach, remarkable in its effrontery – or naïvité – seems to be the first time that it has occurred to anyone in the Godwin household, apart from Jane, that Mary and Percy might be getting close. That's all the more surprising because Mary Jane, no fool when it comes to family matters, is on the alert. She has already sent Fanny away to Wales, possibly to have her health or her character strengthened as Mary's has been by her time in Scotland; but possibly also because she is thought to be falling in love with Percy. (This is something Percy himself seems to believe, as his reaction to Fanny's death will show.)

Percy's behaviour seems less naïve when we remember that Godwin is himself the social revolutionary who declared, in 1793's *An Enquiry Concerning Political Justice*, that man should 'supersede and trample upon the institutions of the country in which he lives', and in particular marriage. But that was two decades ago. Even one decade ago he was already writing in the introduction to his 1805 novel *Fleetwood*, subtitled *The New Man of Feeling* and a study of a *marriage*, that he no longer believes action 'by scattered examples [can] renovate the face of society'. Instead he now thinks radical ideas should be disseminated 'by discussion and reasoning'. And, of course, he is himself twice married.

As a late-flowering paterfamilias, however, his authority over his daughter's relationship with Percy is undermined by the fact that the latter has agreed to be his benefactor to the tune of £1,250. Indeed, a further £1,750 that Percy had originally promised Godwin is now the very money he plans to use to take Mary to Europe. It's easy to see how readily this cross-current of financial implication could be seized on by the teenagers of the Godwin household, brought up to dream of revolutionary action, as proof that it's only grasping materialism that objects to the radical social and sexual rearrangements Percy proposes. The Godwin girls have been conditioned to associate both elopement and a European destination with revolution and freedom. With the double solipsism of privilege and youth, Percy can encourage them to conflate free love with social liberty, possibly even supplying egregious financial detail to the young woman he hopes will run away with him. That he's leaving a pregnant wife penniless and socially in the lurch – that once love wears off a woman can simply be abandoned and, if she is, will have no way to support herself – must seem to the teenagers like the tedious small print of a shining new social contract.

Perhaps Percy isn't manipulative, just thoughtless: or, better still, a true social revolutionary. He is, after all, gambling with his own reputation – to a limited extent. A double standard may make the promiscuous nineteenth-century gentleman into a 'gay dog', but even this differentiates between having affairs and actually abandoning a wife. And Percy does genuinely live by his ideals. After all he was sent down from Oxford, in 1811, as a result of publishing *The Necessity of Atheism* not anonymously but under his own name; and he has subsequently tried out a number of model lifestyles: for example in Wales, at remote Cwm Elan and communitarian Tremadog. Indeed, it was in attempting to raise money for the latter, a model settlement on newly drained land near Porthmadog, that he first met Godwin in 1812. He has also already 'rescued' another sixteen-year-old from what he believed to be the oppression of old-fashioned authority: his wife, Harriet, *née* Westbrook, was a schoolgirl when he eloped with her to Edinburgh shortly after being sent down from university.

Consciously at least, these recurring attempts at liberation and communitarian living cannot be just sexually motivated: shortly after his elopement with Mary, Percy will also contemplate liberating his own sisters, Elizabeth and Hellen, from their school in Hackney. Revolutionary principles genuinely inform his thinking and writing. The former schoolboy chemist, best known at Eton for blowing things up, has by the summer of 1814 already written the short lyric 'Mutability' – which reveals his interest in radical transformation and his sense that 'Nought may endure but Mutability' – and the 2,000-line, nine-canto philosophical fantasy *Queen Mab*, which combines this sense of mutability with the Godwinian idea of 'necessity' to predict social progress for the world. This generalised idealism has been deeply influenced by Godwin's *Political Justice*, and Percy and Mary will reread that book in the first difficult weeks of their post-elopement return to London, as if they hope to find in it some definition or justification of their position.

So it was in a rush of youthful enthusiasm that, on 11 June 1812, Percy wrote to Godwin – a man he hadn't yet met – that 'I will become all that you believe and wish me to be. I should regard it as my greatest glory, should I be judged worthy to solace your declining years.' To the reader who, like Godwin, is aware of both men's respective financial situations, this sounds like a declaration of practical commitment. Indeed it has been elicited (after a pause) by a letter of Godwin's own, in which we hear the older man hinting strongly that he needs the financial support of his wealthy young friend: 'Now I can look on you, not as a meteor & ephemeral, but as a lasting, friend, who, according to the course of nature, may contribute to the comforts of my closing days.'

The question, though, is whether Percy hears the financial nature of these hints. Received wisdom is that he does, and is responding in kind. But it seems just as likely that nothing of the sort is going on. Percy would count it his 'greatest glory' to be 'judged worthy' to be a solace to the ageing philosopher. And look what he says in the sentence before: 'I will become all that you wish and believe me to be.' He is, at nineteen, still little more than a boy, longing to be top of the class as he addresses the intellectual celebrity whose praise he strives for. What he is *not* is a mature adult discussing his inheritance with a potential financial dependant (and nor, one might feel, should he have to be).

Whether or not this exchange initiates a misunderstanding, by 1814 any possible relationship between the two men has become an impacted, attritional form of financial contract. Godwin can be charmless when it comes to money. Even as early as 1812 he's desperate for more of it. His creditors are closing in, and on 8 September one of them obtains an order of execution. As is customary, this gives Godwin three days in which to pay his debt: otherwise he will be arrested. Once he is, all his other creditors will also call in their debts. In that brief window of opportunity Godwin seems to have used Percy's name to persuade his creditor to hold off. He also bolts, heading for the Shelleys' last known address in Lynmouth although, as it happens, Percy and his family have already departed in the opposite direction. It's a typical Godwinian bodge. In the end, the two men meet for the first time when the philosopher returns to London roughly three weeks later after an expensive, time-wasting trip round the West Country.

Despite this, by the summer of 1814 Percy is primed to fall in love with Godwin's daughter. We could say that his choices and actions – even this falling in love itself – represent a whole mixture not only of ideas but also of character traits that Percy himself is probably unaware of. But such mixtures are true of revolutionary Romanticism as a whole. Like all cultural movements, it's being built by a series of human individuals, each with their own personal as well as intellectual motivations. Doubling their significance in this case, however, is the relatively new Romantic concept of the individual. 'Romanticism' is itself a newly minted term: Mme de Staël is credited with bringing it into the mainstream of (the French) language just a year earlier, in her *De l'Allemagne*. Goethe's fiction *The Sorrows of Young Werther* (1774) and Jean-Jacques Rousseau's examination of his own feelings and motivations in his *Confessions* (1789) have initiated an interest in the inner lives of people – and by extension, of things. Arthur Schopenhauer is developing sophisticated notions about the primacy of the mind that, when published in 1818–19 as *The World as Will and Representation*, will revolutionise the old European idea of human beings as subject to divine law. The individual replaces God as the source of meaning: the human becomes the principle that nothing trumps, and so the measure of every action and event.

So when Mary's *Journal* for July 1814 records her own and Percy's responses to the countries she finds herself travelling through, she believes such responses are also part of the observable nature of things. She's undertaking the Romantic project of self-examination: putting herself under the lens along with the places she sees. As we noted in Chapter 2, it's a project that owes much to Rousseau's *Confessions* of 1789. At least, this is a charitable explanation of the several occasions on which the *Journal* dismisses people and places as 'stupid'.

In any case, the majority of these entries are written by Percy. In Paris, for example, he can find only one 'remarkable' picture at the Louvre, while in the gallery's holdings of religious art 'the Blessed looked too stupid', and Notre-Dame 'much disappointed our expectations'. Mary's published account in her first book – the comprehensively titled *History of a Six Weeks' Tour Through a Part of France, Switzerland, Germany and Holland: With Letters Descriptive of a Sail Round the Lake of Geneva. And of the*

Glaciers of Chamouni – replaces such comments with a range of more nuanced reactions. She tells us how, beyond Bar-sur-Aube, 'We travelled for nearly three days through plains, where the country gently undulated, and relieved the eye from a perpetual flat, without exciting any peculiar interest. Gentle rivers, their banks ornamented by a few trees stole through these plains.' This carefully positive account has been developed from the *Journal's* altogether blunter version: 'We have a distant peep at hills. [...] Shelley and I walk to the riverside.'

Mary's book also omits, of course, any account of the trip's 'backstage' story, the material that tells us about *her*. On 16 August at Champlitte-et-le-Prélot, with its pretty downhill side-streets, the travellers have an 'Adventure with Marguerite Pascal – whom we would have taken with us if her father would have allowed us and certainly I never beheld so lovely a child.' Today it sounds extraordinarily cavalier to expect to adopt a child on a dinnertime whim. We aren't surprised that the child's father thought this trio of young adventurers a bad risk for his daughter. Yet in its own context the idea, though odd, is not entirely abnormal. As we've seen, Mary's own mother advocated adoption; her published arguments for nature over nurture are probably familiar to her daughter. Besides, as a maternal orphan, Mary can as yet understand motherhood itself only 'slant'. It's not clear from the *Journal* whether little Marguerite has a mother, an omission that itself suggests genuine ignorance of the maternal role. Still, there may be more of an element of 'rescue' to the enterprise than Mary gets round to explaining.

Either way, her interest in taking on Marguerite Pascal prefigures the way that orphans are to be trigger figures in Mary's fiction in later years. Two years from now, when she begins to write the story of *Frankenstein*, she will invent a strangely distorted form of paternity. By first making – and then rejecting – a living, feeling being, Frankenstein creates a kind of para-orphan. His creature hasn't been bereaved, but is parent-less and alone in the world just the same:

> It was dark when I awoke; I felt cold also, and half-frightened, as it were instinctively, finding myself so desolate. [...] I was a poor, helpless, miserable wretch; I knew, and could distinguish, nothing; but feeling pain invade me on all sides, I sat down and wept.

Two years later again, Mary will invent Maurice, the eponymous hero of a children's story about parents lost and found, which she writes for a family friend. Unlike Frankenstein's creature, Maurice is a real human child. But he too is a para-orphan:

> And then he knew it must be true that his only friend was dead, and that he was now alone in the world. At length quite exhausted by sorrow [...] he got up and opening the cottage door, without eating any supper or striking a light, he knelt down and said his prayers and then went to bed.

Maurice's parents haven't died: he was stolen from them in infancy. Full orphanhood is worse still:

> The condition of her orphan children was peculiarly desolate. Her own father had been an emigrant from another part of the country, and had died long since: they had no one relation to take them by the hand; they were outcasts, paupers, unfriended beings, to whom the most scanty pittance was a matter of favour, and who were treated merely as children of peasants, yet poorer than the poorest, who, dying, had left them, a thankless bequest, to the close-handed charity of the land.

One of these orphaned siblings is Lionel Verney, the eponymous narrator of *The Last Man*, a novel Mary publishes in 1826. Like Frankenstein's creature, Verney ends as he started, a 'wanderer' through a world in which he is alone. It's as if the *peopled* parts of orphaned lives are merely interludes of belonging – within an existential state of isolation. The protagonists of Mary's very last fictions are also orphans. *Lodore*, published in 1835, deals with the effects on the orphaned daughters and widow that Lord Lodore leaves behind after his death in a duel. Two years later, and Elizabeth – the protagonist of Mary's final novel, *Falkner* – is yet another orphan.

Of course, the creators of fictional orphans aren't necessarily revisiting personal experience. Orphanhood is a narrative intensifier – of poverty, vulnerability, sadness – and a conveniently close-packed symbol of pathos, as Charles Dickens, Mary's younger contemporary, knew well. Writers who invent such characters may be doing so not out of imaginative laziness but because of the fierceness of the social and political points they wish, like Dickens, to make. As the plot-driven novel changes and expands during the long nineteenth century, such vivid characters will multiply. From *Oliver Twist* (1838) to *Jane Eyre* (1847), and from *Tom Sawyer* (1876) to the child protagonists of Edwardian classics such as *Anne of Green Gables* (1908) and *The Secret Garden* (1910), a chorus of fictional orphans have entered our collective imagination.

Mary's novels appear relatively early in this development. She uses orphanhood to create degrees of personal isolation for her characters. Of course, for her this *is* a freighted concept. All the more fascinating, then, that she seems less interested in writing family sagas than in exploring what it's like to feel unsheltered in the world at large. Such unshelteredness is a real piece of *zeitgeist*; the dark *tain*, or back of the mirror, which creates the image, the Romantic idea of the individual human who is at the centre of her own universe. To be at that centre means to be no longer sheltered by a notion of God, or even by legal or familial authority. The cost of existential freedom is an equal loneliness.

If Mary and Percy sometimes seem unaware of what they're doing as they set out on their first trip across Europe together, we have to remember not only how young they are but also that they and their peers lack many of the languages for understanding the self that we take for granted. The European mind does not yet even have a formal notion of the unconscious – though there is a sense that some aspects of the psyche are more hidden than others: for example, when Jane 'states her conception of the subterranean community of women' or when the topic of dream and hallucination comes up.

And it often does. In these early weeks of their relationship the *Journal* gives a sense that Mary and Percy are often 'Interrupted by Jane's horrors'. Four days out from Paris, Mary's stepsister even gets into bed with them:

> Jane was not able to sleep all night for the rats, who, as she said, put their cold paws upon her face; she, however, rested upon our bed, which her four-footed enemies dared not invade, perhaps having overheard the threat that Shelley terrified the man with.

I like the dry, sceptical tone of this: that 'as she said', the joking suggestion that rats understand human speech. The implication isn't *quite* that Jane consciously wants to get into bed with the couple and is lying about the rats; more, that they are possibly not the problem she believes them to be. She certainly manages to break in on 'Love in idleness', the reading and talking in bed that are the mortar of the relationship the couple are building.

For not everything on the trip is going swimmingly. On the contrary, things are frequently so frankly uncomfortable that the journey sounds more like a Holiday from Hell than a romantic fantasy. It's hard to be sure whether Mary is truly so happy that none of this matters or whether she simply has to believe in the elopement and so in a sense mythologise it, since she has thrown in her lot with Percy. It may be that he's fairly easy to convince. On 7 August he's once again writing her *Journal*, and records that:

> Mary especially seems insensible to all future evil. She feels as if our love alone would suffice to resist the invasions of calamity. She rested on my bosom and seemed even indifferent to take sufficient food for the sustenance of life.

Yes: or else she's just pregnant.

These 'invasions of calamity' have four main aspects, all aggravating each other. The couple have trouble with travel, with money, with recent political events in the countries they cross – and with Jane. The occasions on which Mary and Percy are alone together are the exception, not the rule. The plan had been to run away to Uri, a picturesque canton in the Swiss Alps which stretches from Lake Lucerne to the St Gotthard Pass, and there to lead the perfect, communal life. But the day after they arrive in Paris they discover that the money Percy was expecting isn't going to be forthcoming. Several days are spent in the capital trying to resolve this financial crisis. In the end, they decide to *walk* the 700-odd kilometres across north-east France and on through Switzerland.

This turns out to mean first buying, in a Paris street market, an ass that is so 'weak and unfit for labour' that the trio have to carry *it* 'like the Miller and his son' before swapping it for a mule the next day in Charenton, where presumably there are fewer donkey sharks, and finally buying a 'voiture' and hiring another mule to draw this as far as the Swiss border. Percy may be experienced at borrowing money, but he is not adept at saving it; as the daughter of a perennially impecunious publisher and bookseller, Mary is. Whether or not she's as blissed out as Shelley claims, her *Journal* entry for 13 August sounds the note of practical intelligence that will all too soon become a refrain of her marriage: 'Shelley […] sells the mule for 40 francs, and the saddle for 16 francs. In all our bargains, for ass, saddle, and mule, we lose more than 15 napoleons. Money we can but little spare now.' Conspicuously, these bad bargains are made whenever Percy and Jane go shopping alone together while the pregnant Mary rests. It's almost as if they are too busy having fun to pay proper attention to their purchases …

Mary may be pregnant, but her travelling companions get to ride in the saddle too. The distances they've set themselves to cover take a toll on everyone. Percy 'sprains his leg' at Trois Maisons, a hamlet beyond Nogent-sur-Seine, while Jane is 'very unable to walk' at Savrine, near the Swiss border, which the trio eventually reach on 19 August. On the far side their postilion, after failing to wait for them at a series of meeting points and telling 'many lies', abandons them. Still, the Swiss scenery duly impresses. They glimpse the Alps for the first time near Neuchâtel, and Mary takes typically Romantic care to note the effect the mountains have on their human observers:

> They were an hundred miles distant, but reach so high in the heavens, that they look like those accumulated clouds of dazzling white that arrange themselves on the horizon during summer. Their immensity staggers the imagination, and so far surpasses all conception, that it requites an effort of the understanding to believe that they indeed form a part of the earth.

On the next day, 20 August, however: 'We consult on our situation' and Percy manages to get £38 out of a Neuchâtel 'banker'. But the lovers consult again on 24 August:

> We cannot procure a house; we are in despair; the filth of the apart-ment is terrible to Mary; she cannot bear it all the winter. We propose to proceed to Flüelen, but the wind comes from Italy, and will not permit. At last we find a lodging in an ugly house they call

the Chateau for 1 louis per month, which we take; it consists of two rooms.

The *History* takes up the story:

> But it was a wretched place, with no comfort or convenience. It was with difficulty that we could get any food prepared: as it was cold and rainy, we ordered a fire – they lighted an immense stove which occupied a corner of the room; it was long before it heated, and when hot, the heat was so unwholesome, that we were obliged to throw open our windows.

The trio have spent more than a quarter of their Neuchâtel haul on getting to Brunnen on the shores of Lake Lucerne, only to find that 'the £28 which we possessed, was all the money that we could count upon with any certainty, until the following December. S***'s presence in London was absolutely necessary for the procuring any further supply.' They decide to return to England; and they need to find a way of doing so that will cost them less than half what the outward journey cost: 'Water conveyances are always the cheapest, and fortunately we were so situated, that by taking advantage of the rivers of the Reuss and Rhine, we could reach England without travelling a league on land.'

No sooner is the decision made than they're off. They wait just one day for their clean laundry, then set out on 27 August. It is still raining 'violently', and all three are travel-worn as well as disappointed by the outcome of their dream of an ideal life. In Switzerland everyone has got on each other's nerves. On 22 August, Percy 'is in a jocosely horrible mood', on the 21st he and Jane have had a 'talk concerning Jane's character'; on the 29th, arriving, 'cold and comfortless' at Basle, they find themselves a bed so uncomfortable that Mary 'groans' (presumably in her sleep).

The return journey is relentless, covering 'eight hundred miles' in eighteen days by way of Dettingen, Basle, 'Strasburgh' (Strasbourg), Mannheim, 'Mayence' (Mainz), Bonn, Cologne, Cleve, Rotterdam, 'Marsluys' (Maassluis, a harbour between Rotterdam and the Hook of Holland) and Gravesend. Downstream from Strasbourg, their fellow passengers in the *diligence par-eau* include three students from the university there:

Schwitz, a rather handsome, good tempered young man; Hoff, a kind of shapeless animal, with a heavy, ugly German face; and Schneider, who was nearly an ideot [*sic*], and on whom his companions were always playing a thousand tricks.

By the time she recalls this, writing some time in the middle of 1817 as she prepares her *History* for publication, Mary has already finished fair-copying the novel that will become her second book – though the first that she completes. In *Frankenstein* she conjures up a German university student whom she enrols not at Strasbourg but at Ingolstadt, Bavarian home of the Illuminati secret society. We don't know whether the real-life Schwitz was studying philosophy and science; we certainly don't know whether he was a particularly driven student. But could Frankenstein, with his good looks and cultivation, be even partly modelled on this young man, who gets so conspicuously better a press than other Germans Mary meets?

Whether through a process of imaginative association or as a codified mnemonic, Mary names *her* student after the Rhineland landmark of Burg Frankenstein above Darmstadt, one of several castles on the Hessian Bergstrasse. Some time on the third and final day that the Godwin–Shelley party spend with the students – by which time barriers of shyness will have broken down through sheer proximity – the boat passes no more than thirty kilometres west of the ruined Burg Frankenstein. The river runs close enough for them to see and talk about the Odenwald on which the thirteenth-century fort is perched, even if not quite near enough to spy its ruins themselves. Situated in a hilly and forested region itself rich in legend, Burg Frankenstein attracts the kinds of stories any group of students would enjoy telling other young people, as they laze together on the deck of a riverboat far into the German summer night. There are rumours of a dragon-slaying von Frankenstein, of buried gold and a fountain of youth linked to Walpurgisnacht superstitions, and about the real-life alchemist Johann Conrad Dippel, a pastor's son who was born at the castle in 1673 and employed as an alchemist there, and who was said to have invented an elixir of life.

For this one night, 1 September – when they even sleep out on deck – Mary and her travelling companions become, briefly, recognisable precursors of today's gap-year adventurers, hooking up with other young travellers to exchange tall tales, and fretting about whether they can get home before their money runs out. But if they do hear local legends as they sit talking in the dark, Mary records none of them in either her *Journal* or her *History*.

Still, the correspondences between Mary's *Frankenstein* and the stories associated with Frankenstein Burg have shorter odds as creative triggering than as pure coincidence. For it's more likely that someone will have told Mary about the castle because of the stories attached to it than because of its name, which to native speakers doesn't sound at all unusual. The Strasbourg students seem the most likely source since Mary, who's handicapped by both lack of German and her gender, can't chat casually with some passing, unrecorded riverboat captain or riverside stallholder.

Reading again her description – 'rather handsome […] a kind of shapeless animal […] nearly an ideot' – it's hard not to feel that this trio could have inspired Frankenstein and his creature in more ways than one. Mary, who is truthfully a bit of an intellectual snob, finds it odd that these three young men should be friends, and we can picture her puzzling over what the attraction could possibly be: intellectual foil – or shadow side?

We know her imagination is at work, because we know she's been writing. On 10 September the travellers are on board the ship that will take them home to Gravesend, and the *Journal* records that Mary begins 'Hate', which sounds like the title of a poem; although she continues work the next day, suggesting a story. An earlier *Journal* entry, dated 25 August, suggests that a certain amount of co-composition is also going on: 'We […] write part of Shelley's romance.'

Whether or not she's allowed much actual creative input, this is the start of Mary's habit of transcribing Percy's work. She's returning to England with a new understanding of herself as an adult embarked on literary life; and it is only in part because she has turned seventeen during the laborious return journey. She brings home with her a travel journal and a memory stuffed with travel notes. It's good that this is so, because a single short story, however fine 'Hate' is – and, as it's never mentioned again, it probably isn't – cannot replace the precious body of material she has lost along the way.

Back near the start of their journey, on 2 August at the Hotel de Vienne, Paris, Percy recorded that:

> Mary looked over with me the papers contained in her box. They consisted of her own writings, letters from her father and her friends, and my letters. She promised that I should be permitted to read and study these productions of her mind that preceded our intercourse. I shall claim this promise at Uri.

But Uri, like so many Shelleyan utopias, is never quite to be reached. And Mary's box, containing all her most treasured correspondence and juvenilia, is lost at Paris. Oddly, unlike the to-and-fro squabbles between the travelling companions, this loss is not recorded in the *Journal*. Yet Mary must have noticed it fairly soon after they left the city to be certain – as she will be in 1845 – that this is where it happened. Why doesn't she mention it? Or is her horrified recognition – rather than, say, pregnancy-related nausea – the 'One horrible spasm' she records in her own first *Journal* entry on 8 August?

We already know how much writing means to Mary; it was her father's work that brought the protagonists of this very literary romance together. And it's the figure of her mother that presides over their elopement. All that the couple read during the entire six-week European trip, apart from a little Juvenal and L'Abbé Barruel's *Histoire de Jacobinisme*, are Mary Wollstonecraft's *Letters Written in Sweden, Norway, and Denmark* and her *Mary, a Fiction*. Her mother's courage in undertaking international travel alone in times of war makes it appear natural for Mary, who is as proud a Wollstonecraft as she is a Godwin, to ignore all warnings and wander fearlessly – if a touch squeamishly – through the recent battlegrounds of the French countryside.

Wollstonecraft, who has symbolised so many things successively over the years to her growing daughter – maternal love and its unattainability, the feminine ideal, the active and intellectual woman, the Romantic, unconventional heroine and lover – is the perfect touchstone for Mary's relationship with Percy. This is every bit as true before the young couple elope. In the secret summer weeks leading up to that departure, their romance is largely carried out in walks, chaperoned by Jane, in St Pancras Old Churchyard where Wollstonecraft is buried. When Jane can be persuaded to withdraw to a discreet distance, they talk at the grave itself. And it's at her mother's grave that Mary declares herself on 26 June and, perhaps, first makes love with Percy in the shelter of the willow trees that early prints show growing near its distinctive monument. It is the closest she can get to 'bringing her young man home' to meet her mother. In the Churchyard she is, so to speak, on home turf.

She's also armed with the absolute confidence of youthful idealism. Mary truly believes Harriet Shelley is in the wrong both politically and personally. Falling in love combines headily with moral and political conviction, and results in a kind of fierce clarity. It's little wonder that, as Percy boasts to Thomas Jefferson Hogg shortly after the runaways return to London, 'her understanding was made clear by a spirit that sees into the truth of things, by affections preserved pure and sacred from the corrupting contamination of vulgar superstitions'.

For nearly three weeks, after Percy's July announcement to Godwin of the young lovers' intentions, Mary is grounded in the upstairs schoolroom at Skinner Street like any other teenager. The lovers' relationship is now briefly sublimated into something entirely literary, as Jane smuggles letters between them. She also smuggles two of Percy's own books into the schoolroom. One is his not-yet-published *A Refutation of Deism*, handsomely bound with Mary's name engraved on the calfskin cover. The other is a copy of his *Queen Mab* inscribed to Mary. The edition includes numerous footnotes expounding its author's views on love and marriage (as well as vegetarianism), and indeed quoting from Godwin: 'The present system of constraint does no more, in the majority of cases, than make hypocrites or open enemies. [...] children [...] are nursed in a systematic school of ill-humour, violence and falsehood.' Mary, living in the shadow of a marriage she longs to see dissolved, needs little persuading as to the rightness of this: besides, isn't it what her father argued in his own famous *Political Justice*?

During her weeks of internal exile Percy's books serve Mary as both reading matter and love-letters – literal letters she stows carefully in the box that will be lost in Paris, and so we don't know the actual words of love Percy writes to Mary. Like Jane at the churchyard, we're forced to withdraw to a certain distance from the lovers' intimacy, though we can still see the affair working itself out as if in mime.

Finally, in the early hours of 28 July, Percy sends word to Mary that a chaise is waiting for her and Jane at the end of his street. Jane – co-conspirator, chaperone and confidante – seems to have become part of the plan to elope almost by default. Some commentators have speculated that she's invited along because she can speak French; but so can Mary and Percy, well enough. It seems more plausible that Percy likes the idea of liberating yet one more damsel in distress. A fortnight into this second elopement, on 13 August, he will even write from Troyes inviting his pregnant wife Harriet, the original rescue project, to come and settle in 'some sweet retreat I will procure for you among the mountains'. Mary, meanwhile, probably feels safer taking along her closest friend and confidante, for all the world like some comfort blanket or favourite toy, as she leaves childhood abruptly behind. She's a young woman who has spent almost all her life living in the same household as her closest friend: when it isn't Jane in London, it's Isabella in Dundee. The idea of setting out not only for another country but to *elope* with no such a companion or witness might be vertiginous.

Sure enough, Mary does waver. In the last hour before the girls, dressed in black silk, slip into his chaise, Mary visits Percy's rooms then goes back to Skinner Street. She has to make a difficult choice. If she stays, her life as the self she knows can continue, though she may have to spend some penitential time away from London and its temptations; cloistered with a family friend perhaps. Her continuing education, and her role in the shop, predictable as both are, offer a shape to her days. If she burns her bridges by leaving, she can expect a more exciting life, but it's also one whose shape is very unclear. It's a weighty decision for a sixteen-year-old. And, ultimately, she must make it alone.

Chapter 5

Becoming a Couple

You must create a female for me, with whom I can live in the interchange of those sympathies necessary for my being. This alone you can do; and I demand it of you as a right which you must not refuse to concede.

'IS THIS THE WAY my beloved that we are to live?' Mary asks Percy, in the very first of her letters to survive. It's late October 1814, fewer than six weeks since the lovers returned from their aborted trip to Switzerland. Mary is writing from rented rooms in a house overlooking the familiar graveyard at Old St Pancras Church. From where she sits she can even see the trees surrounding her mother's grave.

She must feel as though she's tried to take flight, only to crash back to where she started. For all that her mother is a touchstone for Mary's self-belief, Wollstonecraft's grave belongs among her earliest childhood memories: as we've seen, the spot is linked to the time before her father remarried, when she and Fanny still imagined they had him all to themselves. The scene of her recent courtship, it must also remind her of that short period in which she dreamed, too, that she could have Percy entirely to herself.

Their courtship was little more than three months ago, but it belongs to another life: one in which she was her father's proud daughter and an acknowledged member of his well-known, intellectually well-connected household at Skinner Street. By contrast 5 Church Terrace, where she now finds herself with only the increasingly problematic Jane for company, is neither well known nor well connected. It's not even a household, or at any rate not hers – Mrs Page, the landlady, also rents out other rooms. Nor is Mary going to settle here for more than a few weeks.

Coming back to London has not been the homecoming she might have imagined. Instead, it's turning out to be merely a milestone in the huge transition on which she has, knowingly or not, embarked. Every young woman of her generation comes of age when she leaves the family home to get married, but Mary has gone much further, embarking on a course of self-invention. Although she hasn't done anything so simple as marry Percy, she is in the process of changing from Mary Godwin into the eventual Mary Shelley, and these depressing, lonely weeks mark another key juncture in her developing identity.

Much of what has made her what she is at this moment – her looks, her intelligence, her understanding of the literary world – is her birthright. It has come to her just because she's the daughter of Mary Wollstonecraft and William Godwin. Nature or nurture willy-nilly, it's with the daughter of these famous thinkers that Percy has fallen in love. But by leaving home and becoming a young, almost unknown poet's partner, Mary Godwin has chosen to make her own way in life. From now on she will be defined not by her past but by her future, the one she and Percy must make together.

For it's all very well to elope: the continental adventure, however disastrous it may have been on some levels, has an urgency, a momentum that kept Mary and Percy, to say nothing of Jane, living in the moment. But building a life together isn't heat-of-the-moment stuff. It takes time. That's true of both its external elements – where and how to live – and its internal, emotional mechanisms. And this is the chapter in Mary's story, or at least the story of her marriage, where that process takes place most intensively. These first weeks and months with Percy will be lived hand-to-mouth, apparently with little thought for the future. But they set the pattern for the life that is to follow over the next eight years, until – and perhaps even beyond – his death in a sailing accident off the coast of Italy:

a death that is every bit as accidental and unanticipated as the way of life that now emerges.

This hand-to-mouth lifestyle is apparent in the ceaseless comings and going recorded in Mary's surviving *Journal* volumes. But it's also revealed by the loss of whole volumes of that *Journal*, covering the period May 1815 to July 1816: all of what is more or less the couple's second year together. If we can think of Mary's life as a series of portraits, this one is nothing like a painting fixed in oils. It reminds me of the flicker of a video installation: the grainy black-and-white bleached by wilful exposure into near-invisibility, its jerkiness reproducing the apprentice technologies of the very earliest films. We can barely distinguish between the figures themselves and the markings of the wall on to which they're projected. Nothing is certain; everything keeps changing.

On the very first evening of their return to London, 13 September 1814, 'Poor Mary and Jane are left two whole hours in the coach', while Percy, having made a circuit of old friends to no avail, persuades his long-suffering wife Harriet to pay the returnees' fares. They owe not only their coach tickets from Gravesend but their Channel crossing too. Harriet pays these off and gives Percy some cash to spare. The trio are able to spend the night in a hotel in Oxford Street, from where they move to temporary lodgings off Cavendish Square the next day, and 'home' to Somers Town, and Mrs Page's establishment in Church Terrace, on the 27th. It's as if they're still travelling; but London is no staging post on some European Grand Tour. Life is much more expensive here than on the Continent. And the city is home to family and friends who are watching, waiting and coming to their own conclusions about this new ménage.

For, to Mary's astonishment, instead of welcoming her new relationship with Percy, her father disapproves. He does not see her as following in her mother's footsteps, and doing with Percy what Mary Wollstonecraft did with Henry Fuseli (who was married to someone else) or Gilbert Imlay (to whom her 'marriage' was a legal fiction). Or perhaps he does, and can't face the costs of this behaviour a second time. William Godwin may love Mary, and possibly even his stepdaughter Jane. But he has a wife, a son and two further stepchildren still at home, and he's honour-bound to support them. He also has his own literary publishing dreams.

If he loses his business, he will lose both his means of supporting the family and his own identity, and will have spent the last decade struggling in vain.

Caught between the self-protective sternness of the man they're financially and socially dependent on and simple human affection for the two absconding daughters, the remaining Skinner Street women do their best. Three days after the travellers return, 'Mrs Godwin and Fanny pay a visit to the window, but refuse to speak to Shelley when he goes out to them.' They're evidently respecting some paterfamilial, 'you must never speak to that man', injunction to the letter in order to circumvent its spirit. The next time Mary records contact from the Godwin household it is, once again, not her father who makes the move. On 27 October two letters arrive from Skinner Street. 'Fanny's very doleful, and CC [Charles Clairmont] contradicts in one line what he had said in the line before.' Neither of these comments suggests Mary has yet developed a huge capacity for empathy. The runaways have not only diminished Fanny's own life chances at a stroke, by ruining the family's reputation and so her own 'spotless fame'; they seem to be having all the excitement. Yet, loyally, she still writes to them. No surprise either if eighteen-year-old Charles, also left to witness the consequences of the elopement, sends a somewhat contorted letter.

But Mary, forced into defensiveness, already hears those who aren't fully with her and Percy as against them. She's in love with Percy, and he with her: 'dearest & only one I know how tenderly you repine at this absence from me – when shall we be free from fear of treachery?' How can anyone fail to understand how important it is that they're together? The next day, 28 October, her *Journal* records: 'At 6 a letter comes from Mrs Godwin; she is a woman I shudder to think of. My poor Father! if—— but it will not do.' She still doesn't seem to notice – as we, watching across the centuries, can do on her behalf – that it's her stepmother rather than her adored father who is doing the domestic emotional heavy lifting, just as she has since Mary's departure for Ramsgate.

Godwin once again absents himself, both from the process of negotiation and from Mary herself. That this is his *choice* is something his daughter can't allow herself to believe. Later the same evening Mary writes to Percy blaming her stepmother for her father's withdrawal:

> I detest Mrs G. she plagues my father out of his life & then—well no
> matter—why will not Godwin follow the obvious bent of his affec-
> tions & be reconciled to us—no his prejudices the world & she—do
> you not hate her my love—all these forbid it […] press me to you
> and hug your own Mary to your heart perhaps she will one day have
> a father till then be everything to me love.

It's the voice of a hurt little girl. Mary is the good, clever daughter who has
been taught to (mis)take her father's intellectual approval for affection, the
conditional for unconditional love. And now she's transferring this paradigm to Percy, as if *he* were her father. This certainly suggests the 'excessive
& romantic attachment' to her parent that she will confess to in later years.

It also suggests a readiness to jump through similar hoops for Percy.
She continues:

> —& indeed I will be a good girl and never vex you any more I will
> learn Greek and—but when shall we meet when I may tell you all
> this & you will so sweetly reward me.

The 'reward' may be sexual; but it's unmistakeably a treat for good behaviour, as if Mary were truly still the child she's aping. Having been the
'excessive and romantic' girl who wanted to seduce her father, she's now
attempting to turn her lover into a father figure: the usual Freudian rever-
sals that, in 1814, have as yet no name. But at the same time, confusingly
and I suspect confusedly, her 'I will be a good girl' is also a touch flirtatious; in the coming months diminutives such as *Dormouse* and *Pecksie*
will feature prominently among Mary's pet names.

It's hard then as now for a girl who, while she was growing up, gained
parental approval by being intelligent to learn how, as a young woman, to
elicit love and approval in other ways. Less than a week after her 'good
girl' letter, on 2 November, Mary writes to Percy in a completely different
tone. This letter (which unfortunately is badly torn) is full of wise financial advice and starts out sounding thoroughly mature:

> I would not advise you [*tear*] all your estate or to [*tear*]Post obits
> from too many people—Sir John Shelley I think the best to treat
> with—Yet till you have some money from some of them do not break
> with any—

But then, as if suddenly remembering a new lesson about how masculine approval is better won by *not* being intelligent, Mary suddenly changes tack:

> But you know all about this better than I do—So goodnight—may you sleep as well as though it wer [*sic*] in my arms—but I know you won't

Meanwhile, she is rehearsing abandonment weekly. In a sort of bizarre extension of Sunday trading laws, debtors are allowed the twenty-four hours from midnight on Saturday night to midnight Sunday without persecution, but every Sunday night must go back into hiding if they want to evade the bailiffs and imprisonment for debt. Percy, who is heavily indebted, could negotiate with his family for the money he needs. But he resists this idea for weeks, forcing Mary to live apart from him for six days out of every seven. The young couple's Sundays are therefore precious, and Mary and Percy spend large parts of them in bed. On 30 October Mary's *Journal* records: 'Rise late; talk with Shelley all day. [...] In the evening Shelley and I go to an inn in St John Street to sleep. Those that love cannot separate; Shelley could not have gone away without me again.' The following Sunday, 6 November, is 'a day devoted to Love in idleness'.

During the rest of the week, however, Mary can see her lover only briefly, in public places such as churches and gardens:

> will you be at the door of the coffee house at five o'clock as it is dis-agreeable to go into those places and I shall be there exactly at that time and we will go into St Pauls where we can sit down.

It's an appeal whose language has been compressed by stress, and it's not the only one that Mary makes against being left 'walking up an [*sic*] down in a public place'. Her great love story is being reduced from a romantic secret to something merely furtive.

She has also been abandoned by Skinner Street. In the coming spring her father, who hasn't spoken to her since she eloped, will even snub her in the street: a cut all the crueller for being administered less than a month after she has lost her first child, as he well knows. In Mary's own account the pathos of her slip from 'my Father' to 'Papa' is telling: 'As we come home meet my Father and Charles Clairmont. […] Charles Clairmont calls; he tells us that Papa saw us, and that he remarked that Shelley was so beautiful, it was a pity he was so wicked.'

To make matters worse – 'another circumstance has made me feel more solitary' – Mary has also lost contact with Isabella Booth, *née* Baxter. Mary's best friend from Dundee is herself socially compromised by her illegal marriage, earlier in the year, to her late sister's widower. Her husband breaks off the young women's friendship at the start of November – possibly, like Godwin, in an attempt to preserve his own fragile respectability – after Mary has written twice to Isabella and received no response.

Mary isn't completely alone, of course. She has Jane living with her. But this is no consolation for the immediate shock of her isolation; on the contrary, as Jane comes to 'interrupt' the couple more and more, her presence will simply serve to deepen and increase it. For Jane is a flirt, and Mary clearly has no plan to 'share' Percy with her stepsister. Letters apparently written at the time by Mary Jane, and edited by Jane in future decades, claim that in the days leading up to the elopement Percy broke into the Skinner Street schoolroom and tried to persuade Mary into a suicide pact on the grounds that they could not live apart. Passionate stuff, and persuasive to someone like Mary, whose view of love has been shaped by literature and by her own parents' romantic story. Both Jane and her mother can be unreliable witnesses, of course; it's not even certain whether this was Mary Jane's version at the time. But an intense dedication of self to lover does seem to be roughly what Mary is expecting from her relationship.

She certainly doesn't seem to have anticipated sharing her lover's attention, leave alone his bed, with other women. Like so many idealistic young women both before her and since who have fallen for a married man, she seems to believe – at least at the moment when she elopes – not so much in a universal principle of shared love as in the particular failings of her lover's wife. If Harriet is another 'woman I shudder to think of', why should Percy be shackled to her for life? The convention that requires such a thing must be false, Mary's logic goes, following the script prepared for her by her lover's – but also her father's – writings.

In 1814 serial monogamy is widely regarded as radically immoral. But Mary has managed to believe that Harriet is so far in the wrong that it's somehow she, rather than Percy, who has broken up the Shelley marriage. In this context, her own brief *Journal* outbursts are unsurprising – even restrained. On 7 December Harriet 'treats [Percy] with insulting selfishness'. The absent wife's refusal to help a husband struggling socially and financially as a result of marital breakdown would indeed be selfish – if it were of her doing. Even Mary's fury when Harriet writes, on 6 December, with news of the birth of Percy's son 'in a letter from a *deserted wife!!*' (the emphasis is Mary's) is logical if she believes that Harriet is a hypocrite, not deserted but deserting.

But this fury is not *purely* logical. Mary herself is pregnant, by Percy, with her own first child. The birth of Charles Shelley, 'which ought to be ushered in with ringing of bells, &c., for it is the son of his *wife*', is horribly designed to make her realise how close her own and Harriet's experiences are of the man they have in common; and how Harriet, as the legitimate wife, comes first in them. It's a peculiar, intensely corporealised form of sexual jealousy to find yourself bearing your lover's child at the same time as his ex. Besides, the era's high risk of maternal mortality means the stakes for these young women are higher than we can perhaps realistically imagine – and Mary, of course, knows them all too well because of her own mother's death.

In its way, jealousy is the sincerest form of flattery. Today some psychoanalysts even argue that people who have affairs with married men or women want to get *at* or *to* the person on the far side of their psychic threesome. And there's plenty in Mary's past to load the figure of the wife and mother, as personified by Harriet, with meaning. She might well want to *have* what Harriet *is*. Sure enough, as her letters and *Journal* record, her dream seems to be a new monogamy of her own with Percy. She even summons up one of the houses in Wales where he lived with Harriet as her ideal for their own life together:

> But Nantgwilt do you not wish to be settled there at a home you know love—with your own Mary nothing to disturb you studying walking & other such like amusements—oh it is much better believe not to be able to see the light of the sun for mountains than for houses.

It might seem a naïve way to seduce a man who has thrown up exactly this for you. But Mary is simply repeating Percy's own narrative about an ideal lifestyle among the mountains. *This* is what she thought she was going to in Uri.

One of the great conveniences of writing is that it offers so many opportunities for displacement. The fantasy of a good life of remote pastoral domesticity will recur particularly in Mary's early novels. The 'fisherman's cot' of her children's story *Maurice*, written in 1820, certainly differs in its imagined scale from the palatial Windsor homes of the protagonists in Volume I of *The Last Man* (1826), or indeed from the Yorkshire country estate to which the eponymous Matilda and her father retire in Mary's posthumously published second novel, which was composed in 1819–20; but their emotional symbolism is very similar. It's a kind of pastoral – the countryside, at a remove from 'the world', is seen as emotionally healthy and natural – as well as a trace of Rousseau's idea of the original, faultlessly free 'state of nature' with which Mary was raised.

In *The Last Man*:

> We had our separate occupations and our common amusements. Sometimes we passed whole days under the leafy covert of the forest with our books and music. [...] When the frequent rains shut us within doors, evening recreation followed morning study, ushered in by music and song.

But the very first appearance of this fantasy is probably the one that comes closest to Mary's actual experience. In *Frankenstein* Felix, blonde Agatha and their blind father, the 'cottagers' who inadvertently shelter the creature as he learns how to be a human, make up a household of exiled political activists. They live a life of vegetarian simplicity in the German countryside, where their recreations include reading aloud to each other, walking and singing. This is pretty much how, by 1816–17, Mary and Percy will organise their own life in Europe.

In Mary's novel, Felix's lover Safie joins *Frankenstein*'s cottagers in a cohabitation that is portrayed as wholesomely virtuous: the couple may be unmarried but they are monogamous. Back in the real London of 1814–15 however, Percy is planning an altogether different domestic arrangement. He has lent Mary this pastoral ideal, and shares its notion of a collective life based on shared values. But his expectations of romantic love differ from hers. He has already eloped once before, and seen the romantic bloom wear off the subsequent relationship: he knows, as Mary does not, that he is responsible for that break-up. Whether or not he explicitly tells Mary that Harriet has been unfaithful to him, the enthusiasm with which he greets news of the birth of a son and heir makes it pretty clear that he doesn't believe this himself: or at any rate he believes that *this* child is his.

Percy's letters to Harriet now alternate between charm and cruelty, and it's hard not to suspect that this is because he's seesawing between two narratives: one in which he feels frankly and rather mundanely guilty about leaving her for someone else, and one in which he's saddled with a destructive enemy in the person of a wife who doesn't understand that philosophy is calling him to finer things. In a letter of self-justification to his old friend Thomas Jefferson Hogg he has written that, 'ennobled' by Mary's 'genuine elevation and magnificence of the intellectual nature', he can become 'a more true & constant friend, a more useful lover of mankind, a more ardent asserter of truth and virtue [...] above all more consistent, more intelligible more true'. Harriet is indeed uninterested in the alibi of philosophy. She's also unengaged by discussions about whether life as a single mother might be tenable in another and better kind of society: she is living in the all too immediate actual one. Even animals don't desert their pregnant mates, she pleads, to no avail.

In 1820 Percy will set out his doctrine in *Epipsychidion*, where it has the fluency of a well-rehearsed position:

> I never was attached to that great sect,
> Whose doctrine is, that each one should select
> Out of the crowd a mistress or a friend,
> And all the rest, though fair and wise, commend
> To cold oblivion, though it is in the code
> Of modern morals, and the beaten road
> Which those poor slaves with weary footsteps tread,
> Who travel to their home among the dead
> By the broad highway of the world, and so
> With one chained friend, perhaps a jealous foe,
> The dreariest and the longest journey go.

In the meantime, he is already in action to make sure that he himself is not 'chained' to just 'one'. The terms of his letter inviting Harriet to join himself, Mary and Jane in Switzerland, are curiously tortuous:

> I write to you from this detestable Town. I write to shew you that I do not forget you. I write to urge you to come to Switzerland, where you will at least find one firm & constant friend, to whom your interests will be always dear, by whom your feelings will never wilfully be injured. From none can you expect this but me. All else are either unfeeling & selfish, or have beloved friends of their own as Mrs Boinville to whom their attention & affection is confined.

It's hard to not to read anxiety about losing his first partner into this strange mixture of tones which include that old gambit, *no one will love you as much as I do*: 'From none can you expect this but me.' Walking away is different from being walked away from. Mary, Percy's current 'beloved friend', is a very young woman undergoing the stresses of pregnancy with no older female confidante to advise her – exactly the situation he has left behind – and he clearly has no desire to repeat the experience of nuclear domesticity. After all, not only did he invite Harriet along on what was effectively Mary's honeymoon; it is also he who, on its very first day, persuaded Jane not to go home and leave the lovers in peace.

Can we find anything to justify this behaviour? Percy is young, and married too young to sow many wild oats; like many literary young men, he has suddenly discovered himself to be no longer weedy or sissy – but sexy. During these next months in London he continues to charm the teenager who is now effectively his sister-in-common-law. For Mary's stepsister is undergoing her own transformation. By May 1815, when she is first sent away to live at Percy's expense in Lynmouth, Jane will have become 'Claire Clairmont', after spells of trying out 'Clara' (from 24 November, according to Percy's record in Mary's *Journal*), 'Clary' and 'Clare'. More fundamentally, she is transforming her role from that of Mary's sisterly confidante to her sexual rival.

The tentative moves she made in this direction during their European trip – when she slept on the lovers' bed because she was afraid of the rats of Burgundy – might have been no more than childish objections to playing gooseberry. Now Percy encourages her to see herself as a protagonist. She isn't as gifted or as intelligent as Mary; but these are never the qualities that lever literary men into bed. Jane-Clara-Clary-Claire is much the more typical poet's girlfriend. She's no writerly rival but a nice little singer; her dark curls are obviously pretty; and she has no interests (or indeed pregnancy) of her own to get in the way of her continual availability.

She also has her mother's emotional canniness. Over the years to come, as she grows up, Mary will emerge as someone who acts with dignity, certainly in public. Her half-sister Fanny Godwin will write admiringly, in one of her own last letters, about her 'calm contented disposition, and the calm philosophical habits of life which [...] you pursue everywhere'. Jane-Claire, however, has no compunction about acting out, or at least acting up, and pandering to the Romantic preoccupation with *sensibility*.

We find her busily at work on 7 October 1814. Percy takes over Mary's *Journal* to make a lengthy record of an evening during which he and Jane tell each other ghost stories and are fascinated by the hysteria they provoke in each other. Jane has two attacks, one just after midnight and one at dawn. Both times Shelley retreats behind the figure of Mary to calm her down. The first time, he tells Jane that Mary is pregnant; the second, he brings her to Mary, who has been in bed since half past eight trying to get a decent night's sleep.

Mary as comforter and antidote; these are sober, unsexy virtues, and little competition against the drama Jane is creating around herself:

> her countenance [...] beamed with a whiteness that seemed almost like light; her lips and cheeks were of one deadly hue [...] her hair came prominent and erect; her eyes were wide and staring, drawn almost from the sockets by the convulsion of the muscles; the eyelids were forced in, and the eyeballs, without any relief, seemed as if they had been newly inserted, in ghastly sport, in the sockets of a lifeless head.

And not without encouragement. Percy accidently reveals his own come-on face, recording Jane's description of his 'unutterable expression [...] expressing a mixture of deep sadness and conscious power over her'.

But Jane hasn't yet learned that men are seduced when a woman dances to *their* tune. She tries a repeat performance a week later on 14

October after Percy has, in a sudden reversal, given her a telling-off for being 'unformed' and for her 'insensibility and incapacity for the slightest degree for friendship'. That morning he has also ticked himself off for his interest in her: 'Beware of weakly giving way to trivial sympathies. Content yourself with one great affection – with a single mighty hope.' That negative 'content yourself' doesn't bode well: Percy does not customarily 'content himself' with going without what he wants. But for now he means it. So when Jane tries groaning and 'sleepwalking' this time, Percy puts up with the noise for a couple of hours, then makes her sleep with Mary. In the morning, he records spikily, 'the chimney-board in Jane's room is found to have walked leisurely into the middle of the room, accompanied by the pillow, who, being very sleepy, tried to get into bed again, but fell down on his back.'

Infantilising the tale of the pillow is telling. On the earlier occasion this same soft furnishing had a starring role, apparently moving itself to a bedroom chair while Jane's back was turned. Like a child who doesn't want to go to sleep, Jane had come back downstairs, shortly after going to bed, to ask Percy 'if I had touched her pillow': 'I said, "No, no! if you come into the room I will tell you." I informed her of Mary's pregnancy.' It's an apparent *non sequitur* that's really nothing of the kind: I haven't come to your bedroom, Percy is telling her, because I have a sex life with Mary.

But Jane-Claire doesn't give up easily. And her proximity, not to mention her unencumbered freedom, makes her an attractive distraction for Percy on days when it's Mary who has annoyed him instead. A pattern has been set that will last, and in fact outlast, the couple's entire relationship. When Percy is dissatisfied, or just plain bored, with Mary he simply turns elsewhere. Currently and for some time to come this is to Jane-Claire, with whom he increasingly goes out and about even during these first months in London, once his immediate financial problems are solved and he can return to Church Terrace on 9 November. The outcome of this power play is that Mary is unable to negotiate with, for example, Percy's impulsiveness. Instead of being able to capitalise together on their different strengths, including the very qualities for which Percy chose Mary, their relationship remains out of balance, lived on his terms.

During the early months of 1815 the young couple spend time with

Percy's writer friend Thomas Love Peacock, and his portrait of their relationship appears in his début novel *Headlong Hall*, published in 1817. The beautiful Cephalis Cranium is, as her name insists, an intellectual, while Mr Escot is a vegetarian idealist full of theories about how a carnivorous diet is ruining human civilisation. Peacock's heroine is able to contain his protagonist's eccentricities, which may well be the case in conversations Mary, Percy and Peacock share. But in practice Cephalis-Mary is subject to Escot-Percy's every whim: some of the demands he will make in years to come mortally endanger the couple's children. Shelleyan 'free love' is so *very* free that it in fact imprisons his partner, since it's entirely conditional. Yet Mary, schooled by her father's own practice of conditional approval, internalises this way of going on and obeys it.

In any case, she has nowhere else to turn. And so it goes. For the rest of Mary's pregnancy, after the birth of her first child, and on into the weeks after she loses that child, 'Shelley and Jane go to …' or 'Shelley and Clara go to …' becomes a refrain of the *Journal*. At first the reader worries for Mary: hasn't she noticed how much the other two are out and about together? But on 6 December 1814 comes the first explicit acknowledgement that she has: 'Shelley and Jane walk out, as usual.' Positions harden. On 19 December Percy records 'a discussion concerning female character. Clara [Jane-Claire] imagines that I treat her unkindly. Mary consoles with her all-powerful benevolence.' It's hard to reconstruct the tone in which that 'all-powerful benevolence' was written: is it really as sarcastic as it sounds to our ears, or merely clumsy?

In early January 1815, after Sir Bysshe Shelley dies, Percy takes Jane-Claire, rather than the pregnant Mary, with him to the reading of his grandfather's will, something that allows the pair to overnight together at an inn. Do they sleep together? For Mary, meanwhile, is being set her next task. Percy wants her to sleep with Hogg, the same friend whose memoir gave us a glimpse of her sixteen-year-old self. As we've seen, when Hogg himself set Harriet a similar test in 1811, she refused. But Percy has declared himself for free love, and Mary, ever respectful of ideas, is obedient to this 'philosophy'. Alongside *Journal* entries recording Percy and Jane-Claire's many comings and goings, careful notes appear finding the positive in her partner's university friend: 'In the evening

Hogg comes. I like him better each time; it is a pity that he is a lawyer; he wasted so much time on that trash that might be spent on better things.'

She also writes Hogg a number of flirtatious, yet thoughtful, notes after he has declared love and sent her a present of an enamel brooch on 1 January 1815. But she is too conscientious to pretend emotions she doesn't feel, or simply to use Hogg in some rivalrous game with Percy. Instead, in surviving notes she repeats that 'you are so generous so disinterested that no one can help loving you.' These are, of course, virtues every bit as unsexy as her own 'benevolence'.

Nevertheless, Mary battles on. On 7 January – after Percy has passed the previous night away from home, and while he spends the day out and about with Jane-Claire – she sends Hogg some locks of her hair and tells him, 'My affection for you athough [*sic*] it is not now exactly as you would wish will I think dayly become more so'. In the next two months her admirer stays over quite often. Luckily, Mary has her pregnancy as an excuse not to sleep with him just yet. It's characteristic of her emotional plain dealing that she guesses this may make him feel excluded and, rather than whipping up jealousy to increase some sense of personal power, promises him that she isn't sleeping with Percy either: 'I ask but for time—time which for other causes beside this—phisical [*sic*] causes—that must be given—Shelley will be subject to these also.'

Percy, though, remains her first love:

> I who love him so tenderly & entirely whose life hangs on the beam of his eye and whose whole soul is entirely wrapt up in him- […] to see his love his tenderness dear dearest Alexy these are joys that full your heart almost to bursting & draw tears more delicious than the smiles of love from your eyes.

It's a strange passage. Mary is acknowledging that she is in principle prepared to sleep with Hogg (pet name: Alexy) in order to make Percy happy. This isn't tactful, but it is sincere: in fact, it's probably rather an exemplary way to behave within a romantic triangle. But Mary also makes clear that she assumes – or knows – that Hogg is also doing it for Percy: 'your […] your […] to make him happy'. Is this just Romantic overstatement? It's obvious why Hogg might enjoy trading on the conquests of his pretty friend. But how is that disinterested? Perhaps a related question: why does Percy push Mary to sleep with Hogg so early in their relationship?

Several motives suggest themselves. One is truly principled: Percy believes in free love and wants to make sure the pattern of an unconventional relationship is set straight away. Second, principled but less generous, he wants to make sure Mary 'lives up to' these ideals. Less principled, third, he's panicked: here he is once again with a pregnant partner who dreams of monogamy, and who is probably not terribly happy at the moment. Whether or not he can acknowledge it to himself, he finds this tedious and feels trapped. Fourth, and more murkily, he's turned on by the idea of Mary having sex with other men. Fifth, and more depressingly, he has made a mistake. Mary represents all sorts of possibilities – for him she symbolises both her parents, after all – including her own tremendous strength of character; but he isn't actually in love with her. He prefers flighty, pretty girls with whom he has temperamentally more in common. Sixth, and more reprehensibly, he does love Mary but is easily led, or at least easily distracted, and Jane-Claire offers him the chance to have some fun. Dimly aware that to sleep with his partner's (step)sister is probably not a great idea even in the world of free love, he feels that if Mary sleeps with someone else too – ideally perhaps, first – moral responsibility will be evened up. Seventh, more reprehensibly still and somewhat on the elopement principle, if Mary once sleeps with someone else, she will be indissolubly committed to free love, and she will lose the right to ask for any other, more settled kind of emotional life. Eighth, and rather fascinatingly, he is bisexual and – just as Harriet had something Mary wanted and which she may unwittingly have tried to achieve by sleeping with Percy – so Hogg has something Percy wants and which he will achieve if Mary sleeps with both of them. Or else, of course, both men are bisexual, and this is a way for them to sleep (or almost to sleep) together. After all, Percy's prettiness can't have gone unnoticed in the dormitories of Eton, where, as Mary Wollstonecraft had it, the boys 'pig together in the same bedchamber, not to speak of the vices'; but by this stage in their lives the young men have entered the adult world, where 'sodomy' is illegal. Breaking that prohibition is as risky for a young man as the prohibitions Percy expects women to break are for them, and in this case *he* would be bearing the cost and facing down the taboo.

Mary wouldn't be the first woman to find out that, when necessary, desire can be simulated, if not actually manufactured. In her era the sexual obedience of women is the norm, so having to sleep with Hogg may not feel to her like the worst thing that Percy could expect of her. Besides, she likes Hogg – as a friend, at least. When the baby she conceived at the outset of her relationship with Percy, and has been carrying all this time, dies on 6 March, it is Hogg she sends for. At this harrowing juncture Percy, the household's official invalid with a diagnosis of TB, is panicking and 'afraid of a fever from the milk'. Hogg becomes his emotional proxy, giving Mary the support her partner does not.

But love is a different matter. Whatever Percy's feelings for Mary now, she is in love with him; and her jealousy about the liaison between the two people she has left to trust in the world is painful. On 14 March, just a week after she has lost her child, 'Shelley and I go upstairs and talk of Clara's going; the prospect appears to me more dismal than ever; not the least hope. This is, indeed, hard to bear.' Mary has lost not only her child but also her growing sense of herself as a mother, that most loaded figure in her personal pantheon. 'I was a mother, and am so no longer', she notes. Now her beloved Percy seems to be slipping away from her too. Shelley, Hogg, Jane-Claire and Mary have got into the habit of playing chess, and the *Journal* records the interchanging pairings of the players, as intimacies develop between Mary and Hogg and between Percy and Jane-Claire, as if they were dancing sets and pairs in agonising slow motion – until, by 12 May, Mary cannot even bear her stepsister's name. 'Shelley and the lady […] Shelley and his friend', she writes in her *Journal*.

Finally, everything changes at once. Following a successful appeal to the Lord Chancellor on 20 April, Percy and his father reach an agreement under which Sir Timothy pays off Percy's debts – buying-up the 'post-obit bonds' with which the son has bet on inheriting – and settles on him a more generous allowance of £1,000 per year, of which a fifth is to go to Harriet in quarterly instalments. Sir Timothy also gives his daughter-in-law a further £200 against the costs she has run up since being abandoned. Among the debts so cancelled is Percy's £1,200 for Godwin. Percy promptly skims off £200 of this for himself – and in doing so creates a fresh strain in the young couple's relationship with Skinner Street.

Nevertheless, newly solvent, he is able to buy his way out of the problem he has (admittedly not single-handedly) created with Jane-Claire. On 13 May he sends her away to the care of a Mrs Hooper in lodgings in Lynmouth, on the north Devon coast, where he and Harriet stayed briefly in 1812. She will remain there for the rest of the year, turning up in London only on 5 January 1816. But out of sight is not out of mind. After initially declaring her delight at escaping the stormy, triangulated household she has helped to create, the seventeen-year-old quickly becomes lonely, as she's not afraid to inform the couple in her letters. And she remains a powerful loadstone. When Mary and Percy decide to make a new start by moving out of London, it's to Devon that they come, although they choose Torquay, on its other coast. And when Jane-Claire doesn't respond to Mary's letters during Percy's protracted absence and accompanying silence in July – a period during which he is allegedly house-hunting – it begins to seem as if she could be once again cutting in on her sister's relationship.

Sending a young woman away is the traditional way to disguise a pregnancy. The nearly eight months Jane-Claire spends in Lynmouth are certainly long enough to do this, especially if the child doesn't remain with its mother to be nursed. So it is possible that Jane-Claire has a child by Percy in the summer of 1815. But there's no surviving evidence of this. All we can be reasonably sure of is that, if Jane does indeed give birth in Lynmouth, the child does not survive, for, in the years to come, she will live through two great pressure points at which she would surely go looking for it. One of these will be when the daughter she has by Byron dies, the other when Percy himself dies. At neither moment is there any record of such a search.

For Mary, Jane's departure – whether pregnant or not – represents the chance of a fresh start with Percy. 'I begin a new Journal with our regeneration', she writes exuberantly, though unfortunately that new volume hasn't survived to the present day. The move to Devon is the first the couple make alone together, and Mary finds the seaside village so charming that she will remember it five years from now, even from among the beauties of Italy, as she writes her story *Maurice*. But its significance can't disguise the fact that here too their stay lasts for only just over a month.

Soon Percy takes Mary, who is now pregnant again, back into newly built Clifton – smart, yet set on the maritime edge of Bristol, above the Gorge and docks – while he goes off house-hunting near London.

Another month, another address. It's not surprising that so much of what Mary and Percy do at this time seems fractured and incoherent. They simply haven't stopped moving. It was just as bad in London. On 8 November they moved from Church Terrace south of the Thames to 2 Nelson Square, and on 8 February 1815 they moved back north to Hans Place, in what is now Knightsbridge. A month later, and on 2 March they were off again, this time to 13 Arabella Road in Pimlico, from where on 27 April they moved again, to Marchmont Street, near Brunswick Square, before making the shift to Devon. These dates, blocked out in months and one six-week period, suggest nothing so much as a series of flits just before rent falls due.

It's exhausting to keep in mind, leave alone to live. Besides, full of youthful energy or not, Mary is either pregnant or nursing for much of this period. Whatever she didn't know about contraception when she ran away with Percy, she must surely be more clued up about now. But, like her parents, she seems – anyway at this stage in her life – to accept that love means procreation. Her first child, born at Hans Place, dies twelve days later at Arabella Road. It's as if having a baby is so unimportant that it can be fitted in round everything else. The record that remains shows Mary grieving after the death, but Percy largely leaving her to it while he goes out and about, often with Jane-Claire. It's as if he feels no particular grief, and the whole business of his first baby with Mary is unimportant; almost as if he can't countenance having to share her with a child. Even his record of the birth dismisses Mary's labour as 'a few additional pains', describes her as 'Perfectly well, and at ease' and then notes with seeming astonishment that she is 'much agitated and exhausted'. Of course she is: quite apart from labouring without pain relief, she has just gone through the experience that killed her mother – the defining fact of her childhood – and survived.

But then again, everything – pregnancy, repeated moves, emotional stress – is made harder by Percy's vegetarianism in an era before nutrition is well understood, or a wide range of fresh fruit and vegetables readily available. Percy began the diet with Harriet in 1812, leaving Mary with no choice but to at least equal her predecessor's commitment to his demanding belief that meat is the source not only of ill health but also of all violence, including war and colonialism. As he writes in the polemic *A Vindication of Natural Diet*, which was first published in 1813 as part of the notes to *Queen Mab* and reprinted as a separate pamphlet later that same year:

> There is no disease, bodily or mental, which adoption of vegetable diet and pure water has not infallibly mitigated [...] On a natural system of diet we should require no spices from India; no wines from Portugal, Spain, France, or Madeira; none of those multitudinous articles of luxury, for which every corner of the globe is rifled, and which are the causes of so much individual rivalship, such calamitous and sanguinary national disputes [...] How much longer will man continue to pimp for the gluttony of Death?

Mary and Percy are short of money, and prices are high. In March 1815 the Importation Act protects landowners' profits by preventing imports of cheap grain. In doing so it makes bread, the staple diet of the poor, disproportionately – even ruinously – expensive. Among the eventual results of this and the subsequent sequence of Corn Laws will be civil unrest, starvation and an atmosphere of near-revolution that, as we will see, is going to alter the lives of the radical circle in which the couple move. Meanwhile, the food on which Mary must subsist while pregnant and nursing resembles the meatless diet of her poorest contemporaries. What in summer and autumn may be tolerable becomes, as winter draws on and she enters the last months of her first two pregnancies, little more than a slop of root vegetables – turnip, parsnip, carrots and potatoes – served up by inexpert, possibly sceptical cooks.

In years to come, Lord Byron will sneer at the Shelleys' vegetarian diet and associate it with the deaths of their infant children. Admittedly, he does so as part of a campaign to gain custody of his own child. But words spoken in spite can be as insightful as truths spoken in jest. Will Mary secretly suspect he may be right? If she feels she has failed as a parent, the great imaginative leap into the Gothic imaginary that she's soon to make in his company must find at least part of its inspiration in an enduring guilt. In the world of her first novel, to give life turns out to be difficult, and to give life to a full-term, fully human 'progeny' more difficult still. *Frankenstein* is, at least in part, a great statement about the immorality of forcing life on a being whom you have not made well enough to be equal to that burden.

Chapter 6

At Villa Diodati

I remembered also the nervous fever with which I had been seized just at the time that I dated my creation, and which would give an air of delirium to a tale otherwise so utterly improbable.

THE FIRST SCENES OF MARY'S LIFE are brightly illuminated. She spends her childhood in a house lit by huge, modern windows. But by the time she's eighteen a chiaroscuro seems to enclose her. Things have dimmed: her certainty about what she's doing, and ours with it. We get this impression of shadow partly because the loss of *Journal* volumes make it harder to visualise what she's doing. But this is also a time in Mary's life that is murky with cross-currents: a period of personal and domestic upheaval and repeated house moves, but also of wide reading, continued self-education, further pregnancy and the birth of her second child, William.

So it's fitting that the next scene, the most famous tableau of Mary's life, is set indoors and at night. She and Percy are in the drawing-room of Villa Diodati, on the shores of Lake Geneva. The lighted salon seems to float among the dark trees of a hillside high above the darkened water. It is June 1816, and they are visiting George Gordon Byron, sixth Baron Byron, at the house he's rented for the summer. Claire, who is trying to prolong an affair she has been having with the peer, is once again in tow. Also in the room is Byron's young doctor and gentleman's travelling companion, twenty-year-old John William Polidori, who is himself an aspiring writer.

But this is no idyllic summer evening, with a scent of roses and cool drinks on the terrace. For 1816 is the Year Without a Summer. The eruption in 1815 of Mount Tambora on Sumbawa, in what is for now still the Dutch East Indies, has filled the earth's upper atmosphere with volcanic ash, blocking out the sun and creating a volcanic winter. Across the world, average temperatures are one degree centigrade lower than usual; and the anomaly is significantly greater here in Western Europe, a region that is coincidentally already suffering food shortages caused by man-made catastrophe in the shape of the Napoleonic Wars and the British Corn Laws.

Mary and the rest of the group gathered in the lamplight are unlikely to know about the Tambora eruption, even though it's a volcanic event on a scale unequalled since the Hatepe eruption of 180 CE, and kills thousands in its own region. Nor are they likely to be aware that it is the latest in a cluster of major eruptions across the world – in the Caribbean, Japan and the Philippines, as well elsewhere in the Dutch East Indies – which since 1812 have already released large amounts of dust into the atmosphere, so that when Tambora erupts its effects are even more dramatic than they would have been anyway. These European travellers may, though, be anecdotally aware that brown snow has been falling in Hungary and red in Italy; they may also notice that the sunsets they admire are far more colourful than any they've seen before.

Tambora's 'volcanic winter' comes on top of the Little Ice Age, a phenomenon this circle of young writers won't be able to name but will be aware of through the endless British talk about the weather. The European climate has been cooling since the mid-fourteenth century, and British farmland yielding correspondingly less: areas like the Elenydd, the Welsh uplands where Percy stayed in Nantgwyllt, will become known to English Victorian travel writers as 'The Desert of Wales', yet bear the traces of extensive farming and settlement in medieval times. Within this general cooling down, which will continue throughout Mary's life, she's also living through years of particular cold triggered not by volcanic but by solar activity – or rather, its lack. The period from December 1810 to May 1823 is the 'Dalton Minimum', a time of exceptionally low solar activity that further depresses average earth temperatures by one degree centigrade. Even today, two centuries later, May 1816 holds the record for the lowest sunspot activity ever recorded.

All of that means that this summer there are frosts in August, crops have failed, and there's ice in the Swiss lakes where, for example, an ice dam is forming at the foot of the Gietro Glacier in the Val de Bagnes. It's a time of wonders and of suffering. Roughly 200,000 people will die across Europe alone as a result of these climatic conditions. Famine has caused rioting here in Switzerland, where conditions are among the worst anywhere on the continent and where the government has declared a national emergency. A hundred and thirty days of rain between April and September cause Lake Geneva to flood the fashionable city at its southernmost tip.

Yet here Percy, Mary and Claire are on the Genevan shore, where, with some of the same obliviousness that characterised their last European expedition, they have been settled since the middle of May. Tonight's venue, Villa Diodati, is a pretty, boxy eighteenth-century mansion set high above any risk of flooding on the zigzagging Chemin de Ruth in Cologny. Byron describes it as 'a very pretty villa in a vineyard – with the Alps behind – and Mt. Jura and the Lake before'. The Shelleys' own summer rental is the more modest Maison Chapuis on the Chemin du Parc-de-Montalègre, down near the water, where they even have a private dock. What is today an exclusive suburb is then a village, and Lord Byron has followed the Shelleys here in part because it affords him more privacy than he can find in the fashionable city of Geneva itself.

More privacy, but possibly not privacy enough. The hotelier of the Hôtel d'Angleterre Sécheron, where everyone in this drawing-room boarded when they first arrived at the lake, installs a telescope to help his remaining guests speculate about the goings-on at the home of this aristocrat who has become celebrated, since starting an affair with Lady Caroline Lamb in 1812, as 'mad, bad and dangerous to know'. Indeed, it's the series of scandals surrounding his private life that have forced him to leave England permanently. In addition to continuing fiery and very public love–hate encounters with 'Caro' Lamb, there are affairs with actresses, rumours about an incestuous relationship with his half-sister Augusta Leigh and the breakdown of his marriage, a separation formalised in March. His wife Anne has left him after only a year, citing not only the unorthodoxy of his relationship with Leigh but her own belief that he is mad and – most damagingly, since it's illegal – his predilection for anal sex, both in past gay relationships and with her.

Since 25 April, therefore, Byron has been making his way slowly south and east through France; he arrives in Geneva a fortnight after the Godwin–Shelley household. This sequence of arrivals nicely moderates the power relationship between two poets who have yet to meet. Unlike Percy, who is in a way still waiting for his life of adult achievement to begin, Byron is both well known and, because he has already inherited, wealthy. The first two cantos of *Childe Harold's Pilgrimage,* published in 1812, have been an immediate success. Part *bildungsroman,* partly a confession that perfectly matches the *zeitgeist,* the *Pilgrimage* describes the wanderings of a sensitive young man disillusioned with life. In his quest for meaning he travels far from English society, allowing an attractive element of travelogue to enter the poem. Since this is the moment at which European philosophy has settled on such personal development as key to human meaning, the poem also resonates with contemporary intellectual debates.

Besides, Byron is a man of action. Despite his famous limp, he will soon go off to fight for a cause – Greek nationalism – in which he believes. He's already known as an explicitly political writer, opposed to the mechanisation that is encroaching on jobs and livelihoods (he publishes his 'Song for the Luddites' this year) and supportive of Greek opposition to Lord Elgin's removal of the Parthenon marbles to London (in Canto II of *Childe Harold*). He also has, of course, what we now call 'Byronic' good looks – which he's alleged to help along with curlpapers.

All this, and the fact that he is only four years older than Shelley (though half a decade can seem like a generation when we're in our twenties), makes him both desirable and potentially problematic for the younger man, who has obvious, practical reasons for courting his patronage. Yet what's emerging this summer is something like a party of friendly equals. This is a good thing, because Claire has persuaded Percy and Mary to make the journey from England simply in order to meet Byron. If not quite hare-brained, her scheme is certainly built on gossamer foundations. It's also more than a little manipulative, and her true motives for engineering the meeting will by now be clear to the couple, who must be feeling they've been dropped into the middle of a story without getting to read the opening chapters.

Still, Claire's been proved right in guessing that Byron and Percy will hit it off. She's less accurate in her predictions of what will happen when he meets Mary, whom she tries to turn into a figure through whom to flirt by proxy. After bringing her stepsister to meet Byron in London, probably on 21 April 1816, she writes archly, 'Mary is delighted with you as I knew she would be; she entreats me in private [for] your address abroad that we may if possible have the pleasure of seeing you.' By 6 May, already en route to that very end, she writes from Paris: 'You will I dare say fall in love with her; she is very handsome & very amiable & you will no doubt be blest in your attachment.'

But – quite apart from the idiosyncrasies of desire – Mary, unlike Claire, needs no new source of excitement in her life. She already *has* her great love Percy, and her little son William, who was born on 24 January, at a time when what we do know is that she and Percy were still living near Windsor Great Park. William, by now six months old, is just starting to be weaned and is probably teething. There are plenty of ways in which he can absorb her attention. (For example, after the sudden death of a local teenager on 1 June, Polidori helps rush to get the baby vaccinated.) Mary engages Elise Duvillard as William's nursemaid on 27 May, but she's the first in her immediate family to spend periods raising a baby without any such help: even her mother travelled through war-torn Europe with a maid. This doesn't seem to worry her – she will remember these months as one of the happiest times of her life – but it does mean that her child will demand much of her spare time.

It's a good thing she feels so emotionally settled, because the trio's departure from England is being framed as a flight from social ostracism. We get an interesting glimpse of Percy's version of things in Polidori's diary:

Gone through much misery, thinking he was dying; married a girl for the mere sake of letting her have the jointure that would accrue to her; recovered; found he could not agree; separated; paid Godwin's debts, and seduced his daughter; then wondered that he would not see him.

Baby William is named after his Godwin grandfather, but for some months Percy has been struggling with Godwin himself who, while continuing to ask the younger man for hand-outs, has also continued to condemn his relationship with Mary, and refuses to meet the young family. Percy has spent the spring relinquishing the belief that he could be the older man's *de facto* son-in-law and intellectual heir. As he writes from Dover on 3 May (the tone is 'more in sorrow than in anger'): 'You were the philosopher who first awakened, and who still as a philosopher to very great degree regulates my understanding. It is unfortunate for me that the part of your character which is least excellent should have been met by my convictions of what was right to do.'

But it's Percy's letter to Godwin of 6 March that records the turning point in what has become a battle of self-righteous masculine wills, and that perhaps lets us understand why Mary and Percy fall in so readily with Claire's scheme to meet up with Lord Byron in Geneva:

It has perpetually appeared to me to have been your especial duty to see that, so far as mankind value your good opinion, we were dealt justly by, and that a young family, innocent and benevolent and united, should not be confounded with prostitutes and seducers. My astonishment and, I will confess, when I have been treated with most harshness and cruelty by you, my indignation, has been extreme.

That phrase, 'a young family', must have cheered Mary if she managed to read this letter. It suggests a shift in Percy's attitude and narrative: one that she's perhaps enjoying, this summer at Lake Geneva. Claire, absorbed by Byron, is no longer setting her cap at Percy. Byron is turning out to be an intelligent and generous friend. Mary is no longer expected to be so conscientious about free love. (The dashing Byron is probably more of a sexual threat to Percy than Hogg could ever be, and a rather more challenging figure with whom to share Mary.)

In the event it's Polidori, not Byron, who has developed a crush on

Mary. This seems to be a cheering, un-claustrophobic affair: just the kind to massage her self-esteem without the risks of real engagement. The doctor, who is almost exactly two years older than the young woman he calls 'Mrs Shelley', records a stately progress in his journal: 'Read Italian with Mrs S, went into a boat with Mrs S, and rowed all night till nine; tea'd together, chatted, etc.' On 15 June he sprains his ankle jumping off a balcony to offer Mary an arm as she toils up the slope to Villa Diodati. Those around him, and most historians since, seem to take Polidori's interest as a crush, somewhere between laughable and childishly sweet. But we shouldn't forget that his first entry for Mary, on 27 May, reads: 'PS, the author of *Queen Mab*, came; bashful, shy, consumptive; twenty-six; separated from his wife; keeps the two daughters of Godwin, who practise his theories; one LB's.' In other words, he starts from the position of believing that Mary 'practises' *free love* and is not spoken for by Byron: that she is sexually available.

Whether or not there's a rumble of misunderstanding even in Polidori's chivalry, Mary is enjoying herself, and goes exploring as often as she can. On 1 June she writes home to Fanny, with a mixture of boastfulness and frustration:

> An almost perpetual rain confines us principally to the house [...] The thunder storms that visit us are grander and more terrific than I have ever seen before. [...] One night we <u>enjoyed</u> [the underlining is Mary's own] a finer storm than I had ever before beheld. The lake was lit up—the pines on Jura made visible, and all the scene illuminated for an instant, when a pitchy blackness succeeded, and the thunder came in frightful bursts over our heads amid the blackness.

In short, 'it was a dark and stormy night ...', and it's to the accompaniment of this glorious cliché that the Godwin–Shelley household and Byron's often meet in the evenings at Villa Diodati.

On one such evening, most probably 16 June, Mary, Percy, Claire, Byron and Polidori gather to read ghost stories. It's nearly the longest day of the year; but the strange darkness of the skies means lamps have been lit earlier than usual. The book they're reading from is an anonymous French translation of ten German ghost stories, *Fantasmagoriana, ou Receuil d'Histoires de Spectres, Revenants, Fantômes, etc.* The stories it contains are no brief transcriptions of folk traditions and *contes*, but have been worked up in contemporary literary style, as part of a German fashion for the *Schauerroman* ('shudder', or horror, novel) or *Gespenster-roman* (ghost novel), so it's unlikely the friends read the whole two volumes aloud in one evening. We do know, though, that they probably start at the beginning, and read stories numbers two and four, 'Die Bilder der Ahnen' ('Family Portraits'), by Johann August Apel, and 'Die Tod-tenbraut' ('The Death Bride'), from *Das Gespensterbuch*, the five-volume anthology Apel and Friedrich Laun started publishing the year before, because Mary's recollections from 1831 make a stab at the plots of these two stories in particular.

Today a similarly gifted and highly educated house party would read these stories to howls of laughter, and set themselves writing pastiches; these young Romantics do not. To our contemporary imaginations the horror in *Fantasmagoriana* appears very stately; but as genre fiction its stories balance between populism and the literary. Everyone present at Villa Diodati has grown up with the related genre of Gothic novel, an English invention. They all know how it combines up-to-date narrative technique with medievalism, and are aware that this has led to the tradi-tional inclusion of an element of historical mystery or the supernatural. All will be familiar with Horace Walpole's *The Castle of Otranto*, published in 1764 and credited as the first Gothic romance. Its huge success on first publication was partly due to the author's pretending it was the transla-tion of an authentic mediaeval Italian romance. Among the most famous of its successors is Matthew Gregory Lewis's *The Monk* (1796). Byron has praised Lewis – as 'Apollo's Sexton' – in a published poem, and Mary's *Journal* tells us that, on 18 August, the man himself visits Villa Diodati. But when Walpole revealed in *Otranto*'s second edition that he had in fact made the whole thing up, rave reception turned to bitter criticism: the most sensational chill comes from a sense of *authentic* proximity to horror.

The party at Villa Diodati have turned instead to European writing for their thrills. The *Schauerroman* is an altogether darker tradition than English Gothic, combining medievalism and the supernatural most often through stories about necromancy, whose themes of raising the dead are rich in foretastes of the contemporary 'science' of galvanism and fashionable questions about the origins of life. It also has respectable literary antecedents. Friedrich Schiller's drama *The Robbers* (1781) has established the *Räuberroman*, or robber and outlaw novel, a parallel genre within German Gothic; by 1816 E. T. A. Hoffmann, though a generation older than Mary and Percy, is beginning to publish his influential 'Tales'. Of possibly more immediate interest to the June house party is the 'Translator's Preface' to *Fantasmagoriana*, which discusses German research into ghostly phenomena, and an early form of Spiritualism, 'the modern Seers, known in Germany under the denomination of *Stillingianer*. […] This sect […] has a great number of adherents, *especially in Switzerland*' [my italics]. It must all feel more thrillingly proximate than it did in familiar, workaday England.

So it's not surprising that '"We will each write a ghost story," said Lord Byron; and his proposition was acceded to.' That we can narrow down the date for this famous challenge has much to do with Polidori's diary. It tells us that Byron and Polidori don't take possession of Villa Diodati until 10 June, that on the 11th only Percy joins the two men there, and that on the 12th and 13th Polidori is out on the town. It's not until the 14th that 'Shelley etc. fell in in the evening'. On the 15th 'Shelley etc. came in the evening', but the group read Polidori's play and afterwards talk about 'whether man was thought to be merely an instrument'. As both these topics are substantial, it seems unlikely that this was also an evening given over primarily to ghost stories and the challenge that arises from them. However on the 16th, a Sunday, Polidori is 'Laid up. Shelley came, and dined and slept here, with Mrs S and Miss Clare Clairmont', and on the 17th he records that 'The ghost stories are begun by all but me'. The Sunday sleepover seems the most likely occasion for the friends to stay up telling ghost stories, like the kids they still nearly are. A sleepover also means that, in the morning, there are lots of people around to ask each other, 'Have you thought of a story?'

The trouble with a writing challenge is that it produces as much anxiety as inspiration. Polidori isn't the only one to feel left behind; Mary claims that *she* is the last to start. '*Have you thought of a story?* I was asked each morning, and each morning I was forced to reply with a mortifying negative.' She may have ratcheted up the pressure in her retelling, when she says it continued for days. It's possible that both Polidori and Mary measure themselves only against the two poets, dismissing each other's writer's block. Polidori has already noted that Claire and Mary are 'clever', but this is the English nineteenth century, and he's no more likely than the rest of the party are to see Mary as a writer, even in embryo – while she merely views him like a younger brother.

The poets themselves are less anxious about the whole thing. Byron begins 'a tale, a fragment of which he printed at the end of his poem of Mazeppa'. It's an orientalist story – set around the death of a mysterious Englishman, Augustus Darvell, in a 'Turkish' graveyard near Ephesus – which doesn't get as far as the hard work of unravelling the mystery it sets up. Percy starts a story 'founded on the experiences of his early life'. It's intriguing to speculate what such experiences, if not fictional, might be. He has recently disclosed to Polidori that, when he was at Eton, his father tried to have him incarcerated in a lunatic asylum: does he try to recreate the state of mind he was then in?

He's certainly cultivating intense reactions. On the 18th, the friends try once more to feel their way into an encounter with the supernatural:

> Twelve o'clock, really began to talk ghostly. LB repeated some verses of Coleridge's 'Christabel', of the witch's breast; when silence ensued, and Shelley, suddenly shrieking and putting his hands to his head, ran out of the room with a candle. Threw water in his face, and after gave him ether. He was looking at Mrs. S, and suddenly thought of a woman he had heard of who had eyes instead of nipples, which, taking hold of his mind, horrified him.

Of course, they've all been drinking, and perhaps taking laudanum too. Percy has form on staying up late and getting the creeps, although as far as we know in the past he's done this vicariously, by working Claire into a state of hysteria. Now that her attention is taken up by Byron, it's almost as though he feels challenged to recreate his hold on her. Polidori's diary segues so directly from this scene of acting out to Percy's account of himself as a victim 'surrounded' by people who 'feed on him, and draw on him as their banker' that we can almost hear the 'I'm under so much pressure, I'm not myself' excuses.

But Percy's near-manic restlessness and wordy productivity – together with a kind of hyper-real personal quality, a form of charisma – do suggest someone who's slightly more 'high' than the usual. Not all of this can be recreationally induced. Percy resembles a type of highly gifted young man who receives a diagnosis of bipolar disorder but remains high-functioning because manifesting only on the manic end of the spectrum, with no disabling depression. This would certainly explain the sense that those around him – including Mary – have of being simultaneously unable to reason with him yet duty-bound to protect his particular fragility.

And what of Mary herself? No one seems to be protecting her fragility. What on earth does she feel at being the subject of this hallucination that she has eyes for nipples? Percy's so public fantasy makes her simultaneously grotesque and uncanny. Her breasts are frightening instead of nurturing; she's witchy instead of feminine. There's also some symbolic 'seeing through' going on: Percy 'sees through' her clothing to Mary's nipples; and these aren't mute or passive but active: they look back at him, as if *they* can 'see through' *him*. Just as Percy must by now know, or at least suspect, that Mary can. It's a fabulously brazen way to accuse *her* of accusing him – while making out it's 'all a dream'. What neither Percy nor Polidori troubles to acknowledge is that Mary has herself supplied Percy with this image, taken from an earlier version of Samuel Taylor Coleridge's poem with which she's familiar. 'Mrs S', who must be fighting a strong desire to fold her arms, must also be controlling a pretty strong desire to walk out on the whole scenario. Which, if it has indeed been staged either consciously or unconsciously for Claire's benefit, does not in any case have the desired effect: tonight Claire does not end up in the couple's bed.

Perhaps it's because they lack a Coleridgean fluency with the poetics of horror that Byron and Percy soon abandon their ghost stories. As Mary puts it: 'the illustrious poets [...] annoyed by the platitude of prose, speedily relinquished their uncongenial task.' But Mary and Polidori have both set out on longer-term projects: longer-term than they could possibly realise, since both will eventually change the face of genre fiction. Despite this, Mary is dismissive of Polidori's initial attempt:

Poor Polidori had some terrible idea about a skull-headed lady, who was so punished for peeping through a key-hole—what to see I forget—something very shocking and wrong of course; but when she was reduced […] he did not know what to do with her, and was obliged to dispatch her to the tomb of the Capulets.

After she, Percy and Claire leave Switzerland on 29 August, they will never see the young doctor again, and it's not certain that Mary ever reads *The Vampyre*, first published in 1819 and misattributed to Byron. (Both Polidori and Byron will be mortified by this misattribution. They've parted on terms so bad that Polidori even names the first vampire in literary history Lord Ruthven, after the Byron character in *Glenarvon*, Lady Caroline Lamb's hugely successful and highly scandalous *roman à clef* about her affair with the poet.)

But for now, coming and going from their summer home in Cologny, Mary takes Alpine trips with Percy and works intermittently on the 'ghost story' that will become *Frankenstein*. For the first time in their life together she is neither pregnant nor nursing. The result is a tremendous release of energy. At the end of June, when Percy and Byron go sailing round Lake Geneva for a week, she works steadily on the story. On 21 July she leaves the infant William with Elise Duvillard and joins Percy and Claire for an energetic expedition to Chamonix. The Alpine scenery is splendid, with waterfalls and mountains. But it's also cold and wet, the travellers are frequently exhausted, and the bad weather prevents them from seeing everything they'd hoped: 'It rained, and we could not possibly go to Col de Balme, as we intended.' Yet they are delighted by what they do see: 'We arrive at the inn at 6, fatigued by our day's journey, but pleased and astonished by the world of ice that was opened to our view.'

This 'world of ice' is the Mer de Glace. Mary's *Journal* records her first impressions of 'the most desolate place in the world. Iced mountains surround it; no sign of vegetation appears except on the place from which [you] view the scene. We went on the ice; it is traversed by irregular crevices, whose sides of ice appear blue, while the surface is of a dirty white.' In Chapter X of *Frankenstein*, it's across the Mer de Glace that the creature approaches his maker to beg for a companion:

I remained in a recess of the rock, gazing on this wonderful and stupendous scene. The sea, or rather the vast river of ice, wound among its dependent mountains whose aerial summits hung over its recesses.

Their icy and glittering peaks shone in the sunlight over the clouds. My heart, which was before sorrowful, now swelled with something like joy [...] I suddenly beheld the figure of a man, at some distance, advancing towards me with superhuman speed.

It's a larger-than-life landscape fit for Frankenstein's larger-than-life creature. Mary's *Journal* for 1816 records Alpine scenery every bit as uncanny as the apparent warping of the laws of nature in this passage. The travellers see an avalanche, a 'mountain which fell some years ago, and destroyed *many men and cows*', a glacier that's growing at the rate of a foot a day and 'closing up the valley', others that are dangerous to approach, and one, Bossons Glacier, perhaps wishfully recorded in the Journal as 'Glace de Boisson', has 'the appearance at a distance of a foaming cataract'.

Mary's descriptions are surprisingly anthropomorphic. Of waterfalls near Magland, she writes that one, 'struck first on an enormous rock resembling precisely some colossal Egyptian statue of a female deity: it struck the head of the visionary image', while another looked 'rather like some shape which an exhalation had assumed than like water, for it fell beyond the mountain, which appeared dark behind it'. This unhomely sense of a wild landscape that is somehow sentient and observes the human who has strayed into its grip will reappear in *Frankenstein*. The natural philosopher's creation seems almost to become part of the landscapes he haunts as he stalks his maker:

I perceived in the gloom a figure which stole from behind a clump of trees near me [...] A flash of lightning illuminated the object [...] The figure passed me quickly, and I lost it in the gloom [...] another flash discovered him to me hanging among the rocks of the nearby perpendicular ascent.

He could almost be a trick of the light, like the Brocken spectre, a natural illusion of mountain fogs that so terrifyingly enlarges the human figure of which it's a shadow.

Mary's *Journal* records their guide's warnings about the mountainous terrain. But this summer it's not Mary but Claire for whom such an inhospitable landscape poses real challenges. For, though Mary doesn't yet know it, Claire is pregnant, a fact of which both Percy and she are already aware. That Claire has confided not in her stepsister but in her stepsister's partner suggests a number of things: that she's probably a man's woman, but also that she may have been intimate with Percy in the past, for why else would her pregnancy be his business? It's certainly remarkable if Mary, having twice been pregnant already herself, notices nothing; but we shouldn't assume this, since she must surely be aware by now that Claire has been sleeping with Byron while they are in Cologny. Mary has shown herself not only fully capable of putting two and two together, but able too to keep her own counsel in the pages of her *Journal*.

Confiding in Percy rather than Byron further suggests that Claire's affair has not been going well; and indeed it hasn't. In fact, we can see how badly it was bound to go just by its timing. Claire did indeed sleep with 'LB', or *Albe* as the Shelleys come to call him, in England. But whether we can reasonably call this an affair is moot: she only had her chance with him on 20–23 April, during his final three days in London before his departure for Geneva and permanent exile. So he certainly entertained no thoughts of a settled London, or British, relationship with Claire. Nor, apparently, did he envisage a continental one. On what we might call 'the morning after', we've already seen that Claire had to extract his onward address by pretending Mary asked for it. This is a schoolgirl ruse; it also shows a childlike inability to take a hint. Determined to create what she claims to hope will be a four-way ménage, she has simply refused to take no for an answer.

Her earlier susceptibility to Percy, her self-inventing experiments with her own name, so like any bored teenager today practising a signature or a selfie style, the volatility recorded by Percy in Mary's *Journal* – all these suggest that Claire, now eighteen, is just not very grown up. But they also suggest something else: an assumption that she can and will have what she wants, which is modelled at least in part on a seductive, Shelleyan rhetoric.

In the summer of 1816 Percy is still best known for *Queen Mab*, a vision of mind–body separation in which the 'soul' is often frustrated by the limits of embodied circumstance. Human bodies are mortal, and human societies violently unequal; the remedy for these social ills lies in the exceptional individual: 'Some eminent in virtue shall start up, /

Even in perversest time'. Although Book 5 of Percy's poem acknowledges the likelihood in imperfect societies of 'a rustic Milton [...] a vulgar Cato [...] a Newton', immortal 'spirit' – conveniently for a good-looking youngster – resembles the body it inhabits: 'The perfect semblance of its bodily frame / Instinct with inexpressible beauty and grace'.

So exceptional good looks are a promise of the moral perfectibility of the human world. It's an elitist notion, which far in the future can lead to eugenics and indeed fascism. It also has at its heart an assumption of self-evidence. This problematic, but not at the time unusual, idea finds its way into Mary's first novel, where her framing narrator, Walton, assures us that Dr Frankenstein must be an intrinsically good person because his looks and manners are attractive:

> He is so gentle, yet so wise; his mind is so cultivated; and when he speaks, although his words are culled with the choicest art, yet they flow with rapidity and unparalleled eloquence.

Even Byron is briefly attracted to the doctrine during this summer of 1816, while he writes the 1,102-line Third Canto of *Childe Harold*. The poem, which mourns Waterloo as the end of revolutionary political hope, also portrays a tension between transcendent spirit and limited human body that we can immediately recognise as pure Shelley:

> I live not in myself, but I become
> Portion of that around me;
> [...] I can see
> Nothing to loathe in nature, save to be
> A link reluctant in a fleshy chain,
> Class'd among creatures, when the soul can flee.

In Claire the same idea becomes a notion that her own 'eminent [...] virtue' is self-evident because she is so pretty. The tone of her letters to Byron is not exactly will-not-be-baulked; it is more simply assumptive. She wrote to him out of the blue, in early spring 1816, to make her bold offer:

> If a woman, whose reputation has yet remained unstained, if without guardian or husband to control she should throw herself upon your

mercy, if with a beating heart she should confess the love she has borne you many years, if she should secure you secrisy [sic] & safety, if she should return your kindness with fond affection & unbounded devotion could you betray her, or would you be as silent as the grave?

Once they've become intimate, on 20 April, a week before she turns eighteen, she tries to tempt him with more: 'Tomorrow will inform me whether I should be able to offer you *that* which it has long been the passionate wish of my heart to offer you.'

This arch line is read by some as the offer of a child, yet that's not something Claire can guarantee any more than she can possibly know whether she's pregnant by Byron within a day of sleeping with him. So if they have indeed already had sex, what is she offering now? Unprotected sex? Anal sex? She can't be unaware that his predilection is publicly alleged; perhaps it even forms part of his pillow talk. Finally, why does she not yet know whether she will make herself available in whatever way this is? Is she, for example, waiting for her period to end or start? … It's a relief to close the bedroom door on this whole train of speculation; and Byron seems to have felt similar relief. When he finally arrives in Geneva, Claire has to force the issue. Flirtatious on his first arrival, after two days of waiting she becomes charmlessly plaintive: 'I have been in this weary hotel this fortnight & it seems so unkind, so cruel, of you to treat me with such marked indifference.'

Byron's eventual decision to fall in with her demands is unflatteringly framed in a letter to his stepsister and lover Augusta Leigh:

> and as to all these 'mistresses'—Lord help me—I have had but one.—Now—don't scold—but what could I do?—a foolish girl—in spite of all I could say or do—would come after me—or rather went before me—for I found her here […] I am not in love—nor have any love left for any,—but I could not exactly play the Stoic with a woman—who had scrambled eight hundred miles to unphilosophize me—besides I had been regaled of late with so many 'two courses and a *desert*' (Alas!) of aversion—that I was fain to take a little love (if pressed particularly) by way of novelty.

By the time he writes this, in September, Byron knows that Claire is pregnant by him and that he must make a pre-emptive confession to the woman he loves – who is, clearly, not Claire. Making the consequent arrangements, however, falls chiefly to Percy, who now adopts a quasi-familial responsibility for Claire. Indeed, so far is Mary is excluded from these conversations that she may not even be aware that Percy now changes his will, leaving £6,000 to Claire and a further £6,000 to whomever Claire chooses (presumably this is to be the child, though by the time Claire inherits, her child will be long dead).

These practical arrangements, and the somewhat grudging tone Byron adopts towards them ('Is the brat mine?' is his first, defensive response), mean the summer ends prematurely, in anti-climax. On 29 August Mary, Percy, Claire, baby William and the nursemaid Elise are heading back to England and Bath, where the couple will install Claire in some seclusion at a separate address from their own new home beside the Abbey. The agreement they've negotiated with Byron is that he will not put the baby into the care of strangers until he or she has turned seven.

Byron is growing tired of this household of young Romantics. Percy and Mary seem guilty by association of Claire's importunity; besides, talkative vegetarian idealism is nowhere near as much fun as sophisticated society wit. Byron's friend Mme de Staël lives on the opposite shore of Lake Geneva, in the largely seventeenth-century elegance of Château de Coppet. This is the year she commissions the cabinet-maker Samuel Chouet to create an Empire-style library at the château, where in the years since the Revolution she has hosted an extraordinary regrouping of intellectuals exiled or expelled from Paris, along with other non-Parisian intellectuals who include a number of German philosophers. Among many writers and thinkers who have stayed at the château are Francois-René de Chateaubriand, Benjamin Constant, Wilhelm von Humboldt and Friedrich Schlegel. Next year, in his travelogue *Rome, Naples et Florence en 1817*, Stendhal will describe these extraordinary meetings as 'les États généraux de l'opinion européenne', the General Assembly of European Opinion.

Compared with this high table of European intellectual life, Percy Shelley appears little more than a charming autodidact, and in the Fourth Canto of *Childe Harold* Byron will turn on his ideas with ferocity. But for now it's Percy who, on his return to London, will deliver the manuscript of the Third Canto, together with *The Prisoner of Chillon*, to Byron's delighted publisher, John Murray. Later in the year, when they're published together, both works will delight critics and readers.

All the same, Percy is developing. From a vague sense of the attractiveness of perfectibility he's moved to pondering the connection between intellectual animation and the 'spark of life'. Galvinism is still very much part of the *zeitgeist*, and the 'principles' of life, as Polidori calls them, are a theme of the summer. The doctor's diary for 15 June – the night before the *Fantasmagoriana* reading and Byron's ghost story challenge – records the conversation that Mary will later claim is so influential on *Frankenstein*: 'Afterwards Shelley and I had a conversation about principles, – whether man was to be thought merely an instrument.'

In Mary's version Byron replaces Polidori:

> Many and long were the conversations between Lord Byron and Shelley, to which I was a devout but nearly silent listener. During one of these, various philosophical doctrines were discussed and among others the nature of the principle of life [...] Perhaps a corpse would be reanimated; galvanism had given token of such things: perhaps the component parts of a creature might be manufactured, brought together, and endued with vital warmth.

These new ideas may have influenced Mary's story. They have certainly produced the first two major poems of Percy's maturity, 'Hymn to Intellectual Beauty' and 'Mont Blanc'. Both explore how, while 'intellect' – insight, rather than rationality – is evoked by beautiful landscapes and by the occult, landscapes can mean nothing without the human who observes them with awe and understanding.

This portrayal of the push-me-pull-you of awe by Percy's poems is very close to Mary's portrait, in *Frankenstein*, of a wildness that seems to look back at us uncannily through the eyes of her creature: both when he's half-hidden, part of the pattern of a wild landscape, and when we encounter him directly. Awe creates transcendent understanding through its lurch into the exceptional, and the occult produces insight in a similar way.

Awe is, in its way, uncanny. And it's with the uncanny that this chapter ends. Almost the last thing Mary and Percy do before leaving Cologny is to revisit 'Christabel', the poem that so distressed Percy at Villa Diodati. Now they read it to each other with no ill effects but with, for Mary at least, some imaginative consequences. Right to the last, the Gothic hangs in the fog of this strange summer as if it were a Brocken spectre:

He bounded over the crevices in the ice, among which I had walked with caution; his stature, also, as he approached seemed to exceed that of a man [...] I perceived, as the shape came nearer (sight tremendous and abhorred?) that it was the wretch whom I had created.

Chapter 7

A Young Writer

Although I possessed the capacity of bestowing animation, yet to prepare a frame for the reception of it, with all its intricacies of fibres, muscles, and veins, still remained a work of inconceivable difficulty and labour.

IN SEPTEMBER 1816 NINETEEN-YEAR-OLD MARY is settling into yet another new home, this time in Bath. From a distance it could be mistaken for the perfect life. She's the mother of a young child, she is at work on her own writing, and she has a partner who seems, for now at least, engaged by their life together. These late summer days are still long, even if they are unusually rainy and cool. The fashionable resort around her is filled with fellow sophisticates – though admittedly none is quite as interesting as Lord Byron, about whom Mary will note, 'His is a powerful mind: and that fills me with melancholy, yet mixed with pleasure, as is always the case when intellectual energy is displayed.'

The rooms she's taken at 5 Abbey Churchyard afford a close-up view of the abbey and its famous, astonishingly inventive carved west front, where, among crowded Patriarchs, angels continually fall up – or fly down – Jacob's ladder between earth and sky. Mary must be feeling pretty prolix and inventive herself, as she works on two manuscripts at once. Not only is she writing the story that will become *Frankenstein*, but in less than fifteen months' time her first book, the travelogue *History of a Six Weeks' Tour Through a Part of France, Switzerland, Germany and Holland*, will appear.

Yet being in Bath at all is simply another compromise made for her stepsister's sake. Mary and Percy are here to keep Claire's pregnancy secret from London society, and particularly from the Godwins. Far from settling into spa town life, they find themselves once more caught in a perpetually restless motion that starts in their very first fortnight at Abbey Churchyard. This time they visit and revisit the area around Marlow, in Buckinghamshire, as they search for a house to which they can move once the need to conceal Claire's pregnancy is over.

What they had imagined is that they would return to the brick-built 'cottage' – actually a pretty, double-fronted villa – that they've retained right by Windsor Great Park, on Bishopsgate in Englefield Green West. They lived here before they set out for Geneva on Claire's romantic errand; it's the house where their son William was born. But bailiffs have removed the furniture they left against their return, and the place is no longer habitable. Still, the lower Thames Valley appeals to the couple as much as ever. The stretch near Thomas Love Peacock's home in Marlow is near enough to London for visitors such as their old friend Thomas Jefferson Hogg, and soon-to-be-encountered friends Marianne and Leigh Hunt and their children, to be able to come and go easily. It's also very rural, something important to Mary as a second-generation Romantic for whom awe-inspiring and beautiful landscapes can unlock a deep, almost existential understanding of the self. Even as she and Percy make their plans, she's filling *Frankenstein* with Alpine scenery in which 'ruined castles hanging on the precipices of piny mountains […] and cottages every here and there peeping forth from among the trees, formed a scene of singular beauty'.

A decade from now Mary's third published novel, *The Last Man*, will evoke Windsor Great Park as a kind of paradise garden, a fit setting for the ideal life:

> Before it was stretched Bishopsgate Heath, which towards the east appeared interminable, and was bounded to the west by Chapel Wood and the grove of Virginia Water. Behind, the cottage was shadowed by the venerable fathers of the forest, under which the deer came to graze.

But in a way it is a paradise lost. For house-hunting, though tedious, is the least of the shadows that will fall over the next sixteen months. This will turn out to be a time of great creative development and radical shifts in lifestyle, but also of having to mature quickly in response to challenge and tragedy. Claire in particular, just eighteen, pregnant and abandoned by her famous lover, is facing a change in her fortunes more radical than even she had desired. Everything that has remained fluid until now, in both Mary's character and her life, is solidifying and becoming inescapable.

It's she who found the rooms in Bath. She will have been under some pressure to do so quickly. Staying in hotels is expensive, and Percy is in London delivering Byron's manuscripts, among other literary and financial chores. So Mary moves the little household – with her are Claire, baby William and the nursemaid Elise Duvillard, who has accompanied them from Switzerland – into Abbey Churchyard on their very first day in the spa town. She must feel she's made an auspicious choice. The rooms they're renting are above 'Meyler's Circulating Library and Reading Rooms', one of the handful of lending libraries catering to the high demand from Bath's many visitors. In her rush to snap them up, she may not have noticed that the Churchyard, somewhat belying its name, is no discreet Old St Pancras hideaway but abuts the Assembly Rooms, meaning that it's at the very centre of the city's social whirl.

The whole Bath experiment, in fact, will prove less than satisfactory. By Easter, after much planning, Mary's household will have settled instead at Albion House, West Street, Marlow. From outside, Albion House appears intimately proportioned like the little villa at Bishopsgate. Unlike rural Englefield Green, however, it's in the centre of this Thames-side country town, close to the High Street and on the main road from Henley-on-Thames. Not so much a rural retreat as a retreat from fashionable London society, Albion House has Gothic windows and hipped tiled roofs. Although it's twice as big as the Bishopsgate house, its irregular, stepped roofline gives it an informal, cottagey feel. This is certainly not fashionable Bath. Nor is it the progressive architecture of Mary's childhood home in the Polygon. Yet it's at Albion House that Mary and Percy will stage their most successful attempt to build a progressive community of like minds. It's a domestic symposium not unlike that of *Frankenstein*'s 'cottagers', who teach Mary's creature *by example* – that *Looking Glass* educational technique of her childhood – first the language, then the morality and politics, he needs to understand his own situation.

Writing in Bath in the autumn of 1816, this is the life Mary dreams of. But to get to it she will have to live through two deaths, a marriage and a birth, and, as if all that weren't enough, to work through the many difficulties of composing a first novel. Yet her autumn starts quietly enough. The *Journal* records her reading, which includes Richardson's *Clarissa* and *Pamela*, Rousseau's unfinished *Letters from Emile*, *Glenarvon* (Lady Caroline Lamb's *roman à clef* and last year's sensation) and Cervantes's *Don Quixote*.

Wide-ranging, enjoyable stuff: but there's also plenty here to get Mary thinking about the novel form itself. The Richardson novels and the Rousseau are epistolary, told in numerous letters 'from' their characters; *Don Quixote*'s tale of a reader whose imagination has been (mis)fired by reading too many romances plays with the structure of a fiction within a fiction; while *Glenarvon* dresses up fact as fiction – even though in 1815 it is more usual for novels to dress up fiction as fact. It's still quite customary for a novelist to pass a story through a framing device that pretends to demonstrate its truth, and one of the problems Mary is now setting herself is how to create such a frame for her own novel. It's all very well to have Frankenstein explain how he brought his creature to life. But unless we know what we think about the scientist himself, we can't work out his motives, or our own moral position on what he's done; and this matters because *Frankenstein* is above all a story about motivation and morality.

Mary is exploring the mind of what we now call 'blue sky research', which cares about knowledge for its own sake rather than for the sake of its practical applications, and to do so she has to get us to the point of *observing* the researcher himself. She needs to invent a framing witness to observe him on our behalf: what she comes up with is an epistolary solution of her own. Her 'frame' is a series of letters home written by Robert Walton, an explorer who himself mirrors Frankenstein's hubris and who ends up by becoming both the scientist's final interlocutor and his creature's.

In the rooms above the busy Churchyard, reading to the accompaniment

of the voices of passers-by and the sounds of wheels and hoofs, Mary is
certainly a good student. But whether her new fiction habits represent
conscious research or are just what she's attracted to right now, she seems
to be shifting away from trying to perfect herself on Percy's model. The
arduous self-taught Greek of their early days together has been replaced
by drawing lessons. She's also becoming interested in experimental
science, attending lectures at the precursor to Bath's soon-to-be-estab-
lished Royal Literary and Scientific Institution (opening in a splendidly
Palladian terrace in 1824, it will be ennobled later still, by Queen Victoria).

This kind of extracurricular education doesn't come cheap: a series
of private lectures on the model of London's Royal Institution costs at
least a guinea, or more than a month's wages for a labourer. Mary makes
the most of it by reading the 'Introduction' to *Elements of Chemical Philosophy*, by her father's old friend Sir Humphry Davy. This thirty-two-
page essay defines chemical philosophy in terms of what Percy would call
'mutability':

> Most of the substances belonging to our globe are constantly under-
> going alterations [...] The object of Chemical Philosophy is to
> ascertain the causes of all phenomena of this kind, and to discover
> the laws by which they are governed.

Davy goes on to survey various attempts to 'ascertain' these 'laws', from
the pre-Socratics to the author's contemporaries. Along the way he
devotes several pages to medieval and Renaissance alchemy and magic,
which he describes as 'absurdities' and 'prejudices' but – relevantly for
the tangle of motivations Mary creates within *Frankenstein* – dignifies
as relevant forms of experimental knowledge. Her novel levers open that
contemporary term 'natural philosophy' to show how, far from sharing an
approach, the philosopher and the chemist in fact compete even when
they ask similar questions about the nature of life. This competition is
both unacknowledged and dangerous: if he had been content to be what
his mysterious tutor M. Waldman calls 'a petty experimentalist', her
Frankenstein could have lived happily ever after with his Elizabeth.

Davy's verdict carries authority. The celebrity chemist of his day, his
own experimental work with electricity is pioneering. He has discovered

a number of elements of the periodic table by using electrolysis to break down chemical compounds. He is also the discoverer of electromagnetism, as well as the inventor of the Davy safety lamp for miners. True, it wasn't Sir Humphry but Luigi Galvini's nephew who in 1803 staged the famous electrical experiments that triggered the nerves of a recently executed corpse at Newgate Prison, causing its limbs to jump and its face to contort. But Davy is a charismatic public lecturer who has, both Robert Southey and Samuel Taylor Coleridge agree, a poet's way with words.

Mary's own way with words is just beginning to emerge: her *Journal* is still habitually the barest of mnemonic listings. Not until after Percy's death six years from now will she use it to record her thoughts. Some of this is contemporary convention: despite Rousseau's *The Confessions* of 1789, the tone we recognise today as 'confessional' writing has yet to be invented. Still, in bereavement Mary will become as conscientious about using it to study how to live alone as she is about every endeavour. In March 1823 for example, less than eight months after Percy's death, we will find her writing:

> I am beginning seriously to educate myself; and in another place I have marked the scope of this somewhat tardy education, intellectually considered. In a moral point of view, this education is of some years' standing, and it only now takes the form of seeking its food in books. I have long accustomed myself to the study of my own heart, and have sought and found in its recesses that which cannot embody itself in words—hardly in feelings.

The ferocity of this will to self-improvement, even in the early stages of grief, is striking. It's also entirely consistent with the Mary who in 1816–17 is writing *Frankenstein* and applying her fierce seriousness to the art of writing itself.

She will become an expressive letter-writer too. But the letters to Fanny that survive from 1816 aren't so much a personal conversation as the flexing of youthful writing muscles, rehearsals for the travel book she's soon to compile (where she will include them verbatim). The emotional intimacy with which she writes to Percy forms a striking contrast. Mary cross-hatches her letters to him with play and allusion, using nicknames and constant reassurance: that she has no emotional needs, that Percy himself is special and wonderful. This is a real writerly skill. Way back in July 1815 – writing from Clifton during those lost weeks when Claire was apparently in Lynmouth and Percy apparently house-hunting in London – Mary struggles touchingly not to 'nag'. With a sophistication that belies her age (it's hard to remember she's only seventeen) she avoids the accusatory second person – 'you' becomes 'we' – and makes her own right to be impatient into his:

> We ought not to be absent any longer indeed we ought not—I am not happy at it—when I retire to my room no sweet Love—after dinner no Shelley—though I have heaps of things <u>very</u> <u>particular</u> to say—[…] Tomorrow is the 28th of July—dearest ought we not to have been together on that day—indeed we ought my love & I shall shed some tears to think we are not—do not be angry dear love—Your Pecksie is a good girl & is quite well now again—except a headach [*sic*] when she waits so axiously [*sic*] for her loves letters.

The choppy rhythm of this is like driving a car with the brakes on, which metaphorically speaking is just what Mary's doing. She wants Percy back, but knows she 'shouldn't'. Both asking and not asking his plans, both mentioning and not mentioning her pregnancy, her writing falls, whether unconsciously or by design, into Percy's own rhythm of gasping, em-dashed phrases.

Sixteen months on, and the letter she writes from Bath on 5 December 1816 offers a new stylistic place-marker. Well known because of the progress it reports with *Frankenstein* – 'I have also finished the 4 Chap. of Frankenstein which is a very long one & I think you would like it' – it's actually more interesting because it reveals the intimacies the couple still practise when all is going well. Conscious of this, Mary asks Percy not to share the letter, in which she calls Percy 'Sweet Elf […] a winged Elf […] my airy Elf': an endearment which tells us much about a love it can sometimes be hard to understand. Mary has found a way to transmute Percy's flighty, flitting quality, his inconsistency and unreliability, into something desirable and exceptional. Quietly coaching Percy in the art of love – 'Love me tenderly and think of me with affection whenever any thing pleases you greatly' – her chatty letter is a consummate performance that shows just how much Mary has learned by now about the plasticity of words. It also returns, wheedlingly, to the old theme of parting company from Claire: 'give me a garden & <u>absentia Clariae</u> and I will thank my love for many favours.' Evidently a separate Bath address, two blocks away from her own home in Abbey Churchyard is not quite absence enough.

The letter's sunny tenderness, and its continuing preoccupation with Claire, are both all the more surprising because the couple have just been through another, and radically darker, sibling drama. On 26 September, soon after their arrival in Bath, her half-sister Fanny writes to tell Mary that their mother's sisters Eliza Bishop and Everina Wollstonecraft have sailed for Dublin, without taking her along to work with them as a teacher as she had hoped and expected. This may be because Mary's and Claire's escapades have spoiled Fanny's reputation and her chances; it may also be because the aunts have lost income from some London houses that they own and which have been badly managed by William Godwin since their sister's death.

Whatever the reason, it's life-changing news for Fanny. On 4 October another letter from her arrives, vehemently denying that she's been spreading a story that Mary Jane is hounding the Bath household: it's quite bad enough to miss out on the trio's adventures without carrying the can for the bad feeling they've created. She also reprimands Percy for not sending money he has promised 'Papa'. Mary replies, we can presume irritably; and Fanny responds again. Her letter arrives on 8 October. The very next evening, 9 October, another and this time 'very alarming' letter from her arrives. It has been sent from Bristol, where Fanny arrived on the 8th, and from where she has also written her stepfather a letter including the ambiguous phrase, 'depart immediately to the spot from which I hope never to remove'.

This alarms Godwin so much that, unprecedentedly, he stirs from his desk and catches the coach down from London to look for his elder stepdaughter. Typically, his search is unsuccessful and he spends the night of the 8th alone in Bath. Yet even in this emergency he fails to contact Mary, Percy and Claire, who are on hand right here in town and who might not only have offered him a place to stay but might, in Percy's case at least, have been able to help him comb the coaching inns for news. Had

Godwin been more effectual and less stubborn – had he been able to put Fanny first – might things have turned out differently?

As it is, his instinctive alarm proves correct. Fanny kills herself, at one of the leading hotels in Swansea, on the night of 9 October. On 12 October *The Cambrian* leads its domestic news with the story:

A melancholy discovery was made in Swansea yesterday: a most respectable-looking female arrived at the Mackworth Arms on Wednesday night by the Cambrian coach from Bristol: she took tea and retired to rest, telling the chambermaid she was exceedingly fatigued and would take care of the candle herself. Much agitation was created in the house by her non-appearance yesterday morning, and on forcing her chamber door, she was found a corpse with the remains of a bottle of laudanum on the table and a note, of which the following is a copy: 'I have long determined that the best thing I could do was to put an end to the existence of a being whose birth was unfortunate, and whose life has only been a series [*sic*] of pain to those persons who have hurt their health in endeavouring to promote her welfare. Perhaps to hear of my death will give you pain, but you will soon have the blessing of forgetting that such a creature ever existed as …' The name appears to have been torn off and burnt, but her stockings are marked with letter 'G' and on her stays the letters 'MW' are visible. She was dressed in a blue striped skirt with a white body, and a brown pelice with a fur trimming of a lighter colour, lined with white silk and a hat of the same. She had a small French gold watch, and appears about 23 years of age, with long brown hair, dark complexion and had a ridicule [*sic*] containing a red silk pocket handkerchief, a brown-berry necklace, and a small leather clasped purse containing three shillings and five shillings and six-penny piece. She told a fellow traveller that she came from Bath by the mail from London on Tuesday morning from whence she proceeded to Bristol and from thence to Swansea by the Cambrian coach. We hope the description we have given of this unhappy catastrophe will lead to the discovery of the wretched object who has prematurely closed her existence.

The immediacy of this still shocks, as it must have shocked her family if they read it. It's like suddenly seeing the shadowy Fanny in full colour close-up. Her 'long brown hair' may be no surprise, but mention of her 'dark complexion' is. She doesn't share her half-sister Mary's strawberry-blonde pallor; a portrait of Gilbert Imlay, her American father, does indeed suggest something resembling a Mediterranean colouring. May this skin tone, at the time not merely unfashionable but subject to prejudice, be the reason her family have decided Fanny will be the plain, unmarried daughter? (And does it suggest that her radical mother was ahead of racist contemporary attitudes? We shouldn't forget the hopeful sign that in *Frankenstein* Mary gives her cottager Felix an 'Arabian' lover in Safie.)

The details of Fanny's clothes are particularly poignant in a life with little room for manoeuvre. That 'brown-berry necklace': has she decided it's too frivolous a thing to die wearing? Or is it a favourite she didn't want to be without? Her clothes are in good taste; her stockings evidently go to a laundry because they're marked with the family initial. She's wearing her dead mother's stays: does this make her feel somehow closer to Wollstonecraft? Or simply that she's not worth new underwear? And did she wear them often, or are they part of a symbolic suicide 'rite'? The little her reticule contains suggests meagre personal resources. She seems not to have brought anything on her final journey: nothing to read, no treasured letters to keep her company. Unless her belongings were stolen, which that 'fellow traveller' would presumably have noted, she's brought no luggage. She clearly isn't planning to stay with her grandfather in nearby Laugharne, or to follow her aunts to Dublin.

Coming to Swansea is purely symbolic; and not only, it seems, of the aborted Irish trip. Fanny told a fellow passenger that she had travelled first to Bath. Yet there's a direct coach between London and Bristol, and indeed a direct service from London to Swansea itself. What lost hope does the detour to Bath represent? Did Fanny try to visit Mary and Percy when she arrived in the town, on the day before her death? The fastest coach, the London to Bath Mail, takes at least twelve hours, but it runs overnight, and this shy, 'respectable-looking female' may have found that the easiest time to travel, slipping away undetected on the night of 7 October in a kind of dark mirror of her sister's elopement. When she then arrived in Bath on the Tuesday morning, Abbey Churchyard with its famous landmark would have been easy to find. It

1. Frontispiece to the 1831 edition of *Frankenstein*. This engraving by Theodore von Holst is the earliest image we have of the creature and his horrified designer in the 'workshop of filthy creation'. The creature is gigantic, and his head is on a little crooked, but he looks more vulnerable than frightening.

2. The Polygon in Somers Town, where Mary is born and spends the first ten years of her life. This engraving by S. C. Swain is made some decades later, in 1850, by which time the fashionable new district she knew is undergoing rapid decline.

3. Mary Wollstonecraft painted by fellow arriviste John Opie *c.* 1790, around the time she publishes *A Vindication of the Rights of Men* and becomes famous overnight. Despite this success, the young woman with the sensitive mouth and searching eyes is seeing her affair with the married artist Henry Fuseli crumble.

4. Mary Wollstonecraft's memorial in St Pancras Old Churchyard is commissioned by her grieving husband. It's here he teaches the infant Mary to read by tracing the letters of her mother's name. When she turns sixteen, Mary chooses this spot to declare herself to her married lover, Percy Bysshe Shelley.

The Dog strove to attract his attention. — He said, Thou wilt not leave me !

Published by J. Johnson, Septr 1, 1791.

5. One of William Blake's illustrations for the second edition of *Original Stories from Real Life* by Mary Wollstonecraft. First published anonymously in 1788, this book for children *with Conversations Calculated to Regulate the Affections, and Form the Mind to Truth and Goodness* features the benign guidance of 'Mrs Mason'; after whom Margaret Jane King, Wollstonecraft's former tutee and later Mary's friend, will name herself when she too becomes a scandalous woman.

6. The radical philosopher William Godwin, painted by J. W. Chandler in 1798, the year after losing Mary Wollstonecraft to puerperal fever. This is the devoted father that baby Mary and her half-sister Fanny will have to themselves for another three years, and to whom Mary will form her 'excessive and romantic attachment'.

7. Percy Bysshe Shelley, painted in Rome in 1819 by Amelia Curran, the daughter of an old friend of William Godwin. In this portrait he's about to turn twenty-six. He has already lost two children with Mary, and lost custody of the two children of his first marriage after their mother's suicide. In less than a month William, his three-year old son with Mary, will also be dead.

8. Burg Frankenstein, the thirteenth-century castle in the Odenwald where the real-life alchemist Johann Conrad Dippel (1673–1734) was born and lived. Mary, Percy and Claire pass within sight of the Odenwald as they return by Rhine riverboat from the young couple's elopement.

9. The Mer de Glace, a glacier on the northern slopes of Mont Blanc, which Mary, Percy and Claire Clairmont visit in July 1816, about a month after the genesis of *Frankenstein*. It's the setting for the novel's central scene, in which the creature explains himself and challenges his creator.

10. Claire Clairmont at twenty-one, also painted by Amelia Curran in summer 1819. Claire, who is Mary's stepsister, has by now spent some years accompanying the Shelley couple and destablising their relationship. She has also had a child by Lord Byron, who has forced her to hand over the infant, Allegra, to his charge.

11. Villa Diodati, on the banks of Lake Geneva, is Lord Byron's home for the summer of 1816. The Shelleys live in a more modest establishment almost immediately below the villa and right on the lakeshore. This is the setting for the writing challenge that is the genesis of *Frankenstein*.

Mrs Thomas
from her friend – the Author
Mary Shelley

being the copy she made her corrections and additions in for the Second Edition – Geneva, 1823 –

FRANKENSTEIN;

OR,

THE MODERN PROMETHEUS.

My acquaintance with this very interesting person arose from her being introduced to me under circumstances of so melancholy a nature which attended her Widowhood, that it was impossible to refuse the aid asked of me – I gave her all I could and passed many delightful hours with

12. Annotated first edition of *Frankenstein*, held in the Morgan Library & Museum, New York. Many of Mary's marginal emendations enhance the story's Gothic atmosphere, increasing the suspense, drawing out tense moments and elaborating the emotions of Dr Frankenstein. Only some of the revisions in the Morgan's copy made their way into the third edition, which was published in 1831. As the lengthy inscription on the half-title page shows, Shelley presented it as a token of thanks to a woman named Mrs Thomas, who had provided her with much-needed solace soon after Percy had drowned in the Ligurian sea.

13. The Protestant Cemetery in Rome, where Edward Trelawney has himself interred next to Percy's ashes. The grave of little William Shelley, buried here in 1819, has already been lost by the time his father dies, so that they cannot be buried together.

14. Lady Mountcashell, née Margaret Jane King, who will take the pseudonym Mrs Mason when she leaves her husband and settles in Pisa with the Irish writer George Tighe. Mentor to both Mary and Claire Clairmont, 'Mrs Mason' also cross-dresses in order to train as a surgeon, and writes several books for and about children. An engraving made in Paris around 1801 by Edme Quenedey des Ricets.

15. Three-year-old William Shelley, painted by Amelia Curran
in summer 1819, three weeks before his death.

16 and 17. Among Mary and Percy's homes in the Italian countryside are (top) Bagni di Lucca and (bottom) Casa Magni, San Terenzo, near Lerici.

18. George Gordon Byron, 6th Baron Byron, painted by Richard Westall in 1813, three years before the poet starts his permanent exile with the summer at Villa Diodati. Byron, who respects Mary's writing, proves to be a loyal friend after Percy's death.

19–21. Powerful figures in Mary's life in Italy and after. *Top left:* Alexandros Mavrokordatos, Mary's friend and occasional Greek teacher in Pisa, who goes on to become the first leader of an independent Greece. *Top right:* Sir Timothy Shelley, the father-in-law who never forgives Mary for breaking up Percy's first marriage, and who after his son's death lends a meagre allowance to support his grandson on condition that Percy's name is kept out of print. *Bottom:* Percy's last love Jane Williams, when, newly widowed, she returns to London and spreads the rumour that Mary has been an unloving wife.

22. Edward John Trelawny, memoirist and keeper of Percy relics.

23. An early photograph of Field Place in Sussex, the 'desperate…
& so dull' Shelley family seat in which Percy Bysshe was born. Percy
Florence finally inherits the house in 1844, when Mary is forty.

24. Mary in the great 1839 portrait by her friend Richard Rothwell. Still posing in black, seventeen years after Percy's death, Mary appears simultaneously solemn and about to break into laughter.

is, after all, hard by Bath's most famous coaching inn, the White Hart in Stall Street.

If Fanny did try to call on her sister, she may have found Mary absent, at her drawing lesson in the morning and then out walking. The *Journal* records: 'Walk out with Shelley to the South Parade, read Clarendon, and draw.' It's an odd, seemingly arbitrary little perambulation that would take no more than five minutes, and it's unusual to see the unexceptional destination so carefully noted in a diary that understates the most momentous events: almost like an alibi. Three days later, Mary's *Journal* records Fanny's death with similar concision and discreet indirectness: '[Percy] returns with the worst account. A miserable day. Two letters from Papa. Buy mourning, and work in the evening.' The entry forms part of a run written all at once and *a posteriori*. (We know this because 'Shelley' on the 10th becomes 'He' on the 11th and 12th.) This too seems odd, but what could it conceal? Is it possible that Fanny did call on the Shelleys on 8 October, found Mary at home and continued their argument? Or that she asked to join the Bath household, and Mary – still dreaming of *absentia Clariae* and seeing in Fanny another sister likely to set her cap at Percy – said no?

And what if it were the other way around? Supposing Fanny arrived and found Mary absent but Percy at home? That apparently un-monogrammed red silk pocket handkerchief in Fanny's reticule is not her own. It belongs to a man: then, to whom? It's unlikely that it was lent to her by a fellow passenger because that gesture would be so intimate. Besides, coloured silk is expensive and not lightly given away. It implies some closer kind of gallantry, the kind that says, for example, 'I'm sorry, I'm just not in love with you' or 'But you simply can't come and live here.' If he did deliver any such blow, Percy might well want to find ways to keep Mary out of the house for the rest of the day, or at least until the coach for Bristol has left to avoid a showdown.

It's customary to place much of the blame for Fanny's suicide on Percy's charms, and to read his fragmentary 'Misery' as recognition that she had fallen in love with him:

Her voice did quiver as we parted,
Yet knew I not that heart was broken

From which it came, and I departed
Heeding not the word then spoken.
Misery—O Misery,
This world is all too wide for thee.

'The word' is, presumably, either *love* or *death*. And, after all, Fanny does use laudanum to kill herself: the same drug Percy is alleged to have offered Mary, back in the Skinner Street schoolroom, for the suicide pact he claimed was better than life apart. But laudanum is at the time an unremarkable way of committing suicide, and doesn't prove this was a copycat death. It certainly proves nothing about the red handkerchief: maybe this belongs to William or Charles, and Fanny brought it with her from home in a moment of practicality. And perhaps her voice 'quivered', if it ever did, not because she was in love with Percy but simply because the contrast between her life and his, the strain of trying to make peace between two households – neither of which seemed particularly to value her loyalty – was finally too much for her. After all, on 10 September, just a month before her death, she was the go-between in the latest round of negotiations between Percy and Skinner Street. On the strength of Percy's promising him £300, back in May, Godwin had borrowed the same amount on terms he can't afford. It was Fanny who had the unenviable job of explaining this to Percy.

Whatever has or hasn't recently passed between them, he responds to her letter of 9 October with such immediate alarm that it's as if he already knew she was at risk: Claire will later reminisce that he 'jumped up thrust his hand in hair—I must be off'. Percy sets off straight away for Bristol. The next day he goes again, and then on the 11th – following up a 'more certain trace' – to Swansea.

But the news from Wales is final. Like Mary in her elopement, Fanny has followed a course that is dramatic, yet that she probably feels has been approved by both her mother – Mary Wollstonecraft attempted suicide herself when she was abandoned by Imlay – and 'Papa', since Godwin argued in *Political Justice* that suicide can be a rational choice. However, as Mary has found, the world in general is less understanding: Godwin earnestly advises Percy that Fanny is now best served by concealing the fact of her suicide. Her body is left to its anonymous burial, while family and friends are told she died of a fever on her way to Ireland. However good their motives, her family choose to 'forget' her just as thoroughly as she might have feared they would.

Fanny has absented herself, though *absentia Clariae* seems a vain hope. But the other eternal triangle in Mary's life is about to change. On 14 December 1816 Percy arrives home after one of his weeks away. He's asked his old friend Thomas Hookham to search for Harriet and the children, who no longer seem to be living with or near her parents. Hookham's letter follows Percy to Bath the next day, and its news is dramatic. Some time before 10 December Percy's abandoned wife has committed suicide, throwing herself into the Serpentine in Hyde Park.

Unlike Fanny's, this is a very public death; it's also slightly *déclassé*. In early nineteenth-century London, while working-class girls who find themselves pregnant and abandoned may kill themselves by jumping in the Thames or the Serpentine, ladies are more likely to take a poison, such as laudanum, choosing to die in comparative dignity and privacy. Perhaps, then, Harriet's suicide is a cry for help: did she *want* to be witnessed? She didn't choose the more reliably fatal Thames, but, on the other hand, this is December of 1816 – the year of exceptional cold – and she probably jumped after dark, since she wrote her suicide note at evening.

At night the water is clearly icy enough to kill. Besides, since suicide is against the law, unsuccessful parasuicides are arrested: hardly the 'help' a desperate young woman would cry out for. Perhaps, too, such a death contains an element of self-denigration. For not only has Harriet been living as a single parent; she is pregnant again. Fanny seems to have killed herself from a profound sense that she was surplus to requirements. Harriet Shelley's motivation appears altogether less existential and more circumstantial. Her life in the three years since Percy abandoned her to elope with Mary has been a dreary struggle. At first she returned to the Westbrook family home. Chafing at the constraints of her life there, she later moved out again. Since then her family have not been supporting her.

In its coverage of 12 December *The Times* reports that Harriet had been missing for six weeks and was 'far advanced in pregnancy'. Hookham's letter to Percy tells us that her body was discovered on 10 December.

She might, then, have been 'far advanced' any time during those missing six weeks from the end of October; although since there's no suggestion that her body was unrecognisably decayed, it's most likely that she killed herself towards the end of that time – possibly on Saturday 7 December, since her suicide note, in all its hasty urgency, is dated 'Sat eve'. Harriet could have conceived in, say, March 1816, during the period when Percy was still in London before the summer at Lake Geneva.

But why ever might Percy be the father of her unborn child? One particularly unpleasant thought is that William was born on 24 January and Percy, observing taboos of the time, is unlikely to have been enjoying much sex with Mary in the weeks immediately following the birth. Besides, though he may claim to easily fox strangers such as Polidori that Harriet married him for his money, his actual interactions with his young wife are much more emotionally complex. We've already seen how he wanted to keep her dangling – just, not to be 'chained' to her – when he encouraged her to join his European ménage with Mary and Claire in 1814. If we remember all this, Harriet's suicide note sounds in part like a letter of unrequited love – 'I never could refuse you & if you had never left me I might have lived' – and that line *I never could refuse you* stands like an accusation.

Now that she is dead however, Percy decides that Harriet, partially disowned by her family, had been forced to find a man by whom to be 'kept'. To Mary, writing from London the day after they learn the news, he announces that Harriet was 'Driven from her father's house, & descended the steps of prostitution until she lived with a groom of the name of Smith, who deserting her, she killed herself'. But this wouldn't after all be the first time he has invented promiscuity in Harriet for Mary's benefit. And – as Henry Crabb Robinson, writer, friend of many of the older Romantics and himself a barrister, observes sharply some months later – Percy never explicitly denies, even to his lawyer Basil Montagu, that the mystery child Harriet was carrying is his, even though to do so would have immensely strengthened the custody suit for his own living children that follows her death.

Instead, he seizes on the fact that Harriet chose to anonymise herself as 'Smith'. There must, he claims to believe, therefore be a 'Mr Smith', who can be dismissed as 'a groom' – which is to say as someone outside the kind of circles that the Shelleys move in, and so conveniently untraceable. Neither Percy nor Mary seems troubled by the irony of the telling phrase, 'who deserting her, she killed herself'. Percy is eager to spread the blame around: to Harriet herself for sexual incontinence, to 'Mr Smith' the alleged seducer, to Harriet's father and, later in the same letter, to Harriet's sister Eliza, whom he accuses of estranging father from daughter in order to scoop a legacy. It looks like a consummate bit of what conjurors call 'misdirection', but it's actually not quite so consummate. Mary *has* to love Percy, having left herself no other choice, but the same isn't true of the Court of Chancery, which has the power to award or – rare as this would be at the time – to deny him custody of his children by Harriet.

Ianthe, born in 1813, and Charles, born in 1814, have been sent away to the Warwickshire countryside to be looked after by the family of a schoolteacher, the Revd John Kendall. Unsurprisingly, the Westbrooks resist handing them over to the atheist father who abandoned them and the woman for whom he did so. So on 16 December Percy writes to Mary confessing how much he needs her. Much of his letter centres on Ianthe and Charles:

> The children I have not got. […] I told [my attorney] I was under contract of marriage to you, and he said that, in such an event, all pretence to detain the children would cease. Hunt said very delicately that this would be soothing intelligence to you. Yes, my only hope, my darling love, this will be one among the innumerable benefits which you will have bestowed upon me, and which still be inferior in value to the greatest of benefits—yourself.

Mary responds by return: with a letter that reveals her maturity and generosity. No more 'Sweet Elf'; now she addresses 'My beloved friend', and signs herself 'Your Affectionate Companion'. It's a letter presumably written, in part at least, for legal eyes. Already rehearsing the role of wife and loving stepmother, she too centres her letter on Percy's children:

> How very happy shall I be to possess those darling treasures that are yours—I do not exactly understand what Chancery has to do with this and wait with impatience for tomorrow when I shall hear

whether they are with you—and then what will you do with them? My heart says bring them instantly here—but I submit to your prudence.

And she responds to Percy's proposal with even more understatement than his own: 'As to the event you allude [to] be governed by your friends & prudence as to when it ought to take place—but it must be in London.'

If wishes were horses, beggars would ride. The Westbrooks do indeed go to Chancery to fight for custody of Harriet's children, and within a few days Mary is in London, chiefly in order to marry Percy in the presence of her father and stepmother at St Mildred's Church, Bread Street. The wedding takes place on 30 December, and it transforms Godwin's attitude to Percy. Writing to Claire on the very afternoon of the wedding (not, perhaps, a great sign that things are about to change in the ménage), the new son-in-law is able to say: 'Godwin throughout has shown the most polished and cautious attention to me and Mary. He seems to think no kindness too great in compensation for what has past [*sic*].' Godwin's own *Diary* records the day – which starts and ends with the older and new couples eating together – in a special entry that he saves out of chronological place. Mary's *Journal* simply notes, 'A marriage takes place.' The family, aware as ever of the role of historical record in reputation-making, are already starting to disguise the late date on which the partnership was legitimised.

Percy has done the right thing by Mary, albeit to serve his own interests. But it does him no good. His Chancery suit is adjourned on 24 January – which happens to be William's first birthday – first to 8 and then 11 February, and then to 27 March, when, in an at the time almost unheard-of ruling, he fails to win custody of his children. It is an exceptional case, and as exceptional cases will, it drags on: the final legal arrangements for the children's upbringing won't be completed till April 1818, by which time Percy has already left the country for good.

Unlucky for some, but the timing of all this is lucky for Claire. It means that children are on everybody's minds, and the energy that should have been lavished on Ianthe and Charles is instead available for her own newborn, who arrives in the early hours of 12 January 1817: another compromising fact the cautious Mary omits from her *Journal*. Claire's baby is named Alba, a variant of LB, 'Albè', the household nickname for Lord Byron. Around this time Mary herself falls pregnant again, and the household moves again to newly secured Albion House. At the start of 1817 Percy and Mary have spent a large amount of money furnishing their new home; they finally move in on 18 March. Almost immediately, they're joined there not by Ianthe and Charles but by new friends: Leigh and a pregnant Marianne Hunt, the first four Hunt children and baby Alba, whom the Hunts have fostered, passing her off as the child of a distant cousin. The Hunts' ten-week stay at Albion House, from 6 April to 25 June, allows Claire to live with her daughter under a cloak of respectability.

Deaths and births: the period in which Mary writes up *Franken-stein*, from the autumn of 1816 to December 1817, is full of these intensely corporeal changes – the violently painful consequences of embodiment. One reason the novel's parable of created life lacks the slickness of later stories about robots, or even the simplicity of the Jewish golem tradition, is surely that it is written by a woman. Mary cannot avoid knowing both that the creation of life is costly and that the resulting 'animal' (the contemporary word for a baby: her own mother used it, after all, about herself) is autonomous, volatile, the centre of his or her own meaning.

Despite all this, and against the odds, Mary and Percy remain a *literary* couple, and it's a literary friendship that has led to their new experiment in extended domesticity. On 1 December 1816 Leigh Hunt publishes an essay entitled 'Young Poets' in his journal *The Examiner*. He has a radical record, having gained notoriety in 1813–15, when he was imprisoned for libelling the Prince Regent. His recent leader articles have attacked the government for failing to deal with the starvation caused by the Corn Laws, and what he calls 'Sinecurists', or career civil servants, for failing to lower taxes to allow the poor more money for food and the rich more for charity. Now Hunt's editorial on John Keats, John Hamilton Reynolds and Percy Bysshe Shelley claims that they will dispel the neo-Classical shades of Alexander Pope and his eighteenth-century contemporaries by writing about 'real nature and original fancy'.

Of course, this is a young man's Oedipal take on the poetry scene: one that doesn't consider how a previous generation of Romantics, including

Coleridge and Wordsworth, have already done exactly this, and that mentions Byron only in passing. Born in 1784, Hunt is eight years Percy's senior but still only in his early thirties. Today his acuity in picking winners is widely cited as the first recognition of Keats's and Shelley's potential. But Hunt's declaration doesn't so much recognise a generational shift as create it. In her group portrait of this lost, yet so familiar, literary world Daisy Hay points out his power play in positioning himself as the mentor of grateful poets. The mechanism is also simpler and more familiar still: an editor young enough to risk nothing by inventing a 'school' of his as yet not widely published pals, and to enjoy plotting to take over the literary world. And it works. The *Examiner* piece proves important for all three newcomers; especially Percy, who at this date has published – of the major works for which he's known today – only *Queen Mab* and *Alastor*, and who has only recently started cultivating Hunt. Now he is suddenly part of the influential editor's inner circle, and by January is even staying with him.

While this is going on Mary, stuck in Bath with Claire until Alba is born, has continued working on *Frankenstein*. 'Write' and 'work' are regular *Journal* entries until 26 January, when she is at last free to leave for London. There, joining Percy at the Hunts', she's precipitated into a buzzy, arty and intellectual milieu. The Hunts' circle includes not only Keats and Reynolds but also William Hazlitt, Charles Lamb, the musician Vincent Novello and the painter Benjamin Robert Haydon (as well as figures who are less well known today: the Shakespearian scholar Cowden Clarke, poet and parodist Horace Smith, and Bryan Waller Procter, who will later court Mary). Regular visitors, they usually arrive for supper and stay on into evenings full of music-making and intellectual debate in which Marianne Hunt, her sister Bess and the Marys – Mary Lamb, Mary Novello and Mary Shelley herself – all participate. For the first time Percy gets a glimpse of a community that is based not on wifelets but on friendships between artistic and literary peers.

Meanwhile Mary is absolutely at home. This is how her father's circle operated as she was growing up, and it's this that she has been expecting to recreate in Percy's schemes for communal living. (A tragedy of the couple's life is that, while she is her mother's daughter, taking for granted the participation of women as intellectual equals, he remains trapped in traditional roles: a symposium is admirable, one imagines him feeling, but the harem model so much more fun.) Despite this, the Hunts' reciprocal three-month stay at Albion House manages to carry something of this fuller model of community on into the Shelley household. For Mary, as she redrafts *Frankenstein*, the months from February to June 1817 are more intellectually communal and creative than any hitherto; as her *Journal* reveals when it resumes, after the move into Albion House, on 10 April 1817.

Mary is in the second trimester of her third pregnancy, and her energy levels have risen. She's already 'correcting' *Frankenstein*; then, on 18 April, 'Correct' changes to 'Transcribe'. This continues until 13 May, when, at last, 'Finish transcribing' marks the end of fair copying the novel. The next day, 14 May, Mary records that 'Shelley reads "History of the French Revolution", and corrects "Frankenstein". Write Preface. Finis.' Good work indeed for a single day. It also suggests that Percy doesn't spend too much time 'correcting' the novel. This is significant because moot. What we might call The Percy Lobby remains as eager today as in Mary's lifetime to believe that no mere girl could have produced a novel that's become one of the classics of English literature. But the evidence itself is confused.

The final draft of the *Frankenstein* manuscript takes up two notebooks, both of which are held today by the Bodleian Library in Oxford. They're mismatched – one is clearly bought in Geneva and one, of English paper, is assumed to have been bought in Bath – and they don't correspond, either, with the three volumes into which Mary divides her novel. One great difficulty of decoding these notebooks is that, because the Shelleys have very similar handwriting, it's hard to be absolutely clear how many of the corrections are Percy's. Certain pages have clearly been rewritten in stronger ink than those around them, but these seem to mark a fresh dip in the inkpot rather than a new mind at work. Interlinear changes are easier to spot: here Percy's careful hand is both more upright and more ornate than Mary's original. Still, even the 'considerable alterations' by readers, including herself, that her book will eventually undergo at proof stage do not diminish Mary's authorship. They're no more than the usual editorial process novelists undergo even today.

'Finis.' But the difficult part – publication – has only just begun. A week after completing the novel Mary travels to London with Percy to deliver *Frankenstein* to John Murray, her father's friend and Byron's publisher. While there, she capitalises on London's art scene, persuading Percy to join her at Mozart's *Don Giovanni* and the Royal Academy Summer Exhibition. The couple catch up with Thomas Jefferson Hogg, William Hazlitt and John Ogilvie, as well as with family in Skinner Street. Life must feel full of rich connections and possibilities once again, as if Mary is resuming her place in the literary networks that are her birthright. Best of all, as her *Journal* records proudly on 26 May, Murray 'likes "Frankenstein"'.

But on 18 June Murray returns the manuscript. She turns it around the same day, sending it out this time to her father. In the coming weeks, however, neither Godwin nor Percy is able to place the novel with publishers. Perhaps for this reason, on 10 August Mary starts rewriting the *Journal* she kept during her elopement, as a travel book. Once a publisher's daughter always a publisher's daughter, her judgement is sound. *History of a Six Weeks' Tour* does indeed appear very promptly. Out before *Frankenstein*, it's published by Hookham and the Olliers in November 1817. If Hookham is a family friend, Charles and James Ollier are among the publishers to whom Percy unsuccessfully sent *Frankenstein*, and it would be fascinating to know whether they commented encouragingly on the novel's travel-writing.

The two books are in any case necessarily related. Mary has plundered her *Journal* record of dramatic Alpine landscapes for the novel; like a greedy twin, it continues to absorb her attention when she should be thinking about the travel book instead. For the *History* clearly starts out more ambitiously than it ends, probably because, soon after her initial burst of writing up, she hears good news about *Frankenstein*. Some time between 18 and 22 August Lackington Publishers, specialists in books about the supernatural and the occult, write expressing interest.

A busy month follows. Mary's own birthday, on the 30th, is quickly succeeded by the birth of her third baby, Clara, on 2 September. In the same early September days a publishing deal for the novel is finally struck – 'Bargain with Lackingtons concerning "Frankenstein"', the *Journal* records – and the Shelleys welcome a succession of visitors. Finally, on 9

October, Mary reads John Davis's *Travels of Four Years and a Half in the United States of America* (1803) – and remembers her own travel-writing. From the 10th to the 14th she transcribes, but doesn't any longer try to rewrite, the remaining material for her *History*. Letters she and Percy wrote on their 1816 trip, and Percy's poem 'Mont Blanc', also written on the second trip, are added to the *Journal* material as something of a makeweight, and the completed book is indubitably slender. Nevertheless, when it appears on 6 November 1817 – published anonymously, as *Frankenstein* will be – it receives a number of favourable reviews.

Despite or because of this first success, *Frankenstein* continues to occupy the forefront of Mary's imagination. On 24 September 'another proof' – so, not the first – 'arrived tonight', Mary writes to Percy, and comments: 'in looking it over there appeared to me some abruptnesses which I have endeavoured to supply – but I am tired and not very clear headed so I give you carte blanche to make what alterations you please.' The instinct – to manage 'abruptnesses' – is confident, but her mind for detail has been exhausted by a houseful of very young children, not to mention the compound tiredness that must come from breastfeeding while living on an inadequately understood vegetarian diet. There are 'considerable alterations' to the set of proofs Percy forwards to the publishers on 28 October; again, some commentators are tempted to assume these are all his own work. But they come after Godwin, that experienced writer–publisher, has visited Albion House between 19 and 22 October and read his daughter's proofs, and after the *Journal* entry for his departure day records that Mary has once again 'transcribed' *Frankenstein*, surely meaning that she has fair-copied 'alterations' that discussions with her father have produced, not to mention any revisions of her own.

Final proofs arrive just before the end of a year that should feel crowned with triumph – but does not. Percy has revived from the great shocks of 1816, and he no longer seems to need Mary so much. Once again he's frequently absent, often without telling her where he is; Claire, though a loving mother to Alba, is again absorbing much of his imaginative energy. In the early autumn Percy even attempts to place a manuscript of hers with the same publishers he has tried for Mary's far more accomplished work.

And so it starts again. Mary's surviving letters from 1817 to an often absent Percy make sad, and all too understandable, reading. By late autumn one excuse for staying away is that he once again risks arrest if discovered: he has already served two days in prison for debt. But his absences are nothing new. On 28 September, not yet a month after Clara's birth, Mary writes a long letter that tries every angle to reach her husband. It complains about Claire, newly returned from spending time with him in London, and stresses the importance of getting baby Alba to Byron as soon as possible in order not to damage her prospects by breaking that paternal link: 'You do not seem to feel enough the necessity that she should join her father with every possible speed.' *Absentia Albae* has been added to *absentia Clairae* as the longed-for vanishing point of domestic harmony. Mary pushes for more clarity about how the household can afford travel to Italy, and for Percy actually to *send* letters at all: 'and put the letter into the post yourself—be particular in this for Hunt's servant is so neglectful that I did not receive your last letter untill [*sic*] today.'

At the same time, winding him in to his own children's lives, she asks Percy to send a hat for William so the little boy can come out for walks, and to look for ass's milk instead of cow's to augment her own milk for Clara. The note about the hat is full of the kind of detail women give men who won't stoop to such things: 'You can buy it at the corner of Southampton Buildings and send it to the coach at the old Bailey [...] it must be a fashionable round shape for a boy mention particularly [...] and let it be rather too large than too small.' Finally, Mary – who is after all a novelist – resorts to ventriloquism. Apparently 'a friend' of their nursemaid Elise has expressed sympathy for Claire's official plight as an 'abandoned wife' in words that sound suspiciously tailor-made for Mary's own experience: 'Poor dear woman [...] doubtless she loves her husband tenderly and to be separated from him [...] what a cruel thing—he must be such a wicked man to leave his wife.'

Recent biographers have blamed post-natal depression for this pressing tone, but there's no evidence that Mary suffered after her other births. Besides, what could be more rational than to protest at her husband's sustained silence and absence? Now more than ever the description of a charming Dr Frankenstein wrecked by 'the intoxicating draught' of hubristic idealism chimes with Mary's own life:

> His full-toned voice swells in my ears; his lustrous eyes dwell on me with all their melancholy sweetness; I see his thin hand raised in animation, while the lineaments of his face are irradiated by the soul within. Strange and harrowing must be his story; frightful the storm which embraced the gallant vessel on its course, and wrecked it—thus!

The wreck of all Mary's gallant hopes is yet to come, but the storm is already on its way.

Chapter 8

Emigrants

For a long time I could not conceive how one man could go forth to murder his fellow, or even why there were laws and governments.

AS 1818 OPENS WE FIND OURSELVES looking at the map of Europe: its cities, rivers and staging posts, its mountain ranges and borders. It's a colourful image, but the colours aren't quite where we'd expect them to be. Europe is embarking on a period of profound if piecemeal transformation, a domino of changes that won't be equalled in scale and significance until the twentieth century's world wars and ensuing Cold War. After the Vienna Congress of 1814–15, which aimed to resolve a Napoleonic legacy of new and unstable borders, Central Europe is now dominated by the Austrian Empire – extending hugely east to include Galicia and Transylvania, south into Italy and along the Danube to Belgrade – and the German Confederation, which nudges up against Switzerland and Lombardy and includes both Prussian Baltic and Hanoverian North Sea coasts. To the south and east, the Ottoman and Russian Empires press in on the Austrian. Western Europe is a map of kingdoms rather than nation-states. 'Congress Poland' is tiny and still awaits Adam Mickiewicz, Frédéric Chopin and the mid-century surge in Polish nationalism that will produce the inevitably tragic Kraków Uprising of 1846. *Risorgimento*

Italy is 'Young', and just embarking on a long nationalist struggle for unification that will culminate, in 1871, with Rome becoming the national capital. France's Napoleonic 'Republic' has ended with the Emperor's defeat at Waterloo in 1815 and his exile to St Helena.

In this rapidly changing picture it can seem as if only Britain retains its traditional political institutions. But stability comes at a price. Governments who ride out such periods of radical change necessarily fear revolution. In 1817 the British government suspends Habeas Corpus so that it can try suspects (such as revolutionary conspirators who have gone into hiding) *in absentia*, which means that the right to legal self-defence is also suspended. This directly threatens the radical intellectual community clustered around Leigh Hunt and *The Examiner*, who are an obvious target for official British suspicion.

The group are also finding themselves unfashionable. At the end of 1817 the widely read *Blackwood's Magazine* starts a campaign of leader articles against the 'Cockney School' of writers and artists. Sheltering behind anonymity its author, John Lockhart, claims that Hunt and his friends are chaotic, immoral and vulgar. This is a line that countless cultural establishments have used against the 'Young Turks' of the next generation, with their 'small-r' rebellious private lives and artistic perspectives. But it's disproportionately effective here, because many of those whom Lockhart attacks – particularly John Keats and Percy Bysshe Shelley – are relative newcomers, powerless against the reputation-making institution that is *Blackwood's*.

Because he's publishing little, Percy suffers less direct attack; Keats, though, is nearly destroyed. In August 1818 Lockhart sneers that his newly published *Endymion* cannot possibly attain classical beauty because:

> Mr Keats [...] is merely a young Cockney rhymester, dreaming a phantastic dream at the full of the moon. [...] Mr Hunt is a small poet, but he is a clever man. Mr Keats is a still smaller poet, and he is only a boy of pretty abilities, which he has done every thing in his power to spoil.

The snobbery of this throws down just the gauntlet that *Examiner* radicals might be expected to pick up, since they believe precisely that the good things in life should not be monopolised by the wealthy. But much of reading Britain thinks differently. In April 1818, writing in the *Quarterly Review*, John Wilson Croker has already used similar terms to tear into 'Mr. Leigh Hunt and his simple neophyte', who 'is unhappily a disciple of the new school of what has been somewhere called Cockney poetry; which may be defined to consist of the most incongruous ideas in the most uncouth language'. The personal nature of these attacks – Lockhart uses the extended metaphor of a 'sickness' for Keats's work when he is already gravely ill with TB, while describing him not as a medic but as a mere apothecary – is cunningly close to the bone.

And there's something else: Lockhart's review claims that Keats 'has already learnt to lisp sedition' in the opening of Book Three of *Endymion*: 'There are those who lord it o'er their fellow men / With most prevailing tinsel'. The recently passed Seditious Meetings Act of March 1817 is in part a reaction to public displays of disaffection, including the Islington Spa Field Riots and an attack on the Prince Regent. But it's also designed to contain radical groups like the Society of Spencean Philanthropists in London, and the Hampden Clubs in the north of England and the Midlands. In this context, to mention sedition and call *The Examiner*'s writers 'The Cockney School of Politics', as the same piece also does, is to invoke, or at least evoke, the possibility of imprisonment for High Treason. The pressures this places on Hunt and his friends are pernicious, and not everyone in the circle reacts with grace. Hunt's gravitational pull begins to wane as individuals like John Hamilton Reynolds and Robert Haydon drift away, anxious in particular about the notoriety Hunt's poetry collection of March 1818, *Foliage*, attracts. Even Keats himself, perhaps feeling that the price he's paid for mentorship is peculiarly high, becomes more critical, more independent – and more absorbed in nursing his dying brother Tom.

John Keats was not born to privilege but had to work at his medical training. Percy Bysshe Shelley has had no such apprenticeship in difficulty. He cuts an altogether more outward-turned and insecure figure. The intellectual community Hunt has opened up to him is a novelty, but being mentored is not. At Lake Geneva in 1816 he extracted a similar relationship from Byron; earlier, he charmed William Godwin in the same way, and he was introduced to Godwin the man (whose work he already admired) by another – arguably his first – mentor, Robert Southey. For all his self-invention as a brave radical, he still seems to need affirmation, if not adoration. He is also much more warm-hearted and purely social than his poems of transcendence and awe, written in recent months, suggest. As he will write to Peacock in the next year, 'What are mountains, trees, heaths, or even the glorious and ever-beautiful sky [...] to friends? Social enjoyment, in some form or other, is the Alpha and Omega of existence.'

Mary, though adoring, is undeniably Percy's intellectual equal and, with the publication of her second book on 1 January 1818, threatens to become a literary peer too. Her letters to him now shift constantly in tone, as she expresses herself – then remembers to reduce herself to almost simpering admirer. While loyally continuing to agree that every wife is 'a victim of that ceremony', she herself has managed to be restricted *both* by marriage and by Percy's 'free love,' which must be made new, once more with feeling, every single day.

All in all, as 1818 opens, life in the Shelley household is uncomfortable. The intellectual and artistic rewards of living near London don't seem as great as they did just a year earlier. Percy spends January suffering off and on with an eye infection. Even Claire, clear that she will be sharing her life neither with her daughter nor with Lord Byron, who has arranged custody of the baby, offers little lively amusement right now. Worse, the house itself is bitterly cold. Bad for the three very young children – Mary's William, just two, four month-old Clara and Claire's Alba, who is almost exactly a year younger than William – it's also almost impossible to work in. Like the rest of Europe, south-east England remains in the shadow of the Mount Tambora volcanic winter; the Dalton Minimum also continues. The year just ended has been exceptionally wet, with up to 50 per cent more rainfall than is usual. Such conditions are lived as chilblains and draughts, coughs and colds; they translate into black speckles of mould on bedroom walls, steam lingering as dampness after every meal, and asthma-inducing spores of fungi on door and window-frames.

In this miasma of dissatisfaction the possibility of travelling to sunlit, classical Italy to deliver baby Alba to Byron appears a perfect alibi. Very soon, talk of possibility turns into actual planning. By the beginning of

February the lease on Albion House has been sold. Mary spends several days managing the move: 'pack up till Tuesday, 10th, when we leave Marlow'. The household find lodgings close to the British Museum, at the very end of Great Russell Street. There are just four weeks for some cultural immersion; Mary's *Journal* shows her making the most of them. She goes three times to the theatre and three times to the opera (where she sees both *Don Giovanni* and *Figaro*). She and Percy view the Apollonicon, 'the Indian Library, and the Panorama of Rome', and she spends a 'morning at the British Museum, looking at the Elgin marbles'.

But Mary's no genteel, passive consumer of the arts. Reading her *Journal* from these weeks, we get a great sense of lively culture-making and participation in critical combat. There's much exchanging of visits with Leigh and Marianne Hunt, Thomas Love Peacock and Thomas Jefferson Hogg. Mary also sees her family and their old family friend Mary Lamb. She fair-copies Percy's review of Peacock's 'Rhododaphne' for *The Examiner*. There is music-making at the Hunts' home in Paddington with Vincent Novello (whose own splendid home on Oxford Street is tantalisingly just round the corner from Great Russell Street). On 2 March, 'Go to the play in the evening with Hunt and Marianne, and see a new comedy damned.'

It's not surprising that Mary's London month is so active. She's once again in a brief period of respite: neither pregnant nor grieving nor yet coping with another woman attaching herself to Percy (apart, of course, from Claire). More even than this, *Frankenstein* has been published on 1 January. It's destined to have a noisy critical reception. The first glowing reviews won't appear until March and April, but Mary's acquaintances, reading her freshly published book in January and February, are already discussing her work. The novel has been published anonymously; but with its dedication to Godwin and its Preface written by Percy in the persona of the author, it is clear (even to the few who aren't already in the know) that it's written by someone within their circle and, if not by a more established writer choosing to conceal their foray into this genre, then probably by a woman. Precisely because they're part of this critically astute, culture-making milieu, it will also be apparent to them that the novel really is significant, not just within their friend's life but in wider cultural terms. This cannot but shift their attitude to her. She is no longer simply the Godwin daughter who ran away with a young poet; she has emerged as a writer in her own right.

Mary's prose style turns out to be not naïve, as Percy's corrections have implied, but fresh and vigorous. It allows her to tell the story of *Frankenstein* with nuance but also vividly, rather than getting snarled up in anxious formality. This vividness is picked up by reviews: 'One of the productions of the modern school in its highest style of caricature and exaggeration', in the words of *The Edinburgh Magazine and Literary Miscellany*; it is 'a very *bold* fiction', in the verdict of *Bell's Court and Fashionable Magazine*; and displays 'a happy power of expression', according to *Blackwood's*. Hostile reviews will home in on the same quality. The *Monthly Review* calls the novel 'An uncouth story, in the taste of the German novelists', while, according to *The British Critic*:

> We are in doubt to what class we shall refer writings of this extravagant character; that they bear marks of considerable power, it is impossible to deny; but this power is so abused and perverted, that we should almost prefer imbecility; however much, of late years, we have been wearied and ennuied [*sic*] by the languid whispers of gentle sentimentality, they at least had the comfortable property of provoking no uneasy slumber.

Friends will also note that Mary has followed her father in writing a philosophical novel. Like Godwin's *St Leon* (published in 1799), *Frankenstein* is concerned with the meaning of her characters' experiences rather than simply the drama of their actions. *Blackwood's* recognises this – 'The author's principal object [...] is less to produce an effect by means of the marvels of the narrations, than to open new trains and channels of thought' – in a review in the March 1818 issue whose intelligence differs so markedly from the treatment the magazine metes out to Hunt and his circle because it has been written not by Lockhart but by Walter Scott.

Negative reviews point out that this new Godwinian fiction flirts with atheism in its philosophical exploration of materialism:

> This novel is a feeble imitation of one that was very popular in its day,—the St. Leon of Mr. Godwin. It exhibits many characteristics

of the school whence it proceeds; and [...] exhibits a strong tendency towards *materialism*

claims *The Literary Panorama, and National Register,* while the *Monthly Review* reports that

in some passages, the writer appears to favour the doctrines of materialism: but a serious examination is scarcely necessary for so excentric [*sic*] a vagary of the imagination as this tale presents.

'The doctrines of materialism', particularly associated with French Enlightenment thinkers such as Denis Diderot, whose *Encyclopédie* has been intellectually influential for more than half a century, and his fellow Sceptics including Rousseau, have indeed been familiar to Mary since her childhood, which was modelled partly on these ideas. Although her novel doesn't explicitly argue *for* atheism it is *de facto* atheist, by the doctrinal standards of the day, in imagining the possibility of a being brought to life by a German student without help from God. More blasphemously still, Mary's Frankenstein creates a being so self-aware and morally complex as to be quasi-human.

In 1818 being perceived as atheist, like being suspected of sedition, is risky. It's certainly one more reason to have your children christened, as Mary, Percy and Claire do hastily on 9 March at St Giles-in-the-Fields, near Holborn. Percy's atheism and personal reputation have already cost him custody of his first two children; none of the trio wants to lose the infants they still have at home to the care of the Lord Chancellor. In a further securing of safety nets, little Alba is christened Clara Allegra at her father's request.

Nowadays we see St Giles as a fine Palladian church. But in 1818 it is simply old-fashioned. A balcony darkens the interior; there's none of the pastoral flavour of Old St Pancras. The church's traditional associations with the Tyburn gallows, and its current parish which is largely 'rookery' or slum, must concentrate Mary's mind, throughout the ceremony, on the tenuousness of respectability, legality and survival. By now the prevailing social and political atmosphere is so threatening that even this month's repeal of 1817's Habeas Corpus Suspension Act does not seem reason enough to feel settled and secure in England. Sure enough, Mary's

Journal records 'adieus' the very next day, and on 12 March, in capital letters, announces their decision: 'FRANCE. Discussion of whether we should cross. Our passage is rough. A sick lady is frightened, and says the Lord's Prayer. We arrive at Calais, for the third time.'

'For the third time': Mary can't but remember previous crossings. The last, two years ago, led to a productive summer as Byron's neighbour, and so to the birth of *Frankenstein*; the first, two years before that, started her life with Percy. She must hope that they are once again – or at last – embarking on their new life together. It's hard to gauge the temperature of that hope, but it is surely warm. For, in leaving England when she does, Mary walks away from the chance to be fêted in literary-intellectual London, to become a figure celebrated in her own right at the dinner tables and in the salons of artistic decision-makers.

She's making a huge sacrifice for her marriage. Does she do so knowingly? I suspect not. After all, she has form in this area. Not yet twenty-one, she has already walked away from her social and moral 'reputation'. On the other hand, she may feel that the world, having already been 'well lost for love', must now be lost again to make that first wager come true. Percy *has* to mean a great, undying love or else the sacrifices she's already made are pointless.

But perhaps other things are going on. Shyness takes many forms. Maybe Mary feels a certain reluctance to be critically 'visible', having seen her friends and peers bitterly attacked. It's easy to forget, with all that's happened since, that Mary is still only a few years out from the awkward teenager who was sent away from home to find a cure for a disfiguring skin disease. It's all very well to be Percy's 'Maie' – at least, when he remembers – but today's much-admired pale complexion is only a literal thin skin. On the other hand, Mary is the typical daughter of a famous couple who probably doesn't yet realise that reputations are won not only by the quality of work itself but also by other, more occult mechanisms. A *zeitgeist* picks one novelist over all others, rewards one cultural commentator rather than another. Having been born at the centre of things, Mary has no bitter knowledge, as poor John Keats does, of how much depends on being in the lighted room with the opinion-makers. She's innocent enough to walk away from the very thing she wants – a literary life – without realising she's doing so. Finally, to be young is almost by definition not to realise that there will be no second chance. Life, at twenty, seems vast and full of possibility; that others have already fore-closed on you inconceivable.

Mary feels herself to be a veteran of life on the hop. But for all her European experience she knows little about travelling south. In this century before the development of antibiotics any illness can be fatal, especially for infants. Typhoid and dysentery are still rife, even in Britain, and the warm climates of southern Europe encourage such diseases along with cholera. The characteristically ill-prepared little household are racing towards danger, moving south during the first cholera pandemic, of 1817–24, which at its height will travel north from Asia to reach the Mediter-ranean. The risks posed by such diseases are heightened for foreign-born children like William, Clara and Allegra (Byron's daughter is now known by her second Christian name). They lack immunity to local infections and have acquired no useful antibodies from their mothers either. In the next fourteen months, shockingly, Mary is going to lose both her surviv-ing children; four years from now all three of the infants who make that rough March crossing of the English Channel will be dead of infectious diseases.

But that's in the future. For now the party are making fairly rapid progress through France. They reach Turin at the end of the month and spend April in Milan, with trips to La Scala and a side excursion to search for a home on Lake Como. Then, on 28 April 1818, the day after her mother's birthday, Allegra is taken away by the nursemaid Elise. She is to be delivered to her father. Claire has no guarantee that she will see the child again; the separation is recorded with characteristic under-statement in Mary's *Journal*. 'Alba goes with Elise. Finish "Aristippus". Italian exercises.' Discretion combines with, perhaps, the impatience of one whose first-born has actually died to prevent comment on Claire's reaction. Originally the trip's whole excuse, this transaction now seems no more than another step on the lengthy road to life in exile.

So much for the Alps. The party continue south, to the Tuscan Medi-terranean coast and into the sun. The effect, after the years of darkness and cold, can only be astonishing. British amazement at the classical south and its revelatory climate is one of our enduring cultural clichés. In the twentieth century writers as various as E. M. Forster and D. H. Lawrence will find in the warmth and light of Italy, and the *dolce vita* of the Italian lifestyle, a touchstone of human wisdom and emotional intelligence. Mary is no exception. For all that the country is going to cost her, a quarter of a century from now she will still be able to write: 'When we visit Italy, we become enjoyers of the beauties of nature, the elegance of art, the delights of climate, the recollections of the past, and the pleasures of society, without a thought beyond'.

The Shelleys and Claire reach the coast on 9 May 1818. At the smart, historic port of Livorno – which, like all the English of the time, they call Leghorn – light blazes off the waters of canals and the harbour, around which the city spreads its palazzos and belvederes, churches and Renaissance *fortezze*. Livorno suffered economically from the ban on trade with Britain while under recent Napoleonic occupation, ended just three years ago by the Congress of Vienna. Now English residents are welcome, and indeed Mary has old family friends, Maria and John Gisborne, in the city.

Maria Gisborne was William Godwin's friend even before he met Mary Wollstonecraft. Later, she was 'our' Mary's own first foster mother, the woman who looked after her as her mother was dying. That intimate history, and Maria's knowledge of Godwin's early life, make her into the kind of mother figure Mary Jane has never been for Mary: predisposed, connected, a repository of family anecdote. The two women are eager to meet – so eager that the Gisbornes call at the hotel where the Shelleys are staying on the very day they arrive. Mary sees Maria daily for the next week, and has a 'long talk' about her family. This is the start of a lifelong friendship. It's as if, in meeting Maria, Mary has recovered a little piece of her mother.

A month later, and by 11 June the Shelley household have themselves settled in this attractive region. They rent a home about seventy-five kilometres away from Livorno in Bagni di Lucca, a small Tuscan riverside town long seen as a health resort. Life seems good. There's plenty to read, see and do, and the countryside is beautiful, as Mary reports to Maria Gisborne soon after their arrival:

We live here in the midst of a beautiful scene [...] surrounded by mountains covered with thick chestnut woods—they are peaked and picturesque and sometimes you see peeping above them the bare summit of a distant Appenine [*sic*] [...] So we lead here a very quiet pleasant life—reading our Canto of Ariosto—and walking in the evening am[ong] these delightful woods—

Mary is indeed busy reading and writing once again: and not only Ariosto. In May, while still at Livorno, she transcribed John Gisborne's own copy of a story, taken from Lodovico Antonio Muratori's *Annali d'Italia*, of 1749, about the medieval Cenci family. In the coming months she will translate this piece of Renaissance history. When Percy's success *The Cenci*, his verse play based on the tale, is republished posthumously in 1819, she will note that he originally wished her to write this story herself as a novel. Perhaps some part of him, titivated or exasperated by her closeness to her father, would like to see her explore its theme of father–daughter incest, though Mary will claim that 'He conceived that I had some dramatic talent'. In the event, it will be neither of the Shelleys but Stendhal who will transform the story into a novella in 1837, and Alexandre Dumas *père* who will produce a non-fiction account in 1840.

In June 1818 Mary's father suggests to Percy that she might write a book on the 'Lives of the Commonwealth's Men'; which he helpfully outlines. Percy takes it upon himself to dismiss this suggestion on the grounds that it would be hard to get hold of the books necessary to research it in Italy. Despite these near-misses fielded by her menfolk on her behalf, Mary *is* writing – letters – with a new expansiveness and flair. The confident charm of this summer's surviving correspondence with Maria Gisborne and the Hunts is in a different league from the conscientious travelogues Fanny received. Mary suddenly seems like a young woman with a sense of herself: something that being close to an old family friend can only have helped.

As must rumours of literary success, however distant. On 14 June she writes to Walter Scott to thank him for his review of *Frankenstein* or, in other words, to disabuse him of the notion that Percy wrote the novel: 'I am anxious to prevent your continuing in the mistake of supposing Mr Shelley guilty of a juvenile attempt of mine; to which—from its being written at an early age, I abstained from putting my name—and from respect to those persons from whom I bear it.' This is elegantly done, and puts Mary herself beautifully in the frame. The buzz continues, however. By August, Thomas Love Peacock is writing to Percy about how, during a day spent at the races at Egham, everyone was asking him about the anonymous novel. The book 'seems to be universally read', he declares.

But it's in August, too, that her stepsister's frets once again upset the good life Mary's trying to build. Claire is anxious about her daughter Allegra, since the baby's nursemaid Elise has written two agitated letters from Venice about being farmed out with her charge to a foster family. This despite the fact that the home in which she and Allegra are staying belongs to Richard Hoppner, the British consul in Venice, and his wife, Isabella. It's an eminently respectable, comfortable and arguably much more stable environment for a child than Byron's own home in the Palazzo Mocenigo, with its menagerie of cats, dogs, monkeys, birds, fox and wolf. Still, on 17 August Claire and Percy set off for Venice, three hundred kilometres across the country on the opposite coast of Italy, in order to confront Byron and Hoppner.

In their absence baby Clara becomes unwell, but, comfortingly, the Gisbornes come out to visit Mary in Bagni di Lucca. And then a letter arrives from Venice. In order to hide from Byron the fact that he has travelled there alone with Claire, whom 'Albe' by now detests, Percy has pretended to be staying with Mary and his own children in nearby Padua. In response, Byron has offered the household the use of Villa i Cappuccini – a cloistered, former Capuchin convent that is today known as the Villa Kunkler – in the little town of Este, some thirty kilometres south-west of Padua and seventy from central Venice. More than that, he is prepared to let Allegra come and stay with them there for a while. To cover his lie and seal this deal for Claire, Percy writes asking Mary to join him – and urgently, before Byron pays a visit to the villa and discovers her absence.

Mary's rueful *Journal* entry for 30 August says it all: 'My birthday (21). Packing.' She sets out the next day, travelling with Maria Gisborne as far as Lucca, before going on to Florence 'where we arrive late. The day is hot'. Mary has with her the two very young children, an inexperienced nursemaid and the fluent but ultimately dishonest new manservant Paolo Foggi. Early September is still too hot for comfort, and at Florence she must get her passport signed in order to proceed. Then, 'In four days, Saturday 5th, arrive at Este. Poor Clara is dangerously ill', Mary records. Yet in the next sentence it seems life is expected to go on: 'Shelley is very unwell, from taking poison in Italian cakes. He writes his Drama of "Prometheus". Read seven cantos of Dante. Begin to translate "A Cajo Graccho" of Monti, and "Measure for Measure".'

Of course, the *Journal* is the public record. A letter written to Maria Gisborne a few days later is fuller and more honest:

> I hasten to write to you to say that we have arrived safe and yet I can hardly call it safe since the fatigue has given my poor C̲a̲ an attack of dysentery and although she is now some what recovered from that disorder she is still in a frightful state of weakness and fever as is reduced to be so thin in this short time that you would hardly know her again.

Percy meanwhile has enjoyed his time in Venice with Byron. It has made him feel that while, unlike Mary, he may not be pulling in reviews in the national literary press, he is nevertheless seen as an equal by a major poetic figure. He's keen to extend the *entente*, which seems to him of such significance that he will shortly immortalise it in a narrative poem, 'Julian and Maddalo'.

He is also conspicuously more concerned by Claire's health, and his own, than by baby Clara's. On 16 September he accompanies Claire to see a doctor in Padua, possibly because he too is ill (those 'cakes'), or possibly because it doesn't occur to him that Claire might no more need travelling company, in this age of chaperoning servants, than Mary apparently does. The two are off to the doctor's again on the 22nd, when Claire misses her appointment and rearranges for 8.30 a.m. the next day. 'You must therefore arrange matters so that you should come to the Stella d'Oro a little before that hour—a thing only to be accomplished by setting out at half past three in the morning', Percy instructs his wife by letter. And as if she had no choice – as if sleepwalking – Mary obeys, setting out in the middle of the night and bringing with her Clara, who has not only lost weight alarmingly but is feverish with teething.

On 24 September, therefore, when Mary meets Percy in Padua, the baby is unignorably dangerously ill. The young parents start immediately for Venice, where there will at least be expert medical advice. It is probably the last thing they should be doing for 'my poor Clara, who dies the moment we get there'. And then there is the usual blur of grief, the being taken in to stay for five days by the kind Hoppners – the same family who have been fostering Allegra and who by their generosity at this juncture demonstrate that they are ideal people to do so – and the burial of little Clara the next day in the Lido. All this so that Claire can enjoy a month with *her* daughter: which she proceeds to do at Este, where Mary must witness that cosy picture of domestic content. At least, she does so for a fortnight, until little William becomes ill in turn.

This time even Percy does not prevaricate. He and Mary, William and Elise travel together to Venice to see a good doctor, and William does not die. Not yet, at least. The family stay at a decent hotel, and Mary sees the Hoppners almost every day, the friendship confirming for the Shelleys how likeable, like-minded and trustworthy the family are. If Allegra must be parted from her mother – something that's not unusual at this time, however harsh it appears today – it's hard to imagine safer hands for her care. The whole crisis that Claire has manufactured, and its tragic cost, have been unnecessary; and Claire, though she clearly intended no such harm, will never once express a whisper of guilt or regret.

Percy profits from two weeks in Venice to spend plenty of time hobnobbing alone with Byron:

> So, as we rode, we talked; and the swift thought,
> Winging itself with laughter, lingered not,
> But flew from brain to brain

as he will recall in 'Julian and Maddalo', although Mary will remember it differently:

> often I expected S's return from Palazzo Mocenigo, till two or three
> in the morning. I […] saw the palaces sleeping in the light of the
> moon, which veils by its deep shadows all that grieved the eye and
> heart in the decaying palaces of Venice.

We can only hope that Percy didn't act so promptly on his child's behalf this time from mixed motives. After all, the villa at Este, though comfortable, is reasonably plain by Italian standards; Claire is once again briefly unavailable, wrapped up as she is in the returned Allegra; and Mary is grieving. Byron, and Venice, must seem an alluring contrast.

Byron himself, though kept in the dark about any suggestion that Mary's child may have been sacrificed for his own, treats the grieving mother with more care. Although he disapproves of the Shelleys' parenting, he likes and respects Mary, about whom he will write to his own publisher, John Murray: 'Mary Godwin (now Mrs Shelley) wrote *Frankenstein*, which you have reviewed, thinking it Shelley's. Methinks it is a wonderful work for a girl of nineteen,—not nineteen, indeed at that time.' He consults Mary on literary matters: asking her to read his *Memoirs* and advise him whether they're suitable for publication (she thinks they are), and to fair-copy some of his work, including 'Mazeppa' and the 'Ode on Venice'. These tasks, and the straightforward esteem they signal, are like messages smuggled to her in her domestic seclusion and grief.

Grief broods on its own guilt, and the dour lists of reading in Mary's *Journal* this autumn conceal everything that she must think and feel as she goes over and over the unchangeable events of early September. Why, when she knew better than Percy how ill little Clara was, did she decide to obey the summons to Padua? It must be partly down to her sense of responsibility. Mary is after all, in the household's narrative, the 'lucky', married stepsister. She is also precociously mature and has the centred stability that often characterises intelligent women: unlike unanchored Claire, she has, in a sense, nothing to prove. But there's more than simple responsiveness in the way she accedes to Percy's demand that she pack up their entire household virtually overnight and move it across Italy for his and Claire's convenience.

That 'more' takes the shape, of course, of Claire herself. By now even Mary is aware that Harriet really was 'a *deserted wife*!' and not the promiscuous deserter that she herself believed when she ran off with Percy. 'Poor Harriet,' she will write in future years, 'To whose sad fate I attribute so many of my own heavy sorrows as the atonement claimed by fate for her death.' Mary always worries more about Percy's absences when he's with her stepsister: she doesn't want to end up living in her father's house as an abandoned wife herself. She comes to Padua because she cannot be held responsible by Percy for Claire's losing her chance with Allegra.

Sure enough, after a fortnight her husband is once again off to see Claire, who has remained with Allegra in Este. They play at house together for a few days at the Villa i Cappuccini before Percy comes back to Venice in order to return Allegra to Byron. On 5 November the entire ménage – minus those little sacrifices to masculine honour, Allegra and Clara – sets off for Naples via Rome. Conscientious travellers, they admire Classical Rome in particular. On 1 December the women, baby William and the servants rejoin Percy – who has rushed on ahead – in the splendidly ostentatious villa he has rented on the Neopolitan seafront. Contemporary paintings by a local expat, Antonie Sminck Pitloo, show the close-packed but substantial houses of Riviera di Chiaia – where the three adults and two children are installed at number 250 – giving directly on to the beach and the Royal Gardens.

A typically expansive, nothing-but-the-best gesture, 250 Riviera di Chiaia is almost a palazzo. No record remains of what Mary feels about this luxury – although she does admire the view of the Bay of Naples – or about the contrast it forms with life in Skinner Street, where Godwin's household are to a substantial degree depending on Percy's spare cash. Perhaps she simply feels that now is her turn at life. She certainly throws herself into both sightseeing – Vesuvius, Herculaneum, Pompeii, the Tomb of Virgil and Avernus – and background reading of what we could call 'local interest': in particular, the contemporary Genevan historian J. C. L. Simonde de Sismondi's *Histoire des républiques italiennes du moyen âge*, Dante's *The Divine Comedy*, the eighteenth-century German Hellenist Johann Joachim Winckelmann's hugely influential *Geschichte der Kunst des Alterthums* (*History of the Art of Antiquity*) and Virgil's *Georgics*, 'which is, in many respects, the most beautiful poem I ever read—He wrote it at Baiae; and sitting at the window, looking almost at the same scene that he did—reading about manners little changed since his days, has made me enjoy his poem, more, I think, than I ever did any other'. Revealingly, she adds: 'I, although continually seeing novelties, begin to get home-sick.'

Fundamentally, the Shelleys are undertaking their own version of a Grand Tour, fleshing out the Classical education they have both, to different degrees, received. While Percy's health may have contributed to their desire for a southern European climate – he is still officially the household's invalid – it seems no better here in Naples. By 5 March 1819 they and the inevitable Claire are in Rome itself. Over the next three months Mary's letters from the city to Maria Gisborne record much vacillation as they try to find a place to settle. But something more than simple vacillation has underlain the departure from Naples. Once again there is trouble with a child, though this time it's a birth, not a death, that causes Mary much grief. On 27 February 1819 a child, Elena Adelaide, has been registered and baptised as Mary and Percy's daughter.

The child is not, however, Mary's (although she does fall pregnant for the fourth time around now). This leaves two possibilities. One is that Percy, or Percy and Mary, have followed through on their old elopement fantasy of adopting a pretty child from a poor family. This seems relatively unlikely, as Elena Adelaide is only a tiny baby, in an era when babies are routinely called 'animals', rather than a responsive child. What makes it more unlikely still is that Mary's *Journal* for the day the child is registered and baptised records simply, and grimly, 'Pack'; and the next day, when they leave Naples, they leave the child behind. Even if a child had caught Mary's and Percy's eye but the attempt to adopt had gone wrong somehow (perhaps a blackmailing father?), one would expect mention of some first, happy encounter. If Percy has found a little girl for Mary as some consolation for losing Clara – for losing the two Claras; her first-born was also called Clara – would Mary have been able to resist such a gesture of kindness, however appallingly clumsy, from him?

The second alternative asks us to look at a different precedent. In Marlow, after the Hunts left, Mary was happy enough to pretend that baby Allegra (then Alba) was her own foster child in order to spare Claire's reputation. Now it seems as though she has again been asked to protect a baby by lending it the legitimacy of her married status. But whose child needs this protection? Mary's *Journal* records 'A most tremendous fuss' on the day after Elena's birth is recorded, as they leave Naples. One possible reason for such a fuss might be her refusal to take on, in the midst of her grief for Clara, a child she either knows or suspects to be Percy's by another woman.

We know that she wasn't present when Shelley registered the birth because, although he signs, her name has been garbled as 'Marina Padurin', surely by someone misreading a handwritten 'Maria Godwin'. Someone else again will register the little girl's death on 9 June next year, when 'Percy' is misread as 'Bereg' and 'Maria Godwin' becomes 'Maria Gebuin'. This death certificate assumes Elena was born on 27 February 1819, since it records that she died aged fifteen months and twelve days (1820 was a leap year). But the child's birth is registered as having taken place two months earlier than that, on 27 December 1818, even though a child born in Italy at this time is usually registered within a day or two of being born. And on 27 December Mary's *Journal* records that 'Clare is not well'.

So should we suspect that Elena is Claire's child? One reason not to jump to conclusions is the neatness of that two months' delay between Elena's recorded birth date and her registration. It's easy to imagine the registrar, on 27 February, asking Percy how old the child is, and a vague 'Oh, around two months' being translated by bureaucracy into the exactitude of 27 December. Since Percy gives Mary's age as twenty-seven, it may also be that he doesn't know any other numbers in Italian. Also there is family superstition around the number: Mary Wollstonecraft's birth date was 27 April; Mary Jane has always claimed it is Claire's too; and she was living at 27 the Polygon when she started to court her neighbour William Godwin.

There are two further reasons why Claire is often dismissed as Elena's mother. One is the supposition that, because she is so upset to lose Allegra, she would never voluntarily abandon a child. But Allegra is a special case. In bearing Byron's acknowledged, albeit illegitimate, child, Claire has looked for – and gained – certain advantages. She has inserted her own drama at the heart of her friends' lives; time will show her to have inserted herself into literary history by the same means. An unacknowledged child, who brings no such perks, is also liable to lose her the sympathy she has gained through mothering Allegra. Besides, if Claire did have a baby when she was sent away to Somerset, she has form in abandoning children.

The second reason Claire is assumed not to be Elena's mother is that Mary writes a letter denying that her stepsister had a child in Naples: and after all, how could Claire carry a pregnancy to term and Mary not notice?

This reasoning assumes Mary always tells the truth. Her letter, which she will write in August 1821 at Percy's request, is sent to the Hoppners in Venice care of Byron – who holds on to it. The nursemaid Elise, dismissed from the Shelleys' service together with their dishonest manservant Paolo Foggi for being pregnant by him (a situation the employers try to resolve by leaning successfully on the couple to marry), has by now informed the Hoppners – who have told Byron, who has repeated the story to Percy – that Elena Adelaide is Claire's child by Percy. The same story has indeed been used by Foggi a year earlier in an attempt to blackmail Percy. Although this is by now old news, Mary's letter, written at Pisa on 10 August 1821, is vehement and exclamatory: far from the muted grieving tone that sometimes creeps into her more confiding letters to Maria Gisborne, for example. She says she is in tears and that her hand is trembling so much she can scarcely hold the pen:

> That my beloved Shelley should stand thus slandered in your minds—
> He, the gentlest & most humane of creatures, is more painful to me,
> oh far more painful than any words can express.
> It is all a lie—[…]
> Need I say that the union between my husband any myself has
> ever been undisturbed.

Mary's pain is visceral and genuine because she perceives the threat to her relationship with Percy. If Claire has had a child with him, Mary no longer has any first claim on him, since he doesn't recognise the claims of either legal marriage or monogamy. Elise, though, isn't involved in a conspiracy; Mary doesn't realise that her former nursemaid, who by the time she tells the story to the Hoppners is no longer with Paolo, feels *protective* towards her. So do the Hoppners themselves: in the corroborating account they give to Byron, Mary figures as an unwitting victim rather than as complicit in a ménage.

'Claire had no child—the rest must be false': Mary sounds more as though she's arguing with herself than explaining facts to the Hoppners. What makes her denial finally unconvincing is that she bases it, insofar as it *is* based, on claims we know are untrue. 'You knew Shelley, you saw his face', she argues; but we know – and so does she – that Shelley *does* fall for other women. 'Claire is timid': yet Claire is very far indeed from being self-effacing. That the 'union between my husband and myself has ever been undisturbed' will certainly be untrue by the time of Percy's death, if not already. Finally, she says, 'I now do remember that Claire did keep her bed there for two days—but […] her illness was one she had been accustomed to for years.' An odd remark – if the illness was so trivial, why remember it?—and odder still is that in her note to Percy she alerts him to the fact that she's mentioned this.

Old rumours never die. But plenty of other things have happened to 'poor Mrs Shelley', as Hoppner calls her, since that 'tremendous fuss' in Naples in February 1819. On 12 November 1819 she has given birth to her second son, Percy Florence, in the city after which he's named. She toyed with following John Bell, an English specialist met in Rome, south to Naples so that he could attend the birth, but in the event Bell falls gravely ill and becomes unavailable. Nevertheless, her second son is born healthy: 'His health is good, and he is very lively, and even knowing for his age— although like a little dog I fancy his chief perfection lies in his nose.' As 1819 turns into 1820, Mary slowly begins to rebuild her life.

But the task is gigantically hard. For Mary's second son is born an only child. On 7 June 1819, when she is four months pregnant with Percy, her first son, William – her beloved Wilmouse, her 'sweet babe', her 'Blue Eyes' – dies of malaria. Weakened by worms and by the heat, the three-year-old dies after fighting the illness for five days. The family have been living in Rome since March, and he is buried in the city's famous Protestant Cemetery. This interment may feel like some tiny consolation, a way to hold on to a trace of the child: Clara's unmarked grave in the Lido has been lost. But even this will be denied Mary. Three years from now, she will discover William's grave has been 'lost' too – to incompetence or corruption.

Up to the point of William's death Mary applied herself studiously to falling in love with Rome. She has visited the Colosseum, the Vatican, the Pantheon, the Temple of Minerva, the Baths of Caracalla, the Quirinal and the Borghese Gardens, as well as numerous villas and palazzos, and been reading Livy, the Bible and Boccaccio's *The Decameron*. The household have even begun to act like the local expat community, moving away from the downtown heat of high summer on the Corso to the Via

Sistina above the Spanish Steps, on one of the small neighbourhood hills of Rome. This district is home to an old friend of Percy's, the painter Amelia Curran, who completed the famous surviving portrait of little William just a week before his death. Amelia is also the daughter of one of William Godwin's good friends, John Philpot Curran, who was Master of the Rolls in Ireland. Although a generation older than Mary and Percy, she becomes good friends with the couple, and it's on her advice that the young family decide not to leave Rome ahead of the malaria season and instead try to stick it out in this relatively salubrious neighbourhood – with fatal results.

After William's death the Shelleys do at last hurry away from the city. Mary is overwhelmed. As William was fighting for his life, she wrote to Maria Gisborne, 'The hopes of my life are bound up in him.' Now that he's died, it is indeed as if she is without either hope – or life. For she has been battling depression for some time. Already on 22 December 1817, as Marlow became uninhabitable and Percy remained close to Claire, Mary had written in her *Journal*, 'Le rêve est fini' – and then crossed this out. The *Journal* is no place for private thoughts. Since then she has at last found a confidante in Maria Gisborne, to whom she admits that, though she'd at first thought she could escape her troubles by coming abroad again, depression has followed her here. Now she and Percy move to Livorno to be near this good friend, as if retreating to surrogate family.

The cooler coastal climate also helps Mary as her pregnancy advances. From her new address below the hill village of Montenero she writes to other trusted friends. She tells Amelia, who is herself convalescing from malaria, that 'I shall never recover that blow—[…] Everything on earth has lost its interest to me.' To Marianne Hunt she writes:

> I never know one moments ease from the wretchedness & despair that possess me—May you my dear Marianne never know what it is to loose [*sic*] two only & lovely children in one year—to watch their dying moments—& then at last to be left childless & forever miserable[.]
>
> It is useless complaining & I shall therefore only write a short letter for as all my thoughts are nothing but misery it is not kind to transmit them to you—

[…] I feel that I am no fit for any thing & therefore not fit to live but how must that heart be moulded which would not be broken by what I have suffered.

With its mixture of self-loathing, circular thinking and feeling of power-lessness, this is a study in grief turning to depression. But Mary is right: what heart would not be broken by the loss of both children in the space of just nine months?

Part Two

BORNE AWAY
BY THE WAVES

Chapter 9

Le rêve est fini

Every where I turn I see the same figure—her bloodless arms and relaxed form flung by the murderer on its bridal bier.

BOOKS CONCEAL THE VERY things they reveal, packing their sometimes subversive, occasionally revolutionary, content between covers where only a reader can go. In this literal sense they're occult, and their readers share a special intimacy. Little wonder, then, if love affairs start over a book – famously, in the half-legend of Eloise and Abelard – or that Mary might understand her parents' love match as a romantically bookish affair.

She clearly views her own relationship in such terms. The Shelleys' revolutionary take on marriage doesn't extend to real equality. Mary has followed Percy's bidding throughout their life together, accepting his (mis)management of the couple's financial affairs and the frequent uprooting that comes with his bohemian lifestyle. She has befriended his friends and acted as both his secretary, admiringly fair-copying his work for publication, and his housekeeper. But in all this she has dared to dream that, though younger and less well educated than her partner, she too is a writer. Those records of what she and Percy have been reading and writing that so often seem to dominate her *Journal* aren't there just because she's being discreet about other, more personal, concerns. For her this is the heart of what their life together is. And in the spring of 1820, as she embarks on yet more courses of self-improvement (this time in Italian and drawing), Mary still holds on to the belief that her marriage is a meeting of minds.

Since William's death the previous summer, however, her grief at the loss of their first three children has revealed the gulf between her husband's mind and her own. Percy – whose literary career is showing signs of taking off with the success of *The Cenci* – seems to view the enormous shadow this triple bereavement casts from a curiously disengaged distance. And sure enough, another form of disappearance is also beginning to cast its shadow over Mary's life. Claire's near-continual presence may have critically undermined the Shelleys' marriage, but at least it has kept Percy at home. This year, 1820, will be the one in which the much longed-for *absentia Clairiae* finally becomes a reality. But the habit of emotional absenteeism that Percy has acquired from this domestic triangle remains, and it must now find other outlets.

A year from now he will complete *Epipsychidion*, the 604-line poem – of which Mary is unaware – which, as we've seen, includes his famous description of monogamy as a 'chained' life sentence, 'the dreariest and the longest journey', and fidelity as consigning 'all the rest, though fair and wise […] / To cold oblivion'. No surprise that when Percy sends this poem to his publishers, Olliers, he will do so secretly, while out visiting a friend.

As it happens, Mary will also be out that day, 16 February 1821. Ironically, she will be visiting the dedicatee of her husband's poem, nineteen-year-old Emilia Viviani. Since the end of January 1820 Mary, Percy and Claire have been living in Pisa, leaving town for the nearby countryside when the summer gets hot and malarial. It's a way of life they enjoy for the next two years, but though the city suits them well, its society is still highly traditional. The town's governor has confined his teenaged daughter, Emilia, to a convent to await an arranged marriage. When she discovers this, Mary enters into the young woman's situation with characteristic imaginative generosity, writing to Leigh Hunt that 'Now hopeless from a five years confinement every thing disgusts her and she looks with hatred

& distaste even on the alleviations of her situation.' Pert Emilia recipro-
cates with little in the way of either generosity or imagination. 'You seem
to me a little cold sometimes, and awe-inspiring; but I know that your
husband spoke truly when he said that it's nothing but ash covering a
warm heart', she tells Mary, with the confidence of a young woman who
feels she has that husband just where she wants him.

Percy has indeed embarked on this new friendship in a somewhat different spirit from his wife's. But Emilia is not the first young lady to catch
his eye since William's death – or indeed Percy Florence's birth. No more
than a couple of weeks after his new son's arrival and just a month before
the move to Pisa, one Sophia Stacey, the visiting ward of a Shelley relative,
is – Mary wryly records in a letter to Maria Gisborne – '<u>entousiasmée</u>'
to meet Percy. She 'sings well for an English delettanti & if she would
learn the scales would sing exceedingly well for she has a sweet voice. So
there is a great deal of good company for Clare.' This is lovely codified
observation (Mary herself, continually doing the hard yards of study, is
no dilettante. And how neatly she puts Claire in her place by association),
but it stops just short of catty. In three months' time Mary will be able to
write Sophia a letter in the 'Poet's Wife' genre familiar across centuries,
intervening to respond to the female admirer on behalf of the couple: 'I
am afraid that [our plan to spend the summer in Bagni di Lucca] does
not accord with your plans, *bella Sofia*, to pass it there likewise.'

Percy manages to subvert this effect somewhat by adding 'On a Dead
Violet' as a postscript:

> The odour from the flower is gone
>   Which like thy kisses breathed on me;
> The colour from the flower is flown
>   Which glowed of thee and only thee!

… and so on. Which, as love-letters smuggled under the alibi of art go,
is pretty explicit. Loyally, Mary will publish both this lyric, and *Epipsychidion*, without comment in posthumous editions of Percy's work. But it
can't escape her notice that the latter, subtitled 'Verses addressed to the
noble and unfortunate Lady, Emilia V—, now imprisoned in the convent
of –', invokes its Pisan dedicatee as 'my adored Nightingale! [...] Seraph

of Heaven! [...] radiant form of Woman [...] Thou Harmony of Nature's art! [...] Spouse! Sister! Angel! Pilot of the Fate / Whose course has been so starless! O too late / Beloved! O too soon adored by me!' Even Percy is aware that, within the lyric tradition, lines like 'Emily, I love thee' are generally read as confession, and he stipulates anonymous publication to Olliers, 'To avoid the malignity of those who turn sweet food into poison; transforming all they touch into the corruption of their own natures': his code for other people's moral disapproval.

Since, of course, Mary has – unusually – not fair-copied this secret poem, she doesn't read it until the couple's second Pisan summer of 1821, by which time 'Emily' is about to be married and, keen to protect herself from scandal, asks the Shelleys to stop visiting her. The following March, Mary will be able to tell Maria Gisborne that 'the conclusion of our friendship a la Italiana' came when Emilia asked Percy for a substantial sum of money. Whether this was blackmail or simple opportunism, the most convincing supporting evidence of a 'connection' between Percy and Emilia comes, once again, from his own pen. Not only does he rush to reassure Claire that she has nothing to worry about from *la Italiana*; he admits to Byron that 'The whole truth is not known and Mary might be very annoyed at it'.

The trouble with (emotional) infidelity, even when excused by ideals of free love, is that it throws everything around it into doubt. It must be difficult for Mary, as Percy unignorably flirts – at the very least – with Sophia, Emilia and those who follow them, to escape the retrospective conclusion that whatever 'connection' with other women she may earlier have suspected did take place after all. And what does this mean for the times she thought her relationship was happy? Things are shifting, and she can't be quite sure how. Infidelity is particularly abusive in the mixed message it sends; a kind of stop-start *He loves me, he loves me not* that makes it hard for the cheatee either to know where she stands or to move on to better things – whatever those might be for a married woman in the 1820s. As with Harriet, so with Mary: it turns out that, though Percy may want her, he doesn't want to be 'chained' to her. And, also like Harriet, Mary is becoming exhausted by the life he leads her.

By June 1820 the Shelleys' domesticity is a muted affair. 'Our little

Percy is a thriving forward child but after what has happened I own it appears to me – a faded cloud – all these hopes that we so earnestly dwell on', Mary writes to Amelia Curran, who has remained in Rome. In another letter sent the same month she asks Maria Gisborne for a loan of £400 to help settle her father's debts. Trying to make money to this end has even become a motive for starting work on her next novel, the manuscript that will eventually be *Valperga*. For Godwin has continued to harry the household for money, despite the fact that he and Mary Jane have two by now adult sons, neither of whom supports them. Even after little William's death he has paused his campaign only to admonish Mary to pull herself together:

> Remember too that, though, at first, your nearest connections may pity you in this state, yet that when they see you fixed in selfishness and ill humour, and regardless of the happiness of every one else, they will finally cease to love you, and scarcely learn to endure you.

This strikingly brutal and self-serving letter is written a mere three months after the loss of her third child. The pressure her father puts on Mary – and through her on Percy – gets so bad that by their first August in Pisa, Percy, presumably tired of being reminded of financial commitments he doesn't entirely believe in, tells Godwin he will intercept future letters. Rather than change his approach, Godwin seems to lapse into petulant silence.

The Shelleys themselves now live within a network of personal connections on which they rely, and Mary's own letters are busy with practical matters. She's not abashed to ask for advice, for help with shipping goods or delivering Percy's work to publishers – or even for money. But not everything is workaday. Since March 1820 home has been the spacious top-floor apartment in smart Casa Frassi on Lung'Arno, the paved Arno riverbank. 'We have two bed rooms 2 sitting rooms kitchen servants rooms nicely furnished—& very clean & new (a great thing in this country for 4 guineas & a ½ a month—the rooms are light and airy)', as Mary tells Marianne Hunt, ten days after the family and Claire move in.

Meanwhile her correspondence with Maria Gisborne is spotted with requests that tell us a great deal about how she likes to dress. Gone is the eccentric tartan with which she returned to her father's house six eventful years ago. In come smart, luxurious accessories: 'a gown of close pink strip – not like the enclosed but of good material', 'a pair of black [shoes] for the house […] a slim pair of stuff kid or morocco for this they must be made on the same last as my green <u>stuff</u> ones. If he does not remember, I will send him one' and 'I wish you would get me from Arbib's a scarf of China crape. I want it a light pretty colour—lilac, or blue, but not pink.'

Mary's letters to women friends are also full of charm. She has fun with 'the steam engine', a prototype steamboat invented by Maria Gisborne's son Henry in which Percy has invested, and is sympathetic with just a touch of levity when Henry proposes unsuccessfully to the daughter of another friend. Playfully nagging Maria into visiting, she reminds her that she doesn't need to make the trip in a single day: 'Bring your nightcap instead—Do you not know that a lady's frilled Nightcap has the same effect upon night, as the fair moon herself?'

Such friendships are coming to define Mary's life. Just two months before Percy Florence's birth on 12 November 1819, the Shelleys got to know another old friend of Mary's family. 'Mrs Mason', who lives in Florence with the poet and Classicist George Tighe and their two young daughters, ten-year-old Laurette and four-year-old Nerina, is actually Margaret Jane King, countess of Mountcashell. Mary Wollstonecraft's protégée and a child she dreamed of adopting – later, the moderating sensibility with whom Mary Jane corresponded about the Godwin girls – Margaret made an unhappy marriage to Lord Mountcashell in 1791. Although she has escaped, the price has been high: she is not allowed to see the eight children she bore him. Warm, intelligent and full of good practical advice, she has an intimate connection with Mary Shelley, having received from Wollstonecraft the education and mothering Mary herself did not. She has even renamed herself after the wise guide in Wollstonecraft's *Original Stories from Real Life* for children. All this makes her a kind of adoptive mother-by-education to Mary, who is twenty-four years her junior; losing access to the eight children of her marriage also means she can understand something of the compound nature of Mary's loss – and how the deaths of William and Clara make her mother's death not less but more significant.

Casa Silva, the 'Mason'–Tighe home on the outskirts of Pisa, quickly becomes a welcome second home for the Shelleys and for Claire. On 10 August 1820 Mary's diary records 'Write a story for Laurette'. This tale, about a stolen child who believes he is an orphan but who is eventually reunited with his natural parents, is *Maurice, or The Fisher's Cot*. Mary goes to a great deal of trouble over it, fair-copying the novella into its own little notebook and carefully dividing it into three parts just like the three volumes currently fashionable for adult novels. The care with which she does this reminds us again that Mary has herself lost two daughters, the elder of whom would by now be five and a half: quite old enough to have stories read to her (if not quite yet for this miniature novel).

Mary's relationship with Margaret 'Mason' is part of a pattern. All three of her key friendships in the Pisa years – with Margaret, Maria Gisborne and Marianne Hunt – are with older women who, as well as being mothers *like* herself, could be mother figures *to* her. The longest-held of these friendships is with Marianne, after whose growing family Mary enquires wistfully in her letters. Marianne is only a decade older than Mary – though to the twenty-three-year-old this probably seems like a generation – and still leads the relatively settled domestic life, on the outskirts of London, that the Shelleys left behind when they emigrated in 1818. But Percy and Mary have always argued that the Leigh Hunts should follow them to Italy, and in 1821 Marianne's own and her husband's illnesses, his consequent inability to work and the mounting difficulty of the English political situation combine to force them to ask the Shelleys to back their words with action.

However, moving the Leigh Hunts and their seven children turns out to be such an expensively protracted process that the Shelleys will in turn be forced to ask Byron to help with costs. The Hunts set out in December 1821 and, though turned back by bad weather and forced to overwinter in Plymouth, arrive in Genoa in June 1822. Their installation in Pisa will have famously fatal consequences for Percy, but the plan is a good one. Leigh Hunt will work with Byron and Percy on a new quarterly magazine, *The Liberal*, which they will employ him to edit. Being in Italy will allow him to live much more cheaply than in London, and also to publish without fear of arrest. The scheme is one of the few practical arrangements Percy achieves – another is his provision for Claire – although it will only briefly outlive the blow dealt it by his own death, since Byron is not much interested in a publishing a little magazine.

Meanwhile, though, Mary's relations with Maria Gisborne are becoming not so much costly as tangled. In the summer of 1820 the Gisbornes return briefly to London to sort out their financial affairs. While there, they hear the Godwinian perspective on Percy, including complaints about his financial dealings and the accusation that he is Allegra's father: something that not even Lord Byron, who has every reason to wish it were the case, believes. This comes so uncomfortably soon after they've helped deal with Paolo Foggi's blackmail claim that Percy is Elena Adelaide's father, that it's impossible for them not to now revisit that story and reassess the young Shelleys.

The Gisbornes return to Livorno at the start of October 1820; within a fortnight Mary is writing Maria a passionate letter demanding that she choose between the Godwin household and her own. It seems to her as though Mary Jane, that 'filthy woman' she feels has already usurped her father's affection, is now trying to take away her dearest friend. In fact, it is her father who has asserted that Percy 'has a particular enmity against truth, so that he utters falsehoods and makes exaggerations even when no end is to be answered by them', a portrait that cleverly ensures against rebuttal. But little does Mary realise that, earlier in the summer, Percy has already done his bit to erode the friendship (and incidentally help make her father's allegations credible) by trying to enlist Mrs Gisborne in secret negotiations to send money to Naples for baby Elena's keep. In June he even wrote to let Maria in on his plan – in the event, tragically aborted by the little girl's death – to bring the child into his own household. After all this, it's not surprising that the women's friendship takes a good year to mend.

Meanwhile back in Pisa Margaret, the third of this trio, is getting on with some maternal manoeuvring. Her partner, George Tighe, doesn't particularly take to Percy, and it's probable that she herself doesn't either, since Mary Jane Godwin has, in a series of letters written since he eloped with Mary, blamed him for leading her own daughter into harm's way. But 'Mrs Mason' offers the young household a great deal of practical support. She introduces them to the admired Pisan surgeon Andrea Vaccà Berlinghieri, under whom, astonishingly, she has herself managed to study by dint of cross-dressing. Vaccà attends when, for example, the four-month-old Percy Florence has the measles. For a young mother who has already lost three children, the sense of being in expert hands is highly reassuring. The same expertise also cures Percy senior's hypochondria through a magical combination of common-sense remedies and flattering reassurance.

Possibly best of all, Margaret rescues both young women from the Mary–Claire deadlock by the simple expedient of removing Claire from the Shelley household. Biographers tend to suggest she does so because she is particularly close to Claire, for this is another friendship that is more hollowed out than Mary realises. In correspondence with the former Lady Mountcashell, Mary Jane has blamed not only Percy but also, ironically, Mary for Claire's choosing to throw in her lot with the Shelley couple. Indeed, this has become the Godwinian version. In the very month that Margaret is making arrangements to separate the young woman from her dependency on Percy, Mary's father repeats to Maria Gisborne a similar version in which Claire leads 'a life of solitude retirement and indolence, completely disregarded and neglected by her friends, meeting them only at mealtimes'.

Still, in rescuing Claire Margaret is also rescuing Mary and, she must hope, Mary's marriage. So in July, while the Shelley couple are using the absent Gisbornes' Livorno home in order to meet a lawyer who will resolve the Foggi blackmail, Claire goes to stay with Margaret. After some inevitable toing and froing, she moves to Florence in October as a paying guest and trainee governess. Margaret has found her a place with the family of another respected physician, Antonio Bojti, doctor to the Grand Duke Ferdinand III of Tuscany. In a new city, away from her potential notoriety as Byron's discarded mistress, Margaret's mentee has a chance to 'start over'. She can learn German in the Bojtis' bilingual household while teaching the children English, and thus assemble enough skills to become, as she must in order to keep herself, a governess.

Claire will continue to come and go from Mary's home, but her great excuse for staying on – that she has nowhere to go – has finally been quashed. Unfortunately, this astute intervention has come too late. Mary's marriage – and indeed her stepsister's entire life – might have gone differently if someone had intervened to remove Claire at its outset, before Percy got into the habit of having such an attractive alternative to working at the chewy bits of his relationship. It might even have had a chance to work if Claire had stayed away after her West Country sojourn – if, indeed, her teenaged attempt to court Byron had worked out. But by now her presence has starved the Shelley marriage of so much oxygen that it seems unable to restore itself.

Nevertheless, in the summer of 1820 intellectual life continues among the friends in Pisa. Margaret Mason is preoccupied by the possibility of Home Rule for Ireland. Mary and Percy – who in August move to their summer residence at the thermal springs of Bagni di San Giuliano, close by the Apennine foothills – have been translating Spinoza together, as well as reading Thomas Paine's *The Rights of Man*. Percy is also reading Thomas Hobbes, whose *Leviathan* of 1651 argues that the social contract (secured by strong government) is necessary to prevent the 'warre of every one against every one'. This position is, ironically, almost the exact opposite of his own. Far from viewing any social contract as better than none, Percy often seems interested in the overthrow of the status quo for the sake of change itself. In Florence last autumn he composed *The Mask of Anarchy* in response to the Peterloo Massacre of unarmed worker protesters that took place in Manchester in August of that year. But this ninety-one-stanza poem will remain unpublished in his lifetime and its commitment to political change, though genuine, is somewhat naïve. It's easy enough to attack a British Foreign Secretary with lines like 'I met murder on the way— / He had a mask like Castlereagh' from safety on the far side of a continent – 'As I lay asleep in Italy', as the poem itself admits. Politically viable remedies for poor governance are altogether harder to muster, and require both patience and nuance.

An uncharitable observer might assume Percy simply lacks the patience for effective social and political engagement. But he has been interested in the actual nature and instant of transformation itself – whether social, psychological or physical – ever since he was a schoolboy chemist experimenting with electricity and miniature hot-air balloons.

The mature poetic style he discovered in the summer of 1816 doesn't try to pin down or define how things are, but instead to recreate the moment of change that is insight or revelation. Moreover, for all its personal convenience, Percy's resistance to conventional morals does represent a consistently held belief that convention replaces content – in other words, genuine understanding – with empty form. When Mary started to write *Frankenstein* during that same summer at the Villa Diodati, she too picked transformation itself as her theme, choosing to explore the ultimate, and philosophically most mysterious, change of all: the moment of animation.

Four years later, in 1820, Mary has her own reasons for immersing herself in political theory. She's at work on what will become her second published novel, retelling the story of Castruccio Castracani (1281–1328), duke of Lucca. Castracani's life was bound up in the feud between the Guelphs and the Ghibellines, of whom he was one. Two centuries after the duke's death, around 1520, Niccolò Machiavelli wrote a *Life of Castruccio Castracani* to deepen the famous study of leadership and politics in his *The Prince*. Writing another three centuries on, Mary uses the same story to examine not strategy but the unstrategic work of human relationships. Like her husband, she's a writer whose social engagement is 'slant'; her instincts are philosophical rather than political. Indeed all her novels, from *Frankenstein* in 1818 to *Falkner* in 1837, will turn out to explore puzzles in ethics.

In the book Mary starts to write in Pisa, Castracani elects to conquer the fortified territory belonging to his lover Euthanasia, thus forcing her to chose between her love for him and her political independence – her agency – as the ruler of a city-state. Euthanasia chooses to hold on to what she is and, rather than surrender to this imposition, sails away to her death. It's striking that, at this stage in her life with Percy, Mary creates a heroine who refuses a love for which she'd have to sacrifice her entire identity. But she is also writing as a child of her own exciting political times. As she says to Marianne Hunt, 'You see what a John or rather Joan Bull I am so full of politics', although this characteristic wryness follows a rather undistinguished rant about the damage done by the Castlereagh government. That's unfortunate, for the postscript to Mary's letter asks, 'Does [Hunt] think I cd write for his Indicator & what kind of thing wd

IN SEARCH OF MARY SHELLEY

he like.' It's a significant question, for all its throwaway manner – among the first of the many pitches for writing work that Mary will make in the years to come, and a pragmatic acknowledgement that she has graduated into the world of professional writers.

For, despite its emotional freight, *The Life and Adventures of Castruccio, Prince of Lucca* is, like *Frankenstein*, a novel of ideas. The trouble is, though, that political ideas are *held* – in other words the writer 'knows what she thinks before she sees what she says' – and dramatising them can be rather like moving puppets around. *Frankenstein* managed to avoid this effect, breaking free of the ideas that inform it. However important those are, it's the book's characters and their stories that have become world-famous – because they interest us. Even today we want to reread and retell them, and we find in doing so that they are plastic and change according to who is doing the telling. That, of course, is what archetypes do: they work so well as characters – because they're a truth about human nature itself – that we can play with them in all sorts of settings, from clinical psychoanalytic practice to social media meme, and from schlock entertainment to high art.

However carefully she researches and writes, none of Mary's subsequent novels quite achieves this living quality. This is often regarded as a great mystery, as if talent were a tap from which the flow were always at the same pressure. But one reason these subsequent books, though generally significantly longer, seem 'thinner' and 'flatter' than her début is that to write well requires the kind of full-mindedness that stress and distraction destroy. By the autumn of 1820, when Mary is working virtually daily on what will become her second published novel, her life is altogether more complex, emotionally at least, than it was in 1816–17, when she wrote *Frankenstein*. A thrice-bereaved mother, no longer sure of the great love of her life, she's living with a load of emotional ambiguity and grief that will only multiply still further by the time she produces the rest of her books.

Besides, *Frankenstein* creates its new genres and archetypes by being *sui generis*, and by definition what's *sui generis* can't be repeated. If Mary had tried to exploit the success of her first novel directly, writing some kind of sequel, what would she have produced? Probably not science fiction, which she isn't aware of having 'created', but another Gothic romance. *Frankenstein* went out on a limb in its exploration of a taboo. Sure enough, *Matilda*, the short novel she has written next, is indeed a Gothic romance, its protagonist sequestered on a remote country estate, and dramatically violates both incest and suicide taboos. Mary finished its first draft three days before Percy Florence was born, and is still revising the book during the family's first fortnight in Pisa. Yet the story engages neither her husband nor her publisher father, and it remains unpublished in her lifetime mainly thanks to the latter, who refuses either to publish it or – a misplaced censorship, or a gesture of paternal care – to return the manuscript so that Mary can publish it elsewhere.

Moreover Thomas Love Peacock has recently followed up the success of *Headlong Hall* with his *Nightmare Abbey*, published in November 1818. This pastiche of the Gothic romance is a novel in which Mary and Percy once again probably recognise themselves and, even though all three remain good friends, it's impossible to miss the book's satirical message that the genre, far from being profound and awe-inspiring, is actually rather ridiculous.

Mary knows she's a writer, and, like all writers, she wants to be published and taken seriously. She's also living with an increasingly successful fellow author who is in no doubt as to his own talent. Producing a book that will satisfy the criteria for 'literature' in her own environment is key to her writerly survival. So she has embarked on the kind of substantial, three-volume historical drama of political ideas that the men around her produce and approve. Despite this, when she finally sends the Castruccio novel to Olliers in late 1821 they turn it down, and it isn't published until after Percy's death. The book will appear in February 1823 from G. & W. B. Whittaker's, publishers William Godwin secures for it after – once an editor always an editor – cutting some lengthy battle scenes and retitling the book *Valperga*.

Pisa may have become a way of life, but the Shelleys' moves continue. In November 1820 flooding in their Bagni di San Giuliano summer home sends them back to Pisa, where they rent in the Palazzo Galetti. They move to Casa Aulla in March 1821, then a couple of months later back to Bagni de San Giuliano for the summer, this time to a villa that belongs to their city landlords. By late October 1821 they're back in Pisa in the top-floor apartment of the Tre Palazzi di Chiesa, on the Lung'Arno. But it's not all just making do. In these handsome city palazzos had for little rent Mary can arrange her own furniture around her. The great sweep of the River Arno, on to which they face, means that this is no huddled, medieval quarter. Instead there's a bracing sense of being truly 'out in the open'. Sometimes the palatial rooms catch the full sun; at others their shutters tremor in the *maestrale* as it swirls down the wide, navigable waterway.

The Shelleys truly live in splendid isolation. Not merely political exiles from Britain, they are also social exiles from polite society wherever they go. The effects of this fall, as ever, more heavily on the woman than on the man. In December 1821 the Revd George Frederick Nott will invite Mary to one of his services, at which he promptly preaches against atheists, meaning the Shelleys. It's a cruel, public shaming that she has to bear alone (Percy doesn't attend). But things change for the better in the winter of 1820–21. The doctor Vaccà and his beautiful, popular wife, Sofia, do 'receive' the Shelleys and, even better, start to introduce them to the provincial intelligentsia of Pisa, a community whose oddity frankly equals the couple's own.

The legwork of these introductions is done by Francesco Pacchiani, a university professor who, turning fifty in 1821, has largely replaced the grind of libraries and lecture halls with the pleasures of society. At first he's a frequent guest, but the Shelleys quickly tire of his name-dropping: 'there is no truth in him – but a love of wealth and a boasting infinitely disgusting', as Mary tells Claire. Nevertheless, Pacchiani's snobbish ability to 'collect' people he thinks are of note serves the Shelleys well. Among his first contacts Tommaso Sgricci, a public improviser or on-stage rhetorician, captures Mary's imagination, although no particular friendship develops. Another introduction is to John Taaffe, an Irish intellectual exiled because of his rackety private life. One can't help feeling that, in following up these acquaintanceships, Mary is revealing a fatal attraction to charisma. After all, she grew up among the larger-than-life presences of her father's successful, intellectually highly influential friends, and she's still only twenty-four, an age at which attaching oneself to the brightest available star is a normal part of self-invention. Besides, even as it becomes a liability, her own husband's charisma is undeniable. He is what Edward Williams will describe as a 'man of most astonishing genius in appearance [...] his ordinary conversation is akin to poetry'.

Charisma also surrounds the 'Greek Prince' whom Pacchiani introduces on 2 December. Alexandros Mavrokordatos, who is staying with the Vaccàs, is not yet thirty but has already played an active part in Balkan history. He's in exile not as the result of some sexual peccadillo but with the court of his uncle Ioan Georghes Caradja. Caradja and Mavrokordatos are Greeks of largely Byzantine, ennobled ancestry from Constantinople. Their community are known as Phanariots, after the Phanar district, seat of the ecumenical patriarchate on the Golden Horn, where their wooden mansions dominate the streets leading down to the Bosphorus. In 1812 Caradja was appointed ruler, or Hospodar, of Wallachia – the southern part of twenty-first-century Romania excluding Transylvania – by Sultan Ali Pasha of Turkey. His rule, during which Mavrokordatos served in government, was mixed. Although working hard to contain an outbreak of bubonic plague and establish the region's first modern legal code, the Legiuirea Caragea, he also imposed high taxes, increased his personal wealth and faced a series of coup conspiracies – until in September 1818 he was forced to flee to Austro-Hungarian Transylvania.

It must have been a hair-raising ride, with the accompanying retinue of three hundred Albanian mercenaries burning bridges behind the family as they fled. It certainly puts Mary and Percy's elopement dash across Kent in the shade. The court's destination, the old university town of Brasov, is 170 kilometres from Bucharest; their party had a lead of just four hours, meaning that they weren't yet safely across the border when the alarm was raised but had yet to traverse the frankly Alpine terrain of the Bucegi Mountains. So there's no denying that the dark-haired, dark-eyed Prince Mavrokordatos is a man of action as well as an intellectual. No denying, either, that he is the antithesis of dreamy, hypochondriacal Percy.

He also differs increasingly from Percy in his evident admiration of Mary. Characteristically, she takes a while to notice this and makes no second mention of 'a Prince Mauro Codarti' until four weeks after they have been introduced, when in a letter to Leigh Hunt she describes 'a very pleasant man profound in his own language' who 'has related to us some very infamous conduct of the English powers in Greece'. The two begin to meet regularly, at first to help Mary's Greek but later to talk through Mavrokordatos's ideas of Greek sovereignty. He will continue to work out these political beliefs and ambitions with her even after he has left Pisa, in a long series of letters written from the heat of action. For the irony of the young prince's life is that, despite having been born in Turkey and been part of the court apparatus of hated Ottoman rule in Romania, he actively espouses the nationalist desire of Greece – a country he has not yet visited – to escape that rule.

He is, then, a man on the very cusp between tradition and the new, between East and West. In Naples, Sicily, Sardinia and the Italian north as well as in Spain and Portugal and Brazil and Greece, 1820 is a year of revolutions, and Mavrokordatos is no armchair revolutionary. He leaves for the southern Peloponnese on 26 June 1821, three months into the Greek War of Independence. Soon he's helping establish a Greek government, and is voted president of the executive in January 1822. He will serve as prime minister of Greece no fewer than six times between 1833 and 1855, and as Greek envoy to Munich, Berlin, London and Constantinople in the decade 1834–44. Not simply a desk-bound politician, he also leads the Greek troops himself – bravely, if not always successfully – in both 1822–3 and 1825–6.

Mary lacks Percy's knee-jerk sexuality. It's perfectly possible for her to befriend Alexandros Mavrokordatos, and for him to matter to her profoundly, without any sexual *frisson*. It's also entirely possible that any such part of her personality has been squashed by the unromantic role Percy has by now allocated her: for example, in the chilling letter to Maria Gisborne of 20 July 1820 – written in the same month as his celebrated poem of the same name – in which he bemoans the fact that Mary doesn't have the 'wisdom' of a forty-five-year-old about Claire. The fact that there's no recorded hint of any emotional intimacy between Mary and Alexandros may mean just that.

On the other hand, we shouldn't rule out such intimacy completely. By now we know that Mary simply doesn't record feelings and events she wishes to leave unrecorded. And clearly the bright, non-bohemian

Alexandros, who understands her well enough to value her highly, respects either the terms of their friendship or else her need to keep anything of an emotional nature that passes between them absolutely unrecorded. The serious letters he writes from Greece will, after all, in the custom of the day, be read by others in her household. While Percy feels the need to 'write between the lines' in the huge print of his poetic declarations to Sophia Stacey and Emilia Viviani, Alexandros may be emotionally intelligent enough to know that simply continuing to share his deepest political ideas with Mary is a form of intimacy.

And she does have another intelligent male friend. Lord Byron will arrive on 1 November 1821 to take up residence in the Palazzo Lanfranchi, the grand accommodation the Shelleys have found for him across the Arno from their own home. Happily cohabiting with his new mistress, Teresa, Countess Guiccioli, he will remain an ally perhaps not least because Mary makes the effort to be on good terms with Teresa: she understands, after all, what it means to be a poet's mistress. Byron continues to ask Mary to fair-copy his work, a form of first readership that flatters Mary with a high degree of literary trust – and allows the poet to benefit from her accuracy and acuity. Of course, he's not married to her. It's easier to understand a depressed, intelligent woman when she isn't cramping your style as your wife. But despite their lack of sexual 'connection', when, in 1822, Byron plans to stage *Othello* – with himself as Iago – Mary volunteers to play, of all things, Desdemona.

By the time Byron arrives in Pisa, however, the Shelleys are sharing Tre Palazzi with more recently acquired friends. On 19 January 1821 they exchange visits with a newly arrived couple, the Williamses, and this becomes one of their 'friendships at first sight'. Jane and Edward Williams are everything that Mary and Percy should have been: they too eloped unmarried, because Jane was already married to someone else. They too have a child, and Jane is pregnant with their second. And they are in love. Percy can't observe this loving relationship without wanting it for himself. But rather than turning to Mary, he turns *on* her, with an escalating series of accusatory poems and complaints to friends about her coldness. The 'Couldst thou but be as thou hast been' of 'When Passion's Trance Is Overpast' leads to 'The Serpent is shut out from Paradise' and its 'When I return to my cold home, you ask / Why I am not as I have lately been. / *You* spoil me for the task / Of acting a forced part in life's dull scene', while in 'To Jane: The Invitation', the poet's domestic quotidian becomes 'the barren way […] / The wintry world'.

As these poems also record, Percy is, predictably, falling for Jane: in 'Lines Written in the Bay of Lerici', 'Memory gave me all of her / That even Fancy dares to claim'. But for once the woman of his fantasies does not seem to meet him half-way, although she does accept the love poems he writes her. This may be partly because she is a bit dim, rather than busily flirtatious as Claire, Sophia and Emilia have been. Her later portrait by George Clint suggests a smooth-skinned, somewhat equine beauty, doe-eyed but limp-wristed. As Mary remarks to Claire, 'Jane is certainly very pretty but she wants animation and sense; her conversation is <u>nothing particular</u>, and she speaks in a slow, monotonous voice: but she appears good tempered and tolerant.' Percy is forced to do some imaginative heavy lifting to make a muse out of her; the result is some of the most nuanced and interesting of his lyric verse, including 'To Jane: The Recollection', 'Lines Written in the Bay of Lerici' and 'To Jane', where her voice has 'A tone / Of some world far from ours, / Where music and moonlight and feeling / Are one'.

The Williamses and the Shelleys have been introduced to each other by yet another figure in their developing network. Edward's friend Thomas Medwin is Percy's cousin, and he comes to stay with the Shelleys from October 1820 to February 1821. He's not a guest who brings Mary much pleasure, as she tells Claire: 'You have no idea how earnestly we desire the transfer of Mxxxxx to Florence—in plain Italian he is nothing but a Seccatura [nuisance]—He sits with us & be one reading or writing he insists upon interrupting one every moment.' There are, though, more chilly draughts than even this criss-crossing the Palazzo Galetti salon. Claire reads the letter knowing, as this visitor may but Mary certainly does not, that one of Medwin's friends has offered Percy a trip to the Middle East in the spring, and Percy proposes taking along not Mary but Claire.

Medwin may be mimicking Percy's attitude to Mary, all too baldly illustrated by this secret plan, when he peremptorily interrupts while she fair-copies her Castracani novel in early November and experiences the usual authorial second thoughts: 'Correct the novel', as she records without comment on 30 November and 1 December. He probably senses something of her opinion of him too. Mary is less discreet in letters, where she pours scorn on his translations of Dante: 'Not to say that he fills his verses with all possible commonplace', she says, and even more damningly, 'When he cannot make sense of the words that are he puts in words of his own and calls it a misprint.' In years to come, the poetaster will get his revenge by blackmailing a widowed Mary with 'evidence' of Percy's unconventional behaviour, and by publishing a long series of reminiscences of the Shelley circle that undermine her attempts to sanitise the poet's reputation.

But if Medwin is all sourness, the dashing friend the Williamses bring to Pisa a year later is quite a contrast. A *soi-disant* Cornishman, Edward John Trelawny served in the navy from the age of twelve, but resisted service discipline and left at nineteen. He has married against his family's wishes, been cuckolded and undergone a divorce that featured in the popular British press but is not, luckily for him, notorious among literary-artistic expats in Italy. He has been eking out a cheap way of life in Europe; when his father died in 1820, he found he had inherited unexpectedly little. Sympathetic as all this sounds, Trelawny is also good at economising on the truth. He styles himself a captain – which he is not – and has developed a fine line in tall stories about maritime encounters both naval and piratical. With his good looks and his gift for invention, he excels at insinuating himself into interesting company.

This is the 'expert' whom Byron, Percy and Edward Williams invite to join them in mid-January 1822, when they decide that they want to own and sail seagoing boats. It is Trelawny's friend 'Captain' Daniel Roberts who oversees the building in Genoa of both Shelley's shallow-draft go-faster vessel the *Don Juan* and Byron's altogether larger and smarter *Bolivar*. Even Mary enjoys Trelawny's company enormously. Like Alexandros Mavrokordatos, who has now been gone for six months, he is a dark-haired, rugged man of action, although when he follows Byron's lead and goes to Greece to fight, Trelawny will dislike and do his best to undermine Mavrokordatos. But that's in the future, when the piratical gentleman will give Mary a bad press too. In February 1822 the newly arrived 'kind of half Arab Englishman [who] is six feet high—raven black hair which curls thickly & shortly like a Moors' takes her to a ball thrown by Mrs Beauclerc, an active and influential English hostess living in the city, and excitement suddenly wakes in the *Journal*. For two days Mary's entries take stock of what she's feeling about her life: the shape it's taking, and what she might want from it.

Yet if they record excitement, they also record its collapse: 'Some word, some look excite the lagging blood, laughter dances in the eyes and the spirits rise proportionately high', she records on 7 February, and on the 8th, ' I feel a kind of tenderness to those […] who awaken the train and touch a chord so full of harmony and thrilling music.' But later the same day she, Jane Williams and Trelawny spend the evening together, and by the time she returns to the *Journal* her mood has changed. 'I might say, "Thy will be done," but I cannot applaud the permitter of self-denigration, though dignity and superior wisdom arise from bitter and burning ashes.' It reads like excitement in some way rebuffed; Mary never writes so fulsomely about Trelawny again. Although the sailor continues to visit, and 'amuses me as usual by the endless variety of his adventures and conversation', Mary never again mentions his looks, nor do her subsequent *Journal* entries expand with joy in the same way.

Does anything happen between them on these two February evenings? On the night of the ball Percy is away and Mary is not only escorted by Trelawny but is 'home alone' afterwards (Percy and Edward Williams are away at La Spezia). Even in confessional mode, she so codifies her record that we can't be sure what she means: is her 'overflowing mind' stirred out of 'its usual channel' simply by creative and intellectual excitement? More telling than these surviving entries is that she tears out a whole page of the *Journal* here. Trelawny is obviously an operator, and his behaviour after Percy's death will make it clear he doesn't view Mary as the Shelley who will make his reputation by association. Perhaps he gets carried away after the ball, and the next day issues some kind of retraction? We have no way of knowing – which, of course, is just how Mary would have liked it.

Still, life with Percy goes on. By early 1822 the Shelleys are looking forward to the arrival of the Leigh Hunts, for whom they've arranged and furnished an apartment on one floor of Byron's Palazzo Lanfranchi. But the couple themselves are no longer the nexus of their self-styled 'colony'. Instead the men have turned themselves into a gang. Buoyed with masculine self-image, Byron, Percy, Williams and Pietro Gamba, who is Teresa Guccioli's brother, decide to call themselves 'The Pistol Club' and go shooting outside the city walls. After Trelawny joins them and their attentions turn increasingly to sailing, they change their name to 'The Corsair Crew'. It sounds as ridiculous as a children's TV cartoon, and in the early months of 1822 their exploits read like a series of comic rehearsals for tragedy. Percy cannot swim, for all that his 'favourite taste was boating. […] On the shore of every lake or stream or sea near which he dwelt, he had a boat moored.' Trelawny clams that he doesn't even try:

> He doffed his jacket and trowsers [*sic*], kicked off his shoes and socks, and plunged in; and there he lay stretched out on the bottom like a conger eel, not making the least effort or struggle to save himself. He would have been drowned if I had not instantly fished him out.

On 24 March 1822 the Pistol Club are involved in a street brawl that seriously injures an Italian dragoon. The city's authorities banish one of Byron's servants as symbolic punishment, making Pisa altogether less comfortable for the coterie. It is all time-consuming and wearing, and Mary, who is once again pregnant, has less stamina and stomach than usual for looking after the people around her. 'A hateful day', she notes on 31 March, perhaps because she has realised she is expecting for the fifth time in seven and a half years. It's bad enough to have marital sex with a man who's clearly in love with someone else. It's altogether worse to find yourself once again facing all the resulting challenges of pregnancy and birth, especially when you no longer have faith in the child's surviving infancy.

Meanwhile, all through March and April Claire, writing from Florence, is a cat on hot bricks. She has met up with Elise, and the former nursemaid has confessed her own gossip about the Neopolitan baby. Claire declares that she's going to emigrate, demands that her friends help her kidnap her daughter Allegra, and has to be talked down from both positions. In April 1822 she comes to stay with Mary and Percy in

Pisa. She is still visiting when the shocking news arrives that Allegra has died, in a convent at Bagnacavallo, of typhus.

In fact news of the death, which occurred on the 19th or 20th, arrives on 23 April, while Claire is out of town visiting the Williamses, who have already moved for the summer around eighty kilometres up the coast to La Spezia. This makes it easier for Percy and Mary to unite in protecting her from the truth until they can get her safely away from the vicinity of Lord Byron. Claire has not ceased to feel that he abandoned his daughter by placing her with Capuchin nuns the previous spring, even though such placements are fairly customary – even aspirational – at this time, and the nuns clearly adore the little girl they call Allegrina. There is no question in the Shelleys' minds that Claire will blame Byron for her daughter's death.

To prevent a scene that can only do both Claire and themselves harm, they hastily revisit an earlier plan to move the entire 'colony' to La Spezia. Over the spring this idea became bogged down in series of failed house-hunting expeditions. Now Mary snaps up the single gloomy house, directly on the shore, which is still available to rent. It's in an isolated spot, at San Terenzo, outside Lerici; which is itself merely a village ten kilometres from the little town of La Spezia. Nor is the accommodation ideal. The old-fashioned Casa Magni is a lightly converted former monastery, and has just four habitable rooms. There's space only for the Shelleys, the Williamses and Claire, and this at a pinch. The Casa's double-storey seaside terrace hangs exposed above rocks and, at high tide, the sea. The sighing of waves fills the house continually.

The Casa belongs to the Ollandini family, who unsurprisingly prefer to live at another of their properties, the nearby Villa Marigola. The Ollandinis also own the steeply sloping wooded hillsides that surround Casa Magni, closing in on it as if threatening to push it into the water. With typical lack of any pause to reflect, the Shelley party move on 30 April to a house that is quite obviously *unheimlich* in every sense. Cheerless and uncomfortable, it is not in the least cosy. It is also death-haunted from the outset; Claire finds out about Allegra's death just two days into their stay, on 2 May.

Not to be outdone by mere bereavement, and encouraged by the gloomy physical and emotional atmosphere, Percy returns to his old trick of hallucinating ghosts. Is this manipulation? Mary's comment that he has 'often seen these figures when ill' suggests that either a tendency to the high fevers that produce hallucinations or a hypochondriac's heavy laudanum use are also possibilities. Now Percy tells Mary that he has 'had many visions lately', including 'the figure of himself which met him as he walked on the terrace & said to him—"How long do you mean to be content"': a convenient way, whether or not it's conscious, to communicate restlessness without taking responsibility for it. On 22 June he has a transparent anxiety dream about Jane and Edwards Williams 'in the most horrible condition, their bodies lacerated—their bones starting through their skin, the faces pale yet stained with blood'. In the nightmare Edward tells Percy, 'Get up, Shelley, the sea is flooding the house & it is all coming down', and so it appears to Percy, for whom the scene shifts and who suddenly believes himself to be strangling Mary.

The real Mary wakes to find him screaming in her bedroom. She tumbles out of bed and rushes for help to Jane's room – which, tellingly, is on the far side of the central 'large dining hall' next to Percy's – and here her legs give way. For Mary has been in bed for the last seven days, recovering from a near-fatal miscarriage on 16 June:

> This took place at eight in the morning. I was so ill that for seven hours I lay nearly lifeless—kept from fainting by brandy, vinegar eau de Cologne &c—at length ice was brought to our solitude [...] and by an unsparing application of it I was restored.

Much has been made of the fact that it was Percy who saved Mary's life on this occasion by forcing her to sit among ice, though it's no more than anyone would do for a stranger. What this does show, though, is the others in the group failing to act. Claire's usual energy and initiative are presumably absorbed by her own grief, but Jane and Edward simply fail to rise to the occasion, which augurs ill for their own coming emergency.

Later Mary will admit to Jane that she somehow never expected a live full-term birth: 'I wished it—I tried to figure it to myself but in vain', she writes. The dream is dead; it is no longer possible to imagine it sustaining life. Just two days after her miscarriage Percy is complaining to John Gisborne that 'whether from proximity and the continuity of domestic intercourse', Mary does not 'feel, and understand' him. As we've seen, there is something almost hyper even about Percy's charisma, and the faint suggestion of a too-fast-to-touch-the-sides mania. He can tune in brilliantly well to manipulate psychic atmospheres, and particularly the unconscious psyches of susceptible individuals; that's different from understanding the equal, human needs of others. Ironically, Mary can do the latter – but not the former: she and Percy conduct human relationships in completely opposite ways.

Still, in the suffocating, often hysterical psychic atmosphere at Casa Magni, everyone seems to be in love with the *Don Juan*. The sea beyond the terrace offers a mirage of escape. Percy takes possession of his boat on 12 May and makes a number of trips in the weeks that follow. Trelawny is impressed: 'I find she fetches whatever she looks at. In short we have now a perfect plaything for the summer.' The small open-decked vessel, just eight metres long, is the equivalent of a speedboat today. In the second half of June, after the arrival of Byron's much conspicuously larger and more sophisticated *Bolivar* (more equivalent to a luxury yacht), Percy has Captain Roberts modify his vessel, extending the bowsprit and adding a false stern to make it faster still – though possibly also less stable and harder to sail.

On 1 July, just three days after the last of these alterations and before he's had a chance to find out how the modified boat handles, Percy sails to Livorno, taking Edward Williams with him. He is en route to Pisa to see the Hunts, who have finally arrived in the city, as well as to press Byron to keep on with the *Liberal* magazine project that will fund their new life. On 8 July, after their week of meetings, an otherwise fine morning is broken by a thunderstorm. By lunchtime this has passed over, and Percy, Edward and the eighteen-year-old boat boy Charles Vivian set sail for home, despite the fact that such weather is liable to sudden changes. According to Mary's letter to Maria Gisborne:

> Roberts said, 'Stay until tomorrow to see if the weather is settled; &
> S. might have staid but Edward was in so great an anxiety to reach
> home [...]—that they sailed! S. being in one of those extravagant fits
> of good spirits in which you have sometimes seen him.

This rather sounds like self-exoneration on Captain Roberts's part. He clearly knew there was a storm brewing when, a couple of hours later, he went up on the mole to try and see how the *Don Juan* was weathering it, though in the event sea fog meant he could see nothing. There's also a feeling of Roberts trying to appease Mary by blaming Williams, yet at the same time just the ghost of a suggestion that she realises Percy would be quite imperious enough to shrug off the advice of an experienced sailor.

What happens next Mary knows as a gradual, sickening closing in of fact on hope. On 8 July the men don't arrive home as planned, but their womenfolk assume they haven't sailed because of bad weather. It's only at the end of a week of waiting, when on Friday the 12th a letter arrives from Leigh Hunt hoping the trip went well, that they realise Percy and Edward did set out as planned, and that something has gone wrong. Still pale and weak from her own brush with death a month earlier, Mary immediately joins Jane in rushing the seventy kilometres south along the coast to Pisa, a journey that takes about ten hours. 'Two poor, wild, aghast creatures', they are in search of Hunt to ask him what he knows.

Arriving at the Palazzo Lanfranchi at midnight, they rouse not Hunt, who is asleep in bed, but instead Byron and Teresa Giuccioli, who welcome them but can tell them little. Mary by this stage looks 'more like a ghost than a woman'. She and Jane double-back to Livorno, 'with sufficient hope to keep up the agitation of the spirits which was all my life', arriving at two in the morning; but they are directed to the wrong inn. At six in the morning of 13 July, having napped fully dressed where they arrived, they find Captain Roberts at The Globe Inn, and he confirms that Shelley's boat sailed into the storm on the 8th.

By nine the same morning the women are leaving Livorno. Accompanied now by Trelawny, they make their way home via Pisa and the coast. At the village of Viareggio, just north of Pisa, they hear to their horror that a water cask and a small launch, both of which sound like those on board the *Don Juan*, have been washed up just along the shoreline. But there is still hope that these were simply jettisoned and that the boat itself has been driven far off course, perhaps even to safety in Corsica. The trio make it back to the Casa Magni late that night, glimpsing, as they do so, the cruel contrast of a *festa* in the nearby village.

'And thus we waited,' Mary writes to Maria, 'Thrown about by hope and fear. […] Then the sirocco perpetually blew & the sea for ever moaned their dirge.' On Friday the 19th, after a week of this, Trelawny returns to the dreary house at San Terenzo with the news that all three bodies have been found washed up near Livorno:

> I went up the stairs and, unannounced, entered the room. I neither spoke, nor did they question me. Mrs Shelley's large grey eyes were fixed on my face. I turned away.

'All was over—all was quiet now', is how Mary describes the end of hope. 'Well all this was to be endured.'

The very next day she leaves the hated 'dungeon' at San Terenzo for the last time. Trelawny escorts the widows to Pisa along with Claire, who is notably absent from both Mary's and Trelawny's account of these tragic days, and with whom for the next two months he will conduct an affair. On 15 August Percy's and Edward's quarantined bodies, both of which have spent the last month buried in quicklime on the shore where they were found, are released to their friends to be burned on the respective spots. On the 16th, as Mary writes her account of the tragedy to Maria, Byron, Hunt and Trelawny perform 'this fearful office' for Percy at Viareggio, a ceremony immortalised – with artistic licence – in the much later painting by the French artist Louis Édouard Fournier of *The Funeral of Shelley* (1889).

As the body is already decayed even before the quicklime treatment, it cannot be a pleasant task, and Trelawny tells us that only he himself could stomach it. It is also Trelawny who tells us that the body's exposed flesh, including the face, has been eaten away at sea, so that he has to identify Percy by his clothes and by the books in his pockets:

> The tall, slight figure, the jacket, the volume of Aeschylus in one pocket, and Keats's poems in the other, doubled back, as if the reader, in the act of reading, had hastily thrust it away, were all too familiar to me to leave a doubt in my mind.

This may or may not be true, but the self-aggrandising by way of Percy has begun. If Trelawny is possibly the worst offender, he is far from alone. As we'll see in the next chapter, Percy's friends, both women and men, will prove as eager to appropriate him in death as they were in life.

Later still, in September, Roberts supervises the retrieval of the wreck, which has not capsized but has been partly stoved in, possibly by rocks, although rumours will persist for decades that it was rammed by local pirates after the money on board. Another rumour is that Percy refused to let the sails be taken in, while yet another is that he refused to be rescued. The wreck is a natural outcome of risk-taking and inexperience. But it appears mysterious to Mary and her friends. Perhaps this is because it seems to have taken place invisibly yet in plain sight in the bay's natural amphitheatre; perhaps, too, they have been infected by the uncanny, manic atmosphere in Casa Magni.

Jane takes Edward's ashes back to England with her when she departs on 17 September; Percy's are sent to the Protestant Cemetery in Rome, where Mary hopes he will keep Wilmouse company. But little William's body can't be found and eventually, in January 1823, Shelley's remains are buried by Trelawny – next to a plot he buys for himself. We now know, as Mary did not, that Trelawny's piratical way with Percy's bodily remains extends to fragments of skull, which he keeps for himself (and which are now in the New York Public Library and at the Keats–Shelley House in Rome): a kind of gruesome souvenir, half touchstone half fetish, that goes much further than the funerary custom of preserving locks of hair.

It's fairly obviously corruption – at the very least, permissive laziness – that misplaces a child's grave, especially when that child's parents are foreigners who might not be expected to come back looking for it. Of her beloved husband and little son, only Percy's heart survives to Mary for her to perform any kind of obsequy. Trelawny snatched it (or some other gristly organ that passes for it) from the pyre on the shore and gave it to Hunt, who wants to keep it. Not until he has been shamed by a letter from Jane Williams does he allow Mary this relic, which she keeps in a silk purse in her desk until her own death.

This graceless little struggle with Hunt is the shape of things to come. The sour legacy of Percy's complaints about Mary's 'coldness' is just starting to emerge. Friends have been coached to believe that Mary failed him as a wife just as she herself was coached, eight years earlier, to believe that Harriet had failed him. Yet in her grief Mary herself comes closer than ever to her myth of a perfect love shared with Percy:

He, my own beloved, the exalted & divine Shelley, has left me alone in this miserable, hateful world;—on this earth which bears grass only that it may perish again & again.

This latest bereavement follows the deaths of her three eldest children, and it cannot but reawaken a haunting sense of Mary's first loss, the death of her mother. Left unfinished on Percy's desk is his ironically titled masterpiece 'The Triumph of Life', which seems strikingly to make the same link in an image of a storm-haloed moon that 'Doth […] bear / The ghost of her dead mother, whose dim form / Bends in dark ether from her infant's chair'.

Mary is not only bereaved but also – having given up friends, family and country for her husband – acutely alone. In an era when women have almost no opportunity to earn their own keep, without her husband she faces financial ruin, or at best dependency on the whim of hostile in-laws. With her personal reputation in tatters and a child to raise, she cannot work as a governess and is unlikely to remarry. She does not even have a home of her own. Suicidal, she feels bound to survive only for the sake of little Percy Florence, now nearly three years old:

If I could get over the intense hatred I feel to every thing I think, do, or see I might get on—but day after day I long only more & more to go where all I love are save my poor boy who chains me here—

Yet the chain will prove to be her anchor.

Chapter 10

The Mona Lisa Smile

At about two o'clock the mist cleared away, and we beheld, stretched out in every direction, vast and irregular plains of ice, which seemed to have no end.

IN THE FAMOUS PORTRAIT from 1839 by Richard Rothwell, Mary wears black velvet and is seated on a divan whose sumptuous tasselled reds and gold are hinted at rather than detailed. Behind her we glimpse a dim horizon, on which a Classical column gleams and a pinkish sunset – or sunrise – seems to break across what could be a sea. It's a tasteful suggestion, though unfortunately positioned rather like a thought bubble, that her European past with Percy remains with her. There's even the suggestion of a boat silhouetted on the skyline. Mary sits ever so slightly awry, as posing women have down the centuries, and we see a generous expanse of pale, still faultless shoulder sweep down to her lace-edged dress. At forty-two, and after at least five pregnancies, she still has a tiny, sashed waist. Her hair has darkened from the strawberry blonde of her youth to a tawny brown. Her eyes are not quite green but hazel.

This is Rothwell's second portrait of Mary; she first sat for him in 1831, when he was the height of fashion. Over the years leading up to this second painting the handsome Irish artist three years her junior has become a friend.

In his picture Mary regards him, and us, directly. Her expression is one into which we could read tenderness and wisdom, yet she seems about to break into speech or laughter. It's the almost-smile of a Mona Lisa and, like Leonardo da Vinci, Rothwell has captured a particular quality of self-containment which, for all that it's often thought to be annoying, is also seductive.

Rothwell's Mary has all the conventional marks of beauty: clear skin and eyes, a high and unlined forehead, perfectly regular features. But the little down-turned V at the centre of her long upper lip makes her look as though she's about to utter some wryly intelligent, funny *aperçu*, and the slight bags beneath her eyes and the laughter lines at their corners – however much she arranges her hair to hide these – suggest she's supressing a smile. It's a portrait of mobility momentarily at rest, of feminine intelligence and of the paradoxical nature of a woman who has by now been widowed for seventeen years: more than twice the length of the marriage that continues to define her life.

It also shows us someone anchored in the world. That bare spread of shoulder has the accidental effect of suggesting that hers are metaphorically 'broad'. A woman of letters in her own right, she is also a devoted parent to Percy Florence. The Mary we last saw leading a transitory, expat life in Italy in the first days of her widowhood was impoverished, isolated and overwhelmed by grief. That was seventeen years ago, when she was just twenty-five. Now she's a person of substance, and this portrait, painted at what is in many ways the pinnacle of her worldly success, sums up the accomplishments of the intervening years. As portraits do, it both hides and reveals as it tells the story of the struggles and rewards of the sixteen years since her return to England.

Mary has worked particularly hard to see Percy Florence through Harrow School, even moving out of London to live in Harrow on the Hill itself, between 1833 and 1836, in order to save on boarding fees. But this was a sacrifice: Mary returned to town as soon as she could and now, three years on, has settled on the Upper Richmond Road in Putney. For the rest of her life she and her son will live together in guilt-free Oedipal harmony. Their intimacy will change oddly little because Percy Florence never acquires a career or children of his own – although he does eventually marry and, after his mother's death, will adopt a daughter, Bessie Florence Gibson.

Instead he devotes much of his life to following his mother as 'keeper of the flame' of his father's reputation, which sounds at first like history repeating itself. Has Mary, the daughter from whom William Godwin expected too much, similarly pressurised her son to stay close, perhaps even to take his father's place? No: the truth is that this astonishing son has inherited none of his parents' gifts and yet, rather than rebelling, he shares their respect for literary and intellectual accomplishment. Far from holding him back, the pattern of Mary's parenting is to urge him on. A letter to Sir Timothy's solicitor about the ten-year-old records the steps she takes 'to cure a stoop he was getting'. A decade later she acts as go-between for her son and Thomas Love Peacock's daughter Mary Ellen. Fondly, she jokes when he is thirteen that he is 'so fat & so big that I am quite ashamed of him'. He will grow up to be a stolid, hearty man who, portraits reveal, looks like nothing so much as a throwback to the county squire-ocracy from which his father came.

It's now, in the years of her widowhood, that Mary discovers just how inescapable that squire-ocracy is. During Percy Bysshe's lifetime it was the Godwins who filled the couple's familial horizon: partly because Claire, that fixture in their ménage, was also a member of the Godwin family; partly because Mary's father matters so much to her; and partly because the two households shared overlapping professional and intellectual interests. Percy Bysshe's father, Sir Timothy Shelley, figured as little more than a source of inherited income, someone against whose death the son bet with a series of post-obit bonds. Now that unrepaired relationship, and all the father's resentment at the way his son chose to live, are Mary's to deal with alone. Her father-in-law is out to punish the woman who 'in no small degree, as I suspect, estranged my son's mind from his family, and all his first duties in life'. In particular, he doesn't accept that she should raise Percy Florence, and sees no reason to help her do so.

Mary's widowhood is defined on 24 February 1823, when she is still in Italy. Byron – who is one of Percy's executors, with Thomas Love Peacock – forwards a letter from Sir Timothy stating that he will not support her, and will support Percy Florence only if she gives up the child. However, as she points out in the second of two responses she immediately sends Byron, the grandfather has no wish to bring the child up himself: 'He does not offer him assylum [*sic*] in his own house but a beggarly provision under the care of a stranger.' It's possibly tactless, undoubtedly ironic, that she frames her case this way. After all, Byron himself demanded custody of Allegra because he didn't think her mother (or indeed the Shelley ménage) fit to parent – only to put the child in the convent where she later died.

Sure enough, he advises her to hand the child over. Nevertheless Mary reiterates her 'Mothers solicitude'. And she makes another point: 'Besides I loose [*sic*] all—all honourable station & my name when I admit that I am not a fitting person to take care of my infant [...] the advantage to them if the will came to be contested would be too immense.' Mary's marriage, contracted to protect Percy's first two children, now protects her own child as well. He is a part of society, admittedly not yet Percy's heir (since his older half-brother, the tubercular Charles, is alive), but still the second son of the heir to a baronetcy. And Mary herself is no mere mistress but the widow of that heir.

Practised in keeping a household afloat, Mary's first response on learning that Sir Timothy has refused support is to plan where she can earn money by writing. This is the opposite of what he intends: it's a condition of the – *loaned* – annual allowance he eventually grants that he forbids her to write under the Shelley name, or to publish Percy's own life story or work. But as Sir Timothy is already in his seventieth year, it's not irrational of Mary to assume that, if she makes do for a year or two, circumstances will change, and Percy Florence's rights in his father's estate will ensure a living for her and the boy. (This becomes even more the case after 14 September 1826, when Charles Shelley is struck by lightning and dies.) Not surprisingly – given her experience of her husband's dreaminess – her main concern is, as she tells Thomas Jefferson Hogg four days after receiving Sir Timothy's ultimatum, 'what confidence I may put in the validity of his will'.

She must hope, though, that her son won't take after his grandfather: 'he is really very good and above all tractable—which is not quite the virtue of his fathers family', as she tells Sir Timothy's solicitor. The 2nd Baronet of Castle Goring, born in 1753, was nearly forty when his first son, Percy Bysshe, arrived, and he remains a provincial, mid-eighteenth-century country squire. When he came of age in 1774, in the month when Goethe published *The Sorrows of Young Werther*, it was within another world. Shakers were still emigrating to pre-independence North America, Captain James Cook had become the first European to visit Australia just four years earlier, and British and North American complicity in slavery was at its height. Never eager for progress, Sir Timothy did not complete undergraduate studies at Oxford until he was twenty-five; after a pause he entered Parliament, at thirty-seven, to represent the rotten boroughs of first Horsham and then, for sixteen years from 1802, Wareham. The portrait painted by George Romney in 1791, the year he married, shows an unusually high, moony dome of forehead, male pattern baldness, a droopy-eyed, phlegmatic expression. It is not the face of someone who would put himself out for you.

Yet Timothy is the offspring of a landowning American adventurer, and his father must have had some of the genes for charm that Percy Bysshe inherited, since he made not one but two advantageous marriages to English heiresses. Timothy's mother died when the boy was seven. As a teenager, he acquired a stepmother descended from royal courtiers. She passed on to his younger half-brother great Penshurst Place in Kent – the estate, gifted by Edward VI, where Sir Philip Sidney grew up and wrote and where Queen Elizabeth I often stayed: a rather more impressive legacy than the fragile, first-generation ennoblement Timothy himself inherits, with its new-build seaside folly Castle Goring, and the domesticated Field Place, where his own son Percy Bysshe will grow up. Small wonder that he's defensive, a probable domestic bully obsessed with propriety, whose elder son rebels and only one of whose four daughters grows up to marry. (In a double portrait painted by Sir William Ross some time in the 1850s, the surviving unmarried sisters Hellen and Margaret Shelley have an ineffectual, adenoidal air.)

Mary's wish seems to have been granted, for good and ill. Photographs of Percy Florence in his maturity show a warm, if weak, face. Laughter lines crinkle beside his eyes; his half-smile seems not so much mysterious as a polite refusal to impose. He shares his grandfather's male pattern baldness, reminding us that Percy Bysshe would quite probably, if he'd lived, have lost those signature curls. It rather looks, too, as if Percy

Florence shares Sir Timothy's gene for a literal big head. His face seems squashed on one side, as if compressed during a rapid two-hour birth that is, one feels, almost the last thing he did fast. His gaze is a touch vague and, although he sports a dapper beard, it comes as no surprise to learn that, with all the time in the world for hobbies, he becomes a gentleman yachtsman, in love with the sea like his father.

When Mary's portrait is being painted by Rothwell, Percy Florence, now aged twenty, is midway through his time at Trinity College, Cambridge, from where he manages to graduate – although Mary at one point wonders whether he needs private tutoring to help him through. She will continue to worry about her only son, who seems to have inherited his father's dreaminess without his exuberant drive to action. As late as 1843 she will write to Claire:

> with him I ought to be content; & yet from him springs so much of my discontent.—He is happy—I believe that he is utterly free from vice—he has a thousand precious virtues—he has good sense, a clear understanding a charming temper. [But]—there is no aim—no exertion—no ambition. I spent more than I ought […] introducing him to a few distinguished people whom he refuses to cultivate & when he did go into society he put on an air of stupidity anything but attractive.

In the event Sir Timothy skews all calculation on her son's behalf, leave alone her own, by living until he's ninety, testament to the rewards of a comfortable life. Mary famously describes his death on 24 April 1844 to Hogg as 'falling from the stalk like an overblown flower—free from pain—quite comfortable'. He is survived by Percy Bysshe's mother, Elizabeth, *née* Pilford, a woman who seems to have made no effort to help her son's family during Mary's struggling widowhood, though the balance of power will shift when she herself is widowed. Then Mary, accompanying Percy Florence to the family's Sussex estate, will be able to tell Claire, 'They were all immensely civil—& Lady Shelley told Percy she was sorry she did not know me before—Why then did she not?' She will be right to ask. Mary does not attract kindness; never is that more apparent than in her widowhood.

Partly this must be a question of gender. The widely held opinion that she and Percy were moral and social reprobates – based as much on florid false beliefs (Mary sleeping with Byron, Percy fathering Allegra) as on their actual cohabiting – survives his death. And it's not only polite society but also other women within the couple's own milieu who view Mary's belief in Percy's – and earlier her father's – doctrine of free love as consigning her to a pitiless 'those who live by the sword die by the sword' open season on her relationship. The 'muses' who hang round poets are by the very nature of these flirtations in competition with other women, above all poets' wives. They also tend to be resentful of those like Mary who – because they're wives, or are themselves writers, or both – refuse to play the game of romancing for the sake of it.

Nevertheless, Mary finds herself in a peculiarly unpleasant bind. She mourns the man she loved in anguished terms in letters to trusted friends, and in the privacy of her *Journal*: 'Now my heart is truly iced. […] I am a lonely, unloved thing, serious and absorbed. None care to read my sorrow.' But few believe in her grief; her husband's complaints about her cold-ness have undermined her close friendships. Percy's final letter to Maria Gisborne's husband John, for example, written just days before his death – meaning that circumstances intervened to make this angry note his last word on the subject – had complained: 'I can only feel the want of those who can feel, and understand me. […] Mary does not.'

The collapse of the friendship structures on which the couple relied begins immediately. In 1822, alone in Italy after Percy's death, Mary is most let down by those she trusts the most. Leigh Hunt, to whose needs that death could indirectly be attributed, soon manipulates her into subsidising his housing costs. At Trelawny's suggestion she goes house-hunting again and, in the middle of September 1822, finds a forty-room palazzo, Casa Negroto, at Albaro on the coast outside Genoa, to share with the Hunt family; she commits to covering more than half the costs despite the fact that she and Percy Florence will be only two out of its ten (and soon to be eleven) inhabitants. The young widow earns this money by copying for Byron and for *The Liberal*, to which she also contributes a story, 'A Tale of the Passions, or the Death of Despina'. (It is later re-published in *The Weekly Entertainer*.)

Not surprisingly, Hunt is reluctant to see such a useful housemate leave, and Mary feels pressurised to stay on in Italy until Marianne has given birth to a seventh child, on 9 June 1823. It is now nearly a year since Percy died, and in this same month Mary and Hunt have a frank exchange of views which ends in his finally understanding a little more that she is truly grieving: 'she is a torrent of fire under a Hecla snow', as he tells Vincent Novello, in a letter that eases her passage when she returns to London.

He does not, however, ease her passage by paying for it, as he had promised. By the summer of 1823 she's reduced to bargaining with him even to book her ticket. Byron, as one of Percy's executors, offers to fund her journey. But Hunt has interrupted this friendship by showing Mary letters in which 'Albe' disparages the Shelleys, so she refuses to take the money, which the peer is forced to send to Hunt in confidence. Hunt, shockingly, profits from this secrecy. He collects the money from Byron's banker in Genoa and neither passes it on to Mary nor uses it to buy her passage himself. Instead he keeps it and (as people with a bad conscience will) goes on to attack the very person he has let down, publishing a hostile portrait of *Lord Byron and His Contemporaries* in 1828.

Doubtless Hunt is desperate for money, but Byron has already financed his family's move to Florence. A similar disloyalty will characterise the writer-editor's professional dealings with Mary in years to come; he lets her down over writing the preface to her short-lived 1824 edition of Percy's *Posthumous Poems*, even though it is published by his own brother John Hunt. Byron, though, remains loyal in his dealings with Mary, and their misunderstanding is eventually smoothed over, in part by Byron's departure for the war in Greece: he entrusts her with consoling his lover Teresa Guiccioli, left behind in Italy. But by the middle of April 1824 'Albe' himself will also be dead; and Mary loses the friend best placed to treat her with emotional, professional and financial generosity. If Byron is a better friend in her hour of need than she realises, Edward John Trelawny, secret hoarder of Percy's relics and gatecrasher at his grave, is the opposite. He takes credit for paying Mary's passage home: in fact, she has borrowed some money from him, but most of her fare has been paid by Margaret Mason.

Meanwhile, back in London, Thomas Jefferson Hogg – the old friend

Mary has trusted and turned to at such intimate moments as the loss of her first child, a man with whom she shares the special complicity we retain with those who have been in love with us, the friend made at the very outset of her relationship with Percy – is becoming distant too. Hogg has always been interested in Percy Bysshe's women (before Harriet Shelley there was even Percy's literary-minded sister Elizabeth). But at the time of the poet's death 'his woman' appears, to most of those in the know, to be no longer Mary but Jane Williams. This is certainly Jane's own version, and sex quickly trumps friendship when Jane and Hogg are introduced by the Gisbornes, who have now returned permanently to England. Soon the two are close; eventually, in 1827, they will cohabit and have their first child soon after. But in 1823, swallowing wholesale Jane's stories about Mary as a cold wife, Hogg is already able – and perhaps eager, since it lets him off the hook – to call her grief 'imaginary'.

For the first and most intimate of Mary's betrayers is Jane herself, the fellow widow whose shared bereavement is such a touchstone that it takes Mary years to realise what's going on behind her back. It is Jane who poisoned Hunt against her in the weeks before she left for England. Jane arrived back in London on 17 September 1822 and ever since has been enjoying attention – from the very people to whom Mary gave her letters of introduction – as the widowed confidante of the romantically dead young poet Shelley. But she can only do so by portraying Percy's actual widow as unworthy – and keeping her absent. No wonder she repeatedly urges her to stay away in Italy, even advising her to give up Percy Florence to Sir Timothy and remain abroad alone. But she need not have worried. By the time Mary returns to England almost a year later, on 25 August 1823, having travelled alone across France with her child, the damage is done. Mary's 'Hecla snow' is widely perceived as masking no feelings, and Mary herself as deserving little sympathy.

Hogg – who should know better since he knows Mary so well – never redeems his betrayal. Even in 1857, when the adult Percy Florence asks this survivor of his father's youth to write a life of Percy, the initial volumes he produces are so negative about the poet that the Shelley family obtain an injunction preventing further instalments. It's as if the secret, probably unconscious, motivation of a hanger-on is to resent the very success to which he attaches himself.

Astonishingly, Mary doesn't discover the lies Jane has been spreading until another friend, Isabel Robinson, tells her about them directly on 13 July 1827. Mary is overwhelmed, writing in her *Journal*, 'Not for worlds would I attempt to transfer the deathly blackness of my meditations to these pages. Let no trace remain save the deep bleeding hidden wound of my lost heart.' But then, she has form in misreading the apparent friendliness of women who sabotage her behind her back; all her adult life, after all, she has alternately mistrusted and confided in Claire. An exceptional straightforwardness, even a strangely disproportionate literal-mindedness, seems to characterise her reactions.

Mary's own theory is that, because she's a writer, she lives too much in her own mind:

> one who, entirely and despotically engrossed by their own feelings, leads as it were an internal life, quite different from the outward and apparent one! Whilst my life continues its monotonous course within sterile banks, an under-current disturbs the smooth face of the waters, distorts all objects reflected in it.

This *Journal* passage of self-analysis is written in the autumn of 1822, after an evening spent with Byron 'for the first time for about a month'. Mary is deeply moved: she thinks this is because she's used to listening to Byron and Percy converse, and so feels the latter's absence the more. But a sceptical reader might mistrust this entry's typically modest self-portrait – 'incapacity and timidity always prevented my mingling in the nightly conversations of Diodati' – and seize instead on the careful note to self, 'For my feelings have no analogy either with my opinion of him, or the subject of his conversation', that follows. It's as if Mary must make sure that she has no romantic interest in Byron.

Why should this be? Highly experienced with women, Byron is good at putting them at their ease; he also genuinely respects Mary and her writing. Despite his fame, his title and his sexual notoriety – or perhaps *because* of all three: he's a man with nothing to prove, who has a real understanding of literary excellence – he is the friend who recognises that 'I am said to have a cold heart—there are feelings however so strongly implanted in my nature that to root them out life will go with it.' Usually, by contrast, there's a chasm of inexpressibility between Mary's feelings and what she shows the people around her.

Her sadness locks into depression. After Percy's death, the real-life husband who hurt her so much in their last months together is replaced by an idealised version of the poet as a soul mate 'to whom I could unveil myself, and who could understand me!' Mary's grief, so uncompromisingly whole-hearted, has at its outset a Romantic intensity. As the years go on, this will gradually ossify into a typically nineteenth-century hyperbole of mourning. Personal experience becomes difficult to separate from social expectation. Queen Victoria, widowed in 1861, will make uninflected mourning a public affair in the second half of the century. But the fetishisation surrounding bereavement is already current when Percy dies in 1822. Mourning jewellery made from the plaited hair of the deceased is usual, and there are etiquettes for behaviour, costume and the duration of mourning. Surprisingly however, black is expected from a widow for only six months: after this, she can observe a further six months of half-mourning, in subdued colours and styles. The black velvet Mary wears to sit for her Rothwell portrait, seventeen years after Percy's death, is therefore a deliberate statement not only of her grief but also of her continuing identity as Percy's widow.

A certain dogged seriousness was in any case the climate of Mary's upbringing. She missed out on whatever feminising social life her family might have been able to provide (probably not much, judging from Fanny's experience) by eloping at sixteen. She's still the girl who grew up without a mother – no teenager identifies with a bitterly disliked stepmother – and took her beloved, bookish father as role model instead; there's something about her emotional literal-mindedness that we might call geeky rather than girly. For all her pigeonholing by contemporaries as a worldly *émigrée*, part of Percy's sexually irregular ménage, Mary has is in fact less understanding of traditional gender roles than many of her peers. Like Frankenstein's creature, she's an *observer* of the connected social world, learning by conscious imitation what others seem to know by instinct.

But seriousness has its uses. Within the first three months of bereavement Mary has already decided that writing is key to her survival, not only economically but emotionally: 'Literary labours, the improvement of my mind, and the enlargement of my ideas, are the only occupations that elevate me from my lethargy.' This remains the theme of her widowhood. In December 1834 she notes: 'Routine occupation is the medicine of my mind. I write the "Lives" in the morning. I read novels and memoirs of an evening.' Late in 1838 she reflects on her literary ambitions:

> I was nursed and fed with a love of glory. To be something great and good was the precept given me by my Father: Shelley reiterated it. [...] But Shelley died, and I was alone. My Father, from age and domestic circumstances, could not 'me fair valoir.' My total friendlessness, my horror of pushing, and inability to put myself forward unless led, cherished and supported,—all this has sunk me.

So central is writing to her sense of identity that Mary's feelings of literary failure are every bit as existential as John Keats's famously self-dismissive epitaph: 'one whose name was writ in water'. Despite this, the mildly sceptical, sociable, consummate mistress of herself that we see in her portrait by Richard Rothwell *is* a successful writer. Ironically, meeting Sir Timothy's terms by publishing not under the name Shelley but as 'the author of Frankenstein' has probably helped consolidate her literary reputation. And in the years between Percy's death and the 1839 portrait she has published five substantial novels of ideas: *Valperga* has been followed in 1826 by *The Last Man* and in 1830 by *The Fortunes of Perkin Warbeck*, then by *Lodore* in 1835 and *Falkner* in 1837.

Valperga's appearance in February 1823, five days before Mary receives the news that Sir Timothy will not support her, probably helps her meet that blow with greater equanimity than would otherwise be the case. Her next novel, *The Last Man*, is a still bleaker analysis of human motivation and destiny: a three-part study of the effects of political ambition on individuals and relationships, and a dystopian vision of a pandemic that leaves its eponymous narrator alone on earth. Prized by Shelley-watchers for its – somewhat schematic – portraits of Percy (as Adrian) and Byron (Lord Raymond), it contrasts the pleasures of a like-minded intellectual community with the horror of the solitary: a parable against egomania, perhaps.

The book, which appears three years after Mary's return to London, is not a critical success, though it is reprinted later the same year and Colburn, its astute publisher, buys up what remains unsold of the second edition of *Frankenstein* – and will indeed publish Mary's next novel, *The Fortunes of Perkin Warbeck*. Reviewers complain that *The Last Man* is 'removed from nature and probability' and 'perverted and spoiled by morbid affectation […] The descriptions of the operations of the pestilence are particularly objectionable for their minuteness.' *The Literary Gazette* does the most damage, with its comment that, 'When we repeat that these volumes are the production of a female pen, and that we have not ceased to consider Mrs. Shelley as a woman and a widow, we shall have given the clue to our abstinence from remarks upon them,' since by naming Mary it provokes Sir Timothy temporarily to suspend Percy Florence's allowance.

Mary is forced to promise her editor a more commercial return to the historical novel for her next book. Sure enough, four years later *Perkin Warbeck* earns reviews that are a great deal more flattering. But her advance is halved. (The £150 she receives, at a time when labourers earn less than £1 a week and agricultural labourers no more than £1 a fortnight, means that if it had taken her the full three years to write, she would in effect have been paid a male labourer's wage.) It's a compromise, but Mary is still in the game. And the novels continue to map her working widowhood. In 1835 *Lodore* appears from Bentley's – the 'successor to Henry Colburn', as its title page points out – and gains some of the best reviews of Mary's writing life. *The Literary Gazette* now calls Mary, 'One of the most original of our modern writers. Her imagination is of the creative order; and in drawing she analyses the character—thought arising out of invention, and invention out of thought.'

This may be partly because of the fame *Frankenstein* has by now achieved. The book has been reissued, and there have already been numerous stage adaptations: Richard Brinsley Peake's over-egged and frequently revived *Presumption: or, the Fate of Frankenstein* (1823) is only the first – and that by a mere three weeks. Mary went to see this production at the English Opera House (now the Lyceum) on the Strand less than a week after her return to England and reacted with one of her bursts of girlishness, telling Hunt:

> Lo and behold! I found myself famous!—Frankenstein had prodigious success as a drama & was about to be repeated for the 23rd night [...]. The play bill amused me extremely, for in the list of dramatis personae came, ——by Mr T, Cooke; this nameless mode of naming the unameable [*sic*] is rather good. [...] The story is not well managed—but Cooke played ——'s part extremely well—his seeking as it were for support—his trying to grasp at sounds he heard [...]. I was much amused, & it appeared to excite breathlss [sic] eagerness in the audience.

Henry Milner's *Frankenstein; or, the Demon of Switzerland* opened twenty-two days later, just across the river at the Royal Coburg Theatre (now the Old Vic), on 18 August 1823. By the time Milner's (presumably rewritten) *Frankenstein; or, the Man and the Monster* appeared in 1826, there had been more than a dozen further *Frankenstein*s in melodramas and burlesques. In a rare move of practical support, Mary's father made sure she capitalised at least to a limited extent on these plagiarisms, for which she will receive not a penny in royalties, by securing an 1823 reissue of her book. The already broadening cultural presence of this 'splendid fiction of a recent romance' (as it's called on the floor of the House of Commons by future prime minister George Canning) is capped by the novel's widely sold 1831 republication.

Lodore itself, published four years after this reissue of *Frankenstein*, is another story about the tests men set for women. Lord Lodore dies in a duel and leaves his messy financial and legal affairs to be sorted out by the three women who have been dependent on him: his widow, his daughter and the daughter of one of his own childhood friends. Mary uses her trio of female leads to portray three ways of 'doing' womanhood. The widow Cornelia, estranged from her husband and daughter, is concerned with societal norms and worldliness. Her daughter Ethel is hyper-feminised in a different way; all passive obedience. And Fanny, the family friend to whom Mary gives the name of her own dead sister, sounds very like someone we know rather well by now:

> Superiority of intellect, joined to acquisitions beyond those usual even to men; and both announced with frankness, though without pretension, forms a kind of anomaly little in accord with masculine

taste. Fanny could not be the rival of women, and, therefore, all her merits were appreciated by them.

This passage, and especially the preceding sentence in which Fanny is 'more made to be loved by her own sex than by the opposite one', is taken by some readers today to mean that Fanny is 'really' a lesbian. She's just a character, of course, though she does seem the product of a certain amount of self-identification on her creator's part:

> One who feels so deeply for others, and yet is so stern a censor over herself—at once so sensitive and so rigidly conscientious—so single-minded and upright, and yet open as day to charity and affection, cannot hope to pass from youth to age unharmed. Deceit, and self-ishness, and the whole web of human passion must envelope [*sic*] her, and occasion her many sorrows; and the unworthiness of her fellow-creatures inflict infinite pain on her noble heart: still she cannot be contaminated.

Today some observers combine this portrait of Fanny as a woman alone with the closeness of Mary's affection for Jane Williams to suggest that Mary is interested in other women herself. It certainly seems unlikely that this is some slant exploration of her late sister's psyche. The character's whole way of going on – proactive, distinctive, highly intelligent – differs radically from Fanny Godwin's. Perhaps it *is* a self-portrait – offered as a brief, retrospective glance. For in the year *Lodore* is published Mary admits to Trelawny, looking back to the years that followed Shelley's death, that 'I was so ready to give myself away—& being afraid of men, I was apt to get <u>tousy-mousy</u> for women'. 'Towsy-mowsy' is nineteenth-century West Country slang for the female pudenda, and Mary's spelling rather sweetly suggests she hears in it both the Scots 'tousy' for tousled – in widespread use at the start of the century and doubtless a term she heard in her teens in Dundee – and 'mousy', which for the young woman who was once Percy's 'dormouse' probably suggests snuggling. If Mary's term is indeed West Country slang, one answer to how she knows it might be through her correspondent himself. Whether or not Trelawney was truly born in Cornwall, as he claimed, his language must have been salted by his time in the navy.

Mary's letters – by turns serious, loving, flirtatious, even very occasionally bawdy – do show a tendency to cut their language to fit their correspondents. Although there's certainly a romantic and sexual colouring to Mary's letters to Jane, it seems oddly faked up. She writes her most declarative messages in August and September 1827, when she has recently discovered Jane's betrayal but hasn't yet confronted her about it. Here she ties herself in knots in an attempt to be seductively witty:

> Except the feminine what is amiable except our pretty N— the word is too wrong I must not write it, but I shall certainly decline only haec & hoc dilecta vel dilectum Jeff. must not see this.

It's probably wasted effort. Jane is no intellect and, though she will doubtless recognise the allusion to her 'towsy-mowsy', I am not certain she will understand that the Latin declension of *pleasure* ('decline' is itself the first pun) omits the masculine form. Mary tries a similarly overworked pun on the second, sexual meaning of 'die' a month later: 'but of friendship love [...] I cannot go for it—unless it were to seek that sweet Conjunction, whom I die to see again.'

A lifelong pattern of forming close friendships with one woman at a time does look different in the light of what is probably at least a *game* of same-sex desire. In the William Ross portrait Isabella Baxter, the close friend of Mary's teenage years, bears a striking resemblance to Percy; her grandson will recall in 1911 that Isabella 'Had in her youth been exceedingly good-looking. [...] She had a very broad and finely shaped brow, and keen and sparkling eyes.' The girls carved their initials *together* in window glass at the home of David Booth; when he was widowed and asked Isabella to marry him, a whiff of implication did surround Mary. We've seen how Booth travelled to London to consult William Godwin before he proposed; Mary was abruptly recalled to London two months later, apparently when Isabella's brother fell in love with her. David soon forbade his young bride any contact with Mary – ostensibly because of her irregular relationship with Percy. If that whiff were actually a romance between Mary and Isabella, would any of this look much different? Mary Wollstonecraft had pointed out the prevalence of dormitory sex in boarding schools back in 1792; Mary attended boarding school before she went to Scotland. And – at a time when young women talk about friendship in terms of love, and it's quite usual for friends to share beds when travelling, visiting and on other special occasions – how would those around the teenagers know whether anything romantic or erotic was going on?

Just months after Isabella's marriage, Mary demonstrated how attached she was to her stepsister Claire (at the time still 'Jane') by the bizarre decision to elope with her as well as Percy. Claire, early playmate and confidante, became a problem only when she started vying for Percy's affection; Mary manages to remain very fond of her – not a favour Claire consistently returns – after Percy's death. Of course, this is partly because the balance of power between the stepsisters changes once Percy is no longer around. Mary is a published author who remains in literary London among writers and intellectuals, while Claire is forced to become a governess, first in Vienna, then in far-flung Russia (1825–8) and Dresden (from 1828), before returning as a music teacher in 1836 to London, where she stays for only five years before leaving to live with friends in Italy. But still, the fondness is conspicuous. We've speculated that Mary was sent away from home as a teenager for her *mental* health: that is, as a kind of punishment. Could she possibly have got too close to Claire?

There's no doubt that Mary and Percy's union was passionate in those early London days when the couple spent stolen Sundays in bed together. But Mary's expressions of love often focus on Percy's idealism and spirit; calling him 'sweet Elf' doesn't exactly suggest that she fell for his brute *manliness*. During their time together, she seems to join him in becoming fascinated by beautiful young women. (She describes Emilia Viviani as 'this beautiful girl […]—I think she has great talent if not genius—or if not an internal fountain how could she have acquired the mastery she has of her own language which she writes so beautifully.') This might be no more than falling in with Percy's fantasies – Mary becomes in many ways his enabler, as she accepts his ambitions, hobby-horses and *fiat*s – but might it also be something else, something odder and more collusive?

And then there's Jane Williams. At one level, Jane is simply the last of Percy's beauties; she remains in Mary's life partly because he didn't live to tire of her. But Mary doesn't tire of her either: just one letter among many in a similar tone urges her 'best girl', 'the only one I greatly love in the land of clouds', to 'love me ever & confide in the entire affection of—Mary Shelley'. Their friendship survives Jane's slanders because Mary is so eager to forgive her. Even in the first heat of accusation she writes: 'Though I was conscious that having spoken of me as you did, you could not love me, I could not easily detach myself from the atmosphere of light & beauty that for ever surrounds you.' This is more like a declaration of love than an attempt at peace-making.

Where Mary stands on the spectrum of sexual orientation may not be entirely clear even to herself: possibly it's more fluid than polarised. But we know for sure that she at least *sympathises* with same-sex partnerships. In the autumn of 1827 – while renting with friends in Sussex for a few months that she might imagine are a rehearsal for life at nearby Field Place – she helps Isabel Robinson, the friend who revealed Jane's lies and who is herself struggling with life as an unmarried mother, elope to France as the 'wife' of the writer Mary Diana Dods, who is cross-dressing as Walter Sholto Douglas. This story has an unhappy ending for Dods. She dies alone of a degenerative disease in a French debtors' prison less than three years later. But its happier outset unfolds like a sublimation at the very time when Mary feels she has 'lost' Jane Williams twice over: to a relationship with Hogg, and through her betrayals.

Willy-nilly, in daily life Mary keeps on writing – and not only novels. She has become a literary freelancer – a career embarked on even before her return to London in 1823 – and is occasionally even her father's running mate. It is William Godwin who introduces her to Henry Colburn, editor of *The New Monthly Magazine*, for which she will write regularly (he also publishes *The Last Man*). Her father also introduces Mary to the encyclopaedist Dionysius Lardner, who will make extensive use of her writing and researching talents; and she pitches a whole variety of ideas to her father's friend John Murray – who picks up none of them. She writes jobbing articles for any periodical that will take them and genre fiction for magazines, including the *London Magazine* and, at her father's direction, the annuals edited by his friend Frederic Mansel Reynolds. She also tries in her turn to secure a book contract for Godwin.

Both father and daughter sell the copyrights of their best-known works to Bentley's Standard Novels, who reissue *Caleb Williams* in 1830 and *Frankenstein* in 1831. Crucially, copyright restrictions make it a condition of republication that the books are revised. Mary's changes to her famous novel include introducing the contemporary mystery of galvanism. In 1818 it wasn't electricity but 'natural philosophy, and particularly chemistry, in the most comprehensive sense of the term', together with Frankenstein's own *Aha!* insight, that combined as the 'instruments of life' to animate his creature. Now she also takes the opportunity to play up the moral of the tale. Hubris is at the heart of her story. Indeed even the novel's framing story turns on hubris: Walton is only rescued by Frankenstein's intervention from similarly overreaching himself. Perhaps with her sense of this sharpened by events in her own life in the dozen years since the first edition – including Percy's hubristic death – she now underscores these parallels between the scientist's hubris and the explorer's.

Mary's last novel, *Falkner*, appears a couple of years before Rothwell has completed her portrait. It's a sentimental education turned inside out. The protagonist who grows up in the course of a book Elizabeth is a girl. Moreover, rather than *acquiring* emotional wisdom, Elizabeth *teaches* it – to the men in her life: her adoptive father Falkner, and her lover, whose mother he had unintentionally killed. Because it's hard to imagine such a plotline appealing to male readers, this novel has often been dismissed as a conservative, even cynical bid for mass female readership. It's used as ammunition by a line of critique that sees Mary as anti-feminist because she consented to marry Percy, and because she didn't write philosophical-political treatises about the rights of women like her mother's. In 1838 Trelawny makes a similar accusation. Typically, Mary takes this line of criticism to heart and concludes that she lacks the necessary ability:

> In the first place, with regard to 'the good cause'—the cause of the advancement of freedom and knowledge, of the rights of women, &c.—I am not a person of opinions. […] I have not argumentative powers: I see things pretty clearly, but cannot demonstrate them. Besides, I feel the counter-arguments too strongly.

She's selling herself short. In the 1830s, to write a novel like *Falkner* that explores and overturns conventions – around since Aristotle's day – about women as incapable quasi-children is to make a significant contribution towards shifting those notions. But Mary's lacerating self-criticism is nothing new. In 1835 she has written to Maria Gisborne:

> You speak of women's intellect—[…] I know that however clever I may be there is in me a vacillation, a weakness, a want of 'eagle winged resolution' that appertains to my intellect as well as my moral character.

Falkner appears in the year that Mary, having supported Percy Florence through Harrow largely by her writing, sends him off to Oxford. But the novel doesn't only mark the end of raising a son; it coincides with another shift of era. While it's still being written, on 7 April 1836, William Godwin dies. He has been ill for years with a mixture of symptoms: insomnia, cataplexy and vertigo have all mapped through their waxing and waning severity the stresses he's lived under. But that life has been long and ultimately – freed by his eventual bankruptcy in 1825 from the struggle with debt, and dignified since 1833 by a government sinecure – marked by continued reputation. Mary tells her father's old friend Mary Hays, the novelist who engineered her parents' meeting, that he:

> died without much suffering—his illness was a catarrhal fever, which his great age did not permit him to combat—[…] His thoughts wandered a great deal but not painfully—[…] His last moment was very sudden—Mrs Godwin & I were both present. He was dosing [*sic*] tranquilly, when a slight rattle called us to his side, his heart ceased to beat, & all was over.

In effect his literary executor, Mary sets about this task with her usual diligence, although she decides that she can't write his biography because of the reputational risk by association that would entail for Percy Florence.

Mary has achieved her radical aim of leading the writing life as a woman, but not without a great deal of such careful self-invention. And it's not going to get any easier. In 1837 Queen Victoria ascends to the throne. A newly conservative era of gender relations has opened, and will famously be summed up in mid-century by Coventry Patmore's long poem 'The Angel in the House'. Patmore instructs his readers:

> Man must be pleased; but him to please
> Is woman's pleasure; down the gulf

Of his condoled necessities
She casts her best, she flings herself.

And so on. The clever girls who were earlier allowed to take part in literary business – such as Leigh Hunt's sister-in-law Bess, or Mary herself – have had their day. For all Claire's criticisms of her stepsister, Mary's own literary life could be seen as the last stuttering of the revolutionary spark that her mother Mary Wollstonecraft ignited. For example, despite her early career as an editor, Mary Anne Evans will assume the male pen-name of George Eliot by the time her first novel, *Adam Bede*, appears in 1859. The Brontë sisters will choose the same strategy for their *annus mirabilis*, 1847, when *Jane Eyre, Wuthering Heights* and *Agnes Grey* all appear under male pseudonyms.

In the 1810s Jane Austen had solved this problem by publishing anonymously as 'a lady'. That privacy is simply not available to Mary, who is exposed to the prejudices of the critics and reading public of her time. Perhaps not surprisingly, then, her own most widely read work *is* anonymous. By the time of the Rothwell portrait, Mary has produced an extensive series of biographies, each several thousand words long, for *Lives of the Most Eminent Literary and Scientific Men of Italy, Spain and Portugal*, which is published in three volumes in 1835 and 1837 as part of Lardner's 61-title, 133-volume *Cabinet Cyclopaedia*. As well as being a publishing entrepreneur, Lardner is Professor of Natural Philosophy, that fashionable field, at the new University of London. He publishes the *Cyclopaedia* between 1829 and 1846; two volumes of the *Lives of the Most Eminent Literary and Scientific Men of France* to which Mary also contributes appear in 1838 and 1839. It's hard work, but it is not hackwork. Mary has taken the art of biography seriously ever since, at seventeen, she started work on a life of the Girondist J-B. Louvet de Couvrai. She has put a whole series of unsuccessful biographical proposals to John Murray and, among other occasional biographical pieces, publishes a 'Memoir' of her father for the 1830 Bentley Standard Novels reissue of *Caleb Williams*. And she believes in biography as an exploration of character.

In a *Cyclopaedia* entry from 1835, Mary reflects on best biographical practice:

It is from passages […] interspersed in his letters, that we can collect the peculiar character of the man—his difference from others—and the mechanism of being that rendered him the individual that he was. Such, Dr. Johnson remarks, is the true end of biography, and he recommends the bringing forward of minute, yet characteristic details, as essential to this style of history; to follow which precept has been the aim and desire of the writer of these pages.

A 'lady' may write novels: that's different from being the authoritative voice of encyclopaedic 'fact'. But authority *is* the masculine norm Mary aspires to. It's tough to be educated 'like a boy' by her adored father's *fiat*, and surrounded in formative years by fascinating male thinkers, yet be told that this is not for her. Besides, authority suits her. She enjoys evidence-based argument, and biography's obligation to be judicious: 'The custom of publishing biographies totally careless of the feelings wounded or privacies invaded is I think, most censurable', she will say in 1847.

This judicious tone creeps into all her writing. Mary's novels share a tendency to deliver verdicts as they go. Characters experience the usual misunderstandings, misjudgements and mysteries (from *Frankenstein*'s execution of Justine for a murder she didn't commit, to the mixed motivations of the protagonists in *The Last Man*), but the telling itself lacks the fuzzy uncertainty that evokes lived life and is so often the marker of the 'literary' – what another English woman writer, Virginia Woolf, a century from now will call 'the little blur of unconsciousness, that halo of freshness'.

In the 1820s and 1830s the novel is no longer an embryonic form. In full flower across much of Europe and North America, its contemporary exponents include Victor Hugo, Stendhal, Honoré de Balzac, Nikolai Gogol, James Fenimore Cooper, Nathaniel Hawthorne, Edgar Allan Poe, Walter Scott and Charles Dickens. The field is suddenly crowded, and with compelling narratives. But Mary's novels search not so much for the keys to character or the workings of plot as for moral facts: such as, in *Frankenstein*, the nature of hubris. Her interest in such facts is of a piece with her faith in authority, and suggests one reason it can be hard for Mary to fit in with those around her. Because she's a moral realist, she can't understand that her youthful decision to run away with Percy could be misread as self-indulgence rather than passionately held moral and political principle, and her probity consequently viewed as both rigid and hypocritical. Her *Journal* is full of longing for eventual justice: in October 1838 she notes:

> I believe we are sent here to educate ourselves, and that self-denial, and disappointment, and self-control, are a part of our education; that it is not by taking away all restraining law that our improvement is to be achieved.

But this is all part of the tremendous range, from icily furious intellectual to pint-sized blonde in a fit of the giggles, that Richard Rothwell captures the following year in his portrait of his friend. He shows us a woman capable of both intellectual 'sense' and feminine 'sensibility' (to borrow Jane Austen's distinction). And, despite all her difficulties, during her widowhood Mary does attract a number of men. Among these is Bryan Waller Procter, a minor poet but successful dramatist who together with Thomas Lovell Beddoes publishes the first edition (1824) that she edits of Percy's *Posthumous Poems*. However, the book is quickly suppressed by Sir Timothy's objections, and Procter marries a Miss Skepper in October of that year. Next, Mary is courted by the American actor-poet John Howard Payne until the moment, on 25 June 1825, when he declares himself and she gently refuses him. Then the twenty-five-year-old poet and dramatist Prosper Mérimée announces his love while Mary is still recovering from an attack of smallpox – which is, however, mild enough to leave her without permanent disfigurement. It is June 1828, and the thirty-year-old Mary has accompanied her runaways 'Mr and Mrs Douglas' to Paris, though they are eloping and she merely visiting. Mérimée too is rebuffed in a spirit of friendship, though Mary is undoubtedly flattered:

> It was rather droll to play the part of an ugly person for the first time in my life, yet it was very amusing to be told—or rather not to be told but to find out that my face was not all my fortune.

Perhaps she has no appetite for renewing the chaotic, demanding life of an artist's wife. Still, Mary would have married the Anglo-Irish aristocrat Aubrey Beauclerk. Twice she gets her hopes up, and twice has them disappointed. One of Aubrey's sisters, Gee (Georgina), is a close friend, and Mary meets the heir when he returns home from army service. The Beauclerk family are old friends from Pisa days, as well as Sussex neighbours of Sir Timothy Shelley: a telling reminder of where this former revolutionary now locates herself within the English class system. Aubrey has already had two illegitimate children, one of them by a friend of Godwin's. His affair with Mary (for so it seems to become) is therefore marked by a certain equality of experience. Mary allows herself to hope for a happy ending: 'I hope things will turn out well—<u>I trust they will</u>—that is all I know', she writes to Jane Williams – by now known as Jane Hogg – on 5 May 1833. Instead, Beauclerk suddenly proposes to a nineteen-year-old heiress.

It's a blow, and Mary, perhaps because she has dared to hope, collapses under it, succumbing to a bout of what she calls flu. Yet Beauclerk retains her friendship, and in 1839, when his young wife suddenly drowns in a pond on their Sussex estate, Mary allows herself once again to hope, as she tells her *Journal* on 27 November 1839: 'Another hope—Can I have another hope? A friendship secure helpful—enduring—a union with a generous heart—& yet a suffering one whom I may comfort & bless.' But nothing happens. Mary is already committed to an Italian trip with Percy Florence; she receives no heartfelt summons to hurry home. Beauclerk's second marriage, in December 1841, is to a Miss Rosa Matilda Robinson of Kew, a woman twenty years Mary's junior. Time rolls on, and she is no longer the prodigiously gifted youngest in the room.

After discovering that Aubrey was engaged to his first wife, Mary wrote to Claire that, 'I have arrived at my <grand> first climacteric'. She might simply mean by this that she is thirty-five, half of the traditional Biblical three score and ten: and she is. But 'the climacteric' is also the name her era gives the menopause – and to mid-life crises both male and female. Although it's likely that menopause took place earlier nearly two centuries ago, at thirty-five Mary's would be very early. Still, some evidence that it arrives within her next decade comes from a letter written in 1844 to Claire, where she seems convinced this is what's happening to her, after all, slightly younger stepsister:

I own I cannot doubt that your sufferings arise from what they call

the turn of life, & I feel sure that after a time you will get over it—
Women have often mistaken this crisis for a serious internal malady.

Despite all this, what we see in Rothwell's 1839 portrait is a figure of
substance. So what if she keeps her mouth shut to hide the rotten teeth
that, she tells Claire, she always had to have pulled until she discovered
creosote as a remedy? It's now that Mary is at last able to return, armed
with literary authority, to Percy's poems, and to create the careful critical
edition that she has long had in mind, and that will do much to build
his reputation. By 1839 that reputation is already on the ascendant; two
pirated editions currently circulating help Mary persuade Sir Timothy
that the time has come for an authorised version of the work – though
not, he insists, of the life.

In a sense, anyway, Mary agrees with her father-in-law. Percy's verse
has its best chance of success, at least in the short term, if his personal life
is forgotten and his more revolutionary critiques are glossed over. So she
has turned down all requests to write his biography. In 1829 a new edition
of the poems, published in Paris by A. and W. Galignani and introduced
by Cyrus Redding, had made some headway with Percy's reputation and
partly compensated for the speedy suppression of her own 1824 edition:
Mary discreetly supplied the Galignani brothers with useful textual and
biographical material. An equally 'innocent' 1830 edition bowdlerising *The
Beauties of Percy Bysshe Shelley*, published by Stephen Hunt, also received
her unofficial support.

So when, in April 1829, Trelawny asked her for help with biographical information for a memoir of his own life and times among the poets,
Mary refused. She was still busy trying to contain the scandal all too
effectively revived in 1824's *Journal of the Conversations of Lord Byron* by
Percy's cousin Thomas Medwin, who goes on to publish the damag-
ing six-part *Memoir of Shelley* in *The Athenaeum* in 1832, and *The Shelley
Papers* at weekly intervals thereafter. Trelawny – himself neither at risk of
losing an essential allowance, nor nurturing the long-term aim of building Percy's literary reputation, and apparently incapable of calculating
what these obligations must entail – was outraged. Mary had secretly
helped the Irish poet and writer Thomas Moore with his book on Byron.
Trelawny felt his own chance to capitalise through publication on his

famous friends was slipping away. Consumed with impotent jealousy, he threatened to disclose the help Mary had given Moore: a cruel piece of blackmail, since to do so would have condemned both her and Percy Florence to penury.

The actual *literary* work of editing Percy's largely unpublished corpus would be quite challenging enough without this testing context. Percy's handwriting is hard to read, his poems are drafted in every direction and position on the manuscript pages, and the connections between drafts and corrections are often somewhat roughly indicated – in what may effectively have been notes to self. During Percy's lifetime Mary often transcribed his drafts, but now she must do so without being able to check them with him. Her painstaking editorial proficiency is apparent even today, when skilled scholars working with twenty-first-century facilities parallel what she achieved by lamplight, with intelligence and patience, and critique the corpus she established as if she enjoyed the opportunities they do.

The Mary of the Rothwell portrait, then, knows the worst of her self-appointed task of simultaneously recouping and creating Percy's reputation. A long *Journal* entry on 12 February 1839 concludes: 'In so arduous a task others might hope for encouragement and kindness from their friends—I know mine better. I […] have wasted my heart in their love and service.' Is there an echo here of what she once felt about Percy? If so, it goes unacknowledged: 'I desire to do Shelley honour in the notes to the best of my knowledge and ability […] I am torn to pieces by memory.' Mary's friends may compete for posthumous possession of the man, but it is she who must make sense of the work.

The same fractious entry records Mary's responses to the little explosions of outrage to which Percy's friends subject her over *Queen Mab*. First, Trelawney sends back his copy of Volume I of her *The Poetical Works of Percy Bysshe Shelley* (the following three volumes are published later in the spring of 1839) because it omits this poem's political passages – the only way to protect the publisher from prosecution. Then:

> Hogg has written me an insulting letter because I left out the dedication to Harriet. […] Little does Jefferson, how little does anyone, know me! […] Shelley expressed great pleasure that these verses

were omitted [in an 1821 pirated edition]. This recollection caused me to do the same. It was to do him honour. What could it be to me? There are other verses I should well like to obliterate for ever, but they will be printed.

'They will be printed' indeed. Mary's complete edition, with the often biographical explicatory notes through which she cannily circumvents Sir Timothy's interdiction on biography and also keeps the poems themselves foremost in the reader's mind, appears from Edward Moxon, 'edited by Mrs Shelley'. The next year the same publishers issue a handy single-volume edition, with a new postscript. The season of Percy's posterity has begun; Mary's has not quite – yet.

Coda

… borne away by the waves, and lost in darkness and distance.

IN 1834 MARY HAD CALLED her imagination 'my Kubla Khan, "my pleasure dome"' and claimed that though 'occasionally pushed aside by misery […] at the first opportunity her beaming face peeped in and the weight of deadly woe was lightened.' But in her final decade something happens. After 1838 she publishes no more fiction, and after 1844 nothing at all. The tremendous literary productivity of her twenties and thirties slows to a trickle and then stops.

So what has gone wrong – or right? If we track Mary down during these years, we find her not shivering in the guest room of a Swiss *auberge*, or camping in rented rooms above a Bath storefront, but relaxing in a country house of which she is *de facto* mistress. Human in scale despite its formality and antiquity, Field Place overlooks its own rolling estate just outside Horsham in Sussex. Its long, low sixteenth-century frontage is backed by the oak-framed medieval wing of the original house. It's furnished with heavy oak panelling and a series of over-the-top seventeenth- and eighteenth-century fireplaces, and has a library ironically more noted for its fancy stuccowork than for its books.

Mary must laugh when she discovers this, as she presumably does on that first visit, in June 1844, made at the invitation of her newly widowed mother-in-law. She certainly doesn't fall for the house at first sight, telling Claire, in a letter written immediately on her return, that 'Field Place itself is desperate—it is so dully placed—& so dull a house in every way. [...] it would avail little whether I had 300 or 3,000 a year if I am to vegetate in absolute solitude.'

One of the English class system's cruelties is that on Sir Timothy's death the estate passes to the male heir, and his widow and unmarried daughters (though well provided for: he leaves them his entire personal fortune) must move out of their home. Mary has no reason to be fond of the family, but she's in no hurry to seize the house either. Instead, eager not to 'vegetate', in March 1846 she buys a smart London address at newly built 24 Chester Square in Belgravia, a garden square of stuccoed terraces designed by the distinguished architect Thomas Cubitt. Field Place is, after some delays, rented out; it will remain so until 1848, when Percy Florence finally marries.

His bride is Jane Gibson St John. A young widow, she was originally Mary's friend, made through mutual London acquaintances. Her short first marriage (her husband died in 1844, at the age of thirty-six) was childless, as her marriage to Percy will also prove to be. The reason for this is said to be ill health, yet she will live until 1899. Perhaps it's more intentional than Mary realises. Maternity doesn't tempt everyone. Jane is one of nine illegitimate children of a banker, Thomas Gibson, and a certain Ann Shevill, whom he never marries; she must have grown up seeing her mother trapped by these pregnancies in relationship limbo, a position of social and emotional uncertainty and powerlessness.

Jane herself has plenty of common sense and the capacity to be decisive. Like others in this story (Mary Jane Godwin chief among them, though Harriet Shelley was also the daughter of a coffee-shop proprietor and pub landlord who married up), she makes a giant leap through the social ranks when she marries, since her first husband is also a hereditary peer. Such social mobility requires not only a pretty face but a steady will, and indeed in her decades as keeper of the Percy Bysshe flame Jane will prove herself both doggedly determined and strategically creative, as she builds a marketable public identity for the poet.

Mary is an enthusiastically welcoming, though possibly not perceptive, mother-in-law, describing Jane in quite other terms as:

so affectionate so so gentle with a thousand other good qualities—she looks what she is all goodness & truth. She has no taste for society & will thus participate in Percy's taste for a domestic quiet life.

She joins her son and his new bride at Field Place and thus, for the last three years of her life, returns to a kind of beginning. Her own parents, both her half-siblings and even her stepmother are dead, and her step-sibling Claire is living in Europe and, latterly, refusing to speak to her. But here Mary is, living in the house where Percy Bysshe was born. Her life has traced an extraordinary, unexpected trajectory from her own birth with its attendant tragedy, through struggle, risk and adventure to arrive at the starting-point of his: as if this symmetry were inevitable all along, and everything that has happened in that last half-century could be folded back neatly into the Sussex countryside and the landowning life from which her husband came.

That's a deeply conservative fantasy, of course, and Mary herself is not so reactionary. But her attitude to Field Place has changed. Since Sir Timothy's death she has been overwhelmed by financial administration. The estate is no longer worth as much as she'd hoped. Percy Florence inherits both his father's borrowing against it and the substantial legacies made in his will, and must also pay back his own loaned allowance from Sir Timothy. The estate must further provide for his father's mother and two unmarried sisters. Percy Florence has no head for business and, although Mary's tone when she mentions this is protective, the result is that she has to take on the work of organising how the money will be invested, the debts paid and an income provided for various needy acquaintances, such as the Hunts. In late 1844 her letters to Claire about the 'burthened estate' makes depressing reading:

> We have to pay nearly 2000 interest on the mortgage to pay off legacies, younger children fortune & debt to Sir Tim—& when you add to this that our income is derived from rents—frequently in arrear—paid at uncertain periods [...]—All dreams of being a good landlord & taking care of ones tenants vanish.

Mary is too tactful to mention Claire's own legacies – her own and the one designed for Allegra – each of £6,000, a sum equivalent to over half a million pounds in 2017. The result of all these demands is that Mary and Percy Florence have to 'borrow £50,000 and pay it all away'.

Claire havers for months over what to do with her money, full of suspicion about Mary's disinterestedness yet refusing her repeated urging to come to London and deal with the matter in person. In letter after letter, for over a year after Sir Timothy's death, Mary relays options outlined by lawyers, bankers and friends. Just because she has the good sense to do this does not mean she finds it any less tedious than would her stepsister or indeed her son, neither of whom, it seems, can quite be bothered to concentrate on their own financial security. Still, Percy Florence at least is not entirely oblivious: long-stored-up resentment against Claire's legacy will find expression in the 1870s, when he refuses to buy her Shelley papers on the grounds that anything of interest should already have been shared with his mother and that 'Miss Clairmont being a stranger in the Shelley family received £12000 from money raised upon the Shelley estates [...] I think the sum above named ought to have satisfied the lady.'

But by 1844 stability has become of overarching importance to Mary. She describes Percy Florence, with his steady good cheer, as 'the sheet anchor of my life.' And financial security is as important as the emotional kind – indeed, it is itself an emotional matter. About money worries her language has become loaded. In 1843 she's already telling Claire, 'I am going to economize à l'outrance—but the expences [sic] of a house are so heavy I am terrified.' 'You told me not to be frightened about the valuation for the farm but I was & am frightened', she writes to John Gregson – latterly her father-in-law's lawyer, who has continued to act for the Shelley estate in the summer of 1848 – about the farm at Field Place. And to Claire, 'Percy takes the farm into his own hands—& God send he attends to it & will not lose It costs us immensely to get the house & farm into our hands more than £2,000—We have not that nearly on hand and where we are to get it I don't know.'

Perhaps this anxiety has developed Mary's concurrent political quietism. This is the Year of Revolutions that sweep across Europe and on into Latin America, carrying with them ideas about democracy, equality, nationhood and the end of absolute monarchy that are the tenets of her own radical youth. Yet Mary's response, when she anatomises the consequences for the writer George Sand, who is her near-contemporary but who lives in France, is unsympathetic: 'No doubt she lost by the Revolution—all <u>Artistes</u> must—And how can she expect the preaching of Equality to excite any thing but dislike of the preacher who thus arrogates superiority in Wisdom', she tells Claire. It's a glimpse into the mind of someone who's paid too high a price for revolutionary ideals herself; and the notion of arrogated superiority resonates with that long stock we saw Mary take, back in October 1838, of her own failure to become a campaigning writer.

Then she called the 'radicals' who were no longer her friends:

> violent without any sense of Justice—selfish in the extreme—talking without knowledge—rude, envious and insolent.

Whatever the success portrayed by Richard Rothwell in 1839 – whatever her achievement in creating a home and a future for Percy Florence – the lack of support has, finally, brutalised Mary. Modern research tells us that post-traumatic stress is particularly associated with poor cardiovascular health in women; it also tells us that general stress is associated not only with depression and anxiety – both of which Mary suffers – but also with hypertension, depressed immune response and metabolic dysfunction. It's as if all we need to do is wait for Mary to become ill. Sure enough, from 1840 she begins to develop terrible headaches, dizzy spells and 'neuralgia of the spine', the kind of excruciating nerve pain that accompanies back injury. For the just over a decade of life that remains to her, she will be increasingly unwell.

The brilliant teenaged mind that taught itself Ancient Greek from scratch and expected to match the fluency of an Eton-educated Oxford undergraduate; the young woman who studied Italian and translated Renaissance Italian literature; the avid reader, with her annual lists of improving works studied; the novelist and writer brimming with creative ideas: by the mid-1840s this person has all but disappeared. Mary has been ground down by the feckless Shelley gene. Percy Florence appreciates and remains loyal to her – perversely not breaking free into sexual adventure as his father did – even while he cannot bring himself to step up to the plate and manage their joint life. Yet he still contrives to restrict her access to the one pleasure she mentions repeatedly. Mary longs to travel, and especially to return to Italy. In a *Journal* entry of 26 October 1824 she has written, 'Beloved Italy! You are my country, my hope, my heaven!' But in these early days of her widowhood she remained in England for the sake of Percy Florence's education, and as a condition of Sir Timothy's allowance.

Yet as a young man her son remains a reluctant traveller, although – like the mother of some sulky teenager today – she brings his friends along for company. Typically, these young men batten on to Mary for practical or emotional support and advantage. Particularly costly, both financially and emotionally, are Alexander Knox and Ferdinando Gatteschi. Their stories interweave. Knox is a young aspiring poet who has recently come down from Cambridge without a degree – despite holding a scholarship at Trinity College – because of ill health. Mary believes he has a weak heart, though his afterlife will be robust: he becomes a *Times* leader writer and a London magistrate, retiring at sixty but remaining a public figure until his death at the age of eighty-two. Mary, however, makes him her responsibility. At first this is a simple matter of taking him along on her second European trip with Percy Florence, in 1842–3. He's a suitable friend for her son – on whom, perhaps, she hopes some of his more poetic qualities may rub off. Naturally, this means contributing to his travel costs. Once abroad, however, Knox shows himself slightly less able to rustle up sophisticated company than Mary had hoped. Only his equally young and needy pal Henry Hugh Pearson appears. Having charmed her by setting some of Percy Bysshe's poems – and one of her own – to music, Pearson becomes another of Mary's dependants; he is often unwell, and too young to be very socially brilliant.

But Mary is used to living collectively, and to being loyal to her circle. She's particularly used to carrying the social and financial can for arty young men. She has spent years being told by Percy Bysshe that such commitments are purely political, rather than sexual, in nature; her emotional literalism has combined with self-protection to take him at his word. Very soon Mary's conspicuous care for Knox's future is causing friends to joke that the two are having an affair. Claire goes so far as to believe this, especially when Mary confides that she has given the young man £100. (Claire's fury, of course, suggests that, in her own experience, such care – of which she received so much from Percy Bysshe – *is* indeed romantic rather than political in origin.)

A parallel situation develops with Gatteschi, another young and penniless aspiring writer, this time an Italian living in Paris and involved with the Young Italy movement for a unified national republic. Mary meets Paris-based members of the La Giovine Italia movement when, at the end of the fourteen-month-long European trip with Knox and Percy Florence, she spends August 1843 in the city with Claire. La Giovine Italia is a cause that's bound to be close to Mary's pro-Italian heart. She is sympathetic, affectionate and supportive to Gatteschi, and full of plans to find him financial aid. To this end she commissions him to produce an account of 1831's Italian uprisings, hoping to find it a publisher. In the end – it takes him two months to produce – she uses it in her own *Rambles in Germany and Italy in 1840, 1842 and 1843*, the book she plans with her publisher Edward Moxon on her return to London in September 1843, and which is published by August 1844. The project is purely instrumental. As she tells Claire:

> It is true I am writing—there are certain things I could not manage without it—[…] yet I am sorry so to do—I earnestly wished never again to publish—but one must fulfil one's fate.

In the meantime, Mary gets involved in trying to help two of the La Giovine Italia circle to sell a picture of doubtful provenance to the National Gallery. Luckily – since it may well be a fake – this attempt is unsuccessful.

However two years later, in September 1845, Gatteschi has a better money-raising idea. He blackmails Mary, claiming that she's written him love-letters. She is forced to resort to Knox to help her out; possibly he does so precisely because he is in a position to know that Mary's help and friendship for young men such as himself is disinterested, another aspect of her straightforwardness. Rather cleverly, Knox gets the French police involved in the revolutionary affairs of the La Giovine Italia circle, and they raid Gatteschi and an associate. But the affair costs Mary £250 in fees and expenses.

Not all these scrapes are a result of Mary's trusting nature. Only a little less expensive is another fraudster, this time a 'Major George Byron', who passes himself off as the son of Lord Byron. Less than a month after the Gatteschi blackmail has been resolved, 'Major Byron' approaches Thomas Hookham – publisher, bookseller and lending librarian – with forgeries copied from Mary and Percy's early love-letters. Such letters themselves are all too real, and could include those lost when Mary's box went missing in Paris in 1814. By their dates alone they could militate against the image of Percy that, thanks to Mary's patience, is finally being constructed: an image not of the free-living atheist but of a respectable and sensitive lyric poet. Mary ends up buying some of George Byron's copies, but at the lowest price she can negotiate; eventually, in the autumn of the following year, she refuses to do even this. She also refuses Thomas Medwin when, in 1846, he attempts to blackmail her to the tune of the £250 that he claims he's being paid for a biography that will reveal Percy's atheism as well as detailing his private life. With poetic justice it's his greed that makes this scam come unstuck: Mary knows that no publisher would pay such an advance.

Her final decade has opened with her edition of Percy Bysshe's prose, prepared to accompany the 1839 edition of his verse. *Essays, Letters from Abroad, Translations and Fragments* is published, again by Edward Moxon, in two volumes in 1840 and 1841. Apart from the 1844 *Rambles*, it is Mary's last book. Both works are reasonably well received, in the context of a climate of critical opinion in which she is now seen as having 'high rank in the aristocracy of genius, as the daughter of Godwin and Mary Wollstonecraft, and the widow of Shelley'. However, *The Observer* carps that a woman should not be writing about politics in the *Rambles*, and *The Spectator* that, while Percy's prose is good, her selection of it presents 'the weakest and most defective parts' of his oeuvre.

Does Mary notice, in that, in the seven years that follow, she no longer makes time for literary work? Surely she does. Her surviving correspondence reveals a slip into domestic and financial concerns, and a preoccupation with health scares and with births, marriages and deaths, which suggests nothing so much as an end to intellectual and creative stamina. But she's conscientious to the last: her final surviving letter, dated 15

November 1850, is a request that the Royal Literary Fund support her old friend Isabella Baxter Booth, back in contact after the death of her domineering husband. So she will be aware that the practical foreground, always nibbling at her time and energy, has grown up to occlude imaginative and philosophical thought.

Her poor physical health will not have helped. By the start of 1851 it's obvious that Mary, who is staying at her London house in Chester Square, is gravely ill. On 23 January she falls into a coma; nine days later, on 1 February, she dies of 'Disease of the Brain Supposed Tumour in the left hemisphere of long standing'. She had wanted to be buried with her parents in St Pancras Churchyard; instead, they are reinterred alongside her in the churchyard of the fashionable new parish church of St Peter's, Bournemouth. When the residue of Percy Bysshe's heart is found in Mary's desk, the grave is reopened and it is buried with her.

The new family vault is close to her son and daughter-in-law's freshly completed home, fashionably near the sea, at Boscombe Manor. In 1889 and 1899, respectively, Percy Florence and Lady Jane will join her there. It's a gathering-in that is both cosy and tendentious: it signally ignores Godwin's second wife, Mary Jane, and Mary's various step- and half-sisters, Percy Bysshe's lovers and even Percy Florence's own siblings: Mary's lost children remain anonymously buried in London and Italy. Still, this is a kind of domestic canon-building, in which filial and romantic love are at last integrated. As such, it's a monument to Mary Shelley's foundation myth. In death she is confirmed as the daughter and heir of Mary Wollstonecraft and William Godwin, and the wife of Percy Bysshe Shelley: 'high rank in the aristocracy of genius' indeed.

Today, traffic passes close to the family grave. Just like St Pancras Old Churchyard, from which Percy Florence and Lady Jane have 'rescued' Mary and her parents, St Peter's Churchyard has become urbanised. It is locked inside the town's through-way system and overlooked by a department store and, in 2017, by a chain pub named The Mary Shelley. Close by, the Victorian Lower Gardens descend their leisurely chine to the seafront, with its long rows of beach huts and usual municipal paraphernalia: Bournemouth is not Rome, for all its ubiquitous pines. In 1851 the Bourne Mouth where Mary is buried is a provincial spot, without the railway, pier and sanatorium that will prove key to the resort's rapid expansion just a couple of decades later. It's a most unlikely resting place for this uniquely self-made writer, traveller, conscientious social revolutionary and loyal romantic: the larger-than-life, paradoxical figure who is Mary Shelley.

We can imagine her own wry, half-smiling reaction at such an end to her story. But of course it is not the end. This book is about what made Mary into herself. The eventual unravelling of the young woman who could write *Frankenstein*, and of the fiercely proud, exceptional writer she grew up to be, is a different story. Mary's last years as a member of the country gentry balanced greater emotional security than she had ever known with wracking physical pain and the end of the literary career for which she had believed she was destined. She lived them in a domestic triangle that, though certainly not odd by the conventions of her day, was conspicuously a benign reworking of the one that configured her young life with Percy. Happiness is not always found exactly where we look for it. Mary's adaptation to this new normalcy, her surrender of the exceptional in favour of domestic comfort and the hope of a cure for pain and other neurological symptoms, is a search for self conducted along completely different lines from the ones she followed for the first decades of her life.

Mary may have felt this gainsaid, or even betrayed, her earlier selves, but that would not be true. Adaptation is a mark of a survivor's intelligence, and she was a great survivor. Out of material we would most of us find overwhelming she created an astonishing life. Despite being born a girl and motherless in her particular time and place, and despite being almost crushed by the 'great men' around her, she produced, while still only a teenager, the novel that uniquely sums up the restless, experimental spirit of her Romantic times. She changed the face of fiction; she has challenged every 'modern' generation since she wrote her first novel to explore both empirical science and moral philosophy; and in the hubristic researcher Frankenstein and his creature, the nearly human of our nightmares, she created two enduring archetypes.

Above all, she forced open the space for herself in which to write; and it is on the page's white spaces, its 'vast and irregular plains of ice', that we do best to pursue her. At the end of her most famous book, Frankenstein lies in Walton's cabin recuperating from the journey he has made tracking his own creature through Central Europe to the Mediterranean, the Black Sea, 'the wilds of Tartary and Russia' and up into the frozen Arctic Ocean. 'The snows descended on my head', the man of science tells the explorer, and us, 'and I saw the print of his huge step on the white plain.' Mary's print is huge too: huge for writing women, for the always emerging, always creative, scientific imagination and for the dreams and nightmares of the Western world.

Notes

Introduction

p. 1   Directed by James Whale, the 1931 film of *Frankenstein* was written by John L. Balderston, Francis Edward Faragoh and Garrett Fort.

p. 2   Universal Studios' *Frankenstein Meets the Wolf Man* (5 March 1943) starred Béla Lugosi as Frankenstein's Monster. In *Abbott and Costello Meet Frankenstein* (15 June 1948) the comedy duo meet Glenn Strange as the Monster and Béla Lugosi as Count Dracula. Hammer Film Productions' *Frankenstein Created Woman* (15 March 1967) and *Frankenstein and the Monster from Hell* (2 May 1974) both starred Peter Cushing as Baron Frankenstein.

p. 2   The entire Hammer Horror series took off from a Universal sequel, *Son of Frankenstein*.

p. 2   Mel Brooks's 1974 spoof *Young Frankenstein* gets so close to the material it parodies that it even uses props from the 'straight' 1931 film for its lab scene.

p. 3   Mary Shelley, *Frankenstein*, Chapter V.

pp. 5–6   *Frankenstein*, Chapter XXIV.

1: The Instruments of Life

p. 11   Epigraph *Frankenstein*, Chapter IV.

p. 11   On p. 722 of *The Gentleman's Magazine*, Vol. 82 (September 1797), in 'Meteorological Diaries for August and September, 1797', 'W. Cary, Optician, No. 182, near Norfolk-Street, Strand', records the London weather on 30 August as 'showery', with a temperature at 11 p.m. of 60° F, down from a noon high of 68° F. https://books.google.co.uk/books?id=lQ_QAAAAMAAJ&pg=PA722&dq=gentleman%27s+magazine+september+1

797+weather&hl=en&sa=X&ei=OorYVKXhJMXPaJKkgOgK&ved=0CC
IQ6AEwAA#v=onepage&q=gentleman's%20magazine%20september%20
1797%20weather&f=false [retrieved 9 May 2015].

p. 11   In the northern hemisphere the moon on 30 August 1797 was gibbous,
waxing one day past its first quarter. http://www.rodurago.net/en/index.
php?month=8&year=1797&geodata=51.31%2C-0.05%2C0&site=details&lin
k=calendar [retrieved 9 May 2015].

p. 11   In Rembrandt van Rijn's *Joseph's Dream* the Holy Family doze in angelic
light; in his *Holy Family* of 1640, daylight floods the nursing mother.

p. 12   Charles Cocks is the second First Baron. The first, John Somers, was made
a life peer in 1697. Charles Cocks, his great-nephew, is made First Baron
Somers of Evesham in 1784, the year in which he ceases to be an MP. To
make doubly sure, Leroux also calls one block Evesham Buildings.

p. 12   These facts about the consumption of tea and coffee come from Arnold
Palmer, *Moveable Feasts* (London: Oxford University Press, 1953), pp. 12
and 98. Legislation against the reuse of tea-leaves is discussed in Dorothy
Hartley, *Food in England* (London: Macdonald & Co., 1962), p. 573.

p. 13   The Bank Restriction Act 1797 relieved the Bank of England from the
obligation to pay 'the bearer' in gold: from 1793 government overprinting
to pay for the Napoleonic Wars meant that there were more notes in
circulation than the Bank had gold to back, so currency depreciated.

p. 13   The details of the Somers Town estate and its sale are taken from the
notice of sale by Jacob Leroux's executors, published just five weeks after
his will has been proved. Their list also includes '10 very desirable houses
in the Polygon, 11 houses in Charlton-street, 6 houses unfinished in Upper
Evesham Buildings and Phoenix-street, and 14 foundations of Houses in
the Polygon, built up to the ground floor'. *The Times* (15 June 1797), p. 4,
col. 4.

p. 13   The lease-holder of number 29, Miss Leonora Knapp, is an absentee
landlord who lives in Kentish Town.

p. 13   Leroux's mother's name comes from the parish registers of St Paul's,
Covent Garden, where Leroux is listed under Baptisms for 8 January 1738.

p. 13   Estimates of 50,000 immigrant Huguenots include Walloons immigrating
from the Low Countries.

p. 14   William Godwin, *An Enquiry Concerning Political Justice, and Its Influence
on General Virtue and Happiness* (London. G. G. J. Robinson and J.
Robinson, 1793), Book 2, Chapter 2, Appendix 1, p. 93. http://knarf.english.
upenn.edu/Godwin/pj22.html [retrieved 4 February 2017].

p. 14   The phrase 'mediocre respectability' is applied to Somers Town in J. Norris
Brewer, *London and Middlesex; or, An Historical, Commercial and Descriptive
Survey of the Metropolis of Great-Britain: including Sketches of its Environs
and a Topographical Account of the Most Remarkable Places in the above
County* (Illustrated with Engravings), vol. X, (London: J. Harris, Longman
and Co., 1816), p. 185.

p. 14   For the size of the Bow Street force in 1797, see A. Babington, *A House in Bow Street: Crime and the Magistracy, London, 1740–1881* (London: Macdonald and Co., 1969), p. 176.

p. 15   Parts of Jacob Leroux's contract with his builder for the Polygon appear in 'Somers Town' in Walter H. Godfrey and W. McB. Marcham (eds), *Survey of London*, Volume 24, *The Parish of St Pancras, Part 4: King's Cross Neighbourhood* (London: London County Council, 1952), pp. 118–23. http://www.british-history.ac.uk/survey-london/vol24/pt4/ [retrieved 10 February 2015].

p. 15   William Godwin's dismissal of the possible psychic complexities of his stepdaughter Fanny is widely quoted: for example, in Don Locke, *A Fantasy of Reason: The Life and Thought of William Godwin* (London: Routledge & Kegan Paul, 1980), p. 219.

p. 15   For a summary of the weather in summer 1797, see H. H. Lamb, *Climate, History and the Modern World* (London: Methuen, 1982).

p. 16   The poor life expectancy of children in workhouses had prompted the establishment of the Foundling Hospital, whose first admissions were in 1741. But even the Hospital, despite a brief period of 'general reception' in the mid-eighteenth century, when it was expected to accept all comers from anywhere in the country, didn't have places for all the abandoned children of London.

p. 16   Mary Wollstonecraft, *A Vindication of the Rights of Woman*, Chapter 3.

p. 16   Godwin's em dashes are sometimes accompanied by preceding commas and succeeding full stops, which one can only hope aren't an elaboration of the code but a natural cursive.

p. 16   Thomas Stretzer's *A New Description of Merryland Containing a Topographical, Geographical, and Natural History of That Country* had entered a fourth edition in 1741. The free-thinker Richard Carlile, in his 1826 publication *Every Woman's Book, or What is Love?*, was not inventing but advocating existing techniques when he discussed the sponge, the 'glove' (condom), withdrawal and *coitus interfemora*. A book published four years earlier and similarly advocating birth control, Francis Place's *Illustrations and Proofs of the Principle of Population* (1822) was, ironically, a response to William Godwin's own *The Enquirer*, published a month before his wife's death from childbirth.

p. 17   The Polygon appears among fields on 'CARY's New and Accurate Plan of LONDON and WESTMINSTER the Borough of Southwark and parts Adjacent: viz. Kensington, Chelsea, Islington, Hackney, Walworth, Newington &c.', published by John Cary, The Strand, 1 January 1795. http://mapco.net/cary1795/cary.htm [retrieved 9 February 2015].

p. 18   In 2013 the maternal death rate in developing countries was 2.3 for every thousand live births; a high number of pregnancies means women in these countries have a lifetime risk of 1 in 160 of dying as a result of pregnancy. According to L. Say et al., 2014, 'Global causes of maternal death: a WHO systematic analysis', *The Lancet* (2014), 11 per cent of these deaths are due, like Mary Wollstonecraft's, to infection. WHO Fact Sheet no. 348, updated May 2014. http://www.who.int/mediacentre/factsheets/fs348/en/ [retrieved 9 February 2015].

Because maternal mortality wasn't registered by the Registrar General's office until the Births and Deaths Registration Act of 1836, the national average of 7.3 maternal deaths per thousand live births is an estimate by R. Schofield, 'Did Mothers Really Die?', in L. Bonfield, R. Smith and K. Wrightson (eds), *Histories of Population and Social Structure* (Oxford: Blackwell, 1986), cited in *Journal of the Royal Society of Medicine*, Vol. 99/11 (2006), pp. 559–63.

In London death rates come down to 7.8 deaths per thousand live births in the 1790s. Estimates, based on the Bills of Mortality, by Robert Woods, 'Mortality in Eighteenth-Century London: A New Look At The Bills', *Local Population Studies*, no. 77 (autumn 2006). http://www.localpopulationstudies.org.uk/pdf/lps77/article_1_woods_pp12-23.pdf [retrieved 9 November 2017].

p. 18   Mary Wollstonecraft's optimistic take on the rigours of childbirth comes from William Godwin's memoir of his wife. William Godwin, *Memoirs of the Author of A Vindication of the Rights of Woman* (London: Joseph Johnson, 1798), p. 62.

p. 19   'Manfully' is how Mary Wollstonecraft describes the days-old Fanny, on 20 May 1794 to a friend, Ruth Barlow, using knowing italics: 'My little Girl begins to suck so *manfully* that her father reckons saucily on her writing the second part of the R-ts of Woman'. Four months later, in a letter to the child's father on 22 September, Fanny has become 'our little Hercules'. Quoted in Leanne Maunu, *Women Writing the Nation: National Identity, Female Community, and the British-French Connection, 1770–1820* (Lewisburg, PA: Bucknell University Press, 2007), p. 165.

p. 19   Godwin's discussion of his wife's decision-making about the management of the birth comes from *Memoirs* (p. 62).

p. 20   Godwin's version of the events of that night can be found in *Memoirs* (pp. 62–3).

p. 20   Donald H. Reiman notes that Poignand is not listed as either Dr (MD) or Mr (surgeon) in *The Court and City Register* for 1793. Donald H. Reiman, *Shelley and His Circle 1773–1822*, Vol. 8 (Cambridge, MA: Harvard University Press, 1986), p. 189. But one reason for this might be that Poignand had qualified in France. Reiman also records that he is listed as MD in *The Roll of the Royal College of Physicians of London* (William Munk (ed.), *The Roll of the Royal College of Physicians*, Vol. 2, 2nd edn (London: Royal College of Physicians, 1878), pp. 312 and 315, and as both MD and Dr in *The Court and City Register 1807* (Farmington Hills, MI: Gale ECCO Print, 2010), p. 285. This being so, he may well have seemed like the best man for the job.

p. 21   The 'period full of peril and alarm' appears in *Memoirs* (p. 63).

p. 21   The shaking bed is in *Memoirs* (p. 63).

p. 21   Gordon's self-indictment is taken from Alexander Gordon, *A Treatise on the Epidemic Puerperal Fever of Aberdeen* (London: G. G. and J. Robinson, 1795), p. 64.

p. 22   Gordon describes the symptoms of puerperal fever in *Treatise* (pp. 11–12).

p. 22   Godwin's description of his wife's incapacity is from *Memoirs* (pp. 65, 67).

p. 22   Godwin's diary entries for these days can be found at: http://godwindiary. bodleian.ox.ac.uk/folio/e.203_0026r [retrieved 10 February 2015].

p. 23   Godwin's account of Mary Wollstonecraft's last illness is taken from his *Memoirs* (pp. 65, 72, 62, 67 respectively).

p. 23   MS Abinger c. 40, fol. 209, Bodleian Library, University of Oxford http://shelleysghost.bodleian.ox.ac.uk/three-notes-to-william-godwin?item=119#Description [retrieved 9 February 2015].

p. 24   Godwin's portrait of Wollstonecraft is from *Memoirs* (p. 69).

p. 24   *Frankenstein*, Letter IV.

pp. 24–5 Godwin's diary entry recording the death of Mary Wollstonecraft:http:// godwindiary.bodleian.ox.ac.uk/folio/e.203_0026v [retrieved 10 February 2015].

p. 28   The creature comes to life in Chapter V of *Frankenstein*.

Chapter 2: Learning to Look

p. 29   Epigraph *Frankenstein*, Chapter VII.

p. 29   Coal is itself a marker of technological innovation: in the late eighteenth century it has begun to rival wood as the prevalent fuel. Gas and steam power are still just a few years in the future.

p. 30   For a nuanced yet technical outline of differences in domestic window drapery, see http://www.adriennechinn.co.uk/article12.htm [retrieved 15 January 2017].

p. 30   The first iron safety curtain is installed in the Theatre Royal, Drury Lane, in 1794. The wealthy and fashionable have been ejected from on-stage seating only in 1762.

p. 30   Jean-Jacques Rousseau *The Confessions*, trans. and intro. J. M. Cohen (Harmondsworth: Penguin, 1953), p. 17.

p. 30   William Godwin publishes *Memoirs of the Author of A Vindication of the Rights of Woman* just four months after his wife's death, in January 1798.

p. 30   The Italian Renaissance architect Andrea Palladio modelled palaces and public buildings on Classical Greek architecture to evoke a new golden age of civilised achievement. The high ceilings and tall windows that make good practical sense in sunny Italy and Greece are altogether less rational in chilly northern Britain.

p. 31   Plate glass is first rolled in Britain in 1773 at Ravenhead on Merseyside; only around 1800 does the process become industrialised and steam-driven.

p. 32   Samuel Taylor Coleridge to Robert Southey, 24 December 1799.

p. 32   Possibly Fanny, being a little older, has had more opportunities to play
          with the children of family friends.

p. 32   This and much more on nursery rhymes in Iona and Peter Opie (eds), *The
          Oxford Dictionary of Nursery Rhymes* (Oxford: Oxford University Press,
          1951). The Introduction lists collections of nursery rhymes on p. 36. The
          pioneering *Mother Goose's Melody*, first published in the 1760s by John
          Newberry, was much pirated and re-published up to and through the
          1790s. A slightly later specialist, John Marshall, of Aldermary Churchyard,
          brought out a new edition in 1795. The *Melody* collected fifty-one 'rhymes'
          and a Shakespeare selection. Its success inspired the antiquarian Joseph
          Ritson to collect more nursery rhymes in his own *Gammer Gurton's
          Garland, or, The Nursery Parnassus*, of 1784, which was reprinted around
          1799. Many nursery rhymes were composed rather than anonymous, but
          orally transmitted none the less.

p. 33   Percy's entry confirming that these letters were in the lost box: *Journal* 2
          August 1814. Frederick L. Jones (ed.), *Mary Shelley's Journal* (Norman, OK:
          University of Oklahoma Press, 1947), p. 5.

p. 33   Details of his childhood reading come from 'William Godwin' in *Stanford
          Encyclopaedia of Philosophy*. https://plato.stanford.edu/entries/godwin/
          [retrieved 6 September 2015]. Small wonder that Godwin frets when he
          finds Fanny still grappling with a spelling book at the age of six.

p. 34   *The Looking-Glass for the Mind* was abridged and translated by Richard
          Johnson from Arnaud Berquin's *L'Ami des Enfants* of 1782–3, and first
          published by John Newbery in 1787; it remained in print for half a century.

p. 34   Some images, like those illustrating the 1795 edition of *Mother Goose's
          Melody*, are sophisticated miniatures (Opie (eds), p. 86) while others, like
          the earlier, 1770 edition of *Jack Horner* also from Aldermary Churchyard,
          are primitive works which have unlearned the rules of perspective (Opie
          (eds), p. 235).

p. 34   Several writers point to one of Blake's illustrations – in which the girls,
          lying side by side like effigies on their cot, are visited by the nightmare
          figure of a half-naked, disproportionately tall man, with a half-hound half-
          griffin licking his hand – as an original for Frankenstein's monster. But his
          exaggerated height merely matches that of all the book's adults, who are
          pictured from a child's viewpoint.

p. 35   The first cousin once removed who raised Godwin later became Mrs
          Sothren. She seems to have been sufficiently distanced from the strict
          Calvinism of Godwin *père* to take the boy to the theatre and the races.
          'Sent from home to be nourished by a hireling' is Godwin's own verdict, in
          an unpublished autobiographical fragment he writes in 1800, and which is
          dissected in Chapter 1 of C. Kegan Paul, *William Godwin: His Friends and
          Contemporaries* (London: Henry S. King and Co., 1876), Vol. 1, pp. 1–23. By

contrast, Louisa Jones's circle is certainly his own: he sometimes stays with her sisters in Bath.

p. 35   William Godwin confesses paternal inadequacy in a letter to Mrs Cotton. WG to Mrs C. 24 October 1797. Kegan Paul (1876), p. 281.

p. 36   Long before she first employed Fournée, Wollstonecraft had already understood how *modelling* affection develops it: 'to conciliate affection, affection must be shown.' Mary Wollstonecraft, *Thoughts on the Education of Daughters* (London, J. Johnson, 1787), p. 7. Her thoughts on adoption are on p. 5.

p. 36   William Godwin admits that the girls are not brought up entirely according to their mother's wishes. WG to E. Fordham 13 November 1811. http://www.bodley.ox.ac.uk/dept/scwmss/wmss/online/1500-1900/ abinger/images/Dep.b.214.3-40-1.jpg. http://www.bodley.ox.ac.uk/dept/ scwmss/wmss/online/1500-1900/abinger/images/Dep.b.214.3-40-2. jpg. http://www.bodley.ox.ac.uk/dept/scwmss/wmss/online/1500-1900/ abinger/images/Dep.b.214.3-40-3.jpg [retrieved 15 January 2017].

p. 36   Godwin will poke fun in 'Of Phrenology' in his collection of essays *Thoughts on Man, His Nature, Productions and Discoveries* (London: E. Wilson, 1831), pp. 367–75. His thoughts on inequality of talents at birth are given in a 1798 'Note' collected in Kegan Paul (1876), p. 295.

p. 37   Left in charge when Godwin makes his trips is James Marshall, a friend from student days, who lodges at 29 the Polygon as a kind of personal secretary. This letter was sent by WG to JM 11 July 1800. The theme is repeated on 6 August 1800. MS Abinger Dep. c. 214.

p. 38   Johnson's Monday dinners are such an institution that they continue, albeit in the very different surroundings of Newgate Prison, when he spends six months in jail for publishing a 'seditious' pamphlet.

p. 38   WG to Harriet Lee April 1798, MS Abinger box 228/4.

p. 39   The stranger is a Miss Kinsman. WG to Miss Kinsman 26 September 1798, MS Abinger box 227/2.

p. 39   Jane is born in Brislington, now in southern Bristol. There is no record of her baptism in the parish church of St Luke, under any of Mary Jane's usual pseudonyms at least, but Mary Jane is not necessarily Anglican.

p. 40   The story of Mary Jane's courtship of Godwin comes down to us from C. Kegan Paul (1876), Vol. 2, and the Shelley family archive: alas, bias is possible. Mary Shelley was, after all, only four at the time.

p. 40   Marshall's verdict is quoted in Locke (1980), p. 203, and much cited in turn; he gives no reference.

p. 40   Lamb's assessment of the enamoured Godwin comes from CL to John Rickman, 16 September 1801. Alfred Ainger (ed.), *The Letters of Charles Lamb* (London: Macmillan, 1888), Vol. 1, p. 203.

p. 41   From 13 July, to be precise, Godwin's *Journal* once again revealing all.

p. 42   By 1795 Mary Jane was living with a Swiss merchant, Charles (an Anglicisation of Karl Abram Marc) de Gaulis, in Bristol. De Gaulis was her son's father. This research into Mary Jane Clairmont's background by Herbert Huscher (published in the *Keats–Shelley Memorial Bulletin*, vols VIII (1959) and IX (1960)) has been unpacked in William St Clair, *The Godwins and the Shelleys* (London: Faber, 1989), pp. 248–53. See also https://www.myheritage.com/names/charles_gaulis [retrieved 16 January 2017]. Charles Gaulis died in 1796, so could not be Jane's father.

p. 42
Mary Jane's mother came from a prosperous Exeter merchant family, the Tremletts, but married 'down' to Peter de Vial. In November 1791 Mary Jane and her sister managed to sell the Fleur de Luce. https://docs.google.com/viewer?a=v&pid=sites&srcid=ZGVmYXVsdGRvbWFpbnxtYXJ5amFuZXNkYXVnaHRlcnxneDoxZTZhMzNlNzMoNGU3Njhi [retrieved 16 January 2017].

The family property had been kept in a trust for them until they reached the age of twenty-one. https://docs.google.com/viewer?a=v&pid=sites&srcid=ZGVmYXVsdGRvbWFpbnxtYXJ5amFuZXNkYXVnaHRlcnxneDoxZTZhMzNlNzMoNGU3Njhi [retrieved 16 January 2017]. The pub was in a rough area on the corner of the alley leading to Butchers Row, where the Youldon family, butchers with few pretensions, served the smiths of Smythen Street. http://www.exetermemories.co.uk/em/_streets/butchers.php [retrieved 16 January 2017]. http://www.9fairfield.eclipse.co.uk/exeterpubs/bygone/bygwestquarter/bygwestfleur.html [retrieved 16 January 2017]. 'William Hunt' or 'Brown' was presumably the young women's agent or tenant.

A friend and, possibly, landlady, 'A. C.', writes in early December 1797, when Mary Jane has just returned to Bristol, presumably to be closer to Lethbridge: 'for God sake let me know what ensues, and very minutely, if you have found out the reason of his boredom.' 'A. C.' to 'Mrs St Julian' 3 or 4 December 1797. https://sites.google.com/site/maryjanesdaughter/the-dodson-and-pulman-papers/the-letters/letter-1-3-dec-1797 [retrieved 16 January 2017].

Sir John Lethbridge comments on Mary Jane in his letters to his lawyer Robert Beadon: JL to RB 15 January 1799 and 11 June 1799. https://sites.google.com/site/maryjanesdaughter/the-dodson-and-pulman-papers/the-letters/letter-2-15-jan-1799 and https://sites.google.com/site/maryjanesdaughter/the-dodson-and-pulman-papers/the-letters/letter-c31-11-june-1799 respectively [retrieved 16 January 2017].

The Mary Jane [Godwin]/Lethbridge letters are among the records of Dodson and Pulman, Taunton, solicitors, held by the Somerset Record Office. They were discovered by Anne Speight in 2006, when she was doing some unrelated family history research. Digital access to the transcribed letters is via Vicki Parslow Stafford's site, Mary Jane's Daughter. https://sites.google.com/site/maryjanesdaughter/home [retrieved 16 January 2017].

p. 42   To secure the second, 'true' marriage, Godwin has had to lie on oath that he is a resident of Whitechapel. The oath, made a month in advance to the representative of the bishop of London, shows how carefully premeditated these marriage plans were.

p. 42   Godwin's telegrammatic journal entries make it difficult to identify when labour actually takes place.

p. 43   Mary Jane replaces the children's carers with Miss Hooley, a maid called Betsey, Miss Smith as live-in governess and a tutor, Mr Burton.

p. 43   Frankenstein views his creation with disgust in Chapter V; he makes his declaration in *Frankenstein*, Chapter II.

p. 44   The most striking demonstration of 'galvanism' in London has been by Galvani's nephew Professor Aldini 'under the inspection of Mr Keate, Mr Carpue and several other professional gentlemen', who passed an electrical current through various nerves in the body of convicted murderer George Foster, after he had been hanged at Newgate Prison on 18 January 1803. *The Newgate Calendar*. http://www.exclassics.com/newgate/ng464.htm [retrieved 16 January 2017].

p. 45   Mary Wollstonecraft was a governess for the Kingsborough family in County Cork, where her protégée was Margaret Jane King.
         As 'Margaret King Moore', King publishes *Advice to Young Mothers on the Physical Education of Children,* her own reasonably faithful version of the Wollstonecraft approach, in 1823. The approach recommends fresh air, cleanliness and good diet. Wollstonecraft diverged from Rousseau when his *Émile* relegated the girl character Sophie to 'modest' domesticity. Wollstonecraft's own views are in the unpublished *Lessons*, devised as a primer first for Fanny and then, returning to it while pregnant, for her second child. It's circular to assume that what Thomas Paine has already, in his 1775–6 pamphlet, called *Common Sense* – the will of the common man – is always rational.

p. 46   The quotation is from Mary Wollstonecraft, *A Vindication of the Rights of Woman*, Chapter 13, section 5. *A Vindication* also paints a vivid portrait of the distorting effects of exceptionalism on educated women.

p. 47   The term 'scientist' is coined by the Anglican priest and historian of science William Whewell, in a review (of Mary Somerville's *On the Connexion of the Physical Sciences*), in the *Quarterly Review* in 1834. His anonymous authorship is detected by Sydney Ross in '*Scientist: The Story of a Word*' in *Annals of Science*, Vol. 18/2 (June 1962, but published April 1964). tandfonline.com/doi/abs/10.1080/00033796200202722 [retrieved 28 September 2015].

p. 47   Contemporary cabinets of scientific instruments are created at Teyler's Museum, Haarlem, and for the Bavarian Academy, for example. G. L'E. Turner, 'Eighteenth-Century Scientific Instruments and Their Makers', in Roy Porter (ed.), *The Cambridge History of Science,* Vol. 4 (Cambridge: Cambridge University Press, 2003), p. 519.

At the turn of the century distinguished family firms of instrument-makers include the Troughtons and, in Fleet Street, the Adamses. Their premises are in roughly similar parts of East Central London to publishers', including Fleet Street. Turner in Porter (ed.), 2003, pp. 525–31.

p. 48   The references to alchemy are from *Frankenstein*, Chapters II and III. Alchemy remains part of 'natural philosophy' beyond the end of the eighteenth century (cf. Patricia Fara, 'Marginalized Practices', in Porter (ed.) 2003, pp. 499–503). Members of the Avignon Society, known to include alchemical experimenters, include the Godwin family friend William Blake.

p. 48   Number 41 only acquires a 'back' when Godwin acquires the house next door to expand his business. It's unclear who owns the building, which allows Godwin to stop paying rent. Information on the Skinner Street development comes from Ford K. Brown, 'Notes on 41 Skinner Street', in *Modern Language Notes*, Vol. 54/5 (May 1939), pp. 326–32. doi: 10.2307/2912348. http://www.jstor.org/stable/2912348 [retrieved 16 January 2017].

p. 49   Miranda Seymour, *Mary Shelley* (London: John Murray, 2000), has a complete list of the street's booksellers (note 28, p. 579).

p. 49   Other women working the shop include the by now impoverished Eliza Fenwick, here six days a week during that first winter.

p. 50   Born in 1770 and 1771 respectively, William and Dorothy Wordsworth are no more than fifteen years younger than Mary's mother and father, who were born in 1759 and 1756.

p. 51   The quotations are from Samuel Taylor Coleridge, *The Rime of the Ancient Mariner*, Part 1, and *Frankenstein*, Letter II.

p. 52   John Bowlby developed the concept of maternal deprivation after the Second World War: *Maternal Care and Mental Health* (Geneva: World Health Organization, 1951). Often precocious either intellectually or sexually, those deprived of such care may also lapse into babyhood. Their self-mothering includes everything from rocking and thumb-sucking to hair-twiddling and bossiness. They can also be emotionally volatile. Bowlby went on to develop attachment theory, which posited a sustained, loving relationship rather than parental gender as key.

p. 53   In *Mourning and Melancholia* (1917) Sigmund Freud identifies self-hatred as the difference between healthy mourning and unhealthy melancholia.

p. 53   Godwin's boast comes from WG to E. Fordham 13 January 1811, MS Abinger, c. 19, fols 32–3.

Chapter 3: Through a Door Partly Opened

p. 54   Epigraph *Frankenstein*, Chapter III.

p. 54   Hogg's memory appears in Thomas Jefferson Hogg, with intro. by Edward Dowden, *The Life of Percy Bysshe Shelley* (London: George Routledge & Sons; New York: E. P. Dutton & Co., 1906), Vol. 2,

pp. 567–8. https://archive.org/stream/lifeofpercybysshoohogguoft/
lifeofpercybysshoohogguoft_djvu.txt [retrieved 4 December 2015].

p. 55   Thomas Love Peacock's comment on Hogg's biography of Percy is cited in Winifred Scott, *Jefferson Hogg: Shelley's Biographer* (London: Jonathan Cape, 1951), p. 260.

p. 55   The description of Skinner Street is from Hogg's account of his own first sight of Mary.

p. 56   The sketch of the Shelleys' marriage is from Hogg (1906), p. 548; of her post-natal life from p. 547. Confusingly, Eliza is the name of both Harriet's infant daughter and her own sister.

p. 56   Percy's letter to Hogg: PBS to TJH 4 October 1814. Frederick L. Jones (ed.), *The Letters of Percy Bysshe Shelley* (Oxford: Clarendon Press, 1964), Vol I., p. 402.

p. 58   Burr called the three near-sisters of the Godwin household 'the goddesses'. Northcote's anecdote comes from William Hazlitt, *Conversations of James Northcote Esq, RA* (London: Henry Colburn and Richard Bentley, 1830), 'Conversation the First', pp. 3–4.

p. 59   Mary also visits Notting Hill in the summer of 1809.

p. 60   'Age of consent' in the sense of being allowed to marry. Consent to sex was set at ten: that's to say that sex with an under-ten-year-old girl was automatically considered rape, whereas sex with a ten-to-twelve-year-old was only a misdemeanour. http://www.historyandpolicy.org/policy-papers/papers/the-legacy-of-1885-girls-and-the-age-of-sexual-consent [retrieved 14 December 2015].

p. 60   The first edition of Mary's letters was by Frederick L. Jones in 1944; Muriel Spark's 1951 biography was ground-breaking. Frederick L. Jones (ed.), *The Letters of Mary Shelley* (Norman, OK: University of Oklahoma Press, 1944); Muriel Spark, *Child of Light: A Reassessment of Mary Wollstonecraft Shelley* (London: Tower Bridge Publications, 1951).

p. 60   Mary to Trelawney: MWS to EJT 26 January 1837. Betty T. Bennett (ed.), *The Letters of Mary Wollstonecraft Shelley*, 3 vols (Baltimore, MD: Johns Hopkins University Press (1980–88), Vol. 2 (1983), p. 281.

p. 61   Mary mentions her 'girlish troubles' in a letter to Jane Williams in 1823, quoted below, but the context makes clear that she's referring to *emotional* troubles. From commiserating with Jane, 'gone back to [her] Mother's house—to [sister] Maria's temper' she turns to Mary Jane.

p. 61   Migraines appear in the *Bibliotheca Anatomica, Medica, Chirurgica,* printed by John Nott and sold by W. Lewis (London, 1712).

p. 62   Psoriasis is also associated with increased susceptibility to cancers of the lymph system, which can lead to tumours in, among other places, the brain. Mary will die of a brain tumour.

Mary suffers from motion sickness when sailing to Ramsgate and Scotland, and also during the elopement ride to the coast – though on the latter occasion she may also be pregnant.

For more on the history of the treatment of psoriasis see: E. M. Farber, 'History of the treatment of psoriasis', in *Journal of American Academic Dermatology*, 27(4) (October 1992), pp. 640–45; https://www.ncbi.nlm.nih. gov/pubmed/1401327 [retrieved 9 December 2015]; and 'Psoriasis treatment – yesterday, today, and tomorrow' in *Acta Dermatovenerologica Croatica*, 12/1 (2004), pp. 30–34. https://www.ncbi.nlm.nih.gov/pubmed/15072746 [retrieved 9 December 2015].

p. 63   Mary Jane writes to Godwin from Ramsgate as she leaves Mary there about 'the dreadful evil we apprehended'. MJG to WG 10 June 1811, MS Abinger c. 523. William St Clair even diagnoses chickenpox. St Clair (1989), p. 310.

p. 63   It's Aaron Burr who remarks on Mary's air of frailty, at Christmas 1811, on 21 December 1811. Aaron Burr (ed.), *William K. Bixby: The Private Journal* (Rochester, NY: The Genesee Press, 1905 [limited edition 250 copies]), Vol. 2, p. 270. Even when she is well, her pallor will be remarked on for the rest of her life.

p. 63   WG to MJG, 4 June 1811. http://www.bodley.ox.ac.uk/dept/scwmss/wmss/ online/1500-1900/abinger/images/Dep.c.523-31-1.jpg; http://www.bodley. ox.ac.uk/dept/scwmss/wmss/online/1500-1900/abinger/images/Dep.c.523-31-2.jpg; http://www.bodley.ox.ac.uk/dept/scwmss/wmss/online/1500-1900/abinger/images/Dep.c.523-31-3.jpg [retrieved 17 January 2017].

p. 64   Godwin's famous message to Mary appears in WG to MJG, 18 May 1811, Kegan Paul (1876), Vol. 2, p. 184, and at http://www.bodley.ox.ac.uk/ dept/scwmss/wmss/online/1500-1900/abinger/images/Dep.c.523-31-2.jpg [retrieved 17 January 2017].

p. 66   Between 25 August and 2 September, Baxter visits the Godwins twice with his daughter and twice without, as Godwin's *Diary* records: http:// godwindiary.bodleian.ox.ac.uk/people/BAX01.html [retrieved 20 December 2015]. 'Baxter of Dundee' is not mentioned again until three years later, when Godwin writes to initiate the invitation. There is some uncertainty as to which daughter accompanies Baxter to London in 1809. The digital archive of the *Diary* assumes it is Isabella: http://godwindiary. bodleian.ox.ac.uk/people/BOO03.html#BOO03-bio [retrieved 20 December 2015]. The family account gives credence to Christy's reminiscences in old age and believes it to be her: 'On one of his visits to London in 1811 Baxter took his daughter Christina ('Christy Baxter') with him to meet Godwin, and Mary, who was about the same age, was so charmed with the Scottish lassie that they became fast friends, and Christy remained guest in Godwin's house in Skinner Street for several days.' There is no record of this [in] Godwin's *Diary*: http://www.doig. net/ROBX1713.html [retrieved 20 December 2015].

p. 67   William Godwin's letter to William Baxter is dated 8 June 1812. Quoted in Anne K. Mellor, *Mary Shelley: Her Life, Her Fiction, Her Monsters* (London: Routledge, 1990), pp. 15–16.

p. 67   For more on the *Osnaburgh*, see *The Register of Shipping for 1821, Instituted in 1798 By a Society of Merchants, Ship-Owners and Underwriters*: https://books.google.co.uk/books?id=7Mk_AQAAMAAJ&pg=RA1-PA80&lpg=RA1-PA80&dq=osnaburgh+packet+1812&source=bl&ots=6K o3Y_Xjvy&sig=-z6zTX-i3HIgt7dISYweDgHylKk&hl=en&sa=X&ved=0a hUKEwjJ_YmF_efJAhWDQhQKHbMABisQ6AEIPjAJ#v=onepage&q =osnaburgh%20packet%201812&f=false [retrieved 19 December 2015].

p. 68   In John Wood's 1821 *Plan of the Town of Dundee from Actual Survey*, 'The Cottage' seems to be called a 'manor house'. http://www.waughfamily.ca/ Aimer/1821dundeemap.jpg [retrieved 20 December 2015].

p. 69   The description of icebergs comes from *Frankenstein*, Chapter XXIV. So too does the monster's description.

p. 71   For more on Glasite dogma, see James Gardner, *Faiths of the World* (London: A. Fullarton & Co., 1860), p. 976.

p. 71   Like Fanny, Christy will never marry. Perhaps she's inoculated against matrimony by the unhappiness of the early marriages that take place around her. Unlike Fanny, she will long outlive Mary, dying in Dundee 'in reduced circumstances' in 1886. http://wc.rootsweb.ancestry.com/cgi-bin/ igm.cgi?Op=GET&db=robx1713&id=I215 [retrieved 20 December 2015].

p. 72   His temper may not be helped by the fact that David Booth is, according to his grandson, 'an extremely little man'. Stuart also remembers Isabella, who was his grandmother, with whom he spent time as a child: There is no doubt that my grandmother's mind had a gloomy turn, in which she differed widely from my mother. [...] My sister has an oil-painting of her, with dark hair curling close round her brows, [...] by William Ross, when she was twenty-three, as a study for a picture of Lady Jane Grey with Roger Ascham. The same volume of reminiscences is the source of the detail about Mary's long goodbye, from 'a diary kept by Christy Baxter, which was in the possession of the late Mr Walter Baxter, solicitor, Dundee'.

James Stuart, *Reminiscences* (London, Chiswick Press, 1911), pp. 12 and 93–4. https://archive.org/stream/reminiscencesoostuaiala/ reminiscencesoostuaiala_djvu.txt [retrieved 15 December 2016].

p. 73   MWS to JW 7 March 1823. Bennett, ed. (1980–88), Vol.1, p. 322.

p. 73   MWS to EJT 26 January 1837. Bennett, ed. (1980–88), Vol. 2, p. 280.

Chapter 4: Elopement

p. 75   Epigraph *Frankenstein*, Chapter X.

p. 75   On sailing the Channel, see: http://www.sailingalmanac.com/Almanac/ Navigation/doverstraits.html

pp. 75–6 Most of these descriptions of elopement are from Mary's *Journal* 28 July 1814, in Jones, ed. (1947), pp. 3–4. Details of 'a hotter day than has been known' and 'reefing the sail' come from Mary's later account in *History of a Six Weeks' Tour through a Part of France, Switzerland, Germany and Holland*:

With Letters Descriptive of a Sail Round the Lake of Geneva, and of the Glaciers of Chamouni (London: Hookham and Ollier, 1817), pp. 2 and 4.

p. 77   On 26 June Mary declared her love; so it is possible that the 27th is the date on which the relationship is consummated. Or Shelley may just have got the date wrong in the *Journal*; or this may be an early appearance of his superstition around the 27th.

p. 78   Mary's account of her own seasickness is from *History of a Six Weeks' Tour*, p. 3.

p. 78   She writes of the 'first and most perilous instance' when she 'had the opportunity to look at Death in the face' that 'I was then at Lerici': *Journal* 5 October 1839. Jones, ed. (1947), p. 208.

p. 79   Mary's descriptions of Calais's inhabitants come from *History of a Six Weeks' Tour*, pp. 5–6, and those of nearby countryside and roads from *History of a Six Weeks' Tour*, pp. 7 and 10. *Journal* entries complaining about French rural hygiene and attitudes, even while acknowledging that the region has recently been sacked, suggest a lack of political awareness. Echemine 'is entirely ruined by the Cossacks; but we could hardly pity the people when we saw how very unamiable they were'; *Journal* 12 August 1814. Jones, ed. (1947), p. 8.

p. 79   Mrs Godwin's arrival is recorded in the *Journal* 29 July 1814. Jones, ed. (1947), p. 4.

p. 81   Percy on rebuffing Mrs Godwin: *Journal* 30 July 1814. Jones, ed. (1947), p. 4.

p. 81   The full story of Fanny's suicide appears in Chapter 7.

p. 81   Godwin is thirty-seven by the time William junior is born.

p. 81   We must note in passing that Percy has already tried a similar arrangement with his first wife and her sister; it ended badly, with the departure of his sister-in-law.

p. 81   Godwin's letter to Percy is whereabouts unknown: WG to PBS 25 July 1814, now known only in transcript in the Southeran Sale Catalogue #784, item 841, 1923.

p. 82   Fanny is summoned back to Skinner Street when Mary and Jane run away, presumably to take their place in domestic and shopkeeping duties. It can't escape her notice that no one seems particularly concerned to rescue her.

p. 82   Preface to *Fleetwood, or The New Man of Feeling*, Vol. 1 (New York: I. Riley & Co., 1805). http://dwardmac.pitzer.edu/Anarchist_Archives/godwin/fleetwoodpref.html [retrieved 19 January 2017].

p. 82   That Percy has promised something in the region of £3,000 (we must allow for Godwin's tactical exaggeration) we know from a letter he writes to Josiah Wedgwood a year earlier, asking for an advance of this sum and claiming it can be insured against a baronet's estate. WG to JW 30 August 1813, Josiah Wedgwood & Sons Archive, University of Keele. Godwin and his allies have spent the intervening year working through substantial difficulties to make it possible for Percy, who as yet has only an allowance, to access this sum against his inheritance. The hoops they jump through are detailed in St Clair (1989), Chapter 26, pp. 344–55. Godwin has inadvertently financed Percy's elopement with his own daughter.

p. 83   One can't help noticing that Percy lived not in the model village but in the home of its developer, a Regency manor whose name, Tan yr Allt (In the Heights), says it all.

p. 84   Percy's declaration to Godwin: PBS to WG 11 June 1812. *Letters from Percy Bysshe Shelley to William Godwin*, Vol. 1 (London, privately printed, 1891), p. 65. https://archive.org/stream/lettersfrompercy01shelrich/ lettersfrompercy01shelrich_djvu.txt [retrieved 20 January 2017].

p. 84   Godwin's letter was temporarily lost in the post while the Shelleys moved from Ireland to Wales. WG to PBS 30 March 1812. MS Abinger c. 524. http://www.bodley.ox.ac.uk/dept/scwmss/wmss/online/1500-1900/ abinger/images/Dep.c.524.04-2.jpg [retrieved 20 January 2017].

p. 85   Friedrich Nietzsche's *The Gay Science*, which proclaims explicitly that 'God is dead', will not be published until 1882; his better-known restatement appears in *Thus Spake Zarathustra*, first published (in four volumes) in 1883–91.

p. 85   Percy receives 'a cold and stupid letter from Hookham' two days before he is a grumpy tourist: *Journal* 3 and 5 August 1814. Jones, ed. (1947), p. 5.

p. 86   *History of a Six Weeks' Tour*, p. 30.

p. 86   Mary's entry on Champlitte in the *Journal* 16 August 1814. Jones, ed. (1947), p. 9.

p. 86   For more on Mary Wollstonecraft's *Thoughts on the Education of Daughters* see Chapter 2.

p. 86   Frankenstein's creature tells his maker what it was like to become aware of himself as an emotionally isolated, physically unsheltered being in *Frankenstein*, Chapter XI.

p. 87   It's Mary's own mother who was governess to the mother of *Maurice*'s eleven-year-old dedicatee. Laurette is the daughter of 'Mrs Mason'/Lady Mountcashell née Margaret Jane King. Mary Shelley, *Maurice, or the Fisherman's Cot*, ed. and intro. Claire Tomalin (London: Viking, 1998).

p. 87   *The Last Man* (London, Henry Colburn, 1826), Vol. 1, Chapter 1. http:// onlinebooks.library.upenn.edu/webbin/gutbook/lookup?num=18247 [retrieved 5 February 2017].

p. 88   Jane states her views on 7 October, interrupts the couple with her horrors on 27 August and gets into bed with them on 12 August. *Journal* 7 October 1814, 27 August 1814 and 12 August 1814. Jones, ed. (1947), pp. 18, 12, 7.

p. 89   Mary and Percy manage 'Love in idleness': *Journal* 6 November 1814. Jones, ed. (1947), p. 24. Mary 'seems insensible'. 7 August 1814, Jones, ed. (1947), p. 5.

pp. 89–90   The money for the trip was to have come from the de Boinvilles via Thomas Hookham; this is why his letter is 'cold and stupid'.

     Mary's reports on the costs of these modes of transport: *Journal* 8 and 13 August 1814. Jones, ed. (1947), pp. 6 and 8.

p. 90   The postilion's lies appear on *Journal* 18 August 1814; the Alps on 19 August 1814. Jones, ed. (1947), p. 10.

p. 90   Mary is so pleased with her description of the Alps that it reappears almost verbatim in her *History of a Six Weeks' Tour*.

p. 91   The house at Brunen appears in the *Journal* 24 August 1814 (Jones, ed. (1947), p. 11) and in *History of a Six Weeks' Tour*, p. 52. The account of the travellers' return is taken from *History of a Six Weeks' Tour*, pp. 53 and 54.

pp. 91–2   The detail on the state of the travellers is taken from Mary's *Journal* 21, 22 and 29 August 1814 (Jones, ed. (1947), pp. 11–12); but the claim of 'eight hundred miles' and the description of the students come from *History*, pp. 54 and 64 respectively.

p. 92   On the boat from Mainz to Cologne, 'nothing could be more horribly disgusting than the lower order of smoking, drinking Germans who travelled with us; they swaggered and talked, and what was hideous to English eyes, kissed one another'. *History of a Six Weeks' Tour*, pp. 67–8.

p. 93   Mary's 'Hate': *Journal* for 10 and 11 September 1814. Jones, ed. (1947), p. 14. Her co-writing: 25 August 1814. Jones, ed. (1947), p. 11.

p. 94   Percy records the contents of her box in the *Journal* 2 August 1814. Jones, ed. (1947), p. 5.

   Mary notes the loss of her box at Paris in a letter to Thomas Hookham written decades later, in October 1845, in response to blackmail threats by 'Major George Byron', who claims to have some of her correspondence, which he offers to sell back to her via Hookham. MS to TH 28 October 1845. Bennett, ed. (1980–88), Vol. 3, p. 245. For more on this see the Coda.

p. 94   Or perhaps Percy writes the *Journal* on the day Mary's loss is realised.

p. 94   The Wollstonecraft books were presumably brought with them, left out of Mary's box by happy oversight. Mary Wollstonecraft, *Letters Written during a Short Residence in Sweden, Norway, and Denmark* (London: J. Johnson, 1796). Mary Wollstonecraft, *Mary, A Fiction* (London: J. Johnson, 1788).

p. 95   PBS to TJH 3 October 1814. The first page of this letter is neat, but the handwriting grows larger and more hasty, racing across the sheets, as Percy expounds his love for Mary. https://repository.tcu.edu/bitstream/handle/116099117/6183/97743_Shelley_Hogg_October_3_1814.pdf?sequence=1&isAllowed=y [retrieved 23 January 1817].

p. 95   Percy's notes on marriage gloss his line in V. 189, 'Even love is sold.'

p. 95   Edward Dowden, in *The Life of Percy Bysshe Shelley* (London: Routledge and Kegan Paul, 1969), p. 226, claims that Mary's copy of *Queen Mab* has a note by Percy contradicting the dedication 'To Harriet' by aspersion: 'Count Slobendorf was about to marry a woman who, attracted solely by his fortune, proved her selfishness by deserting him in prison.'

p. 96   Percy's letter inviting Harriet to Switzerland doesn't propose a ménage: he writes as a 'firm and constant friend' suggesting she would have a home of her own in the country. PBS to HS 13 August 1814. http://

shelleysghost.bodleian.ox.ac.uk/copy-of-a-letter-from-shelley-to-harriet-shelley?item=29; http://shelleysghost.bodleian.ox.ac.uk/copy-of-a-letter-from-shelley-to-harriet-shelley?item=133 [retrieved 23 January 2017].

Chapter 5: Becoming a Couple

p. 97   Epigraph *Frankenstein*, Chapter XVII.

p. 97   Mary's first surviving letter is MWG to PBS (25 October 1814 – date established by Betty T. Bennett in her edition of *The Letters of Mary Wollstonecraft Shelley*. It's from this letter that her 'treachery' comment also comes.

p. 98   A blacksmith's family also live in the house; Mary records his son's birthday party: *Journal* 8 November 1814. Jones, ed. (1947), pp. 24–5.

p. 99   As the *Journal* is shared with Percy, it's hard not to see the phrase 'poor Mary' as a protest. *Journal* 13 September 1814. Jones, ed. (1947), p. 15.

p. 99   The temporary lodgings are identified as 56 Margaret Street in Newman I. White, *Shelley* (New York: Alfred A. Knopf, 1940), Vol. 1, p. 364.

p. 100   Entries recording contact from Skinner Street: *Journal* 16 September 1814, 27 October 1814 and 28 October 1814. Jones, ed. (1947), pp. 15, 23.

p. 100   William Godwin's *Diary* does not mention his daughter all autumn. A brief entry on 16 September – 'Letter from Shelley' – is followed by one on 22 September, 'Write to PBS' and, on 7 November, 'Meet PBS'. http://godwindiary.bodleian.ox.ac.uk/diary/1814.html [retrieved 7 May 2016].

p. 101   Mary's emotional evening letter is MWG to PBS 28 October 1814, Bennett ed. (1980–88), Vol. 1, p. 3. Her famous phrase about her fifteen-year-old self, 'Mrs Godwin had discovered long before my excessive & romantic attachment to my father', comes from a letter to Maria Gisborne written just after own her child, Percy Florence, turns fifteen. MWS to MG 17 November 1834. Bennett, ed. (1980–88), Vol. 2, p. 215.

p. 101   Mary's financial advice is given in MWG to PBS [2 November 1814 – date established by Bennett]. Bennett, ed. (1980–88), Vol. 1, p. 4.

p. 102   Mary records the lovers' Sundays: *Journal* 30 October 1814 and 6 November 1814. Jones, ed. (1947), pp. 23–4.

p. 102   Mary's requests to be met promptly are from her letters to Percy [25 October 1814] and [2 November 1814]. Bennett, ed. (1980–88), Vol. 1, pp. 1 and 4.

p. 103   Godwin's snub is *Journal* 23 March 1815. Jones, ed. (1947), p. 42.

p. 103   Mary receives a letter from David Booth on 3 November.

p. 103   Copies of 'Mary-Jane's letter' about Percy's laudanum suicide pact are variously dated, according to Miranda Seymour, 16 and 20 August and 2 September 1814. It seems likely that she did send it in some form to Lady Mountcashell. This emotional blackmail sounds perfectly in character for Percy; Seymour also astutely points out that laudanum, easy to come by, is no proof that Percy was serious. Seymour (2000), p. 97 and note 15, p. 581.

p. 104   Mary's outbursts: *Journal* 6 and 7 December 1814. Jones, ed. (1947), p. 28.

p. 104   Nantgwyllt was built between 1792 and 1812 by Shelley's uncle, 'Mr Grove of Wiltshire'; in a photograph taken just before the Claerwen and Elan valleys were flooded to supply Birmingham with drinking water, it's a homely, large, stone-built house in late eighteenth-century style. http:// history.powys.org.uk/history/rhayader/nantgwyllt.html [retrieved 25 June 2017]. MWG to PBS 3 November 1814.

p. 105   Windsor particularly attracts Mary. The family reunited in the third chapter of *Maurice* also live 'near Windsor Park', so that their son can go to Eton. Mary's pastorals may be inspired partly by her childhood home overlooking the fields of Middlesex. None of Mary's fictional protagonists lives well when alone. Mary Shelley, *The Last Man*, http://onlinebooks. library.upenn.edu/webbin/gutbook/lookup?num=18247 [retrieved 5 February 2017]. Mary Shelley, *Maurice*, ed. Claire Tomalin, p. 86. Mary Shelley, *Matilda* (Santa Barbara, CA: Bandana Books, 2013), p. 36.

p. 106   Percy's letter to Hogg is the one we cited in the previous chapter: PBS to TJH 3 October 1814. https://repository.tcu.edu/bitstream/ handle/116099117/6183/97743_Shelley_Hogg_October_3_1814. pdf?sequence=1&isAllowed=y [retrieved 23 January 1817].

p. 106   Percy Bysshe Shelley, *Epipsychidion* (London: C. and J. Ollier, 1821), lines 150–60. https://archive.org/stream/epipsychidionooshelrich/ epipsychidionooshelrich_djvu.txt [retrieved 25 January 2017].

p. 107   Percy's letter inviting Harriet to Switzerland is at: http://shelleysghost. bodleian.ox.ac.uk/copy-of-a-letter-from-shelley-to-harriet-shelley?item=133 [retrieved 23 January 1817]. The allusion to Mrs Boinville's 'beloved friend' sounds remarkably like the jealousy of an unsuccessful lover.

p. 107   In flirting with Jane, Percy flirts with the very taboo David Booth has broken by marrying Mary's friend Isabella.

p. 108   Less than a fortnight after complimenting Mary, on 9 October, Fanny would kill herself. FI to MWG 26 September 1816. Marion Kingston Stocking (ed.), *The Clairmont Correspondence: Letters of Claire Clairmont, Charles Clairmont, and Fanny Imlay Godwin, 1808–1879* (Baltimore, MD: Johns Hopkins University Press, 1995), Vol. I, p. 74.

pp. 108–9 Percy and Jane scare themselves silly: *Journal* 7 October 1814. Jones, ed. (1947), p. 18. Percy refuses to play along: *Journal* 14 October 1814. Jones, ed. (1947), pp. 20–21.

p. 110   Thomas Love Peacock, *Headlong Hall* (London: T. Hookham, Jun., & Co., 1816).

p. 111   'Clara' and her behaviour is recorded in the *Journal* on 19 December 1814, Hogg's virtue on 24 December 1814. Jones, ed. (1947), pp. 30–31.

p. 111   Mary's letters complimenting Hogg, and her promises to try for a sexual relationship with him after the baby is born, are: MWG to TJH 1 January 1815 and 7 January 1815. Bennett, ed. (1980–88), Vol. I, pp. 6 and 8.

p. 111   Hogg's pet name 'Alexy' derives from his self-published, fictional *Memoirs of Prince Alexy Haimatoff*, which Percy has reviewed in Hookham's *Critical Review* (December 1814).

p. 112   For Mary Wollstonecraft on boys' boarding schools, see Chapter 2. For what happens when Lord Byron falls foul of the prohibition on anal sex, see Chapter 6.

p. 113   Mary asks Hogg to comfort her in Percy's place in MWG to TJH 6 March 1815. Bennett, ed. (1980–88), Vol. 1, p. 10. She confides her recurring thought that 'I was a mother, and am so no longer' to her *Journal* 13 March 1815. Jones, ed. (1947), p. 40.

p. 114   Mary writes Percy an anguished letter, carefully putting the blame for any possible meeting on to Jane-Claire. She assumes that the two would be in London not Lynmouth: suggesting either that she's unaware of any pregnancy or that, having been up and about herself so quickly after the birth of her first child, she assumes her stepsister will be too. MWG to PBS, 27 July 1815. Bennett, ed. (1980–88), Vol. 1, pp. 15–16.

p. 114   Exmoor National Park has convincingly narrowed down a tangle of conflicting claims about Percy and Harriet's lodgings to Woodbine Villas, now destroyed but roughly on the site of the present Shelley's Cottage Hotel:

> The favoured site was known as 'Blackmore's Lodgings' […] This later became 'Woodbine Villas'. It was later demolished and a new cottage near the site became known as 'Shelley's Cottage', which, as 'Shelley's Cottage Hotel', was rebuilt following damage in the 1952 flood disaster. Evidence for this comes from an article in the '*North Devon Herald*' of 1901. In the article, Agnes Groves, celebrating her 100th birthday, is quoted as remembering the Shelleys staying with her in 'Woodbine Villas' when she was ten. Local people also claim to have seen Shelley's signature in the visitors' book for 'Woodbine Villas'. […] Another theory is that they stayed in the top cottage on Mars Hill. Evidence of this comes from a newspaper of 1907 reporting a fire at 'Shelley's Cottage' on Mars Hill. It seems that Mary Blackmore moved to Mars Hill in 1854 […]. To add to the confusion, another account suggests that they did not stay with Mary Blackmore at all but with a Mrs Hooper.

http://www.exmoor-nationalpark.gov.uk/Whats-Special/culture/literary-links/percey-bysshe-shelley [retrieved 7 May 2016]. 'Mrs Bicknell', the name recalled by Mary-Jane, is a conceivable misremembering of 'Blackmore'. The association with Mrs Hooper is demonstrated by a receipt that Richard Robinson records among the Shelley's Cottage Hotel's papers: *The Telegraph*, 2 October 2002. http://www.telegraph.co.uk/travel/725229/Devon-In-search-of-Shelleys-muse.html [retrieved 7 May 2016]. So possibly Mrs Hooper wasn't the landlady but a lady's maid or maidservant; probably not a midwife. Midwifery fees 'in the late eighteenth century were generally half a guinea, fifteen shillings, or one guinea, with only a few billed at one to three guineas for more affluent patients'. In 'Rules and Regulations Agreed and Entered into by the Medical Gentlemen of Blackburn 1819', a class-3 patient was charged 19 shillings, a class-2, 21 shillings, with 'fee and a half' for 'Difficult' and extra half fees for 'Turning' and 'Use of forceps': very far from the '£30' on the bill that the *Telegraph* uncovers. Anne Digby, *Making a Medical Living: Doctors and Patients in the English Market for Medicine, 1720–1911* (Cambridge: Cambridge University Press, 1994), pp. 254–5. https://books.google.co.uk/books?id=n_uUJyNy9LcC&pg=PA255&lpg=PA255&dq=midwife+fees+nineteenth+century&source=bl&ots=adC1G5yrXw&sig=HIntebQnIObg1skKT6QI8GB-TOg&hl=en&sa=X&ved=0ahUKEwjf49SPrsjMAhVhD8AKHSS3Bjo4ChDoAQgcMAA#v=onepage&q=midwife%20fees%20nineteenth%20century&f=false [retrieved 7 May 2016].

p. 115   Percy records Mary's labour: *Journal* 22 February 1815. Jones, ed. (1947), p. 38.

p. 116   Percy Bysshe Shelley *A Vindication of Natural Diet* (London, J. Callow, 1813). http://knarf.english.upenn.edu/PShelley/mabnotes.html [retrieved 26 January 1817].

Chapter 6: At Villa Diodati

p. 118   Epigraph *Frankenstein*, Chapter VII.

p. 118   'Claire' has by now settled on this name, which she keeps for the rest of her life and we use for the rest of this book.

p. 119   The Dutch East Indies becomes Indonesia in the twentieth century.

p. 119   Around 41km³, or 10,000 million tonnes, of pyroclastic trachyandesite were ejected by Mount Tambora in April 1815 in what's thought to have been the most dramatic sulphur dioxide (SO_2) environmental event in five thousand years. The eruption column, more than 43km high, reached the stratosphere; it included exceptional amounts of the powerful atmospheric coolant SO_2 and had an exceptional volcanic explosivity index (VEI) of 7. Richard B. Stothers, 'Density of fallen ash after the eruption of Tambora in 1815', *Journal of Volcanology and Geothermal Research*, Vol. 134/4 (2004), pp. 343–5. Bibcode:2004JVGR..134..343S. doi:10.1016/j.jvolgeores.2004.03.010. Clive Oppenheimer, 'Climatic, environmental and human consequences of the largest known historic eruption: Tambora volcano (Indonesia) 1815', *Progress in Physical Geography*, Vol. 27/2 (2003), pp. 230–59. doi:10.1191/0309133303pp379ra.

p. 119   Although something of an exaggeration, 'Little *Ice* Age' is the scientific term, introduced in 1939 by François E. Matthes. 'Desert of Wales' is cited, but no source given, by John Henry Cliffe in *Notes and Recollections of an Angler: Rambles among the Mountains, Valleys, and Solitudes of Wales* (London: Hamilton, Adams, & Co., 1860).

p. 120   The Dalton Minimum was identified by the scientist and meteorologist John Dalton, who also gave his name to the phenomenon of colour-blindness.

p. 120   Figures for European deaths from the Year without a Summer come from an unreferenced 'BBC documentary' cited in Wikipedia: https://en.wikipedia.org/wiki/Year_Without_a_Summer [retrieved 27 January 2017].

p. 120   The Val de Bagnes ice dam breaks in 1818, with catastrophic results.

p. 120   Byron's description of Villa Diodati: LB to John Cam Hobhouse, 23 June 1816. Richard Lansdown (ed.), *Byron's Letters and Journals: A New Selection* (Oxford: Oxford University Press, 2015), p. 224.

p. 120   These are today's street names; since the two are connected by a 'Chemin Byron' we can't assume these were current in 1816.

p. 120   The Sécheron hotelier, M. Dejean, may resent the loss of his celebrity guest.

p. 120   Although Lady Caroline is credited with coining the epithet 'mad, bad and dangerous to know', Paul Douglass points out a lack of contemporary evidence for this attribution. Paul Douglass, *Lady Caroline Lamb: A Biography* (London: Palgrave Macmillan, 2004), pp. 109–18.

p. 121   Byron's opposition to the removal of the Parthenon marbles appears in stanzas xi–xv of *Childe Harold's Pilgrimage*, Canto 2.

p. 121   I can't find any source for the repeated myth of Byron's curlpapers.

p. 122   CC to LB, 21 April 1816 and 6 May 1816. Marion Kingston Stocking, ed. *The Clairmont Correspondence: Letters of Claire Clairmont, Charles Clairmont and Fanny Imlay Godwin, 1808–79*, Vol. 1, pp. 40–41.

p. 122   What is William vaccinated for? Local worries about typhoid are mentioned in Polidori's diary, but a typhoid vaccination won't be developed until 1896. Polidori records the sufferings of young Percy on 1 June, and William's vaccination on 2 June 1816. William Michael Rossetti (ed.), *The Diary of Dr. John William Polidori: 1816, Relating to Byron, Shelley, etc.* (London: Elkin Mathews, 1911), p. 116. https://archive.org/stream/diaryofdrjohnwiloopolirich/diaryofdrjohnwiloopolirich_djvu.txt [retrieved 26 June 2016].

p. 123   PBS to WG, 6 March 1816 and 6 May 1816. Olwen Ward Campbell, *Shelley and the Unromantics* (London: Methuen, 1924), pp. 137–8. Mrs Julian Marshall (ed.), *The Life and Letters of Mary Wollstonecraft Shelley* (London: Richard Bentley & Son, 1889), Vol. 1, p. 130. https://books.google.co.uk/books?id=BTPtJYcPNfgC [retrieved 31 January 2017]. George Edward Woodberry, *Studies in Letters and Life* (Boston, MA, and New York: Houghton, Mifflin & Co., 1890), p. 140. https://en.wikisource.org/wiki/Page:Studies_in_Letters_and_Life_(Woodberry,_1890).djvu/150 [retrieved 31 January 2017].

p. 124   Polidori is introduced to Mary the day after his note on her sex life. He seems to have paid more attention to this 'fact' than to details he finds less salient: Percy, who is twenty-three, not twenty-six, has been cleared of having TB; Claire is not Godwin's daughter. The doctor often uses the verb to tea in his diary, where it joins the more familiar gustatory verbs to breakfast and to dine. At least, we think these are his words, but the version eventually published in 1911 is his sister's transcription, and she destroyed the original. He omits mentioning helping Mary from his diary, which records only that he received a sprain 'jumping a wall'; 31 May 1816, 15 June 1816 and 27 May 1816. https://archive.org/stream/diaryofdrjohnwiloopolirich/diaryofdrjohnwiloopolirich_djvu.txt [retrieved 17 January 2017].

p. 124   Mary's letter to Fanny reappears in her first book. It's hard to say whether this is in good taste, given that the book is published a year after Fanny's suicide. *History of a Six Weeks' Tour*, pp. 99–100.

p. 124   *Fantasmagoriana, ou Receuil d'Histoires, d'Apparitions, de Spectres, Revenants, Fantômes, etc.*, 2 vols (Paris: F. Schoell, 1812). The translation is by the distinguished geographer, and translator of travel literature, Jean-Baptiste Benoît Eyriès; he's anonymous in the edition the group reads. An English edition has already introduced its own variations to the collection: Sarah Elizabeth Utterson (ed. and trans.), *Tales of the Dead, Principally Translated from the French* (London: White, Cochrane and Co., 1813).

p. 125   Other famous Gothic novels include Ann Radcliffe's *The Mysteries of Udolpho* (1794). Byron praises 'Monk' Lewis in Lord Byron, *English Bards and Scotch Reviewers: A Satire* (London: James Cawthorne, 1809), lines 265–78:

> Oh! wonder-working LEWIS! Monk, or Bard,
> Who fain wouldst make Parnassus a church-yard!
> Lo! wreaths of yew, not laurel, bind thy brow,
> Thy Muse a Sprite, Apollo's sexton thou!

Although by this time hard at work on *Frankenstein*, Mary chooses not to go with Percy to meet Lewis. *Journal* 18 August 1816. Jones, ed. (1947), p. 57.

p. 126   I'm quoting from the Translator's Introduction to *Fantasmagoriana*'s contemporary English translation; Utterson, ed. (1813), p. vii.

p. 126   Geneva is in Romandy, or French-speaking Switzerland. Further contemporary references to the *Stillingianer* seem be exclusively in German (and cease after the mid-nineteenth century).

p. 126   Mary's eyewitness account of Byron's challenge is from her 1831 'Introduction' to *Frankenstein*. Polidori's account is from his 1911 edition of his diary, 10–17 June 1816, pp. 121–5. She is telling a story *about* telling stories, and writing fifteen years after the event. He is writing his diary at the time, and, although we know that he had been commissioned to keep it by John Murray publishers – and although it does contain passages of 'purple' descriptive prose – often simply writes telegraphic notes to self. On 30 May 1816 Percy, Mary and Claire are 'All clever, and no meretricious appearance'. Mary's version does leave open the possibility that the challenge is issued on the 14th, or even the 15th, the conversation about 'principles' of life is on the 16th, and she starts to write on the 17th, leaving only Polidori on the starting blocks.

p. 127 Many of the autobiographical 'facts' Percy feeds Polidori are untrue. But his disclosure of an early diagnosis of madness is on 1 June: 'Shelley is another example of wealth inducing relations to confine for madness, and was only saved by his physician being honest', the diary notes. http://archive.org/sFream/diaryofdrjohnwi1oopolirich/ diaryofdrjohnwi1oopolirich_djvu.txt [retrieved 17 January 2017]. The surviving 'Fragment of a Ghost Story' by Shelley is doggerel verse, apparently written for children. 1 and 18 June 1816. Polidori (1911), pp. 112 and 128.

p. 127 That Mary gives Percy Coleridge's original image of the woman with eyes for nipples is uncovered by Charlotte Gordon in *Romantic Outlaws: The Extraordinary Lives of Mary Wollstonecraft and Mary Shelley* (London: Windmill Books/Penguin, 2015), p. 191. Perhaps not coincidentally, Percy's coinage appears in 'The Witch of Atlas', stanza xi, line 136, with its cruel opening addressed to Mary 'How, my dear Mary, — are you critic-bitten / (For vipers kill, though dead)' placed directly below the 'Witch' of the title.

p. 129 Mary's dismissal of Polidori's first story is also from her 1831 account.

p. 129 Many sources repeat variants of this myth of *The Vampyre*'s indebtedness to Byron, claiming that it is inspired by Byron's *Fragment*. Yet the entire focus of Polidori's story is completely different from Byron's.

pp. 129–30 Mary's visit to the Mer de Glace is recorded in her *Journal* 22 July 1816. Jones, ed. (1947), p. 52. The fallen mountain is 26 July 1816 and the waterfalls are 21 July 1816. Her Frankenstein visits it in Chapter X.

p. 130 Frankenstein's creature haunts Plainpalais, just outside Geneva. Chapter VII.

p. 131 'They have the custom here of marrying very early', Mary comments, citing an eighteen-year-old marrying a sixteen-year-old – the age at which she herself ran away with Percy. It's easy to forget how important a part youth plays in Mary's elopement story. Brought up as the bright child of her precociously achieving father, she is likely to value precocious achievement as an end in itself: she may be proud of how youthfully she has 'achieved' Percy. *Journal* 26 July 1816. Jones, ed. (1947), p. 54.

p. 132 Percy Bysshe Shelley, *Queen Mab: A Philosophical Poem*, Canto 6, lines 33–4; Canto 8, line 134; Canto 5, lines 137–146; and Canto 1, lines 133–4, respectively.

p. 132 Walton describes a gentlemanly Frankenstein in Chapter I.

p. 132 Lord Byron, *Childe Harold's Pilgrimage*, Canto 3 (London: John Murray, 1816), stanza 72, lines 680–86. http://knarf.english.upenn.edu/Byron/ charold3.html [retrieved 29 June 2016]. In the John Murray digital archive: http://digital.nls.uk/jma/gallery/title.cfm?id=29 [retrieved 31 January 2017].

p. 133   Claire's letters to Byron are, respectively, undated in March/April 1816, 20 April 1816 and 27 May 1816. Kingston Stocking, ed. (1995), Vol. 1, pp. 25, 39, 47.

p. 133   Byron's account of the affair with Claire is LB to AL 8 September 1816, in Richard Lansdown, *Byron's Letters and Journals: a new selection from Leslie A. Marchand's Twelve volume edition* (Oxford: Oxford University Press, 2015), pp. 229–30.

p. 134   Little does Claire know the pathos with which these negotiations echo those surrounding her own infancy, as we saw in Chapter 2. The pivotal date seems to be 2 August. Mary's *Journal* records: 'In the evening Lord Byron and [Percy] go out in the boat, and, after their return Shelley and Clare go up to Diodati; I do not, for Lord Byron did not seem to wish it.' In her next sentence, 'Shelley returns with a letter from Longdill, which requires his return to England. This puts us in very bad spirits.' This 'lawyer's letter' is the alibi to get the pregnant Claire home to England, and Mary is clearly excluded from this new, secret reason for everyone's 'bad spirits'. *Journal* 2 August 1816. Jones, ed. (1947), p. 55.

          Mary and Percy are indeed loyal to Claire; if they ever suspect that throwing her hat at the more famous Byron was an attempt to best them, they give no sign of doing so.

p. 134   'On me raconte qu'il y a eu, cet automne, sur les bords du lac la réunion la plus étonnante; c'étaient les états généraux de l'opinion européenne. […] À mes yeux, ce phénomène s'élève jusqu'à l'importance politique. Si cela durait quelques années, les décisions de toutes les académies de l'Europe pâliraient.' Stendhal, *Rome, Naples et Florence, en 1817* (Paris, E. Champion, 1854), p. 423.

p. 135   Mary's account in 1831 of this conversation about 'principles', and her portrait of Frankenstein as a man who understands his place in the world are in the Introduction and Letter IV.

p. 135   Among *Journal* entries recording work on her story, Mary notes that she is reading the Geneva-born Jean-Jacques Rousseau, whose educational theories influenced her own upbringing.

p. 136   The description of the giant creature is from *Frankenstein*, Chapter X.

Chapter 7: A Young Writer

p. 137   Epigraph *Frankenstein*, Chapter IV.

p. 137   Mary's nostalgia for Byron is triggered by publication of the Third Canto of *Childe Harolde*, written during the Villa Diodati summer.

          Since this is our chapter in which Mary marries, her initials now change from MWG to MWS. MWS *Journal* 28 May 1817. Jones, ed. (1947), p. 80.

p. 138   Some of this feeling about Bishopsgate may be pure sentiment, as the household had moved back to London before they left for Geneva.

          Mary's description of the cottage comes from *The Last Man*, Vol.

1, Chapter 3; http://onlinebooks.library.upenn.edu/webbin/gutbook/
lookup?num=18247 [retrieved 5 February 2017].

p. 139   Mary is no fan of house-hunting: 'I know what *seeking* for a house is and
           trust me it is a very *very* long job [...]—we shall both of us be put off day
           after day with the hope of the success of the next days search for I am
           frightened to think how long—' MWS to PBS 27 July 1815. Bennett, ed.
           (1980–88), Vol. 1, p. 15.

p. 139   For information about Mary's Bath neighbourhood see: http://
           www.coalcanal.org/history/Shareholders/Meyler.php and http://
           paintedsignsandmosaics.blogspot.co.uk/2010/07/circulating-library-and-
           reading-rooms.html [both retrieved 4 July 2016].

p. 141   The *Frankenstein* Notebooks are digitalised in facsimile: http://
           shelleysghost.bodleian.ox.ac.uk/Frankenstein-notebook-reader#page/1/
           mode/2up and http://shelleysghost.bodleian.ox.ac.uk/Frankenstein-
           notebook-reader2#page/2/mode/2up [retrieved 5 February 2017].

p. 141   Similarly, Mary studies Gothic material when she's first at work on her
           'ghost story'. On 26 and 27 August 1816, when the *Journal* records a rare
           instance of her re-reading, it is Samuel Taylor Coleridge's *Christabel*. Jones,
           ed. (1947), p. 61.

p. 141   For the cost of attending public lectures, see Laurence Brockliss, 'Science,
           universities and other public spaces', in Roy Porter (ed.), *The Cambridge
           History of Science*, Vol. 4, *Eighteenth-Century Science* (Cambridge:
           Cambridge, University Press, 2003), pp. 78–9.

p. 141   Source for labourers' wages: http://www.afamilystory.co.uk/history/wages-
           and-prices.aspx [retrieved 27 April 2016].

p. 141   Humphry Davy, *Elements of Chemical Philosophy* (London: Johnson and
           Co., 1812). pp. 1–32.

p. 141   Waldron tempts Frankenstein to broaden his studies in Chapter III.

p. 142   For more on the 1803 experiments with galvanism, see Chapter 2. Davy's
           poet admirers are named but no source is cited in 'Davy, Sir Humphry',
           Encyclopædia Britannica, 11th edn, ed. Hugh Chisholm (Cambridge:
           Cambridge University Press, 1911), Vol. 7, pp. 871–3. https://en.wikisource.
           org/wiki/1911_Encyclopædia_Britannica/Davy,_Sir_Humphry [retrieved 3
           February 2017].

p. 142   Mary takes herself to task for her 'tardiness' on 19 March 1823: Jones, ed.
           (1947), p. 189. The sentiment is of a piece with many entries from 1822–6:
           'So much for philosophising. Shall I ever be a philosopher?' *Journal* 3
           December 1815. Jones, ed. (1947), p. 197.

p. 142   Where other young ladies might paint a watercolour to send home, Mary
           sends description.

p. 143   At this time, sharing a letter with friends and family is customary. MWS
           to PBS 27 July 1815 and 5 December 1816. Bennett, ed. (1980–88), Vol. 1,
           pp. 22–3.

p. 144   By December 1816 Claire, in the last month of her own pregnancy, is
          unafraid to remind Mary that Percy's second partner may not come first
          with him in other ways either. 'My William who will lose his preeminence
          as eldest and be helped third at table—as his Aunt Claire is continually
          reminding him.' MWS to PBS 17 December 1816. Bennett, ed. (1980–88),
          Vol. 2, p. 25.

p. 144   The aunts' houses are in Primrose Street, EC2.

p. 144   Fanny also writes 'Mamma' for Mary Jane: she must know that both terms
          are honorifics.

p. 145   The report of Fanny's suicide is dated 11 October, and is from *The
          Cambrian,* 12 October 1816, p. 3. http://newspapers.library.wales/
          view/3323870/3323873/12/ [retrieved 5 February 2017].

p. 146   Mary Wollstonecraft seems to have been completely grey by the time
          of the Opie portrait of 1790–91, painted when she was no more than
          thirty-two. Perhaps she's portrayed wearing a hat because she went
          grey early. Imlay is an old American surname of Scottish or Irish rather
          than Mediterranean origin. But could he be partly native American? It
          would be wonderful to find that Mary Wollstonecraft was sufficiently far
          ahead of her time to fall in love with someone of mixed ethnicity; but no
          mention of either Imlay or Fanny uses the blunt or racist terminology of
          their day.

p. 146   From Bristol to Swansea the post coaches offer a direct service via
          the Bush Inn, Bristol, and the Bell Inn, Gloucester. The journey takes
          seventeen hours. The Spencer Godwin and Co.'s 'Original Gloucester
          Coach the Prince of Wales' runs three times weekly direct between the
          'Bolt in Tun, Fleet Street, London' and the Bush Inn, Swansea. Advertised
          in *The Cambrian* (5 October 1816); http://newspapers.library.wales/
          view/3323865 [retrieved 5 February 2017].

p. 147   'Men's handkerchiefs were […] often coloured for day use […] Generally
          of silk, cotton not being known among the middling ranks since the duty
          has been taken off silk […] Women's handkerchiefs, for day use, were
          of white cambric, linen or cotton; for evening, they were often of lace or
          edged with lace or embroidery.' http://www.bergfashionlibrary.com/view/
          bdfh/bdfh-div11644.xml [retrieved 13 August 2016].

p. 148   Godwin has borrowed £300 from William Kingdon, a 'stockbroker' or
          moneylender.

p. 148   Claire remembers Percy's reaction in Silsbee Papers, Bodleian Library, Box
          7, folder 2.

p. 148   William Godwin (1793), Book 2, Chapter 2, Appendix 1, p. 93.

p. 148   Does Percy show Mary the newspaper article? Would she recognise that
          handkerchief?

p. 148   Not only does suicide by poison ensure that the body is more decently
          covered; the suicide itself also stands more of a chance of being covered
          up.

p. 149   Harriet's suicide letter, with its touching scrawl and protestations of love, makes it clear that she is about to do the deed: 'oh I must be quick'. http://shelleysghost.bodleian.ox.ac.uk/harriet-shelleys-suicide-letter#Description [retrieved 5 January 2017].

p. 149   Neither Hookham's letter nor *The Times* article clarifies who identifies the body as 'Harriet Smith', or 'Harriet Smith' as Harriet Shelley. The Westbrooks have presumably withheld her suicide note from the inquest, which returns the verdict 'found drowned'. Edward Dowden (1969), pp. 334–5.

p. 150   'It is singular that it was not suggested to Basil Montagu by Shelley that he was not the father of his wife's child.' *Henry Crabb Robinson on Books and Their Writers*, ed. Edith J. Morley (London, J. M. Dent and Sons, 1938), Vol. 1. p. 211 (transcribing a *Diary* entry from November 1817.) Crabb Robinson doesn't take to Percy. Meeting him for the first time at Godwin's a few days earlier, he describes his conversation as 'vehement, and arrogant, and intolerant'. Thomas Sadler (ed.), *Diary, Reminiscences and Correspondence of Henry Crabb Robinson* (London: Macmillan and Co., 1869), Vol. 2, p. 67. https://archive.org/stream/diaryreminiscenco2robiiala/diaryreminiscenco2robiiala_djvu.txt [retrieved 5 January 2017].

p. 151   Bizarrely, Percy had also tried to live his first marriage in a trio with Eliza. On 18 December he foolishly writes to Eliza that Mary is 'the lady whose union with me you may excusably regard as the cause of your sister's ruin'. Leslie Hotson (ed.), *Shelley's Lost Letters to Harriet* (London: Faber, 1930), p. 175.

p. 151   Percy's proposal: PBS to MWS 16 December 1816. https://www.bl.uk/collection-items/letters-concerning-the-relationship-between-p-b-shelley-and-mary-godwin [retrieved 6 February 2017].

pp. 151–2   MWS to PBS, 17 December 1816. Bennett, ed. (1980–88), Vol. 1, p. 24. In her letter to Byron announcing the birth of his daughter by Claire, Mary is charmingly unable to resist telling him that: 'Another incident has also occurred which will surprise you, perhaps; It is a little piece of egotism in me to mention it—but it allows me to sign myself—in assuring you of my esteem & sincere friendship. Mary W. Shelley'
MWS to LB 13 January 1817. Bennett, ed. (1980–88), Vol. 1, p. 26.

p. 152   Godwin's change of attitude: PBS to CC 30 December 1816. Dowden (1969), p. 339.

p. 152   Ianthe and Charles are placed in the care of Revd Jacob Cheesborough of Kent and Cheshire, under the supervision of the royal physician Dr Hume and his wife, guardians selected by Percy. Monthly supervised visits are allowed to the father (not that he makes them: by the time of the ruling he is in Europe), monthly unsupervised to the maternal grandparents, and unlimited access to the paternal grandparents. Dowden (1969), pp. 341–51.

p. 153   Percy submits the 'Hymn to Intellectual Beauty' to *The Examiner*. Hunt loses the poem, which remains unpublished in Percy's lifetime, but the editorial arguably does his reputation more good.

p. 154   Daisy Hay analyses Hunt's editorial strategy in her *Young Romantics* (London: Bloomsbury, 2010), pp. 99–100.

p. 154   Mary joins the Hunt household at first intermittently and then, after disagreements at Skinner Street, continuously. Not everything there is perfect: Haydon and the married Leigh Hunt are both interested in Hunt's sister-in-law Bess.

p. 155   Percy's interlinear markings are clear on p. 12 of Notebook B of the Frankenstein manuscript, but the contrast between the same notebook's ultimate and penultimate pages is surely only a question of ink.

p. 155   Though Percy may only be correcting *part* of *Frankenstein* on 14 May 1817.

p. 156   The Shelleys bargain with Lackingtons some time between 2 and 19 September: *Journal* 19 September 1817. Jones, ed. (1947), p. 84.

p. 157   Healthy vegetarian diets are based on dietary *knowledge*: long regional tradition or contemporary scientific research, neither of which underpins Percy's doctrine.

p. 157   Mary asks Percy to help with proofs. Bennett, ed. (1980–88), Vol. 1, p. 42.

p. 157   Mary writes to Percy about revisions in MWS to PBS 24 September 1817, second letter. On 3 December she dedicates *Frankenstein* to her father.

p. 158   Mary writes pleadingly to Percy: MWS to PBS 28 September 1817. Bennett, ed. (1980–88), Vol. 1, pp. 45–7.

          'Pauvre, chere dame [...] Sans doute elle aime tendrement son mari et en etre separèe [*sic*] pour toujours [...] – quelle cruelle chose – qu'il doit etre un mechant homme pour quitter sa femme [...]'

p. 159   *Frankenstein*, Letter IV.

Chapter 8: Emigrants

p. 160   Epigraph *Frankenstein*, Chapter XIII.

p. 161   *Blackwood's Magazine* attacks Keats on August 1818: https://en.wikisource.org/wiki/Blackwood%27s_Magazine/On_the_Cockney_School_of_Poetry_IV [retrieved 10 September 2016].

p. 162   *Quarterly Review* attacks Keats on April 1818: http://spenserians.cath.vt.edu/TextRecord.php?textsid=7900 [retrieved 10 September 2016]. Keats has already learned that life is cruelly arbitrary as his family die one by one of TB.

p. 163   Percy's letter about sociability is PBS to TLP, late summer 1819, quoted in Dowden (1969), p. 429.

p. 163   Mary describes her childhood friend Isabella, *née* Baxter, whose husband is 'illtempered and jealous', as 'a victim' of marriage. Isabella's father suspects his son-in-law of being a bullying, possibly abusive husband. MWS to PBS 24 September 1817. Bennett, ed. (1980–88), Vol. 1, p. 41.

p. 163   'The anomaly [in England and Wales] is given as 149% of LTA
          (1916–1950).' http://booty.org.uk/booty.weather/climate/1800_1849.htm
          [retrieved 11 September 2016].

p. 164   Hunt doesn't, in the event, publish Percy's review of 'Rhododaphne'.

pp. 164–6 Mary's reviews are from: *The Edinburgh Magazine and Literary
          Miscellany; A New Series of 'The Scots Magazine'* 2 (March 1818), pp. 249–53.
          La Belle Assemblée, or Bell's Court and Fashionable Magazine, 2nd ser., 17
          (March 1818), pp. 139–42. *The Monthly Review*, n.s., 85 (April 1818), p. 439.
          The British Critic, n.s., 9 (April 1818), pp. 432–8; also reprinted in *The Port
          Folio* [Philadelphia] 6 (September 1818), pp. 200–07. *Blackwood's Edinburgh
          Magazine*, no. xii, II (March 1818), pp. 613–20; reprinted in Susan J.
          Wolfson (ed.), *Frankenstein: Longman Cultural Edition* (New York:
          Longman, 2007), pp. 377–82. *The Literary Panorama, and National Register*,
          n.s., 8 (1 June 1818), pp. 411–14. She is also reviewed in: *The Gentleman's
          Magazine* 88 (April 1818), pp. 334–5. *Quarterly Review* 18 (January [delayed
          until 12 June] 1818), pp. 379–85 (by John Wilson Croker). All via: https://
          www.rc.umd.edu/reference/chronologies/mschronology/reviews.html
          [retrieved 12 September 2016].

p. 166   Diderot and Jean le Rond d'Alembert took over as editors of the
          Encyclopédie in 1747.

p. 167   Mary records the crossing. *Journal* 12 March 1818. Jones, ed. (1947), p. 93.

p. 168   We don't know whether Claire behaves with dignity or hysteria as she
          parts with her daughter, though it's tempting to guess. *Journal* 28 April
          1818. Jones, ed. (1947), p. 97.

p. 169   Mary's invocation of the English experience of Italy comes from her
          Preface to *Rambles in Germany and Italy in 1840, 1842, and 1843* (London:
          Edward Moxon, 1844), Vol. 1, p. xvi.

p. 170   Mary's description of Bagni di Lucca: MWS to MG 15 June 1818. Bennett,
          ed. (1980–88), Vol. 1, p. 72.

p. 170   Mary's tie to her father is one Percy is never able to break, and it's based
          on just the mutual intellectual respect he longs for. Mary's thank you letter
          to Scott is MWS to WS, 14 June 1818. Bennett, ed. (1980–88), Vol. 1, p. 71.

p. 171   Mary's *Journal* records her hesitation over Percy's request as a 'consultation'
          with Maria Gisborne, 28 August 1818. Jones, ed. (1947), p. 104. Her
          letter: MWS to MG, [13] September 1818. Bennett, ed. (1980–88), Vol. 1,
          pp. 78–9.
              Percy issues his summons to Mary in PBS to MWS 22 September 1818.
          Jones, ed. (1964), pp. 39–40.

p. 173   Mary records Clara's death in her *Journal* 24 September 1818. Jones, ed.
          (1947), p. 105.

p. 173   Percy Bysshe Shelley, 'Julian and Maddalo: A Conversation', lines 28–30.

p. 173   Mary's recollection of this time in Venice appears in her last book,
          Rambles, Vol. 2, Part 3, Letter vi, p. 81.

p. 174   Byron admires *Frankenstein* in LB to John Murray 15 May 1819. https://web.archive.org/web/20080310063903/http://engphil.astate.edu/gallery/byron8.html [retrieved 9 February 2017].

p. 174   Mary writes about Harriet in her *Journal* 12 February 1839. Jones, ed. (1947), p. 207.

p. 175   MWS to MG 22 January 1819. Bennett, ed. (1980–88), Vol. 1, p. 85.

pp. 176–7   Elena's birth is registered at: http://www.antenati.san.beniculturali.it/v/Archivio+di+Stato+di+Napoli/Stato+civile+della+restaurazione/Chiaia/Nati/1819/004907061_00147.jpg.html?g2_imageViewsIndex=0 [retrieved 14 February 2017].

'Shelley' is written by ear on Elena's death certificate, using the Germanic spelling – *Schelly* – that comes naturally within the Austrian Empire. Percy is accurately described as a '*possidente*' or landowner, and the couple as 'domiciled in Livorno'. https://familysearch.org/search/collection/results?count=20&query=%2Bgivenname%3A%22Elena%20Adelaide%22~%20%2Bsurname%3AShelley~%20%2Bbirth_year%3A1818-1819~&collection_id=1937990 [retrieved 3 October 2016].

'Italia, Napoli, Stato Civile (Archivio di Stato), 1809–1865', database with images, *FamilySearch* (https://familysearch.org/ark:/61903/1:1:QJDQ-LGMW: 31 December 2015), Elena Schelly, Death, citing Quartiere Montecalvario, Napoli, Napoli, Italy, Archivio di Stato di Napoli (Napoli State Archives); FHL microfilm 1,981,140.

p. 177   It's not just the little girl they wanted to adopt at Champlitte-et-le-Prélot in 1814. At Albion House in 1818 they took in Polly Rose, a girl who was both local and poor, and though when they left for Italy Polly became a servant in the Hunts' household, while she lived with the Shelleys it was as a child of the household.

p. 178   Mary must feel the household's dirty linen is being washed in public when, during June 1820, they stay with the Gisbornes at Livorno in order to consult a lawyer over blackmail attempts.

p. 178   Mary's letter denying Elena is Claire and Percy's child is MWS to Isabella Hoppner. Her cover note to Percy urges, 'Do not think me imprudent in mentioning Clares illness at Naples—It is well to meet facts.' MWS to PBS 10 August 1821. Bennett, ed. (1980–88), Vol. 1, p. 204–8.

p. 178   Hoppner's allegations to Byron extend to the suggestion that Claire and Shelley's visits to doctors while little Clara was dying were to procure an abortion; made in a letter of 16 September 1821, cited in Bennett, ed. (1980–88), Vol.1, p. 205.

p. 178   Is it possible that Claire has difficult periods and that any incriminating blood Mary saw at the time was put down to this?

p. 178   Mary's misunderstanding of Elise's motivation has led some commentators to conjecture that the child is not Claire's but Elise's, by Percy, and that her 1821 disclosures are revenge for the death, on 9 June 1820, of a baby she has been forced to give up. If Percy *had* seduced Elise, there might indeed be an attempt to marry her off. Mary's letter claims Elise was pregnant when the household was in Naples. Elise by her own account had a daughter, born on 3 February 1821 and so conceived not long after Elena Adelaide was left behind in Naples: this would fit a pattern of compensatory pregnancies that marks Mary's own life. Elise might equally have been pregnant by Byron: by August 1819, after all, she had been agitating to return to the Shelleys' household and away from both Byron and the Hoppners, hinting that Byron was a sexual threat even to his own infant daughter. Percy's eagerness to look after the famous poet's accidental children might be a pattern established by Allegra, but Percy, not Byron, makes payments for Elena's care in Livorno in March 1820.

p. 179   Mary describes the newborn Percy Florence: MWS to MG [13] November 1819. Bennett, ed. (1980–88), Vol. 1, p. 112.

p. 179   Ironically, Mary writes, 'We are delighted with Rome, and nothing but the Malaria would drive us from it for many months', to Maria Gisborne two months before William dies of the disease. MWS to MG 9 April 1819. Bennett, ed. (1980–88), Vol. 1, p. 93.

p. 180   Letters: MWS to MG 5 June 1819 and MWS to MH 29 June 1819. Bennett, ed. (1980–88), Vol. 1, pp. 98, 101–2.

Chapter 9: Le rêve est fini

p. 185   Epigraph *Frankenstein*, Chapter XXIII.

p. 186   Percy posts his poem while out visiting 'Mrs Mason'. Percy Bysshe Shelley, *Epipsychidion*, lines 149–59.

p. 186   Emilia's real name is Teresa. Mary tells Leigh Hunt about her: MWS to LH 29 December 1820. Bennett, ed. (1980–88), Vol. 1, p. 172.

p. 187   Emilia tells Mary: 'Tu mi sembre un poco fredda, talvolta, e mi dai qualche soggezione; ma conosco, che tuo Marito disse bene, allorchè disse: *che la tua apparente freddezza, non è che la cenere che ricuopre un cuore affettuoso.*'

p. 187   Mary on Sophia: MWS to MG 2 December 1819. Bennett, ed. (1980–88), Vol. 1, p 118. Her letter to Sophia: MWS to SS 5 March 1820. Bennett, ed. (1980–88), Vol. 1, p. 130–31.

p. 188   PBS to CO 16 February 1821, quoted in the introductory note to *Epipsychidion* by H. B. Forman in a private edition, 1876. https://books.google.co.uk/books?id=viI_vmWNZSAC&pg=PA2&lpg=PA2&dq=shelley+epipsychidion&source=bl&ots=d [retrieved 16 October 2016].

p. 188   PBS to LB 14 November 1821. Seymour (2000), p. 269.

p. 189   Mary writes about Percy Florence: MWS to AC 20 June 1820. Bennett, ed. (1980–88), Vol. 1, p. 150.

p. 189   Her request for £400 to help her father is unsuccessful. MWS to MG 30 June 1820. Bennett, ed. (1980–88), Vol. 1, p. 151.

p. 189   Her father's letter of 9 September 1819. No other letters from this period survive, which proves nothing, but Mary frets over how few letters are arriving from Skinner Street, which possibly does. It's as if Godwin can think of nothing else to write to his daughter except demands for money.

p. 189 Mary describes their accommodation: MWS to MH 24 March 1820. Bennett, ed. (1980–88), Vol. 1, p. 136.

p. 190 Her requests for clothes: MWS to MG [13] December 1819, 22 March 1820, [21 March] 1821. Bennett, ed. (1980–88), Vol. 1, pp. 120, 135, 185.

p. 190 The nightcap: MWS to MG 19 February 1820. Bennett, ed. (1980–88), Vol. 1, p. 128.

p. 190 Nor does Claire's own acerbic note of 4 July 1820 accord with the picture of a withdrawn Mary: 'Heigh ho, the Claire and the Maie/Find something to fight about every day.'

p. 190 Mrs Mason's predicament reminds us that Claire's loss of custody is not unusual. Finally widowed in 1823, she will marry Tighe in 1826.

p. 191 The Tighe family recognise Mary's care. The notebook is rediscovered in fine condition nearly two centuries later by Cristina Dazzi, and authenticated and transcribed by Claire Tomalin for its first complete publication in 1998.

p. 191 Perhaps not coincidentally, in the first week of June 1820 Mary rereads her mother's own works and her father's memoir of Wollstonecraft.

p. 191 Byron had been interested in Hunt because he believed he was still at the high-profile *The Examiner*. But the Hunts stay on in Italy until 1825.

p. 192 As we saw in Chapter 8, Elena Adelaide dies of typhus in Naples on 9 June 1820.

p. 192 Maria Gisborne records Godwin's comments on Percy in her journal, 4 July 1820 and 9 July 1820. Frederick L. Jones (ed.), *Maria Gisborne and Edward E. Williams, Shelley's Friends: Their Journals and Letters* (Norman, OK: University of Oklahoma Press, 1951), pp. 38–9. Mary writes furiously to Maria: MWS to MG 16 October 1820. Bennett, ed. (1980–88), Vol. 1, pp. 160–61.

p. 194 Percy Bysshe Shelley, *The Masque of Anarchy* (title changed by publisher of first edition: London: Edward Moxon, 1832), lines 1, 5–6. http://knarf. english.upenn.edu/PShelley/anarchy.html [retrieved 16 February 2017].

Yet Percy's friendship with Leigh Hunt hiccupped in September 1819, when *The Examiner* felt unable to publish this poem.

p. 195 Euthanasia's story is a new paradigm. The tragic 'Classical' heroines – Dido abandoned by Aeneas, Cleopatra losing Mark Antony – see love sacrificed to the great game of public service. Euthanasia's lover simply wants to annex her.

p. 195 Mary is a Joan Bull in MWS to MH 24 March 1820, Bennett, ed. (1980–88), Vol. 1, p. 138.

p. 195 In 1819 Percy self-publishes his five-act verse-play *The Cenci*. Distributed in London in 1820, the book is a critical and commercial success and goes into a second edition. In early summer 1821 Percy publishes *Adonais*, which attracts further widespread attention.

p. 198   Mary on being preached against: MWS to MG 7 March 1822. Her verdict
          on Pacchiani: MWS to CC 14–15 January 1821, Bennett, ed. (1980–88), Vol.
          1, pp. 223, 175–8.

p. 198   Taaffe's fascinated admiration of Percy's work is apparent in his copious
          annotations of the 1821 Pisan edition of *Adonais*. http://blogs.libraries.
          claremont.edu/sc/2009/06/shelleys-adonais-1821-pisa-edi.html [retrieved
          22 October 2016].

p. 199   The description of Percy is from Edward Williams's letter to E. J. Trelawny
          19 April 1821; Jones, ed. (1951), p. 158.

p. 199   The Ottoman empire's Grand Dragoman and Grand Dragoman of the
          Fleet, and the Hospodar of Moldavia, are always appointed from the same
          Phanariot community.

p. 199   The Bucegi Mountains are part of the Southern Carpathians, also known
          as the Transylvanian Alps.

p. 200   Mary's letters to Mavrokordatos don't survive the battlefields and public
          service of his life. She describes him to Leigh Hunt: MWS to LH 29
          December 1820. Bennett, ed. (1980–88), Vol. 1, p. 173.

p. 200   There's something mysterious about Alexandros's subsequent romantic life.
          He marries twice, and in the late 1830s he will father two sons by his first
          wife, Chariclea Argyropoulos, who is a fellow Phanariot – but who lives in
          Italy, not Greece.

p. 201   Jane Williams was married to John Edward Johnson, who seems to have
          been violently abusive. To place Percy's lyrics see Hutchinson (1929).

p. 202   The Williamses share the Shelleys' apartment in the month of November,
          before moving to their own rooms within the Palazzo. Mary on Jane's
          dullness: MWS to CC 21–4 January 1821. Bennett, ed. (1980–88), Vol. 1,
          p. 180.

pp. 202–3 Mary's description of Medwin: MWS to CC [14–15] January 1821.
          Medwin's friend's offer conveyed to Claire by Percy: PBS to CC 29
          October 1820. Bennett, ed. (1980–88), Vol. 1, p. 178.

p. 203   Strictly speaking, Daniel Roberts only reached the lower rank of
          Commander during his Navy service, but 'Captain' would have been the
          usual address by his crew.

p. 204   Two days later Mary adds: '[Trelawny's] company is delightful for he
          excites me to think and if any evil shade the intercourse that time will
          unveil.' MWS to MG 9 February 1822. Bennett, ed. (1980–88), Vol. 1, p. 218.

p. 204   *Journal* 7, 8 and 9 February 1822. Jones, ed. (1947), p. 167–8.

p. 205   Trelawny's reminiscence comes from Edward John Trelawny, *Records of
          Shelley, Byron, and the Author* (London: George Routledge & Sons, 1878),
          Chapter VII, p. 61. https://archive.org/stream/recordsofshelleyootrel/
          recordsofshelleyootrel_djvu.txt [retrieved 17 February 1817. Nevertheless, in
          1821 Percy had already built a kind of coracle, 'a boat such as the huntsmen
          carry about with them in the Maremma […] a boat of laths and pitched
          canvas', for use on the Arno. Unfortunately it overturns in the sea canal

one day in April, but 'a wetting was all the harm done, except that the intense cold of his drenched clothes made Shelley faint'. Details of the men's sailing activities are Mary's own. Mary Shelley 'Notes on Poems of 1821', *The Complete Poetical Works of Percy Bysshe Shelley*, ed. Thomas Hutchinson (Oxford: Oxford University Press, 1929), pp. 656–7.

p. 205   The dragoon, named Masi, survives.

pp. 206–10   Details of the unfolding tragedy at Casa Magni are taken from Mary's letter to Maria Gisborne, which omits any mention of Claire and Allegra. MWS to MG 15 August 1822. Bennett, ed. (1980–88), Vol. 1, pp. 244–50.

p. 207   Mary on her miscarriage is MWG to JW 31 May 1823. Bennett, ed. (1980–88), Vol. 1, p. 341. Percy's letter to John Gisborne survives in transcript 18 June 1822. *The Letters of Percy Bysshe Shelley*, ed. Frederick L. Jones, 2 vols. (Oxford: Clarendon Press, 1964), Vol. 2, p. 435.

p. 208   Edward Trelawny's approving comment on the *Don Juan* is a diary entry, for 12 May 1822, quoted by Mary Shelley in 'Notes on Poems of 1822', *Complete Poetical Works of Percy Bysshe Shelley* (1929), p. 670.

p. 208   Although Trelawny and Williams pull out of the plan to *pay* for the boat in partnership with Percy, Trelawny names the vessel. Percy wanted to call it *Ariel*, but the boat arrives 'disfigured' with 'Don Juan' painted on its mainsail. MWG to MG 2 June 1822. Bennett, ed. (1980–88), Vol. 1, p. 236.

p. 208   Charles, one of three English seamen who delivered the boat to Percy, stays behind for the job of boat boy.

p. 210   Trelawny's description of how he breaks the news to Mary is in *Records* (1878), p. 161.

p. 210   Mary calls Casa Magni a 'dungeon' in an extraordinary letter warning Hunt off the place. MWS to LH [30] June 1822. Bennett, ed. (1980–88), Vol. 1, p. 238.

p. 210   Trelawny's detailed description of Percy's body comes from Trelawny (1878), pp. 128–9.

p. 211   Trelawny records a deathbed confession in the 1860s by 'a boatman dying near Sarzana' that the *Don Juan* was rammed for 'gold' on board. Trelawny (1878), p. 165.

p. 211   Trelawny and Hunt seem to have held on to some fragments of skull, however. These are now held in the Keats–Shelley Archive in Rome and at New York Public Library. http://www.atlasobscura.com/articles/shelley-skull-fragments-at-nypl [retrieved 28 October 2016].

p. 212   Mary confides her true feelings to Mara Gisborne: MWS to MG Genoa 17 September 1822 and 6 November 1822, Bennett, ed. (1980–88), Vol. 1, pp. 260, 287.

Chapter 10: The Mona Lisa Smile

p. 213   Epigraph *Frankenstein*, Letter IV.

p. 214   The teachers, who take in boarders, seem like hucksters, misquoting fees and charging for extras such as furniture. MWS to John Gregson 16 December 1832. Bennett, ed. (1980–88), Vol. 2, p. 177.

p. 214   The name of Bessie's birth mother's name has not come down to us, but her father shares a name with Percy's brother-in-law, so it seems likely that she was an 'accident' by whom the family do right.

p. 215   She describes the teenaged Percy to Elizabeth Stanhope 17 May 1833. Bennett, ed. (1980–88), Vol. 2, p. 191. See note to p. 218.

p. 215   TS to Byron 6 February 1823. http://shelleysghost.bodleian.ox.ac.uk/letter-from-shelleys-father-refusing-to-help-mary [retrieved 23 October 2016]. Sir Timothy himself has an illegitimate oldest son, to whom he gives his name but not inheritance rights. 'Captain Shelley' even marries his lawyer's daughter. The gentry's 'first duties' are to secure legitimate family fortune and title. An accidental child before marriage denotes sexual laxity, but not straying from this task.

p. 216   Mary's response to Sir Timothy's terms: MWS to LB [25] February 1823. She thinks of writing for Hunt's *The Liberal*. Bennett, ed. (1980–88), Vol. 1, pp. 315–16.

p. 216   Mary worries about Percy's will: MWS to TJH 28 February 1823. Bennett, ed. (1980–88), Vol. 1, p. 318.

p. 217   Elizabeth Jane Perry married Sir Bysshe Shelley in 1769.

p. 217   In the Shelley sisters' portrait thought to have been arranged by Lady Jane Shelley after Mary's death, Margaret wears a mourning necklace woven from Mary Wollstonecraft's hair by Antony Forrer, 'Artist in Hair Jewelry to Her Majesty', who ran an atelier with more than fifty employees: presumably this was also commissioned by Lady Jane. From the necklace dangle two lockets containing hair, initialled PBS and MWS respectively.

p. 218   'He has an hereditary passion for the sea', Mary comments wearily about Percy Florence to the Australian Alexander Berry, who married her first cousin Elizabeth, *née* Wollstonecraft, and is in partnership with Elizabeth's brother Edward. MWS to AB 17 August 1847. Bennett, ed. (1980–88), Vol. 3, p. 326.

p. 218   Oxford University's records show Percy Florence received his BA in 1841. http://venn.lib.cam.ac.uk/cgi-bin/search-2016.pl?sur=&suro=w&fir=&firo=c&cit=&cito=c&c=all&z=all&tex=SHLY837PF&sye=&eye=&col=all&maxcount=50 [retrieved 11 December 2016].

p. 218   Mary on Percy Florence: MWS to William Whitton 2 December 1829; MWS to CC London 30 August [1843]. Mary on 'his fathers family': MWS to William Whitton 2 December 1829. Bennett, ed. (1980–88), Vol. 2, p. 91; Vol. 3, p. 83.

p. 218   Mary on Sir Timothy's death: MWS to TJH 24 April 1844. On Lady Shelley: MWS to CC 4 June 1844. Perhaps this civility is not just self-interest but also 'the natural sense of propriety' as Mary calls it in a letter to Claire the year before. MWS to CC 30 August 1843. Bennett, ed. (1980–88), Vol. 3, pp. 124, 135, 85.

p. 218   See, for example, both the article and the References in Lilian MacNell, Adam Driscoll and Andrea N. Hunt, 'What's in a Name: exposing gender bias in student ratings of teaching', in *Innovative Higher Education*, Vol. 40/4 (August 2015), pp. 291–303.

p. 219   Mary tells Byron that she has feelings: MWS to LB [25] February 1823, Bennett, ed. (1980–88), Vol. 1, p. 316. Mary on her 'iced' heart: *Journal* 31 December 1822. Jones, ed. (1947), p. 186.

p. 219   Percy complains about Mary: PBS to JG 18 June 1822. *The Prose Works of Percy Bysshe Shelley*, ed. Harry Buxton Forman (London, Reeves and Turner, 1880), Vol. 4, pp. 279–82.

p. 219   Hunt records this for posterity as: 'We were to live in the same house with her […] The rent of this house was twenty pounds a-year.' Leigh Hunt, *Lord Byron and Some of His Contemporaries, with Recollections of the Author's Life and of His Visit to Italy* (London: Henry Colburn, 1828), p. 61.

p. 220   Hunt's letter to Novello is LH to VN 24 July 1823 (Brotherton Collection, Leeds Novello Cowden Clarke Papers). It does indeed ease her passage. Mary visits the Novello family so often at their home in what is now Hackney that gossip that she is having an affair forces her to break off the friendship in March 1828. MS to VN 11 March 1828. Bennett, ed. (1980–88), Vol. 2, pp. 28–9.

p. 220   Mary on Trelawny and Greece: MWS to LB 14 June 1823. Bennett, ed. (1980–88), Vol. 1, p. 343.

p. 221   Hogg writes to Jane sceptical of Mary's grief. TJH to JW 17 April 1823. MS Abinger Dep. c.211. Although his first child with Jane does not survive infancy, a second, born in 1836, does.

p. 221   We know Jane is the source of Hunt's misconstrual from Hunt's letter of rebuke once the record is eventually put straight.

pp. 222–4   Mary's self-analysing *Journal* entries are 13 July 1823, 10 November 1822, 2 October 1822, 19 October 1822, 2 October 1822, 2 December 1834 and 21 October 1838; Jones, ed. (1947), pp. 199, 185,181, 183–4, 181, 203, 205.

p. 224   John Keats chose his own epitaph, 'Here lies One Whose Name was writ in Water', shortly before his death in 1821; he was buried in the same Protestant Cemetery in Rome as Wilmouse and Percy Bysshe Shelley.

p. 225   Reviews of *The Last Man* are from *The Monthly Review* (March 1826). Cited by Betty T. Bennett, 'Radical Imaginings: Mary Shelley's *The Last Man*', in Steven E. Jones (ed.), *The Last Man by Mary Wollstonecraft Shelley: A Romantic Circles Electronic Edition*. https://www.rc.umd.edu/editions/mws/lastman/bennett.htm [retrieved 14 February 2016] and *The Literary Gazette* (18 February 1826).

p. 225   For more on working men's wages see: https://www.measuringworth.com/datasets/ukearncpi/earnstudynew.pdf [retrieved 14 December 1816].

p. 225   *Lodore* is reviewed in *The Literary Gazette*, Vol. 19/949 (28 March 1835),
          p. 194. https://books.google.co.uk/books?id=VuVGAQAAMAAJ&pg=PA
          194&lpg=PA194&dq=%22one+of+the+most+original+of+our+modern+writ
          ers%22+gazette&source=bl&ots=GG-dFhGpEg&sig=Ygd8y52ho1ArljxRp
          vnc2OiiGqo&hl=en&sa=X&ved=0ahUKEwj39KbN4_bQAhUGDsAKH
          fP8CHgQ6AEIIDAB#v=onepage&q=%22one%20of%20the%20most%20
          original%20of%20our%20modern%20writers%22%20gazette&f=false
          [retrieved 15 December 1816].

p. 225   Mary wrangles with Ollier for review copies of *Lodore*: MWS to CO 25
          March and 6 April 1835. Bennett, ed. (1980–88), Vol. 2, pp. 237, 239.

p. 226   Mary finds herself famous: MWS to LH 9 September 1823. Bennett, ed.
          (1980–88), Vol. 1, p. 259.

p. 226   *Lodore*, Vol. 3, Chapter 1: https://ebooks.adelaide.edu.au/s/shelley/mary/
          lodore/v3.1.html [retrieved 22 December 2016]. *Lodore* Vol. 3, Conclusion:
          https://ebooks.adelaide.edu.au/s/shelley/mary/lodore/v3.19.html [retrieved
          22 December 2016]

p. 227   Mary tells Trelawny she was apt to get tousy-mousy: MWS to ET 12
          October 1835. Bennett, ed. (1980–88), Vol. 2, p. 256.
          'Towsy-mowsy (DORSET)' appears next to 'Towdie (DUNBAR)',
          which suggests an alternative, Scottish source in the poet William Dunbar
          for this part of Mary's vocabulary. John Stephen Farmer, *Slang and Its
          Analogues Past and Present: A Dictionary* (London: Harrison and Sons,
          1896), Vol. 4, p. 40.

p. 228   Mary's Latin joke: 'this' is only feminine and neuter, not masculine ('hic').
          'Corpus delicti', with the masculine of 'delicta', means the evidence of a
          crime. MWS to JWH 23 September 1827. Bennett, ed. (1980–88), Vol. 1,
          p. 573. MWS to JWH 28 August 1827. Bennett, ed. (1980–88), Vol. 2, p. 9.

p. 228   'Mrs David Booth (*née* Isabel Baxter)' is glimpsed in a painting by
          William Ross in the possession of her granddaughter Isabelle Stuart, and
          in Stuart (1911), pp. 93–4. Miranda Seymour points out the resemblance in
          Seymour p. 75.

p. 228   Notably, when the friendship resumes in 1828 after David Booth's death,
          Mary is eager both to tell Isabella that 'one of the cleverest men in France,
          young and a poet' admires her, and to note that 'I am in no danger of
          permanent disfiguration' from smallpox. MWS to IBB 15 June 1828.
          Bennett, ed. (1980–88), Vol. 2, pp. 46–7.

p. 228   Although scandal surrounding Mary's elopement would be reason enough
          to forbid contact.

p. 229   Some vocabulary existed for sex, but not for love, between women.

p. 229   After nursing her mother, who dies in 1841, Claire will go to live with
          Mrs Mason in Pisa, and then, in 1870, with her niece Paulina in Florence,
          where she will die at the grand old age of eighty on 19 March 1879. During
          the 1840s, however, she also spends some time in Paris, and Mary visits her
          there in 1843.

p. 229   Mary describes Emilia in a letter to Hunt: MWS to LH 29 December
         1820. Bennett, ed. (1980–88), Vol. 1, p. 172.

pp. 229–30 All these endearments are from a single letter: MWS to JW 31 May 1823.
            Bennett, ed. (1980–88), Vol. 1, pp. 340–42.

p. 230   Mary's angry letter is written on the Thursday following an initial 'scene'
         of accusation that Monday. MWS to JW 14 February 1828. Bennett, ed.
         (1980–88), Vol. II, p. 25.

p. 230   Betty T. Bennett revealed Dods's identity in *Mary Diana Dods, A
         Gentleman and a Scholar* (New York: William Morrow, 1991). Miranda
         Seymour unpacks the story of the Douglases in Chapter 25, pp. 378–89.

p. 231   The 1818 version of Frankenstein's knowledge remains in 1831 at the start of
         Chapter IV.

p. 231   Mary critiqued as insufficiently feminist: http://www.victorianweb.org/
         previctorian/mshelley/bio.html [retrieved 12 January 2017].

p. 231   Trelawny's motives are not unmixed. He has moved in with Mary's friend
         Augusta Goring – they have an illegitimate child together in 1839 – and
         is experiencing at first hand the costs for women who fail to follow moral
         conventions.

p. 231   Mary agonises over her apolitical writing in her *Journal* 21 October 1838.
         Jones, ed. (1947), pp. 204–5. She writes to Maria Gisborne about her
         'weakness' on 11 June 1835, Bennett, ed. (1980–88), Vol. 3, p. 246.

p. 232   Godwin's *Diary* reveals that after the bankruptcy he remained friends with
         Lamb, Scott, Coleridge, Wordsworth and others.

p. 232   Mary's description of her father's death: MWS to MH 20 April 1836.
         Bennett, ed. (1980–88), Vol. 2, p. 270.

p. 233   Jane Austen's *Sense and Sensibility* was published in 1811.

p. 234   Mary on biography MWS to [?] 4 December 1847. Bennett, ed. (1980–88),
         Vol. 3, p. 330.

p. 234   Virginia Woolf ascribes the lifelike blur to Thomas Hardy in 'The Novels
         of Thomas Hardy', in *The Common Reader,* second series (London:
         Hogarth Press, 1935), pp. 224–5).

p. 235   Mary on self-improvement: *Journal* 21 October 1838. Jones, ed. (1947),
         p. 204.

p. 235   Mary describes her courtship by Mérimée: MWS to IBB 15 June 1828.
         Bennett, ed. (1980–88), Vol. 2, pp. 46–7.

p. 235   http://drc.usask.ca/projects/lives/plaintextview.php?chapter=10&volume=2
         [retrieved 23 December 2016], p. 206. Ibid., pp. 194–5.

p. 235   Discreet Mary uses only Aubrey Beauclerk's initials in her *Journal*, where
         she writes 'Farewel [*sic*]' on the date of his wedding on 13 February 1834
         and, a year later, 'An anniversary strange & bitter', as Miranda Seymour
         points out, p. 426.

p. 236   Mary's premature confidence: MWS to JH 5 May 1832. Bennett, ed.
         (1980–88), Vol. 2, p. 189.

p. 236   Rosa, born 9 July 1818, is the daughter of Joshua Robinson, a
          'gentleman', recorded in the baptismal register of the parish of St
          Marylebone: http://interactive.ancestry.co.uk/1558/31280_194654-
          00489?pid=1102352&backurl=//search.ancestry.co.uk//cgi-bin/sse.dll?indi
          v%3D1%26db%3DLMAbirths%26h%3D1102352%26tid%3D%26pid%3D%
          26usePUB%3Dtrue%26usePUBJs%3Dtrue%26rhSource%3D1623&treeid=
          &personid=&hintid=&usePUB=true&usePUBJs=true [retrieved 8 January
          2017].

p. 236   Mary's hope: *Journal* 27 November 1839. [Not in Jones, etc. (1947)]

p. 236   For more on Jane Gibson's background see Betty T. Bennett, *Mary
          Wollstonecraft Shelley: An Introduction* (Baltimore, MD: Johns Hopkins
          University Press, 1996), p. 119.

p. 236   Darrel W. Amundsen and Carol Jean Diers, 'The age of menopause in
          Medieval Europe', *Human Biology*, Vol. 45/4 (December 1973), pp. 605–12.
          https://www.jstor.org/stable/41459908?seq=1#page_scan_tab_contents
          [retrieved 7 January 2017]. Mary suggests it to Claire: MWS to CC 7
          December 1844. Bennett, ed. (1980–88), Vol. 3, p. 164.

p. 238   *Journal* 12 February 1839. Jones, ed. (1947), pp. 206–7.

p. 238   At Christmas 1839 Mary refuses another approach by a would-be
          biographer of Percy, this time the twenty-two-year-old George Henry
          Lewes.

Coda

p. 240   Epigraph *Frankenstein*, Chapter XXIV.

p. 240   *Journal* 2 December 1834. Jones, ed. (1947), p. 203.

p. 242   Mary tells Augusta Trelawny about her daughter-in-law MWS to AT 10
          June 1848. Bennett, ed. (1980–88), Vol. 3, p. 339.

p. 241   Mary on Field Place's dullness: MWS to CC 4 June 1844. Bennett, ed.
          (1980–88), Vol. 3, p. 135.

p. 241   Jane meets Percy because her relatives are Mary's neighbours. Bennett, ed.
          (1980–88), Vol. 3, p. 339.

p. 242   Another possible reason for Jane's childlessness, and a speculation
          prompted by Percy Florence's rather weak and dapper appearance in
          surviving photos, is that this is a lavender marriage.

p. 242   Mary writes about the 'burthens on the estate' MWS to CC 6 December
          and 27 October 1844. Bennett, ed. (1980–88), Vol. 3, pp. 157, 162–3. Lady
          Shelley 'removed every thing worth having, & sold the rest by auction. She
          wanted to take out the grates & fixtures but was stopt.' MWS to CC 7
          December 1844. Bennett, ed. (1980–88), Vol. 3, p. 163. Even moving to Field
          Place is tricky: the incumbent, Sir James Duke, has to be bought out of
          his lease. Bennett note to MWS to John Gregson 7 July 1848. Bennett, ed.
          (1980–88), Vol. 3, p. 343.

p. 243   For 2017 equivalents to prices see http://inflation.stephenmorley.org
          [retrieved 8 January 2017]. The same site calculates Mary's borrowed

£50,000 as equivalent to £5.75 million in 2017. MWS to CC 7 December 1844. Bennett, ed. (1980–88), Vol. 3, p. 163.

p. 243   It would cost too much to set up home in Castle Goring, which Mary sells as soon as possible, for £11,250, paying off some debts and enabling her to buy the London house.

p. 243   'I should have liked to have made [Percy Florence] more a man of business—but for his own happiness he could not be altered for the better.' MWS to CC 27 October 1844. Bennett, ed. (1980–88), Vol. 3, p. 157–8.

p. 243   Percy Florence's letter is to an unnamed intermediary via 'Mr Rt Browning', her neighbour in Florence 1847–61. http://shelleysghost. bodleian.ox.ac.uk/draft-letter-from-sir-percy-florence-shelley-to-mr-cartright?item=194#Description [retrieved 17 April 2017].

p. 243   Mary's 'sheet anchor' is also MWS to CC 27 October 1844. Bennett, ed. (1980–88), Vol. 3, p. 158.

p. 243   Mary's financial fears: MWS to CC 11 September 1843. Bennett, ed. (1980–88), Vol. 3, p. 89. MWS to John Gregson 7 July 1848. Bennett, ed. (1980–88), Vol. 3, p. 343. MWS to CC 28 July 1848. Bennett, ed. (1980–88), Vol. 3, p. 345.

p. 244   Mary on 'Artistes': MWS to CC 28 July 1848. Bennett, ed. (1980–88), Vol. 3, p. 344.

p. 244   Mary on Radicals: *Journal* 21 October 1838. Jones, ed. (1947), p. 205.

p. 244   According to the research published in the *American Heart Association Journal* and the UK Government Health and Safety Executive. http:// newsroom.heart.org/news/ptsd-traumatic-experiences-may-raise-heart-attack-stroke-risk-in-women; and http://www.hse.gov.uk/stress/ furtheradvice/signsandsymptoms.htm [both retrieved 9 January 2017].

p. 245   Mary's love of Italy is not in Jones, ed. (1947).

p. 245   Knox's later life is according to Cornelia Crosse, *Red Letter Days of My Life* (London: R. Bentley & Son, 1892). pp. 146–59. https://archive.org/ details/redletterdaysmyooocrosgoog [retrieved 9 January 2017].

p. 245   Making Knox a travelling companion 'Will fall rather heavily on my purse', Mary notes ruefully. MWS to CC 2 June 1842. Bennett, ed. (1980–88), Vol. 3, p. 28.

p. 245   Knox has only found 'two stupid Englishmen as yet'. MWS to CC 28 June 1842. Bennett, ed. (1980–88), Vol. 3, p. 32.

p. 246   That writing *Rambles* is purely expedient: MWS to CC 10 November 1843. Bennett, ed. (1980–88), Vol. 3, p. 105.

p. 247   'Had he said £100 there had been a semblance of truth', as Mary tells Jane Hogg. MWS to JH 30 May 1846. Bennett, ed. (1980–88), Vol. 3, p. 286.

p. 247   Mary's poor review is 'Shelley's Posthumous Prose' in *The Spectator* 14 December 1839. http://archive.spectator.co.uk/article/14th-december-1839/14/shelleys-posthumous-prose [retrieved 22 February 2017].

p. 248   Mary is re-evaluated in Richard Horne (ed.), *A New Spirit of the Age* (London: Smith, Elder & Co. 1844), Vol. 2, p. 232. https://archive.org/

stream/newspiritofage02horn#page/n5/mode/2up [retrieved 9 January 2017].

p. 249   Bournemouth population 1851: http://www.localhistories.org/bournemouth.html [retrieved 18 April 2017].

p. 250   The quotations are from *Frankenstein*, Letter IV and Chapter XXIV.

Further Reading

Letters and Journals

The Shelley family gave the first two parts of their family archive to the Bodleian
Library at the University of Oxford in 1893–4 and 1946–61. The final selection – known
as the Abinger papers – was bought by the Library in 2004. Ninety per cent of the
Godwin and Shelley family manuscripts are held by either the Bodleian or New
York Public Library; these are gradually being digitised and placed online at http://
shelleygodwinarchive.org. The Bodleian Library also holds William Godwin's Journal,
which they have digitised and made available online at godwindiary.bodleian.ox.ac.uk.
Good editions of the non-digitised material include:

Betty T. Bennett (ed.), *The Letters of Mary Wollstonecraft Shelley*, 3 vols (Baltimore, MD,
  and London: Johns Hopkins University Press, 1980–88)
Paula Feldman and Diana Scott-Kilvert, *Mary Shelley, Journals*, 2 vols (Oxford: Oxford
  University Press, 1987)
[There is also an alternative, single-volume edition, referred to in the Notes here:
  Frederick L. Jones (ed.), *Mary Shelley's Journal* (Norman, OK: University of
  Oklahoma Press, 1947)]
Frederick L. Jones (ed.), *Maria Gisborne and Edward E. Williams, Shelley's Friends: Their
  Journals and Letters* (Norman, OK: University of Oklahoma Press, 1951)
Frederick L. Jones (ed.), *The Letters of Percy Bysshe Shelley* (Oxford: Clarendon Press,
  1964)
Marion Kingston Stocking (ed.), *The Clairmont Correspondence: Letters of Claire
  Clairmont, Charles Clairmont, and Fanny Imlay Godwin, 1808–1879*, 2 vols (Baltimore,
  MD: Johns Hopkins University Press, 1995)
Richard Lansdown (ed.), *Byron's Letters and Journals: A New Selection* (Oxford: Oxford
  University Press, 2015)

William Michael Rossetti (ed.), *The Diary of Dr. John William Polidori: 1816, Relating to Byron, Shelley, etc.* (London: Elkin Mathews, 1911)

Primary Works

Listed as first published: where there's an in-print or widely available edition, this is also given. Other works are digitised or available as print on demand.

William Godwin, *An Enquiry Concerning Political Justice, and Its Influence on General Virtue and Happiness* (London. G. G. J. Robinson and J. Robinson, 1793)

William Godwin, *Caleb Williams: or, Things as They Are*, 3 vols (London: B. Crosby, 1794); repr., ed. Maurice Hindle (Harmondsworth: Penguin, 2005)

William Godwin, *Memoirs of the Author of A Vindication of the Rights of Woman* (London: Joseph Johnson, 1798); repr. in Mary Wollstonecraft and William Godwin, *A Short Residence in Sweden & Memoirs of the Author of 'The Rights of Woman' AND Memoirs of the Author of 'The Rights of Woman'*, ed. Richard Holmes (Harmondsworth: Penguin, 1987)

William Godwin, *Fleetwood, or The New Man of Feeling* (New York: I. Riley & Co., 1805)

Mary Shelley, with Percy Bysshe Shelley, *History of a Six Weeks' Tour through a Part of France, Switzerland, Germany and Holland: With Letters Descriptive of a Sail Round the Lake of Geneva, and of the Glaciers of Chamouni* (London: Hookham and Ollier, 1817)

Mary Shelley, *Frankenstein: or, The Modern Prometheus* (London: Lackington, 1818); rev. with new preface (London: Colburn and Bentley, 1831); repr., ed. M. K. Joseph, Oxford World Classics (Oxford: Oxford University Press, 1980)

[Mary Shelley's *Frankenstein* notebooks are held at the Bodleian Library and have been digitised and are online at http://shelleygodwinarchive.org/contents/frankenstein/]

Mary Shelley, *Valperga; or, The Life and Adventures of Castruccio, Prince of Lucca* (London: Whittaker, 1823)

Mary Shelley, *The Last Man* (London, Henry Colburn, 1826); repr., with intro. and notes by Pamela Bickley (Ware: Wordsworth Classics, 2004)

Mary Shelley, *The Fortunes of Perkin Warbeck: A Romance* (London: Colburn and Bentley, 1830)

Mary Shelley, *Lodore* (London: Bentley, 1835)

Mary Shelley, *Falkner: A Novel* (London: Saunders and Otley, 1837)

Mary Shelley, *Rambles in Germany and Italy, in 1840, 1842, and 1843* (London: Edward Moxon, 1844)

Mary Shelley, *Maurice, or The Fisher's Cot*, ed. and intro. Claire Tomalin (London: Viking, 1998)

Mary Shelley, *Matilda* (Santa Barbara, CA: Bandana Books, 2013)

Percy Bysshe Shelley, *The Complete Poetical Works of Percy Bysshe Shelley*, ed. Thomas Hutchinson (Oxford: Oxford University Press, 1929)

Percy Bysshe Shelley, *Poems*, selected by Fiona Sampson (London: Faber & Faber, 2011)

Edward John Trelawny, *Records of Shelley, Byron, and the Author* (New York: Scribner and Son, 1887); repr., ed. and intro. Rosemary Ashton (Harmondsworth: Penguin, 2013)

Mary Wollstonecraft, *Thoughts on the Education of Daughters* (London, J. Johnson, 1787); repr. (Altenmünster, Germany: Jazzybee Verlag, 2016)

Mary Wollstonecraft, *Letters Written during a Short Residence in Sweden, Norway, and Denmark* (London: J. Johnson, 1796); repr. in Mary Wollstonecraft and William Godwin, *A Short Residence in Sweden AND Memoirs of the Author of 'The Rights of Woman'*, ed. Richard Holmes (Harmondsworth: Penguin, 1987)

Mary Wollstonecraft, *A Vindication of the Rights of Woman*, in Janet Todd (ed.), *Mary Wollstonecraft: Political Writings* (Oxford: Oxford University Press, 1994)

Secondary Materials

This short list of key contemporary works includes *Fantasmagoriana*, which inspired the writing competition that was to produce *Frankenstein*.

Jean-Baptiste Benoît Eyriès (trans.), *Fantasmagoriana, ou Receuil d'Histoires de Spectres, Revenants, Fantômes, etc.*, 2 vols (Paris: F. Schoell, 1812); ed. and trans. as Sarah Elizabeth Utterson (ed. and trans.), *Tales of the Dead, Principally Translated from the French* (London: White, Cochrane and Co., 1813)

Thomas Jefferson Hogg, with intro. by Edward Dowden, *The Life of Percy Bysshe Shelley* (London: George Routledge & Sons; New York: E. P. Button & Co., 1906)

C. Kegan Paul, *William Godwin: His Friends and Contemporaries*, 2 vols (London: Henry S. King and Co., 1876)

Mrs Julian Marshall (ed.), *The Life and Letters of Mary Wollstonecraft Shelley*, 2 vols (London: Richard Bentley and Son, 1889)

Thomas Love Peacock, *Headlong Hall* (London: T. Hookham, Jun., & Co., 1816)

Jean-Jacques Rousseau, *The Confessions*, trans. and intro. J. M. Cohen (Harmondsworth: Penguin, 1953)

Three group biographies give a fascinating fuller account of Mary Shelley's context:
Charlotte Gordon, *Romantic Outlaws: The Extraordinary Lives of Mary Wollstonecraft and Mary Shelley* (London: Windmill Books/Penguin, 2015)
Daisy Hay, *Young Romantics* (London: Bloomsbury, 2010)
William St Clair, *The Godwins and the Shelleys* (London: Faber, 1989)

Finally, there have been numerous biographies and other studies of Mary Shelley. For me, three key accounts are:

Miranda Seymour, *Mary Shelley* (London: John Murray, 2000)
Muriel Spark, *Child of Light: A biography of Mary Shelley* (London: Tower Bridge Publications, 1951)
Emily Sunstein, *Mary Shelley: Romance and Reality* (New York: Little, Brown and Co., 1989)

Index

Harold's Pilgrimage 50, 121, 132, 134 ; blames vegetarianism for death of Shelley children 116; 'Song for the Luddites' 121; and Claire Clairmont 121–2, 130–31, 132–4; proposes writing of 'ghost story' 126–9, 135; 'Mazeppa' 127, 174; moral worth of beauty 131–2; Claire Clairmont pregnant 133–4; birth of Allegra 152–3; gains custody of Allegra 163; visited in Venice by PBS and Claire Clarimont 171–3; 'Ode on Venice' 174; respect for MS 174; return of Allegra 175; starts *The Liberal* with PBS 191–2; moves into Palazzo Lanfranchi 201; buys *Bolivar* 203; and 'The Pistol Club' 205; death of Allegra 205–6; woken by MS and Jane Williams when PBS missing 209; informed of death of PBS 210; executor for PBS 215, 220; forwards letter from Sir Timothy Shelley 215; treatment of Allegra 216; departure to Greece 220; continuing friendship with MS 222–3; as character in *The Last Man* 224; early biographers 237

Byron, 'Major George' 247

C

Carron, Abbé 14

Cervantes, Miguel di
Don Quixote 140

Chapman, John
engraving of Mary Wollstonecraft 25

Chateaubriand, Francois-René de 134

Chouet, Samuel 134

Clairmont Manoeuvre, the 41

Clairmont, Charles (son of Mary Jane Godwin, née Clairmont) 39, 100

Clairmont, Claire (daughter of Mary Jane Godwin, née Clairmont)
childhood friend of MS 39–40; accompanies MS and PBS as they elope 79–81, 96; lives with MS 103; changes name from Jane 107; designs on PBS 107–8; possible child with PBS? 114; meets Lord Byron 121–2; pregnant to Lord Byron 130–31; offers herself to Lord Byron 132–4; pregnancy 138; birth of Allegra Byron 152–3; affair with PBS? 157–9; Allegra Byron taken 168; visits Lord Byron in Venice with PBS 171–2; mother of Elena Adelaide? 176–9; leaves Shelley house 192–3; death of Allegra 205–6; later life as governess and music teacher 229

Clairmont, Jane *(see Clairmont, Claire)*

Clairmont, Sophia 42

Clarke, Cowden 154

Clint, George 202

'Cockney School', the 161

Cocks, Charles First Baron Somers of Evesham 12

Colburn, Henry (publisher) 225

Coleridge, Samuel Taylor, 154
joins Wordsworth in Lake Disrict 30; visits 29 the Polygon 32; *Lyrical Ballads*, the (with William Wordsworth) 50; visitor to the Godwin house 59; 'The Rime of the Ancient Mariner' 51; 'Christabel' 127, 136

Constant, Benjamin 134

Corn Laws 116

Cowper, William 38

Croker, John Wilson 162

Curran, Amelia 180, 189

Curran, John Philpot 180

Cushing, Peter 2

D

Dante
Divine Comedy, the 175, 203

Davis, John
Four Years and a Half in the United States of America 157